WITHDRAWN

NEITHER FRIEND NOR FOE

Also by Jerrold M. Packard

SONS OF HEAVEN

PETER'S KINGDOM

AMERICAN MONARCHY

THE QUEEN & HER COURT

NEITHER FRIEND NOR FOE

The European Neutrals in World War II

JERROLD M. PACKARD

CHARLES SCRIBNER'S SONS
New York

MAXWELL MACMILLAN CANADA
Toronto

MAXWELL MACMILLAN INTERNATIONAL
New York   Oxford   Singapore   Sydney

Copyright © 1992 by Jerrold M. Packard

Charles Scribner's Sons
Macmillan Publishing Company
866 Third Avenue
New York, NY 10022

Maxwell Macmillan Canada, Inc.
1200 Eglinton Avenue East
Suite 200
Don Mills, Ontario M3C 3N1

Macmillan Publishing Company is part of the Maxwell
Communication Group of Companies.

Library of Congress Cataloging-in-Publication Data

Packard, Jerrold M.
Neither friend nor foe: the European neutrals in World War II/
Jerrold M. Packard.
p.   cm.
Includes bibliographical references (p. 401) and index.
ISBN 0-684-19248-9
1. World War, 1939–1945—Diplomatic history.   2. Neutrality—
History—20th century.   I. Title.
D749.P33   1992
940.53'2—dc20   92–5960   CIP

Macmillan Books are available at special discounts for bulk purchases
for sales promotions, premiums, fund-raising, or educational use.
For details, contact:

Special Sales Director
Macmillan Publishing Company
866 Third Avenue
New York, NY 10022

10 9 8 7 6 5 4 3 2 1

Printed in the United States of America

CONTENTS

ACKNOWLEDGMENTS

This book was researched primarily at the following libraries: the Library of Congress, the library of the University of Oregon, the library of Portland State University, the Multnomah County Library, and London's Wiener Library. The staffs of all of these institutions proved unfailingly helpful.

For their generous help, I owe a special debt to Professors Franklin C. West and Jim F. Heath of the History Department of Portland State University—my sincerest thanks to both these scholars for reading the manuscript and making many corrections and suggestions. My thanks, also, to Lt. Col. (Retired) John P. Duggan of the Irish Army, whose insights on Eire's path through World War II I immensely appreciated.

The guidance and advice given by Erika Goldman, my editor at Scribners, was always on the mark. For her care with the manuscript—not least the judicious trimming—I am indebted and grateful.

This book is for Merl Grossmeyer, the extraordinary man who made it possible.

INTRODUCTION

For the sixty-eight months from Blitzkrieg to V-E Day, Europe suffered a war of unprecedented barbarity. Just five nations on that tormented continent managed to keep their peace. This is the story of how, against overwhelming odds, they did it.

Nearly half a century after the end of the fighting, the dominant perception of World War II Europe is one of an entire continent caught up, with little regard to traditional conventions of neutrality, in the most all-embracing military struggle mankind had yet descended to: national sovereignty ignored, innocent populations turned into armies of refugees, governments mired in megalomania, and nations flirting with annihilation. The continent did indeed undergo a nearly mortal convulsion, one transcending the slaughter of the Thirty Years' War, that put in shadow the dislocations of the Napoleonic campaigns, incalculably surpassing the havoc of World War I.

But lying uneasily between the warring nations, a handful of states managed for nearly six years to remain apart from the fighting, to cleave to a fragile peace. Two of the states were fully democratic, notable exceptions in a decidedly nondemocratic world order. Two were authoritarian, but at opposite ends of that imprecise category. The fifth was a full-fledged dictatorship newly born of war itself. Though characterized as neutral, they were more accurately Europe's "successful nonbelligerents." Continually under pressure to bend to the demands of the side currently in the ascendant, these few nations nonetheless aspired, to the extent dangerous circumstances and their own domestic politics permitted, to a formal neutrality, to be *officially* neither consort nor adversary to the warring states.

Neither Friend Nor Foe is the story of how Switzerland, Sweden,

Spain, Portugal, and Eire[1] succeeded in staying out of the war: how they reacted to and eventually overcame the enormous pressures from the belligerents, what the consequences of their neutrality were, how their peoples lived on the edge of a maelstrom that threatened at any moment to spill over their borders. The format is chronological, a year-by-year accounting of the events and forces that caused these five countries to accommodate first the Axis and later, as the conflict's tide began to turn, the Allies.

When war broke out in Europe in 1939, more than thirty independent states blanketed the continent. Six years later, when the aggressor was finally crushed, only five had managed to remain at peace.[2] But none of the five had been completely "neutral" in practice. Each had instead swung precariously from one camp to the other in attempts, often desperate, to appease warring neighbors. Until the latter part of 1942, Germany's interests were usually favored because Hitler appeared to be winning. After that pivotal year, the neutrals came more and more to hedge their bets in favor of the Allies as the Reich's military edge began to blunt and that of its united foes to sharpen.

Though none was a world power, neither was any a remote backwater that might ride out the conflict undisturbed. Each had something both sides would want: raw or finished materials, tactically useful ports, manpower, control of important land or water passageways, potential moral support. Primarily it was their locations and resources that brought them unwanted attention. And while none of the neutrals was itself an economic powerhouse, their total assets could contribute very materially to a belligerent's cause, as we'll see they did, in the aggregate, to Germany's. Of critical importance to their behavior, all were deeply suspicious of and usually unreservedly antagonistic toward the Soviet Union.

Despite professions of neutrality, such status always stands in danger of violation when the interests of war-making neighbors override the counterbalancing costs of warring against the neutral. To be effective, a state's policy of neutrality must, almost always, be backed with both the determination and the military capability to defend itself. It must as well know when and how much to bend in the face of unavoidable pressure. And in spite of their best efforts, all the neutrals discussed in this book understood the underlying reality of their plight: that their neutrality finally depended more on Germany than it ever did on their own actions.

Throughout World War II, Iberia[3] remained the one solidly neutral quadrant of Europe. The two peninsular states were each ruled by right-wing, fascist-leaning leaders, men who had risen to power in the chaos of the depression decade. In 1932 the conservative and scholarly finance minister, Dr. Antonio de Oliveira Salazar, became Portugal's premier, ending years of political chaos with the relative order of a military-supported system. By 1939 he was widely regarded as the world's "best" dictator. Salazar's one-party *Estado Novo*, the self-consciously "New State," would from the outset model itself on the example provided first by Mussolini and soon afterward by Hitler. After war broke out in Europe, Salazar's cardinal policy became the conviction that Portugal should remain neutral *and* do everything in its power to see that Spain did likewise. The dictator was convinced beyond any doubt that if his peninsular neighbor either entered the conflict as an Axis co-belligerent or was invaded by Hitler, Portugal would inevitably be dragged into the war.[4] And through the struggle's early years, Salazar was both torn and molded by the parallel belief that his country couldn't hope to maintain its colonial empire intact in the event of Britain's defeat, the Royal Navy acting as the guarantor of Portugal's colonies against a German takeover.[5]

Of the five nations examined here, Spain's behavior has generally been accounted the least "neutral," bringing it closest to actually entering the conflict—on the German side. But with Spain suffering its own mutilation from civil war from 1936 to 1939, Francisco Franco judged his country too weak to risk participation in the broader European war.

Franco, who held unprecedented fourfold authority in Spain—as commander-in-chief of the armed forces and as head of state, government, and Falange—deemed himself and Spain under obligation to both Hitler and Mussolini, the Axis leaders who by providing critical military matériel and air support had helped him achieve victory during the Civil War. Though it is indisputable that Spain sympathized ideologically with the dictators, a sympathy especially acute after Germany attacked the hated Soviet Union, Franco shrewdly and successfully forestalled the Axis with assurances to both Berlin and Rome of his loyalty and support, and his unshakable determination to join them in battle when "conditions" allowed. Instead, he kept the Wehrmacht out of Spain and Spain out of Hitler's war, and in the doing bestowed a bounty on the Allies of gigantic magnitude.

Switzerland has been the European state most identified with formal, traditional, institutionalized neutrality. Landlocked and (after June 1940) surrounded by Axis-controlled territory, Switzerland could in World War II ill afford to assume that its historic neutrality would continue to be respected. Forced by the sober reality of its dilemma to oblige Berlin, especially in granting unrestricted access to the critical Alpine tunnels linking Germany and Italy, the Swiss nonetheless informed Berlin with glasslike clarity what the cost to the Reich would be if the Wehrmacht attacked Switzerland. If physically transgressed, the Swiss would totally and without hesitation destroy those tunnels, the great Simplon and St. Gotthard rail conduits that kept the Duce's war economy viable.

If Spain was the neutral coming closest to allying militarily with the Axis, Sweden was the neutral most narrowly avoiding German occupation. Since 1870, strict noninterference in the affairs of other nations had in this Nordic state been raised to the level of national doctrine. After World War I the Swedes agreed—reluctantly—to join the League of Nations, but the rise of the dictators and the League's tragic debasement led Stockholm in 1938 to renounce its obligations to participate in the organization's sanctions, the single chink the Swedes had allowed in their wall of impartiality to the outside world's concerns. Instead, the kingdom turned in the direction of Nordic security with its Scandinavian neighbors, a kind of isolation based on achieving and maintaining a common policy of neutrality.[6] Possessed of two commodities vital to Germany's maintaining its war footing—ball bearings and high-grade iron ore, both sold to the Reich in enormous quantities—Hitler, clearly warned of Sweden's intentions to destroy these assets if attacked, decided against chancing any interruption in their delivery.

The world's sole English-speaking nation and the only British dominion not to militarily take up the Allied cause in World War II was Eire—Ireland's southern and western twenty-six counties.[7] The fact that the island's six northeastern counties continued to comprise a part of the United Kingdom, a partition Dublin viewed as an iniquitous and unjustified British occupation of its own territory, was the single most important moral justification in Irish prime minister Eamon de Valera's determination not to join Britain's war against the Axis. Ironically, it was this Irish partition that became the chief protection of Eire's neutral status from *British* threat: if Britain had possessed no Northern Ireland bases from which to protect its forward shipping lanes, a British occupation of Ireland would very likely have proven an irresistible necessity for the United Kingdom's survival.

· · ·

One or two points might be made at the outset. Foremost, I will attempt to demonstrate that successful neutrality is not absolute. It must be earned, and continue to be earned. Even Switzerland, the nation that in 1939 came closest of any European state to possessing something like "natural" neutrality, still found itself continually obliged to demonstrate that it would do whatever was necessary to protect its most treasured asset—its independence. Further, a state doesn't achieve "neutrality" simply because it wants to. To continue earning that station, it almost always will have to compromise in greater or lesser degree with those who would threaten it.

The reader should, when judging the behavior of the neutrals in World War II, bear in mind the factors and forces operating at the time. To condemn or criticize based on an ex post facto understanding of the *totality* of the Nazi evil would be unjust.

At the end of the war, Dean Acheson, who presided over the economic destiny of the neutrals as American assistant secretary of state, made a comment accurately reflecting a very great part of popular Allied opinion toward these nations whose policies had kept them safe from the fray. "At home the public, almost to a man, regarded arrangements to supply the neutrals as traitorous connivance at treating with the enemy. Neutrals were judged to be enemy sympathizers."[8] It is hoped this book will give the reader a better understanding of what *really* happened in these five countries in those tragic and momentous years.

NEITHER FRIEND NOR FOE

CHAPTER I

PROVENANCE

The last European war began with four belligerents: Germany the aggressor, Poland the victim of aggression, Britain and France the guarantors of Poland from that aggression. Every other European state would within hours of Germany's attack on Poland rush to declare its neutrality in an effort to keep clear of a tempest about to rain six years of hellfire on Europe.

. . .

Just as forecast by the Polish State Radio, Friday, the first of September 1939, dawned over the plains of Poland with promise of another golden day to add to what had already been a memorably golden summer. This dawn, though, brought not just another new day but a new age. With it came the opening scherzo of World War II, the multifronted attack on a still semi-medieval nation by a supremely well-primed German invasion force of a million and a half men. By the time the sun had risen to its zenith that September morning, Poland—and the world—were forever changed. The world didn't yet realize, of course, that more than just another bloody page in time turned that day. But in truth never had Europe experienced so sharp a rupture between one phase of its history and the next, between one way of life and another.

EUROPE

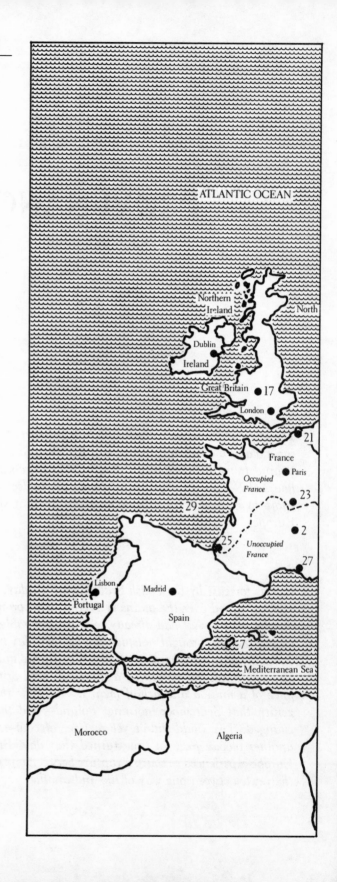

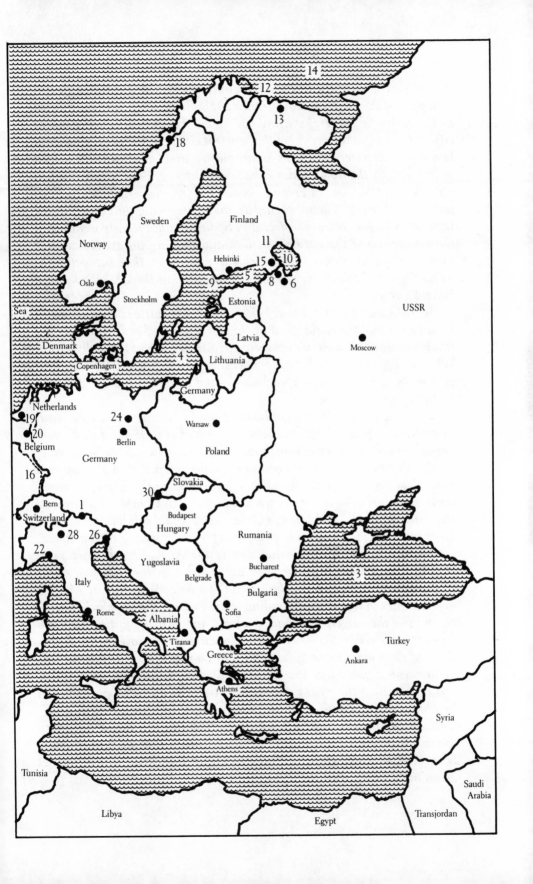

The first salvo of the war had been unleashed before dawn, the eleven-inch guns of the German Navy training ship Schleswig-Holstein, *moored in the harbor of Danzig, spitting out fire at the artificially independent city-state; it was the removal of that ancient city from German hands that had been such bitter bane to its former masters and had done much to lead to this day. By the time the day's shadows shortened, Panzer divisions had already swept well across Poland's border regions, converging on the capital city of Warsaw. Clouds of Stukas, many practicing the aerial warfare their pilots had so recently perfected in Spain, simultaneously went about the destruction of the nation's civilian and military infrastructure—the roads and power plants, the airfields and batteries that supported the gallant but pathetically vulnerable horse cavalry at the symbolic heart of Poland's army.*

By the time the sun set that Friday, the death rattle of a people could be heard around the world. And by the end of the weekend, with Poland's fate irreversible, Warsaw was pleading to a stunned world for deliverance. What the continent's diplomats pondered as they listened to the broadcast cries of the wounded nation was when—and how—Poland's British and French allies would respond.

From the prime ministries of London and Paris, the response was swift in contrast to years of appeasement. The reaction in the British Foreign Office had initially been understandable confusion in light of the speed of events. But by the first afternoon of the crisis the British ambassador in Berlin had been instructed to deliver a "warning" to the German government, stating that unless the Reich was prepared to promptly withdraw its forces from Poland, His Majesty's Government would fulfill its promises to Germany's victim. A French response along the same lines quickly followed.

The genesis of those promises and of the Anglo-French reaction to Hitler's rape of Poland lay in the Nazi invasion earlier that year of the emasculated remains of Czechoslovakia. Hitler's 1938 deal at Munich provided that in return for the ceding to the Reich of the so-called Sudeten territories—the largely German-speaking and heavily fortified margin lands of Czechoslovakia—Berlin would guarantee the sovereign independence of the remainder of the country. Half a year after that promise, the Wehrmacht marched into Prague, demonstrating finally, beyond any further equivocating the Nazi menace, that Hitlerism was not a phenomenon in which trust or honor or limits were relevant. In response to this realization, both Britain and France promised Poland—a promise made with seeming impetuousness in light of its enormity—that should it be invaded, both countries would consider it an attack upon themselves, and would act accordingly.

When Hitler took the risk that the Anglo-French guarantee was a bluff and invaded Poland, there was clearly little likelihood of either Western partner actually rescuing the Poles from their tormentor. Instead, London and Paris could only declare themselves at war with Germany—unless Germany were to give up its prey. The diplomatic minuet danced that weekend in the government salons of the four principals hung on that proposition.

In Berlin, the Reich's leadership engaged in a ludicrous attempt to convince the world that it was Polish "aggression" that had pushed German endurance beyond its limits, that in response to such aggression Germany's actions were justifiable as "self-defense." "I have therefore resolved to speak to Poland in the same language that Poland for months has used toward us . . . ," Hitler thundered to the German people.[1] Forty-eight hours later, the United Kingdom and the French Republic declared war on the German Reich, a declaration immediately reciprocated by Berlin.

·   ·   ·

As war was breaking out that weekend, so was neutrality. All over the continent, governments rushed to assert their national eagerness to stay out of the German-Polish fight, a conflict showing unmistakable promise of sucking nations into it like a whirlwind gathering the dust. For every nation, an eagerness to avoid the devastation all had witnessed a generation earlier was, of course, the paramount motivation for keeping clear of the fight. So it was for the five nations of this book, and their expressions of neutrality were somber, urgent, varied. But avoiding the winds of war would mean walking the firebreak between unambiguous neutrality and as strong a defense as each could muster.

Of the five, only Switzerland could with any hope of success assume its neutrality might be taken for granted. It was, everyone knew, "permanently neutral," a condition its Federal Council—and its army—guaranteed and one its powerful neighbors had since the wars of the Napoleonic era honored. Switzerland aimed simply to keep clear of the belligerents, fulfill its economic obligations, take care not to provoke the dictators,[2] prepare militarily as best as possible, hope that the need for an entity like Switzerland would be recognized in Berlin, and in the doing of all this be spared invasion. Time would shortly prove how formidable this course would be.

Peaceful and insular Sweden threw its chances of remaining at peace in with the so-called Oslo group of states of Scandinavia and the Low

Countries, all of which except Belgium and Luxembourg had achieved success in remaining unentangled in the Great War and which now hoped to keep out of this war with a commitment to neither rile nor aid either side in the latest fight. But Sweden knew it would have to go further to get through the approaching storm. Its government judged it couldn't depend on respect from Hitler for the rights and desires of Europe's smaller and weaker states, but he might respect Sweden for its strengths and resources— iron ore, ball bearings, the waters of the Baltic, military capability—and a steely determination to thwart any invader. The Swedes decided to make Sweden too valuable to destroy and too costly to take on.

And how would the Irish react to the war Britain and France were throwing themselves into? This would be the first chance in the island nation's history to present itself on the international stage independent of Britain. But the government of this young state ominously sensed that if all-out war developed between Germany and Britain, the initial danger to Eire's existence might come not from the Germans, but from the British. For centuries, England's first line of defense had been its navy, and that navy had long relied on Irish ports and Irish naval bases to help it maintain a long arm into the Atlantic and the North Sea. Ireland knew that if Chamberlain had not handed the Treaty Ports back only a year earlier, it would surely have been treated by Germany as a part of the United Kingdom and thus a legitimate military target for the Reich. Would Britain now try to regain the ports over Ireland's opposition? If it did, and if it survived a war, would the newly free Irish be lucky enough to get the British out a second time?

Tethered to the edge of Europe off the continent's main concourses of war, the two states sharing the Iberian Peninsula felt a degree of immunity from the storm breaking over Europe. But Spain and Portugal's strategic importance would not be ignored by the belligerents. In their possession of the portal to the Mediterranean as well as island colonies positioned astride Atlantic trade and submarine lanes, both countries stood in danger of being pulled into the conflict.

In September 1939, Spain was an economic and social wreck. Exhausted by war, terrorized by Franco's retaliation against his defeated but still defiant enemies, the nation was utterly unprepared to oppose a military threat from either warring camp. While Franco pondered his options, his brother dictator in Lisbon worried most about the possibility of Spain joining the Axis. It was a scenario Salazar believed had to be avoided at all costs, for if Spain's debt to Hitler translated into Spanish co-belligerency with the Reich, Portugal would be swept down the same road, with all Iberia becoming just another German satrapy. The two men, one running his country with a velvet-gloved fist and the other with brass knuckles, knew above all else that whatever Iberia's participation in a world war would bring to their peninsula, it very well might mean the end of their power.

Bern

On September 1, 1939, the hardworking burghers of Bern were as nervous as the legislature whose presence made their city the confederal capital. Cloistered in the massive gray stone pile that served as the National Parliament building, the lawmakers had just granted the Federal Council, the nation's unique seven-man executive, total authority to maintain the "security, independence, and neutrality" of Switzerland in whatever way it saw fit. Both the government and the governed were acutely aware that their country was at immediate risk of invasion if the Western democracies made good on their pledge to go to war with Germany over the invasion of Poland.

While the Poles endured the first waves of Hitler's blitzkrieg that eventful weekend, the Swiss were enjoying a national festival. Styled the National Exhibition and staged in Zurich, the confederation's largest city, the show was meant to showcase—primarily for domestic edification—Switzerland's multitude of achievements as well as give the nation's citizens a chance to see up close the technological strides their country had made. When the exhibition first opened, there was still extant in Switzerland the widespread notion, perhaps only wishful thinking, that European war would somehow be avoided, that the glorious summer of 1939 would be extended into years of peace. But the events in Poland shattered this mirage beyond repair.

It seemed odd to the logically minded Swiss that Britain and France should have gotten themselves backed into such a corner over Poland in the first place. With British prime minister Neville Chamberlain proclaiming "peace in our time" after receiving Hitler's flimsy pledge that the dismemberment of Czechoslovakia meant the end of German territorial demands, it appeared to the world the worst had passed. Germany got the Sudeten periphery of Czechoslovakia it wanted, and the potential (and considerable) Czech military threat to the Reich was virtually nullified—as was, of course, Czech trust in the West. But in turn, and seemingly well worth the high price, the likelihood of war between Germany and the Western democracies was turned around.

The fact was that Hitler's ambitions were nowhere near satiated with

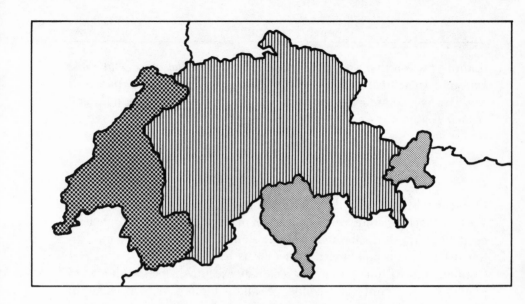

SWITZERLAND

1. Simplon Tunnel
2. Saint Gotthard Tunnel
3. Zurich
4. Schaffhausen
5. Geneva
6. Rütli Meadow
7. Basel
8. Belfort
9. *Dreiecke*, or Three Corners
10. Fortress Saint-Maurice
11. Fortress Sargans
12. Lugano
13. Dübendorf
14. Stein am Rhein
15. Ruti
16. Tuttlingen
17. Lake Constance (Bodensee)
18. Lake of Zurich
19. Lake of Lucerne
20. Lake Geneva

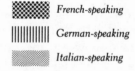

French-speaking

German-speaking

Italian-speaking

------ *Railway links used by the Germans*

General area of the Redoubt

Guisan's 1940 defense positions

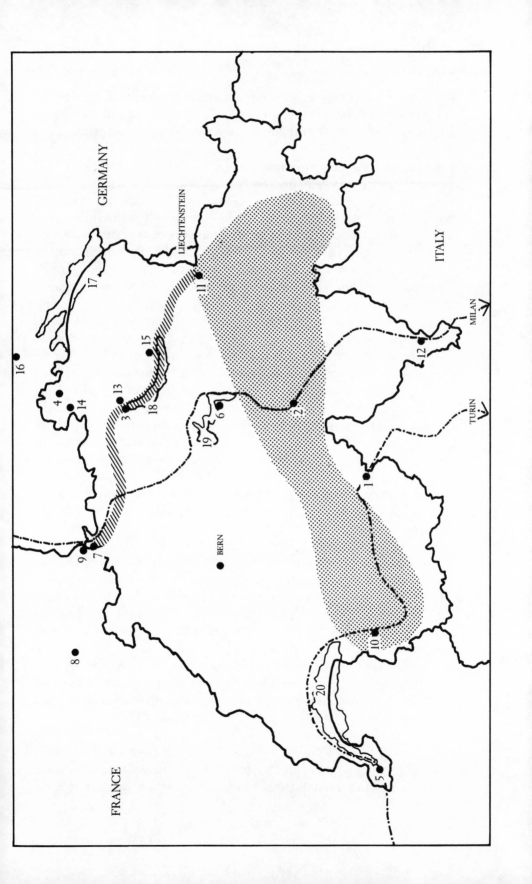

the Sudeten gain to the Reich. In terms of the "geopolitical" ideology of Nazism, most of the remaining rump of Czechoslovakia still constituted a metaphorical dagger thrust directly into the "heart" of Germany. Consequently, in March 1939 the Wehrmacht marched into Bohemia and Moravia, the bulk of what remained of Czechoslovakia, and declared it a protectorate of the Greater Reich; rump Slovakia, nominally "independent," also soon received German "protection." With this act of breathtakingly brazen aggression, Britain and France finally realized the game was up with Hitler, and concluded that the next such aggression would mean they would have to act against him or see their credibility as European powers vanish. The result was a promise to Poland, Hitler's obvious next victim, that they would guarantee its sovereignty against attack from Germany.[3] It was a pledge that on September 1, 1939, both would be called upon to redeem. For the Swiss, three-quarters of whom were German-speaking and considered in terms of Nazi racial ideology to be *Volksdeutsch*—ethnic Germans—and thus a legitimate target for either voluntary or forcible incorporation into the Reich (since the birth of the Nazi state German maps had included Switzerland as a part of the Grossdeutsches Reich), the danger inherent in these events was manifest.

Not that there wasn't a noisy minority in Switzerland who would have welcomed assimilation into the Reich. As in most European countries in the 1930s, Switzerland too possessed a sizable domestic movement allied with the social and political goals of the party that had been in charge in Germany since January 1933. The largest of the Swiss versions was the National Front, whose members sought to emulate their big brothers across their northern border by faithfully adopting the costumes, insignia, terminology, and ideology of the National Socialist German Workers' Party—the Nazis. Not entirely new in the 1930s, like-minded groups had gained a toehold on Swiss soil in 1923, encouraged by the fascist victory in Italy. One historian ascribed the formation of such anti-democratic organizations less to steadfast conviction and more to the penchant for glory on the part of some Swiss dissatisfied with the perceived slight size and statues of their country.[4] By 1939, there had been at least a dozen totalitarian Swiss organizations (including a small but feverish Communist Party), many merging, dissolving, combining, renaming themselves, but their overall membership—perhaps 40,000 in all—never exceeded a tiny fraction of the total Swiss population of 4,200,000.[5]

The best-known icon of the Nazi-style groups was one Wilhelm Gustloff,[6] held as Swiss "Führer" by his adherents until assassinated in February 1936 by a young Yugoslavian Jew; unsurprisingly, Germany blamed his murder on the "inflammatory anti-German rhetoric" of the free Swiss press. Gustloff's and similar groups imported many of the Nazi trappings found in Germany itself: a full-fledged *Hitler Jugend* for boys, a *Bund deutscher Mädel* for girls, and assorted other clublike groups whose purpose was to merge personal identities into an all-powerful ideology. The German government brought strong pressure on Germans living in Switzerland to join these organizations, all of which were thoroughly inimical to Swiss notions of democracy. Yet for Switzerland to have simply banned such bodies was almost impossibly difficult, Bern knowing Berlin would have considered such a move a hostile act, one that could easily boomerang against the nation's efforts to stay on the Reich's friendly side.

Despite the small but strident and potentially dangerous minority agitating for *Anschluss*[7] with the Reich, the Swiss tradition of neutrality ranked among the most immutable customs of European diplomacy. The unshakable rock of the confederation's neutrality meant keeping out of other countries' affairs, especially their wars; expecting other countries to stay out of its affairs; and treating all other nations with a theoretical evenhandedness. The great majority of the Swiss people regarded this policy as the cornerstone of their nation, and Switzerland was widely viewed internationally as the prime example of the archetypal rigidly neutral state.

In point of fact, Swiss neutrality was a condition that could be said to be older than the Swiss Confederation itself. As a nation composed of three ethnic groups speaking four languages and practicing two religions, neutrality was as necessary for internal peace and stability as it was for external security.[8] Peacefully maintaining their diversity required not only putting aside domestic differences but also refusing to take up the cause of related ethnic groups or co-religionists abroad.

The genesis of the Swiss Confederation—the birth of Switzerland as an identifiable nation—dates back to what was called the "everlasting" pact, the *Ewiger Bund* among the forest cantons (or communities) of Uri, Schwyz,[9] and Unterwalden, the founding trio of the eventual twenty-three cantons that today make up the twentieth-century nation. The alliance contesting Habsburg power was signed on August 1, 1291, at a place called the Rütli, a meadow hugging the forested shores of the Lake of Lucerne. Six and a half centuries later, on this same historic spot that had long since become a shrine to Swiss independence, the determination to thwart Nazi Germany would be firmly and solemnly articulated.

With the success of this "primeval" trio of cantons, within a century the original nucleus would begin to be joined by neighbors in a wider confederation, some as full partners, others initially as protectorates seeking a shield against the Habsburgs, who continued to try to retain their control over the Alpine districts. The number of partners grew to thirteen by 1513, when the confederation closed its doors to any more expansion until the Napoleonic era. Despite periods of internal bickering, nothing bad enough ever happened to break up the ever more firmly tied cantons, and the provision in the Rütli pact requiring that disputes between the partners be resolved peaceably firmly instilled a tradition of arbitration in the Swiss political fabric.

One of the taproots of Switzerland's freedom from a military caste and all the difficulties that flow from that social disability lies in the historical reality that the Swiss were the first European people to emerge from the chaos of feudalism. But when the cantons stopped fighting each other, they had to figure out what to do with an overgrown military establishment that had suddenly become superfluous. The solution was to export it. Swiss mercenaries became the best in the world, much sought after by the princes and prelates of Europe, who always found themselves short of homegrown cannon fodder with which to attack their neighbors. Eventually some 750 of these exports became marshals and generals in other rulers' armies.[10] All through the Middle Ages, Swiss soldiers-for-hire meant the home front stayed relatively demilitarized.

The formal Swiss intention to keep out of Europe's disputes is most commonly dated from 1515, when Switzerland was defeated by the French in the Italian wars' Battle of Marignano.[11] Reversing its drift toward Great Power status, the Swiss instead withdrew into a sort of neutral buffer status between France and Austria; the first use of the term "neutrality" itself appeared in an official document from 1536.

A century and a half later, the Federal Diet—the country's legislature—formally proclaimed a neutral position between warring France and the Netherlands. Conferring with the country's neighbors, Swiss statesmen worked out treaties meant to keep the confederation out of the myriad wars endemic to the European states in this Absolutist Epoch, an age so called for the virtually unrestricted power of the monarchs occupying Europe's thrones. One of these treaties was the hopefully named Perpetual Peace, an accord with France bringing Switzerland harmony with its largest neighbor. This protective relationship helped ensure the success of its buffer status, at least until the passions generated in the Napoleonic era again forced the Swiss to take up arms. It was Switzerland's involvement in these wars, an unending series of conflicts ransacking the continent from 1798 until 1815, that pressured the confederation to finally codify its neutralist policy in the form of international conventions.

Modern Swiss neutrality was born with the Act of Paris. Signed on

November 20, 1815, by Austria, France, Great Britain, Prussia, and Russia, the declaration decreed the "formal and authentic acknowledgement of the perpetual neutrality of Switzerland."[12] The signatory powers did not require that the Swiss forsake any of their sovereignty as quid·pro quo for this recognition, and Switzerland's neutrality in European affairs was thereafter assumed.

The corollary was that the Swiss ceased to be power players in European affairs. But by turning a seeming weakness into an asset, the confederation became the trusted representative of belligerent countries—the source of information, of prisoner exchanges, of welfare and succor; the development of the Red Cross was a direct outcome of Switzerland's new status. It also—less fortuitously—became a magnet of international espionage as well as a safe haven for troublemakers and revolutionaries. But significantly, the country prospered as the locus of lucrative and uninterrupted trade and commerce with all sides in any given war.

The neutral confederation got through Bismarck's three limited late-nineteenth-century wars of Prussian aggrandizement unscathed, as it would World War I, though in the latter conflict the nation's linguistic groups strongly (and potentially dangerously) identified with their co-linguists among the fighting states. When two years after the end of World War I Switzerland joined the League of Nations—which organization it hosted on its own soil—the nation permitted a crack in its neutrality; the post-Great War euphoria of the "brotherhood of man" and the "end to war" led many Swiss to believe the old Great Powers' enmities were dead.[13] The confederation agreed to "conditional neutrality," meaning that only under limited circumstances would it participate in coercive, but nonmilitary, measures to thwart a breaker of the League's covenant.[14] But after watching as the road to a future war was paved by the totalitarian powers and the League's inability to stop them, Switzerland renounced this policy. In October 1938 Bern reestablished absolute neutrality, relieving itself of any obligation to enforce League sanctions. In light of this new position, in the war-clouded summer of 1939 the Swiss government undertook to avoid any public official utterances designed to influence the about-to-be belligerents, Bern fearing that such a course could be interpreted as taking sides as Germany and its opponents squared off.

But in the tangled circumstances of 1939, Switzerland's ability to maintain its protective coat of neutrality seemed ominously threatened. In the first place, the potential enemy the Swiss now faced was wholly different from those who had menaced the country in earlier years. The Nazi craving for Switzerland was unambiguously founded both in the country's strategic geographical position and in the rich fruits of Swiss industriousness. Even more important was the racial consideration, with the Nazi catechism having clearly mandated the "return" of all ethnic Germans to the Fatherland. National Socialist cant may have had the German-speaking Swiss as fellow Volksdeutsch, but the Swiss themselves took quite a different view of the matter. German-speaking Swiss are *not* German, indeed commonly scorn the Germans, and have never been a part of anything remotely resembling a historic German national state. These facts were irrelevant to Hitler, of course, who simplistically viewed the German-speaking majority of Switzerland as Volksdeutsch who would eventually be returned to their true home in a Greater German Reich.

To maintain any chance of frustrating such notions, a few Swiss understood the overarching fact of European life in 1939: they would have to make swallowing their country too formidable for an easy Wehrmacht victory—or else suffer the consequences. Although this nation of only a little over 4 million people couldn't possibly field a military force capable of withstanding an army drawing on a population of 80 million people, Switzerland did possess a combination with which it might be able to keep Berlin at bay: mountains and tunnels.

In terms of strategic geography, the Swiss are singularly blessed. Switzerland's location as the roof of Europe positions the country to dominate the vital international rail axes connecting the major Western European powers. For the two Axis partners, Germany and Italy, those routes were of overriding strategic importance: communication by sea was effectively controllable by British naval blockade, leaving the rails the sole means by which Germany could reliably keep its Italian junior partner supplied with coal, vital to Mussolini's war-making capability.

In 1939, Germany, France, and Italy were connected by four primary rail links. Two were in Switzerland, with the other two flanking the country on the east and on the west. The latter, to the west, was France's nearly eight-mile-long Mont Cenis Tunnel coupling France with Italy, and the least consequential of the four links. On the east, the Brenner Pass, a series of twenty-one tunnels and sixty bridges built in the 1860s, constituted the lowest of the principal Alpine passes and the main link between Italy and Austria (the latter since 1938 called the Ostmark and no longer an independent state but an integral part of Germany).[15] At the critical center of this strategic quartet of rail connections were the two Swiss tunnels, the St. Gotthard and the Simplon.

It was once the case that winter brought much of Central Europe's communications to a standstill. But the Swiss outclassed nature by building a pair of rail-threaded tunnels penetrating the most important of the

Alpine barriers. Beginning in the 1870s and the start of construction on the St. Gotthard, within a decade the first of the pair was finished and ready for the steam locomotives used to pull the early trains. Almost ten miles long, the St. Gotthard connected central, German-speaking Switzerland with its southern, Italian-speaking Ticino canton, gateway to Italy and the salient factor in the tunnel's international significance.

The younger of the pair was the Simplon. Piercing twelve and a half miles of Alpine massif and thus the longest in the world in 1939, the tunnel directly crossed the frontier between Switzerland and Italy some 7,000 feet below the crests of the mountains it foiled. About forty miles southwest of the St. Gotthard, it, like its partner, was blasted by Swiss engineers through solid rock, the engineers mindfully providing both with fortifications at the time they were built.

Both Italy and Germany contributed to the cost of building the St. Gotthard, meaning that the Swiss were obligated to guarantee the two nations the right to haul both freight and passengers through the tunnel, rights that could not be legally curtailed by Switzerland and which in effect constituted a kind of abridgment on Swiss sovereignty over the route. In 1909, an expanded agreement between the three countries formally extended privileges to Italy and Germany to the use of all Swiss railways for any purpose but the transportation of war matériel.

In World War II, this agreement would exercise a crucial effect on Switzerland's wartime relationship with the belligerents. In the event of war, Hitler's generals knew the two flanking arteries, the Mont Cenis and the Brenner, would be required to serve primarily as troop and war matériel shipment routes to their Italian allies, while the two central, Swiss tunnels would act as passages for the coal and other vital and technically nonmilitary supplies needed for Mussolini's war machine.

·   ·   ·

Regardless of Switzerland's natural and man-made advantages, in the war's early days ambivalence concerning the seriousness of the Nazi threat undermined the Swiss government's resolve to stand up to German aggression. Since the first intimations of the danger almost a decade earlier, it had not been the government that served as the primary wellspring of Switzerland's resistance to Germany. Opposition instead came directly from the average Swiss citizen's deep-seated hatred for Nazi methods and ideology. At the civilian level, the confederation's journalists, particularly those of the German-language press, were the most articulate champions of Swiss independence.

Paradoxically, the nation's German-speakers in general best compre-
hended the dangers of the Nazi siren call. With their ability to understand radio broadcasts from the Reich, programs bloated with the saber-
rattling speeches and fatuous ceremonies central to National Socialism,
Swiss Germanophones understood more clearly than their French- and
Italian-speaking countrymen the idiocy of Nazi doctrine and values.
Francophones in the *Suisses romandes*—the French-speaking cantons of
western Switzerland—were less aware of the moral bankruptcy in Germany and were more swayed by the neighboring French radio broadcasts
which tended to moderate the Nazi menace; they thus had come to think
of National Socialism in comforting terms, as something like a German
bulwark against Russian Bolshevism.[16] Menacingly, it was in the French-
speaking parts of the country, most susceptible to influences from soon-
to-be Vichy France, where one most often heard German-style jargon,
expressions such as "rethinking" and "relearning" and "resettling," the
prophetic catchphrases of the New German Order.

Measured in terms of newspaper readership, the Swiss were among
the most literate people in the world. Yet with its 400 papers, Switzerland's problems with the press would prove among the most difficult of
any state in the run-up to and during the early days of World War II.
Sensitive to threats from Berlin about the anti-Nazi tone of the vast
majority of those papers, the government reluctantly but nonetheless
passively instituted censorship designed to stop the country's press from
printing negative articles about the policies of the behemoth to the north.
The employment of anti-Nazi German refugees in the newspaper industry was also curtailed as a sop to the tetchy Reich. Germany did gain some
benefit from this effort to keep the Swiss ignorant of the Reich's aggressiveness. Within a year of the Polish invasion and the German victories
in the West, there would be many Swiss finding themselves advocating
even greater accommodation to the seemingly invincible Reich's demands, rationalizing the censorship of their own news with the slogan
"Why die for the press?"

As war hung like a headman's ax over the peaceable confederation,
the men entrusted with the nation's future traveled from their various
cantons to Bern in the migratory nature of their calling. The unique
government they came to serve provided one of the truest representative
democracies in the world. All other countries have a head of state—a king
or president or some such, and perhaps a separate head of government,
or prime minister. But the Swiss possess, as befits their confederal system,
an all but literally plural executive, with one of its members rotating
annually in the wholly nominal presidency so as to make one man

available to nominally personify the nation's sovereignty; the system creates the near virtual anonymity of the Swiss head of state. This Federal Council—that is to say, the executive—is a group of seven men, elected every four years by a joint session of the two legislative chambers, the upper Council of State and the lower National Council. The chosen seven represent the seven departments of state, each assuming responsibility for one of the portfolios: Foreign Affairs, Interior, Justice and Police, Military, Finance, Agriculture and Industry, and Posts and Railways.[17]

From among these seven federal councillors are elected each year two who will serve as president and vice president—technically President of the Confederation and Vice President of the Federal Council. Neither may immediately succeed himself, but has to wait a year before being named to either office again; the vice president normally succeeds the president. Many men have served in both offices many times in their tenure as members of the Federal Council. The president possesses no significant constitutional powers beyond those of any other of his six co-councillors—he has no veto power or qualification to conduct diplomacy, and he has no responsibility for choosing fellow councillors, and thus the office in no way resembles a prime ministership. In emergencies, the council may authorize the president to act in its name, but any act performed in this function must later be approved by the rest of the council. In short, the head of the Swiss Confederation becomes, for most purposes, an individual only when the nation is being represented on ceremonial occasions.[18] In 1939—as today—even an informed Swiss might have had trouble saying which of the federal councillors was president.

It was this group of men who would be responsible for deciding what the nation's response to the Nazi menace would be. Though Switzerland's natural defenses as well as its capacity for destroying Central Europe's key rail links were formidable, without the political will backed by a national consensus to use these assets, the danger of the loss of the nation's independence was immense. And it was in this uppermost rank of Swiss society where that political will looked to be the most critically deficient.

· · ·

If the crisis threatening Europe were to transform itself into another general continental war, Switzerland's principal defense would, of course, be the responsibility of its army. That army, soon to find itself facing at point-blank range the most dangerous threat in the confederation's history, was a very different force—in makeup as well as size—from that of its potential foe.

In almost all of the countries neighboring Switzerland, most particularly in France and Germany, professional military service was a calling largely alien to civilian life. In the typical army or navy of the time, officers formed a caste that demanded and was accorded high class standing in society. Enlisted ranks were very often composed primarily (or at least most importantly) of men in for a lifetime's full occupation. The prestige conferred on the military, where the working and peasant classes contributed very few of their members to the officer class and the enlisted members derived from hardly any other classes, ensured most of Europe's military establishments a clout often central to government policy.

By 1939, the evolution of Switzerland's military service had arrived at a wholly different pattern, having emerged into a kind of national militia. For the Swiss man, being in the military simply meant "service"—service to his nation and to the fundaments on which that nation stood. The oath each recruit recited on enlistment required allegiance not only to the state but to his nation's constitution—a remarkably singular concept on a still largely authoritarian continent. Every male Swiss had by the weight of the confederation's history come to accept intermittent and compulsory military service as much a part of his routine life as was his work or his family. Very few exemptions from service were granted, and those that were were related almost entirely to physical disabilities, with those men exempted being required to pay a special tax. It was an obligation entirely different from the conscription, or draft, of most other European nations—Swiss duty was not for a single fixed period of one's young manhood, but for short stretches every year lasting well into middle age, from one's eighteenth birthday to the end of the forty-eighth year. These citizen-soldiers would then remain liable for call-up in a national emergency until the end of their sixtieth year. They spent these periods during the first twelve years in front-line guard duty, and those in the remaining years in increasingly less onerous rear-guard service. Only during mobilization were service periods open-ended. The entire army—40 percent of all Swiss males—could be mobilized at a moment's notice, as it would be in two days in September 1939.

Schools exclusively for officers, in the style of a British Sandhurst or a French St. Cyr, had never been established in Switzerland. The military training schools that did exist educated all ranks in common. Different classes of Swiss mixed in their military training, and although officers tended to come from the educated middle class, even officers served mostly as part-time soldiers, just as did their enlisted subordinates. Every effort was made to ensure that officers commanded men of their own language group,[19] the military units as a result generally being linguistically homogeneous. Even when not in uniform, the part-time officers maintained a paternalistic attitude toward their outfits, the officer becoming a kind of adviser in helping solve his men's personal family problems. Most of the Swiss soldiery returned to civilian duties for the bulk of the year, each man keeping his rifle and a generous supply of ammunition at home with him when not on active duty, a custom most European governments on their own turfs would have considered foolishly dangerous. In consequence of all these factors, the outlook of the overwhelming majority of the military assumed a strongly civilian perspective.

The professional, full-time officer class represented a small part of the Swiss military, and for the most part was controlled by the cantons, whose governments were responsible for all promotions through the rank of captain. This "standing" army was essentially a nucleus of military instructors, general staff officers, and divisional and corps commanders. No general officer existed except for a single major general in wartime,[20] and much of the story of World War II Switzerland revolves around the personality and resolve of that individual. That solitary general was the man who more than any other person would be responsible for the course Switzerland pursued through the next six harrowing years.

Stockholm

Until August 23, 1939, Sweden had enjoyed as safe a position as was possible for any country in a Europe clearly set on a course for war. Secure in the North behind its Baltic moat and the shield of traditional neutrality that had brought it unscathed through the Great War, the Swedes believed—hoped—they would be able to stay clear of the coming conflagration. But the earthshaking pact that the German and Soviet foreign ministers signed at Moscow on the twenty-third not only stunned the Swedes into a new sense of danger, it also effectively ended the likelihood of pan-Scandinavian neutrality in Hitler's approaching war.

Before the bombshell of the Molotov-Ribbentrop pact, the Swedes had founded their faith in neutrality on the two comforting strategic realities of the nation's existence: Sweden's geography had fortuitously placed it in an enviable position, one that seemed to promise it safety from Europe's twentieth-century quarrels; and its soil produced an ore

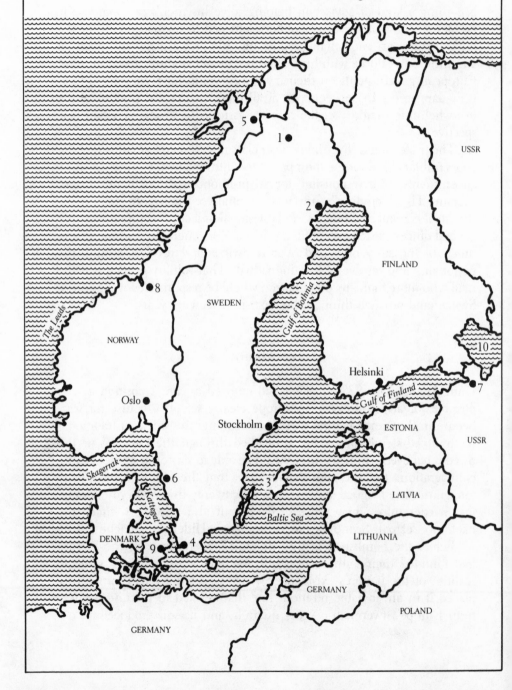

SCANDINAVIA

1. Kiruna
2. Lulea
3. Gotland
4. Malmö
5. Narvik

6. Gothenburg
7. Leningrad
8. Trondheim
9. Copenhagen
10. Lake Ladoga

whose importance to the Nazi capacity in maintaining its war machine made the benefits of German cooperation with Sweden clear even to Berlin's most restless militarists.

As with its Norwegian neighbor, the waters forming the Swedish coastline acted as a kind of moat, separating and shielding the two northern kingdoms from potential European aggressors: Germany lay across the Baltic and the Soviets were walled off by the Gulf of Bothnia. But Sweden differed in one major respect from its western neighbor. It did not share in an Atlantic coastline, the strategically fatal component of Norway with respect to the belligerents' needs. Though Sweden was thus contained in the Baltic and thereby inaccessible from the west should Germany overrun Denmark, this geographical reality also meant that Sweden's central position wasn't nearly as important to Germany. Furthermore, on the east, Finland as well as the Gulf of Bothnia stood between the Swedes and their anciently despised Russian arch-nemesis. In the context of the approaching war, it indeed appeared that the vagaries of the geographic gods had been generous to the Swedes.

The other dominant ingredient in the Swedish recipe for safety from a European war—its iron ore—was buried in the soil of its arctic north. The extraction of iron ore is by far the oldest Swedish industry, and for many centuries the most economically important. The industry's roots stretched back to the Viking era and had been a mainstay in the strength of that virile civilization; by the eighteenth century, the Swedes would hold a world monopoly on iron ore exports. What made the ore particularly valuable from Sweden's standpoint was the fact that the mineral was contained in well-defined geographic areas, thus making it easier to protect: Lapland, beyond the imaginary line of the Arctic Circle, and the Kiruna fields near the head of the Gulf of Bothnia contained the bulk of the precious mineral. The Swedes employed two principal routes to export the ore from the far north. One was across the narrow Swedish corridor bordering northern Norway, to the seaport of Narvik, buried deep in the glaciated fjords of the Atlantic coast. The second was from its own port of Luleå, at the head of the Gulf of Bothnia.

In 1939, the Swedes were the world's largest exporter of iron ore; other countries—France, the United States, the Soviet Union—produced greater quantities, but also used vastly larger proportions of their own output domestically. Further, it wasn't just the quantity of Sweden's iron ore capacity that was so important. Its *quality*, the percentage of iron in the ore, was what gave Sweden's black treasure its prized value—the Swedish ore contained roughly twice the percentage of iron as that from the mines of the French deposits in Lorraine.

The paradoxical downside of this situation for Sweden was that the country possessed far more than it could use domestically, but other nations—principally Germany—could use its ore very profitably indeed. The capital its mineral wealth added to the Swedish coffers was pleasant, but it appended an *un*pleasant note of danger to the country's desire to stay unoccupied by any of the potential belligerents. Now events in Moscow were about to radically alter hitherto sustainable equations.

• • •

Since the Swedes' last experience with war 125 years earlier, the un-alloyed consensus of the nation's polity demanded that the country pre-serve its neutrality—at whatever cost. And they had seen as the final guarantor of the ability to maintain that neutrality the balance of power between Europe's great nation-states, a balance that had existed since the close of the Napoleonic era, when Sweden's adoption of neutrality be-came the foremost principle of its foreign policy.

Until the end of World War I, European power remained essentially balanced between the continent's great nation-states, a condition provid-ing a stability that protected Sweden from threatening moves from any quarter. This reassuring equilibrium was shaken first with the rejiggering of the European power structure in the wake of Versailles and then again with the rise of Nazi hegemony in Central Europe. But the Swedes still trusted that German ambitions would continue to be counterbalanced by the interests of the democracies on its western flank as well as those of the Soviet Union on its east. It was this comforting calculation that came crashing down on Sweden's hopes with the utterly unexpected pact signed between Germany and the Soviet Union on August 23, a pact that Stockholm interpreted as Berlin granting Moscow free rein to do as it wished in the North.

Knowing the story of the metamorphosis of the Swedes from one of the fiercest people on earth to among the most pacific helps in under-standing this nation's reasons for and deep attachments to neutrality. The passage of the Swedes from the wild men "mighty in ships and arms" of whom Tacitus first wrote in 98 A.D. to a people thoroughly ingrained with the values of living at peace with their neighbors in the twentieth century was a journey with spectacular highs and crushing lows, one in which Sweden was far more often at the center of the world's political stage than it would be in our own century.

The earliest "Swedes" to be recorded with any historic certainty were really two groups: the Svears (a word eventually transformed into

"Swedes"), a people who settled around Lake Mälaren, west of modern Stockholm, and, to the south, the Götars—or Goths, a tribe that lived in the central part of the Swedish mainland and on the Baltic island of Gotland. It was clusters of the island Götars who two or three centuries before the advent of the Christian era sailed across the Baltic to the Oder and Vistula estuaries on the European mainland, there establishing a complex matrix of interrelated East Germanic tribes.[21] Many eventually returned over the centuries to their original homeland, introducing into Sweden bits of Greco-Roman lore and civilization, including the written script called runes.

The heroic age of the peoples of the North began in the ninth century. This was the inception of the Viking era, the time when Scandinavia's protohistory segues into true history—a dependably reliable record of the times. The word "Viking" is an all-encompassing term for the tribes who populated the states that make up modern western Scandinavia—Sweden, Norway, and Denmark. During the Viking age, the Scandinavians grew to become the masters of the European seas, setting out from their forested encampments in longboats manned with twoscore or more warriors, pulling oars and hoisting sail that would carry the ships as far distant as Greenland and North America, Africa and Asia.

In 862, these Northmen interrupted their wanderings in the east long enough to establish a city, called Novgorod, or New Town, still standing today with the monumental church dedicated to its Swedish founder, Rurik. Novgorod, expanded into a city-state, would come to be synonymous with the realm of Russia: the native inhabitants of the region had called the Swedish invaders Ruotsi, shortened to Rusi, eventually to become the name of the entire land itself.[22]

Back in Sweden, by the mid-1100s Christianity had grown strong enough so that King Eric, called Eric the Holy, felt able to justify a military mission to conquer Finland, wrapping it in the banner of a Christian crusade of the sort then devastating much of Eurasia. The campaign proved a success, and the now subjugated Finland was added to the Swedish domains.

In 1521, at the end of the so-called Union Epoch of Scandinavian history in which Denmark tried—at times successfully—to politically unite the Danish, Norwegian, and Swedish crowns, the Swedes under the twenty-three-year-old nobleman Gustavus Vasa rose against the interference of these despised Danes. The successful Gustavus, founder of the modern Swedish state and of its greatest royal dynasty, assumed the crown two years later, becoming in the bargain the country's first absolutist monarch.

The reign of Gustavus II Adolphus brought Protestant Sweden squarely and victoriously into the middle of European power politics. The king and his army acted as major players in the most destructive so far of the continent's armed struggles, the gruesome Thirty Years' War. The 1648 Peace of Westphalia ending the war guaranteed Swedish freedom of conscience from the Catholicism of Rome and brought the northern kingdom to the most militarily powerful standing it had ever attained or that it would ever attain again.

After endless decades of warfare, years in which the Swedes wrested the south of their peninsula from Denmark to gain what have ever since remained their natural water frontiers, Sweden took a breather from battle for the relatively pacific reign of Charles XI. When that monarch died of stomach cancer in April 1697, with the country's resources at the highest level in its history, Sweden's destiny fell into the hands of his fifteen-year-old son, the new Charles XII, a monarch whose actions shaped Sweden's future to the present day. The absolutist state nurtured by his predecessors proved a disaster: his kingdom would be reduced to penury, its military strength wasted, and the balance of power between itself and Russia permanently cast—in the latter's favor.

Charles's fellow sovereign and arch-nemesis reigned with a passion over the great Russian empire whose nucleus the Swedes of a millennium before had wrested from the Slavic wilderness. Tsar Peter—to all the generations in his wide wake known as Peter the Great—had with the kings of Saxony, Poland, and Denmark formed an alliance to thwart the Swedish power all Europe's monarchs saw as a threat to their own interests. Charles's defeat came in 1709 when his capabilities finally exceeded his reach, and all the Swedish monarch's initial victories against Peter counted as nothing in the reckoning brought about by his final battle. Determined to put an end to what he considered the Russian menace to the unity of the Germanic peoples, Charles set out on a campaign to destroy Peter. But in a herculean struggle at the little Ukrainian town of Poltava, it was Peter who emerged victorious, with the Swedish sovereign losing virtually his entire 32,000-man army. The Swedish ascendancy on the continent would rapidly end as his enemies turned on him, evidently ungrateful for the latter-day Viking king's effort to keep Russia from Western Europe. After he pressed from his deeply exhausted people yet another army to take the field against the Norwegians, recently allied to Russia, the Carolean saga finally spun itself out when Charles was shot and killed at the Battle of Fredriksten on the first Sunday in Advent in 1718, the last of modern Europe's monarchs to fall in battle. In the end, his legacy to his country proved to be a negative one:

a lasting hatred of the Russians, an attitude fully in play when World War II started.

Gustavus IV Adolphus stuck closely to Britain and its allies during the Napoleonic wars, but his place in Baltic history is secured by the unhappy fact that losing a war in 1809 against Russia led to Sweden's loss, first of Pomerania, then of Finland, the latter after six and a half centuries of that nation's control by its Scandinavian neighbor. The disaster enabled a revivified parliament—called the Riksdag—both to compel the king to abdicate and then to put a new constitution into effect, one that crippled the monarch's powers. The ex-king's uncle was called in to reign as Charles XIII. But the by then venerable Charles was both old and childless, a situation leading to one of the strangest royal personnel hunts in history, as well as the establishment of the dynasty still reigning in Sweden.

Knowing he wouldn't be fathering a child, and seeing Prince Christian Augustus, Stadtholder of Norway and his first choice as successor, predecease him by way of a stroke, Charles and the Riksdag went looking for an heir. What they hit on was one of Napoleon's marshals, Jean Baptiste Jules Bernadotte, Roman Catholic, son of a southern French petit bourgeois, out of favor with the emperor though recently created Prince of Ponte Corvo, hawkish, possessor of few significant military credits—but available and willing. Bernadotte went through the motions of asking his emperor's permission. Napoleon reputedly exclaimed, "Preposterous! Absurd!" but he nonetheless granted the request. Duly elected by the Riksdag as Crown Prince Charles John, he arrived in Sweden in October 1810, where almost immediately the new heir assumed complete dominance over his adoptive father, the tottering Charles XIII. The house of Bernadotte de Ponte Corvo had set up shop and Sweden's modern era had begun.

The new crown prince's energies found their outlet in matters military. Having gained the consent of Great Britain, Russia, and Prussia in accepting his Swedish position, Charles John led a Swedish contingent into Germany and assumed command of the northern army assembled to defeat Napoleon. One of the dividends for turning against his old boss was recognition by the powers of Swedish domain over Norway. That recognition led to the union of the two countries' crowns in 1815 after a short, sharp military campaign a year earlier waged to extinguish a burgeoning Norwegian independence movement. Disappointing the hopes of the Riksdag that had put him forward for his position, the crown prince decided, however, not to try to regain Finland from Russia. By the time Charles XIII died in 1818, and Charles John became King Charles XIV

John, Sweden had with the Norwegian episode four years earlier shed its last blood on the battlefield. What was more, power in Sweden was at the same time being irreversibly transferred from the palace to the elected parliament and its responsible ministers, where it has resided ever since.

Sweden's *real* golden age was now beginning. Maintaining peace and neutrality and putting the collective national muscle into rebuilding Swedish prosperity from its state of war-induced impoverishment, the new Bernadotte dynasty was off to a brilliant start. Reforms begun by the ex-marshal continued under his son, Oscar I, and grandson, Charles XV. The latter inaugurated the modern representative constitution, importantly guaranteeing religious equality for all Swedes, including the country's several thousand Jews.

Charles was succeeded by his brother, Oscar II, in whose reign Norway peaceably broke off from the Swedish crown, founding its own revivified throne under the rule of the Danish Prince Charles as its new King Haakon VII. Two years after the dissolution of the Swedish-Norwegian union, Oscar's son—and Bernadotte's great-grandson—succeeded as Gustav V. It was this monarch who at the age of eighty-one found himself on Sweden's throne as Hitler marched into Poland.

· · ·

Sweden's mission throughout the 1930s had been to suckle and nourish Scandinavia's neutrality, virtually at any cost. One of the primary tools to ensure this undertaking's success was through the consolidated determination of an organization called the "Oslo States"—a convention of seven nations originally conceived in 1930 as a group committed to opposing tariff increases. Initially meeting in the Norwegian capital, thus giving it its name, the loose union was conceived by the Dutch soldier-administrator-statesman Dr. Hendrikus Colijn. The Northern nations of Sweden, Norway, Denmark, and Finland were joined in the pact by the contiguous continental states of the Netherlands, Belgium, and Luxembourg. As the decade's woes increased, the organization switched to the far more important concern of keeping its members neutral instead of tariff matters.

The Scandinavian members of the convention formally notified the League of Nations that they would no longer participate in the League's military sanctions, reasoning—with some logic—that the League was too weak to make its sanctions stick, but in the doing hammering another nail into the already moribund organization's coffin. The problems the Oslo group faced were much the same as those faced by all the other European states then scurrying out of harm's way: how to survive in case of general war among the continent's Great Powers, and how to convince those powers that the self-declared neutrals should be left in peace.

Until the shock of the Russo-German pact, the Stockholm government was convinced the Oslo group's fervent protestations of noninvolvement might be successful in exempting Sweden from Hitler's rapacity. It also hoped to be thus spared the enormous cost of building up its own military defense to a level necessary to give an aggressor second thoughts about an attack. Though cognizant of the brutality of Hitler and the Nazis, most Swedes had so far believed the North wouldn't be drawn into a continental war. But the Moscow agreement and the new wild card in the European balance it represented changed the formula drastically: the Soviets would no longer be a brake on German-Italian ambitions against the democracies, and Moscow now seemed militarily free to do pretty much what it wanted north of the Baltic.

Sweden's defense buildup had been allowed to lag far behind both its capabilities and a credible condition fitting to its policy of neutrality. Though by the late summer of 1939 Sweden's determination to defend itself in a worst-case scenario had translated into a stronger defensive military posture than any of the other Oslo states possessed, the Social Democratic (Labor) government led by Prime Minister Per Albin Hansson had so far rejected the Conservative opposition's demands for greatly increased military spending. Hansson's policy had until recently met with the electorate's approval. In the September 1936 elections the voters returned the socialists to office with the greatest popular vote that a party had ever received in Sweden—and the party's platform was squarely based on opposition to increased defense spending.

But when the reality of fascism's unappeasability sank in with the signing of the Munich Pact in September 1938, the government began its first tentative steps toward substantially preparing the country for what might lie ahead. The prime minister notified Europe's strongmen that his country's policy was neutrality and its values peace and liberty, but that despite the former it would defend the latter "with all its might." In a speech, Hansson affirmed that "we look on no one as our enemy [but] the strengthening of our defense preparations serves merely to underline our fixed determination to keep our country outside the conflicts among others and, during such conflicts, to safeguard the existence of our people."[23]

As fortune would have it, a completely unexpected war, one between

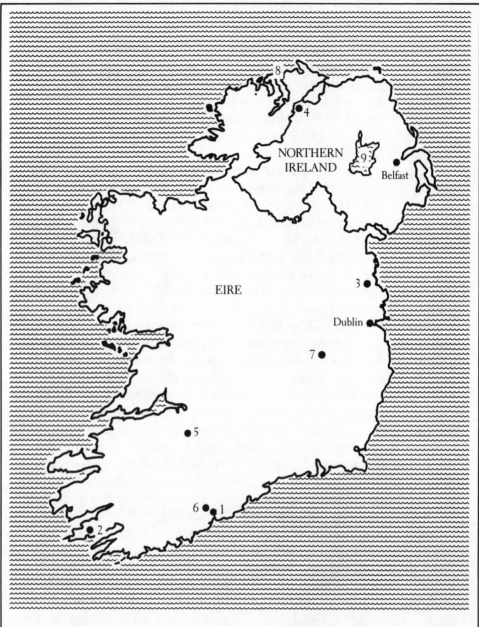

IRELAND

1. Cobh
2. Berehaven
3. Battle of the Boyne
4. Derry (or Londonderry)
5. Bruree

6. Cork
7. Curragh, the
8. Lough Swilly
9. Lough Neagh

the giant Soviet Union and its peaceable Finnish neighbor, would within weeks break out just across the Gulf of Bothnia. And for the second time since August 23, all of Sweden's bets would be off.

Dublin

For this sundered island, the first weekend in September was endured in two entirely different frameworks. In the north—Ulster—the first three days of this historic month signaled that the province would almost certainly soon be at war with Germany. For the far larger south, the overriding issue was how neutrality in the looming war could be preserved. For Ireland as a whole, that dichotomy, one fostered by a tragedy-filled history leading to a siege mentality, would underscore a bitterness that in the half century since has come to create an unbridgeable chasm.

In London, the king's first minister, Neville Chamberlain, and his cabinet had a great deal more to worry about this summer weekend than the question of Eire's loyalty to Britain in the catastrophe overtaking Europe. As with the other dominions—Canada, New Zealand, Australia, South Africa—Ireland's complete fidelity was, despite the provisions of the External Relations Act of 1936 whereby Dublin virtually declared its total independence, simply expected. What was most assuredly *not* expected was the firm resolve on the part of Eire's prime minister, Eamon de Valera,[24] that his nation should stay out of this war, whatever the price.

If the British thought relatively little about the "loyalty" of its dominion, the German Foreign Office had given close attention to the question of Eire's actions if hostilities were to break out. On August 29, two days before Germany's attack on Poland, Hitler's foreign minister, Joachim von Ribbentrop, instructed Eduard Hempel, the German minister resident in Dublin, to clearly apprise de Valera's government of Germany's offer of normal relations so long as Eire remained neutral if war came. Ribbentrop wrote Hempel:

> In accordance with the friendly relations between ourselves and Ireland we are determined to refrain from any hostile action against Irish territory and to respect her integrity, provided that Ireland, for her part, maintains unimpeachable neutrality towards us in any conflict. Only if this condition should no longer obtain as a result of a decision on the part of the Irish government themselves, or by pressure exerted on Ireland from other quarters, should we be compelled as a matter of course . . . to safeguard our interests in the sphere of warfare in such a way as the situation then arising might demand of us.

. . . Furthermore the German government would make every effort to restrict as far as possible to an absolute minimum any unavoidable repercussions which might arise for Ireland and Irish trade from Germany's conduct of the war. We are, of course, aware of the difficulties involved in the geographical position of Ireland.[25]

After two days of digesting his prickly superior's instructions, the careful Hempel wired back to the Foreign Ministry in Berlin:

. . . De Valera repeated the statement that the Government's aim was to remain neutral. The final decision would have to be taken by the Irish Parliament in due course. . . . He said that in spite of the Irish Government's sincere desire to observe neutrality equally toward both belligerents, Ireland's dependence on Britain for trade vital to Ireland on one hand, and on the other the possibility of intervention by Britain if the independence of Ireland involved an immediate danger for Great Britain, rendered it inevitable for the Irish Government to show a *certain consideration* for Britain, which in similar circumstances they would also show for Germany. . . .[26]

In theory, Eire was in 1939 (and would remain throughout World War II) still—at least symbolically—a British dominion and still a member of the Commonwealth of Nations, the United Kingdom's configuration of colonies, former colonies, and dependencies whose focal point and principal glue was the British monarch. But its dominion status did not, in the eyes of its government, require it to fight alongside Britain in this or any other war. Of vital importance to understanding Eire in World War II is the fact that Dublin's determination to remain neutral was firmly supported by the overwhelming majority of the country's people and by virtually every interest group—politicians, diplomats, writers, the press, the church. Though the Irish government was sympathetic to the fate of Poland, the concerns and limitations of its own partitioned island homeland took precedence over that sympathy. The people of Eire overwhelmingly ascribed their partitioned status to British policy, and to fight at Britain's side while their island was divided was anathema to them—and anathema to their prime minister. Partition was not, of course, the only reason for the policy Eire would follow for the next six years, and had the island been politically whole de Valera still would not necessarily have brought his state into the war. As Lord Longford concluded in his biography of the Taoiseach (the Gaelic word for "prime minister" and de Valera's title throughout the coming conflict), though a lack of partition would have transformed the situation, "one can only speculate as to what path [an undivided] Ireland would or would not have taken"[27] in World War II.

.   .   .

The sources of that wound and many others were concealed under countless layers of the Irish psyche. Though Ireland had been a semi-colonial
dependency of the British crown since the seventeenth century, the troubles between it and the more powerful island to its east are buried in a far
more distant past. In the Europe of 1939, only Poland shared with Ireland a condition in which politics were so largely the result of an ancient
legacy.

The Celts, a race whose ancestors once peopled almost half of Western Europe, were the first to settle the island.[28] Culturally precocious,
these prolific nomads were first cousin to the Scots and the Angles who
populated Britain before the stronger Saxons supplanted their dominion.
But these early Irish dissipated their strength in the feuds of rival kinglets,
economically exhausting the island and their culture along with it. In the
late twelfth century, the Plantagenet King Henry II became the first
English sovereign to plant his standard and England's claim on Ireland's
soil, near today's Dublin. In what thereafter became known as "the Pale,"
English law took root, but the invaders themselves soon assimilated with
the native Celts into a kind of common gene pool. A native parliament
was established, albeit one hedged closely with English infringements.

Though a "high king" had for a brief period presided over the island's
lesser kings, no true politically united Ireland had ever existed, and what
limited measures of self-government the Irish enjoyed continued to be
steadily whittled away by the English interlopers. Both within and without the Pale, English suzerainty was maintained by a Lord Deputy representing and appointed by the Crown and free from any encroachments
on his authority by the native parliament in Dublin.

The break that would most fundamentally estrange the smaller island
from the larger came in the sixteenth-century reign of Henry VIII, who
transferred his realm's supreme religious authority from the pope to himself. The Irish would not follow this apostasy, remaining steadfastly—
some would have said virulently—adherent to the old faith. In the
following century, the character of the northern part of the island—
primarily the province of Ulster—would be transformed into a British
image when King James I decreed the settling of that corner of Ireland by
native English and Scots in what was called the Plantation. The lands
thus confiscated from the indigenous Ulster Irish became heavily British
and Protestant in character, the native Irish Catholics forming a minority
of Ulster's population to beget a conundrum that lasts to the present day.

James's less able successor lost almost all of Ireland for England. But though the Irish in revolt against Charles I were triumphant in the short term (their sixteenth-century massacre of newly settled Protestants in Ulster left bitter memories—predictably exaggerated—to be revenged), they were tragically unsuccessful in the longer run. When Oliver Cromwell and his Roundheads—so called from the close-cropped haircuts favored by these Puritans—overturned the monarchy, with their leader creating himself Lord Protector of the new republican Commonwealth, Cromwell saw it as his duty to reclaim Ireland and in the doing begot a sea of hatred of Irish for English that knew no shores. Large parts of the island were distributed to Cromwell's officers, turning countless Irish hearts unexpiable in bitterness.

This so-called Cromwellian Settlement—really an English political rape of the island and extension of Protestant settlement island-wide—was in effect in 1689, when the deposed Catholic king, James II, attempted to utilize Ireland as his route back to the throne. Landing on the ill-used island and receiving the support of all Irish except the Ulster Protestants, the incompetent James led his fellow Catholics in Ireland in a crusade against the English throne. But he—and they—were so badly beaten at the Battle of the Boyne a year later that their English oppressors were able to forestall any more Irish attempts at rebellion for more than a century. So severe did English repression of the Irish become that the latter were by the end of the seventeenth century probably the most thoroughly downtrodden people of Western Europe.

The Napoleonic wars perhaps economically weakened Britain, but not so much that it couldn't crush with practiced brutality whatever revolutionary ambitions the Irish people got themselves up to—specifically, their 1798 rebellion against the Crown. The British government "scientifically" regarded the constitutional union that followed in the wake of this aborted uprising as a "structural" answer to the Irish problem. London hoped that a heavy dose of forced Irish assimilation of English truths might go a long way toward reducing Ireland's troublesome sectarianism. The parliament in Dublin was abolished, but the British viceroy remained in his Dublin Castle headquarters, with Ireland's parliamentary representation now installed in Westminster. Britain saw the new arrangement as a "true" United Kingdom, and William Pitt, the prime minister responsible for the undertaking, hoped the Act of Union would be beneficial to the Irish. The Irish—aside from Ulster's Protestants—saw it as continued oppression from across the water, particularly in light of the vicious reprisals that followed the crushing of their rebellious aspirations.

The Act of Union resulted in relatively quiet times in Anglo-Irish relations for more than forty years—until the mid-1840s. Irish history and Ireland today are still shaped by the events of what next transpired: the horrendous potato famine and the resulting halving of the island's population, partly by emigration to America, partly by death from starvation. The blight knew no nationality, but the policies that worsened its effect were indisputably British, a fact no Irishman was likely to forget. By mid-century, Daniel O'Connell began to effectively champion an Irish quest for "home rule," a political pursuit meant to allow the Irish to govern their own affairs while remaining under the ultimate authority of the United Kingdom. Home rule advocates succeeded by 1873 in creating an Irish Nationalist Party in the House of Commons, with Charles Stewart Parnell its charismatic leader. Parnell finally persuaded Liberal prime minister William Gladstone to introduce an Irish home rule bill in Parliament. The bill provided Ireland with a legislature responsible for all matters Irish, leaving imperial affairs to Westminster. The semi-autonomous island was to contribute one-seventeenth of the expenses required to run the empire, but was not to be represented any longer in the British parliament, this last provision—in effect, taxation without representation—highly repugnant to the Irish Nationalists, as the same thing had been a few decades earlier to the American colonists.

Nonetheless, Parnell won widespread Irish support for Gladstone's bill. What killed it—and any hope of averting the tragedy which would in a few years overtake the Anglo-Irish relationship—were the anti-home rule forces in Westminster, ironically led by Liberals from the prime minister's party, who now styled themselves Liberal-Unionists. A new Liberal-Unionist-dominated ministry finally snuffed out the bill wholly.

Gladstone in his next ministry tried again, this time in 1893. The new measure would allow Ireland eighty representatives in the British House of Commons, members who would be permitted to vote only on Irish matters. Though the Commons passed it, the far more conservative Lords then vetoed it—by a huge majority. Ireland regarded the measure's fate as another English knife in its already badly scarred back. Though by the turn of the century the worst excesses of the Protestant "Ascendancy"— the political and social overlordship of Ireland by an Anglo-Irish oligarchy—were over, the embittered relationship between Ireland and Britain was not, by any means, on the mend.

The Parliament Act of 1911 at last curbed much of the Lords' power to thwart the will of the elected government, and a new prime minister tried a third time to get Irish home rule passed. This latest measure was a mix of the first two, and it successfully passed the Commons in 1912. The still recalcitrant Lords again defeated it, but procedure now allowed the bill to go into effect against such veto after a two-year waiting period. A sizable measure of hard-won Irish independence was thereby set for the summer of 1914, despite the resistance of Ulster's Protestants, who objected bitterly to the idea of being ruled by Dublin instead of Westminster and whose leaders promised civil war rather than acquiesce.

World War I put off the reckoning. All parties decided to place home rule on hold while Britain and its empire went off to the continent to fight the Hun. The politicians agreed to wait until the war's end to put home rule into effect, and also promised to find some way to accede to Ulster's desire that that province continue to be run by fellow Protestants from London. Senior Irish politicians may have put loyalty to king and empire ahead of Ireland's aspirations for freedom, but very many young and headstrong Irish believed that Britain's emergency was Ireland's opportunity—indeed its best opportunity to secure freedom since Napoleonic days. Many urged striking for complete independence while England was mired in the mud of Flanders and running to put out fires on an array of other war fronts. Naturally, Germany obliquely agreed to help these anti-British patriots in any way it could—specifically with money, arms, and ammunition.

Leading the movement in Ireland for independence from Britain was a republican organization that took its poetic name, Sinn Fein,[29] from the Irish-Gaelic for "ourselves alone." Sinn Fein found little difficulty in attracting adherents at a time when thousands of young Irish soldiers were being sacrificed into the bottomless maw of the Western Front for an amorphous cause in which Ireland and its interests seemed to be far removed. (Of the quarter million enlisted Irish who fought in the war, 27,405 were killed.) Finally, at Easter 1916, the republicans rose in the opening act of the final assault against the British in Catholic Ireland. Though this Easter Rising proved a military failure, it (abetted by the terror and executions it spawned) resulted in giving birth to far more militant and virulently anti-British feelings, feelings that would no longer be satisfied with the kind of prewar home rule bills that issued stillborn from Westminster.

Not surprisingly, the British took the rising, coming in the middle of their war, as the most dastardly kind of treason, and hounded many of its principal participants all the way to the gallows. There was, significantly, never any meaningful German help; all that Ireland provided was the occasional sanctuary the Kaiser's U-boats found in remote west Irish harbors. Eamon de Valera himself was in 1917 sentenced to death by a military tribunal on charges of conspiring with the Germans, after which he was briefly imprisoned; when the British found out their prisoner had been born an American, he was released: Westminster was most anxious that the United States should come into the war and therefore shrank from giving that country's large Irish population any possible offense. [30]

Though he is now so much a part of Ireland's modern history that his existence as the father of the Irish Republic seems somehow to have been ordained, de Valera got to the shamrock isle very nearly by accident. The future Taoiseach was born in October 1882, not in Ireland, but in New York City. His mother, from County Limerick, had migrated to New York in 1879 and went into domestic service, sharing the fate of tens of thousands of young uneducated immigrants. Of the man she married, little is known. Vivion de Valera was born in Spain, possibly with the original name Vevian De Valero. He died in Denver in either 1884 or 1885—the date is uncertain. Eamon's birth record said his father's occupation was an artist. Other than these sketchy facts little is known with certainty about the father of the father of modern Ireland.

Ireland's future protagonist arrived on that island in 1885, when at three years of age he was brought by his uncle. He first lived with his grandmother and another uncle in a laborer's cottage in Bruree, County Limerick. His higher education came by winning school prizes and was fleshed out by teaching. At the age of twenty-eight, the now professor of mathematics married Sinead Flanagan, the lifelong companion who would give him six sons and a daughter, all of whom survived the considerable dangers of childhood, and all of whom—except Brian, killed in a riding accident in 1936—rose to positions of stature in their own adulthoods. [31]

The Easter Rising of 1916, now regarded as a glorious icon of the nation's will to independence though it was in reality a military failure, gave the gawky math professor—up to then only a minor figure in the Irish independence struggle—a substantial position in the struggle's pantheon. Assigned command of a battalion, de Valera was detailed the task of holding two miles of a strategic Dublin railway line and canal. At Boland's mill, where he made his battalion headquarters, the British were fast closing in on him and his 50 men. His celebrated exhortation to his troopers—"You have but one life to live and one death to die. See that you do both like men"—became the genesis of the de Valera legend.

His men fought their British attackers bravely, wounding 300 Britons and keeping the enemy—some 2,000 Sherwood Foresters—from crossing the Mount Street Bridge and marching to the center of the rebellion at the General Post Office. When the fight ended, the Irish overwhelmed, de Valera was the last commander to surrender. A month later, the professor-cum-revolutionary was condemned to death. Unlike the others similarly sentenced, de Valera's condemnation was commuted to life imprisonment in Britain for reasons we've seen.

When the future Taoiseach was released from his English jail in the 1917 general amnesty, he returned to Ireland acclaimed a hero. Thousands of Irish men and women who idolized him wore little badges bearing his picture, even though to do so could still lead to arrest and imprisonment by the British authorities. Many—some said most—of the nation's homes hung his picture in places of honor, and Irish Republicans sang, inconsistently, "We'll crown de Valera King of Ireland."[32]

In June 1918, Britain put forward conscription for Ireland, prompting the republican-minded Nationalists and others to disown any allegiance to the British parliament. Six months later de Valera declared an Irish Republic, with himself as president of the Dáil—the new legislature's House of Commons.[33] With Britain's quick suppression of the Dáil and within months of the ending of the European war, the final Anglo-Irish struggle got well and truly underway, Sinn Fein—by now a coalition of different interests—leading the republicans in the fray.

In May 1920, to reinforce its Irish constabulary and put down the quickening revolt, Britain began shipping to Ireland reserve troops—the infamous Black and Tans, so called for the colors of their uniforms and soon to be internationally notorious for the ferocity of their methods. The British ruthlessly carried out their mission with wholesale reprisals and multiple hangings. For over a year, the two forces—the Black and Tans and the IRA—fought an unrelenting but undeclared war all over Ireland, with bombs, arson, torture, and hostages its weapons. Finally and after excesses reflecting the Great War itself, the British public came to question their nation's right to continue to repress the beleaguered island. Another home rule bill, hurriedly passed by Parliament, would be rejected out of hand by the now far less tractable Irish leadership.

Though considerations of national defense and atavistic maintenance of the empire's status quo were still high on Britain's list of reasons to retain Ireland, much of London's quandary centered on the problem in the north, the problem of a people who wanted neither rule by Dublin nor "freedom" from the protective bonds of the United Kingdom. But Britain came increasingly to recognize that the war with Ireland could not continue indefinitely, at least not without the expenditure of an enormous cost in blood and coin. Negotiations for ending the struggle had to be opened, the alternative being that Britain would find itself required to send a very considerable and very expensive force to the island to maintain the Crown's hold. To pursue a compromise, the prime minister, David Lloyd George, invited Sinn Fein leaders to London.

There a settlement was at last reached. Most of the island—the part in which Catholics predominated—was to become a semi-independent entity called the Irish Free State, a self-governing dominion on the lines of Canada or Australia. Six of the nine counties of Ulster, the heavily Protestant province in the north (800,000 Protestants lived with 400,000 Catholics in the six counties), were to become an autonomous region of the United Kingdom called Northern Ireland, with both its own parliament and the right to send representatives to Westminster.[34] It should be noted that there are absolutely no natural boundaries between the two political parts of the island—the new border would arbitrarily cut farms in half, separate villages, split highways. Furthermore, there would be substantial parts of Ulster where Catholics were in a majority, Derry City (called Londonderry by the British and Protestant Ulstermen) the most prominent example.

The proposed treaty solution didn't work. At least not to the satisfaction of the less moderate-minded southern republicans who saw it as a form of second-class citizenship for their northern brethren. With de Valera at the helm (and losing overnight his immense nationwide popularity for turning on his former comrades), the radicals tried to continue the war against Britain in order to avoid partition. But the war-sickened British soon opted out of a continued fight. The conflict thus turned into civil war, between the anti-treaty de Valera-led radicals and the pro-treaty moderates who wanted to accept the Irish Free State, imperfect but at peace.

The armed struggle of republican Irishman against his republican brother went on interminably, the barbaric instruments of assassination and arson used against the British again being taken up by Irish against Irish. Finally, constitutional means to breach the deadlock between factions were turned to by de Valera in 1923. Breaking with the most die-hard radicals, de Valera walked out of the Sinn Fein and founded a new party called the Fianna Fail—"Soldiers of Destiny." Winning a legitimate seat in the Dáil, he began a drive against his former IRA companions which would invoke draconian methods to break their continued resistance. Within a few years, de Valera had become his nation's undisputed international spokesman and, in 1932, its head of government as well. But from the moment his faction gave up the fight, de Valera started to plan the demise of the Free State and the birth of a completely free and independent Ireland.

In 1933, the prime minister began a campaign of total independence from Britain by insisting that the right to choose the governor-general—the Crown's chief representative in Ireland and theoretically its ranking personage—be exercised from Dublin rather than from London. Widening the breach, he further demanded that the governor-general forswear the right to withhold the royal assent from legislation enacted by the Irish parliament. The Taoiseach then abolished the Irish citizen's right to take appeals from the Irish Supreme Court to the British Privy Council. Finally, in 1937, de Valera took the step that would permit Irish neutrality in World War II—the promulgation of a new constitution with its near-abrogation of the fifteen-year-old Free State. There was by this time little Britain could do to stop him.

The constitution of 1937 turned the twenty-six counties of southern Ireland into what was virtually an independent nation—a near-republic, at least near enough that it would in the future conduct its affairs entirely independent from the United Kingdom. It was still—certainly in London's view—a dominion, like Canada and Australia and New Zealand, and it was a member of the Commonwealth and theoretically recognized the British monarch as the head of that Commonwealth,[35] but the single substantive hedge on its sovereignty was that of guaranteed use of three of its ports by the British Navy in time of war. Yet the fact was that by its unilateral constitution, the legal status of Eire—the official name of the state according to the 1937 constitution[36]—was entirely clear neither to itself nor to the United Kingdom, and, because of the matter of the ports, its declaration of intention to remain neutral in any international conflict certainly was not clear to any potential belligerent. The most important strategic question bearing on the relationship between Britain and Eire remained this thorny matter of the "Treaty Ports."

Part of the price Eire paid for the 1921 treaty with Britain involved the mandatory lease for the Royal Navy's use in time of war of three of the island's finest and safest harbors (outside of British Ulster): Lough Swilly, on the north Donegal coast, commanding the route passing to the north of the island; Berehaven, in the extreme southwest, commanding the south coast; and Cobh,[37] in the southeast, a major port of call for Atlantic shipping. All had been of immense importance to Britain in World War I, when Lough Swilly sheltered thirty British destroyers operating in the North Atlantic, Berehaven provided dockyard facilities to heavy Royal Naval units controlling the North Atlantic, and Cobh based thirty-four American destroyers holding open the southern approaches to England.

Lough Swilly lies in County Donegal, at the top of Ireland. Its deepwater harborage is impregnably situated at the end of the eighteen-mile fjordlike passage bored between the Knockalla Mountains and the Inishowen peninsula. The guns of Forts Dunree and Lenan protected its naval facilities. At the southwest of Ireland, directly addressing the heavily traveled Atlantic sea lanes, Berehaven nestles hidden behind the fortified Bere Island in Bantry Bay. The harbor is nearly the last landfall of the Old World, and, like Lough Swilly, was one of the assembly points for Great War convoys to the New World. The last of the three, and a hundred miles to the east of Berehaven on the south coast, is Cobh, the former Queenstown, which had been regally renamed in honor of being the first place Queen Victoria landed on her 1849 visit to Ireland. Hidden behind Spike Island and serving as port for Ireland's third-largest city, Cork, Cobh had functioned longest of the three as a naval anchorage. Flanking it were two strongly fortified army posts, Forts Camden and Carlisle, as well as a network of lesser facilities designed to enhance the impregnability of the site. For the three ports together, nearly four thousand officers and men guarded their facilities, which in the aggregate could provide moorage for more than a hundred of Britain's warships.

In light of those critical services, Britain's retention of the ports and their bases in the agreement giving Ireland semi-independence in 1921 was considered to be vital to British security. They controlled access to the open Atlantic and gave far wider control of the North Sea than was possible from Britain itself. Because of their superb ship basing and repair facilities, works into which the Admiralty and the Department of War had sunk millions of pounds since the beginning of the nineteenth century, they were among the empire's most strategically and economically valuable harbors. Whitehall and the Admiralty calculated that the ports acted as a 500-mile semicircular ring of protection around the kingdom's western perimeter, an estimation that in light of their Great War role caused them to figure importantly in British demands when negotiations got underway with Irish republicans at the end of that war.

But by 1938, the prime minister, Neville Chamberlain, decided a grand gesture would go far in mending still bruised Anglo-Irish relations. Anxious to assuage Irish nationalism, Chamberlain—almost infathomably, in retrospect—decided to permit the bases' leases to lapse, characterizing the gesture as an "act of faith."[38] The British premier assumed, perhaps naively, that in the event of war Dublin would lease them to Britain again, but the provision of the 1921 treaty—specifically, Article 7 and its Annex—by which the former Irish Free State was to be a cobelligerent of Britain in any war in which it might engage was also abrogated by Whitehall (it had already been abrogated in Dublin's estimation in its 1937 constitution). The British military chiefs concurred, apprising the government that a British division would be required to hold each port if Ireland were actively hostile and that Britain's forward Atlantic sea lanes could always be protected by use of French ports instead of Irish ports. Usually a voice in the political wilderness in these years, Winston Churchill strenuously objected to what he considered folly. Railing against the ports' loss in a May 1938 speech in the House of Commons, he characterized the three as the "sentinel towers of the western approaches."[39] Speaking hotly, he warned that "the dark forces of the Irish underworld had already tried to stab Britain in the back during the World War and de Valera would not be able to control them if he assumed a friendly attitude toward Britain."[40]

To de Valera, the issue of the ports represented a foreboding. Anticipating the war Europe was heading into, he judged that Ireland would not be able to maintain a policy of neutrality if Britain were allowed the use of the ports, a situation which would permit Germany to disregard any profession of neutrality on Eire's part and consider the south as much a belligerent as it would undoubtedly regard Ulster. The result would be an Ireland dragged into any war despite its efforts to stay out. On top of that concern, de Valera equally believed that if Britain once again gained access to these significant bits of independent Ireland, it might never again be so foolish as to leave. When Chamberlain solved the problem for him, de Valera would come to look upon the return of the ports as one of the greatest political successes of his public life. He knew that the end of partition would not in the short term be politically possible, but the return of the ports, which would allow Eire's neutrality in a European war, was indisputably a victory.

• • •

For most of the rest of the world, including Ulster, the calamitous events of 1939–45 were "World War II." For Eire, they were, officially and popularly, "the Emergency." It was a term that came to dominate life on the island, as the Taoiseach gingerly led his country along the tightrope— the only neutral behind what were, in effect, the Allied lines. High on de Valera's list of priorities was convincing the world that his neutrality wasn't a tilt toward Germany on the part of a people whose resentment for the British never sank very far below the surface. And what became the enduring fear in Eire for the next two years was invasion—not from Germany, but from Britain.

Though the Irish leader had formally stated seven months earlier in 1939 that Eire would remain outside any European conflict, it was still by no means clear to Whitehall that he would carry out his pledge if Britain actually went to war with Germany. Even when the Dáil officially adopted neutrality on September 2—the day after the German attack on

Poland—Irish neutrality didn't, in London's estimation, carry any internationally recognized "validity," as did that of the Swiss.[41] After all, Britain was by far the largest trading partner for Ireland, and the Twenty-six Counties would obviously be unable to defend themselves in any battle with the Wehrmacht. It was held by the British cabinet that an invasion of Britain itself might well be preceded by a German landing in militarily weak Ireland, both to better position the Wehrmacht for an attack on the west of England and to more securely control the sea lanes around Ireland.

Although de Valera firmly held the backing of the vast majority of the Irish people in the neutrality policy, there were still influential voices in the Dáil not ready to accept it. Some opposed neutrality on a moral stand, deeming the Allied cause to be patently morally superior to that of the Germans and thus worthy of being fought for. The more sanguine among the opposition deputies believed neutrality couldn't represent more than a gesture, that Eire couldn't possibly maintain such a stance lying as it did athwart Britain's vital trade routes. They further reasoned that the presence of a British province in the northern part of the island would inevitably bring the war to the south.

In any event, some British concluded that Irish neutrality wasn't serious—or at least could be breached without serious costs. Some ten minutes after Neville Chamberlain's BBC announcement on September 3 that Britain was at war with Germany, the crew of an RAF Sunderland seaplane touched down in Irish waters off the Skerries, a group of islets in the Irish Sea. The Garda, Eire's police force, didn't know whether or not to intern the fliers, word apparently not having been received from the authorities in Dublin on what to do in such a happenstance. After some dithering, the Garda allowed the plane to be refueled and it took off on its watery runway in the direction of home.

To the hard-pressed British, the issue of a single flying boat couldn't have had much importance in the first confused hours of the war. But to de Valera, any incident reflecting on his nation's determination to remain neutral was critical. Though he tried to suppress any mention of the matter, the natural worry to the Taoiseach was that the Germans would view any such acts as decidedly unneutral, and they would thus provide the Reich the excuse it needed to attack Eire or its interests.

The reality of war became quickly apparent in the hamlet of Pettigo, sitting smack on the frontier between dominion and province. The halves of the village presented very different looks after sundown, when on the Ulster side every light from September 3 onward was extinguished in the general blackout. In the peaceful Eire part of the sundered town the usual

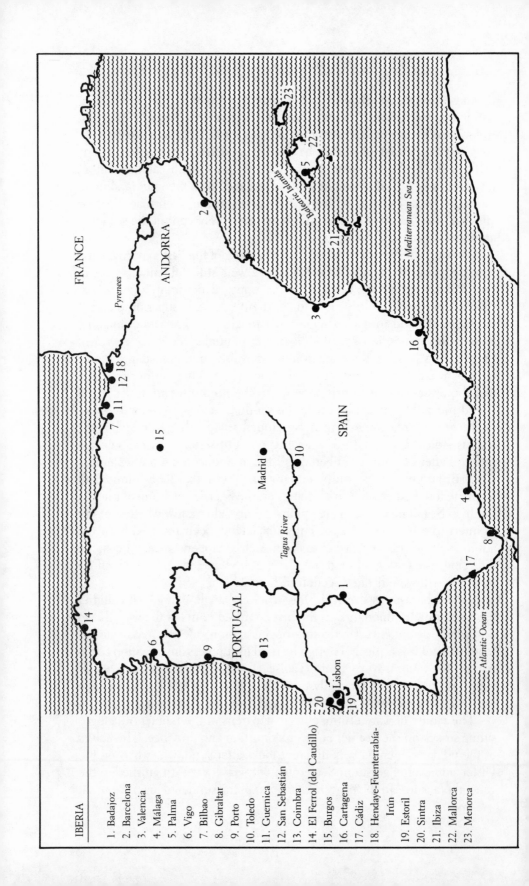

IBERIA

1. Badajoz
2. Barcelona
3. Valencia
4. Málaga
5. Palma
6. Vigo
7. Bilbao
8. Gibraltar
9. Porto
10. Toledo
11. Guernica
12. San Sebastián
13. Coimbra
14. El Ferrol (del Caudillo)
15. Burgos
16. Cartagena
17. Cádiz
18. Hendaye-Fuenterrabia-
    Irún
19. Estoril
20. Sintra
21. Ibiza
22. Mallorca
23. Menorca

FRANCE

ANDORRA

Pyrenees

SPAIN

PORTUGAL

Madrid

Tagus River

Lisbon

Balearic Islands

Mediterranean Sea

Atlantic Ocean

soft glow continued to radiate from cottage windows. This telling division between the two was but a small taste of what would be a six-year-long split between the two peoples, the two countries, the two parts of the island.

Madrid

For many historians, the story of the neutrals in World War II commences inevitably with that war's opening act: Spain's three-year-long drama of national self-destruction. Involving many of the same players, issues, and atrocities, the Spanish Civil War painted an ominously accurate portrait of the larger conflict that would commence in its wake. For what was taking place in the maelstrom that would ravage both Spanish landscape and Spanish society was truly the rehearsal for the twentieth century's second general European war.

Spain of a half century ago was genuinely a nation in agony, a place and a time of great and far from quenched hatreds. For the thirty-two months ending in April 1939, Spaniards had torn each other and their nation apart with an unparalleled fury, Spain's 25 million people turning the country into a battleground for a deadly and decisive duel between ideologies. That the war so thoroughly exhausted Spain would, together with the single-minded will of its new dictator, prove the decisive factor in Spanish neutrality in World War II. And that neutrality would in turn prove important almost beyond measure to the Allied victory.

In many ways, Spaniards entered the 1930s as walking wounded from the Middle Ages. In the early centuries of the second millennium, most of Western Europe grew from the superstition-drenched introversion of feudalism into the dynamism of modern nation-statehood. But Spain and its people remained behind, in the half light of superannuated practices, even as its explorers and captains of the sea put it for a time at the front of the human stage in a towering age of world domination and military virility. And eventually, while Britain and France, Prussia and America, Russia and the Netherlands grew and prospered, Iberia would tumble, almost as if in free-fall, into an abyss from which it never redeemed itself.

For a time, though, Spain seemed to have it all. The reign of the dazzling royal cousins and spouses, Ferdinand II of Aragon and Isabella of Castile, witnessed Spain's conquest of a vast uncharted world, a conquest propelled by the lure of gold and carried out in the name of God. The mountains of bullion brought back from the Americas made many Spaniards—chiefly the aristocracy and the clergy—fabulously rich, and secondarily financed a golden epoch in the arts; much of the Prado collection was amassed at the time by buying the masterpieces of Italy, where a steep slide into stagnation greased such acquisitions as Europe's focus of power drifted westward. By 1493, when with his famous Line of Demarcation Pope Alexander VI divvied up the New World between Portugal and Spain, Spain gloried at the zenith of its international power.

On the deaths of its two seminal sovereigns, the crown of Spain circuitously passed to a foreign dynasty, the Austrian Habsburgs. The nation would coast along for a few more decades, its surface sheen seemingly undiminished. But with the Habsburgs came the extinguishment of its halcyon days, Spain getting itself involved in continental wars and being obsessed with colonial politics while much of the rest of Western Europe blossomed into new science, philosophy, and technology.

Yet once again, a glorious spiritedness briefly surfaced with Charles V, both king of Spain (as Charles I) and emperor of the Holy Roman Empire. Though much of the nation's wealth was transferred to maintain the Habsburgs' non-Spanish domains, the monarch himself was the paramount sovereign on the continent, Spaniards basking briefly but luxuriantly in his eminence. After his monastic retirement he was succeeded by his son, Philip II, who wed Mary of England (a marriage honored little in the symbolism and less in the observance) and was thus fleetingly "king" of England in, if not the English parliament's, at least his wife's estimation. Spain incorporated Portugal during Philip's reign, to which kingdom the Portuguese remained a part for sixty years, from 1580 to 1640.

Philip ruled Spain in the most literal of senses. Though he maintained elaborate councils of advisers, it was the monarch who decided every question of importance. He was a royal bureaucrat par excellence, and his imprint, emanating from the Escorial, marked all facets of Spanish life. The court developed a fantastically intricate etiquette, and much of the rest of Europe drew from Spain standards by which it measured its culture. The trouble was that Spain was rapidly falling apart, victim to both its military expenses and the bureaucratic calcification so central to the governing style of King Philip.

To pay its debts, the wealth from the New World drifted away like gold dust in the wind. Holland, for example, prospered mightily on what it loaned the Spaniards to pay for their army. To make matters worse, the court bled dry its own citizens with taxes, thereby fatally stifling investment. Plague and emigration reduced the population. And the 1588 defeat of Philip's Grand Armada by Elizabeth of England's fleet transferred irreversibly the world's sea primacy to that island kingdom.

The decline that had set in in the sixteenth century became by the seventeenth century a national rout on all fronts—military, social, economic, and political. The Habsburg dynasty itself finally petered out in 1700 on the death of the sadly inbred and childless Charles II, thus introducing to the peninsula the Bourbon infelicities as the grandson of France's Louis XIV ascended the greatly devalued throne on which Ferdinand and Isabella had once sat so proudly.

The War of the Spanish Succession, a horridly complicated, multinational affair that amounted to a twelve-year-long European catastrophe, savaged the ascent of the Bourbon monarch two years after he was installed. In part a world war and in equally brutal part a Spanish civil war, the Spanish Succession conflict devastated as never before large parts of Spain, principally Catalonia. Britain gained Gibraltar, Spain lost its Italian and Dutch possessions, and on the signing of the peace treaty Madrid was forced to undertake that Spain and France would never be united under the same crown. All in all, Spain came out very much poorer than it was before the war, though the victors leniently allowed it to retain its colonial possessions.

Absolutist monarchy, lack of any liberalization of land ownership, and the hindering of the rise of a middle class meant that Spain would slumber through the 1700s as a sort of continuing medieval holdover. The advent of republican France at the end of the century further complicated Spain's existence. Eventually Napoleon and his armies invaded the peninsula, the French emperor installing his elder brother Joseph on a shaky Spanish throne. The attempt to dislodge the Bonapartist interloper became indelibly imprinted in Spanish history through the electrifying etchings of Goya, the artist capturing in all its brutality the excesses the two antagonists dealt one another. Eventually, with the help of the British, the French were finally ejected from the peninsula.

Unfortunately, the unity displayed by nearly all elements of Spanish society fighting the War of Independence, as this last struggle came to be called, evaporated after victory. The nineteenth century saw a succession of buffoons, incompetents, and libertines occupying the throne in Madrid. The still intractable Carlist quandary was born when Ferdinand VII left the throne to his daughter. This wasn't supposed to happen in a Salic monarchy—one in which females are barred from sovereignty—but Ferdinand ignored the so-called Salic law. Ferdinand's earlier heir, his brother Don Carlos, contested the succession. Don Carlos lost, but he left miffed adherents to his cause whose descendants have continued to plague Spanish monarchial politics and who have every once in a while taken to the sword to express their persistent outrage.

Socially, economically, and every other way, Spain wasn't much better off in the nineteenth century than it had been in the eighteenth. Spaniards tried a republic in the mid-1870s, but it failed due to the country's utter lack of experience with republican (let alone democratic) forms of government. The army brought back the monarchy, this time under Alfonso XII, supposedly liberal and supposedly restrained by a constitution. But Alfonso saw to it that the Spanish church, an institution steeped in ignorance and reaction, retained its preeminence, a step virtually guaranteeing that Spain would remain in the figurative Dark Ages. Alfonso died when his wife was pregnant; thus their only son—Alfonso XIII—was sovereign from the moment of his birth.

The immediate harbinger of its twentieth-century troubles was Spain's defeat at American hands in the humiliating war of 1898. The Spanish-American War wrote a finale to whatever lingering pretensions Spain retained of being a Great Power, the loss of most of its remaining colonies in the conflict sadly mocking the giddy heights it had achieved in its days of global exploration. The war secondarily lifted the lid on the corruption and decay of official Spanish life, prompting popular pressure for reform.[42]

In the 1920s, a monarchy under the nominal rule of Alfonso XIII and the real rule of military dictator General Miguel Primo de Rivera (whom the king allegedly once presented to Italy's King Victor Emmanuel as "my Mussolini"[43]) became the platform on which the state uneasily rested. The armed forces, the Roman Catholic Church, and the landed aristocracy made it their most vital business to perpetuate their own power. In reality, Spain had ceased to be a monolithically clerical nation, most Spaniards ignoring Catholic practice except for perfunctory weddings, baptisms, and funerals.[44] But with 5,000 religious communities housing some 20,000 monks and 60,000 nuns, the Spanish church remained a rich and, above all, powerful institution.

In 1931, after the dictator's demise, King Alfonso tried direct rule through an oligarchy representing the traditional underpinnings of the state. But the Spanish were fed up with royal misrule and overturned this outmoded tableau. A national election transformed the kingdom into a republic when Alfonso correctly interpreted the results as a broad repudiation of monarchy and the past. Yet even with the king gone, the triple pillars of army, church, and aristocracy that had propped up the *ancien régime* remained ominously in place.

If the new Republic's leaders were long on the rhetoric of universal rights, they were tragically short on the wherewithal to implement them. The conservatives, who naturally felt threatened by the new government, took no immediate steps to destroy it. But if the liberal government had to keep a wary eye on these potential adversaries on the right, it also faced an appalling array of enemies from the left. Communists and socialists representing a rainbow of political permutations considered the Republic's well-intentioned measures far short of what was necessary to remedy the abuses of centuries of reaction.

Understandably, though, it was the propertied and privileged classes on the right that the Republic regarded as its most dangerous enemy. Its program commendably sought to narrow the gaping chasm between the haves and the have-nots, to bring Spain closer to the liberalized standards of post-World War I Western Europe. But governing under the constricting framework of its admirably liberal constitution, the hamstrung Republic's leaders couldn't effectively attack the traditional forces of reaction. Land reform was halfhearted, the church's power was only nominally curtailed (though it lost its throttlehold on education), and army restructuring brought no lessening in the threat the military represented to the new state. The government's liberal measures ensured the enmity of the right, while doing little to decrease its threat.

After a failed army coup in 1932, the first real blow to the Republic came, predictably, from the right. In the fall of 1933, a coalition of conservative parties forced liberal president Manuel Azaña out of office. In reaction, a year later socialists attempted a counter-coup against what had been, in effect, the rightist takeover of the moderately leftist Republic. The socialists were crushed with a bloody vengeance. When the politically organized miners rose in Asturias (in northwestern Spain) and formed a "soviet," while murdering in their revolutionary zeal a number of clerics and other middle-class civilians, the right-wing government responded in a blitz that resulted in the deaths of 1,400 revolutionaries, mostly at the hands of colonial Moorish troops. Nor was this state counter-terror confined to Asturias. By 1935, the government, its original ideals long dead, had in jail some 30,000 of its "left-wing" opponents.[45]

The Republic, in its now right-wing reincarnation, altogether abandoned any pretense of the reformist zeal of 1931–33. It managed to stay in power, drifting from one cabinet crisis to another, but in February 1936 it finally was forced to confront a challenge from the regrouped left—the so-called Popular Front. The Front was a new political stratagem advanced by the Soviet Union in which various countries' Communist parties were ordered by the Comintern to enter coalitions with socialist and liberal parties. In Spain it was a mélange of leftist forces representing opinion on the ideological spectrum from Azaña's moderation to the Communists' fiery radicalism, its simple goal to try to dislodge the right-wing government. The Front eked out an extremely narrow polling victory, but it nevertheless took its win as license to reconstitute its own vision of the Republic. And it made no pretense that in spite of its narrow win it wouldn't break all legal bounds and launch a real social revolution. Although it was unquestionably aiming at a more just and equitable society than Spain had so far known, the confabulation that was the new government unfortunately embodied all the tensions and strife that had so wounded Spain in the previous century. The right, remembering the Asturian soviet, feared Spain itself was about to become a soviet.

Unlike in 1931, this time the Republic's left-wing government would immediately face a mortal challenge from the right. One source of resistance came from the fascist Falange, a party which had achieved little national importance before the spring of 1936. But it now attracted large numbers from the frightened middle class, becoming with the Carlists[46] one of the two leading right-wing parties.[47] The party promised to dispense with parliament, censor the press and individual expression, control business, regulate wages and hours, and attempt to fix prices.[48]

Named for the ancient Macedonian military unit, one that had prophetically been responsible in the fourth century B.C. for destroying Greek democracy, the Falange was the personal creation of José Antonio Primo de Rivera. Son of the 1920s dictator and a charismatic and compelling proponent of conservative values, José Antonio (he was always called by his given name rather than his family name) represented a right-center political course that if taken might have averted the coming civil war. But waiting, barely concealed in the wings, was the army.

The hatred of faction for faction, of one segment or class of the Spanish people for another, continued to fester. Eventually, a set of murders provided the sparks that brought the hatred to a head and Spain to war. On July 12, a young leftist in the Assault Guards, Lieutenant José Castillo, was murdered by rightist gunmen, their motive retribution for Castillo's participation in the murder three months earlier of José Antonio's cousin, the Marquis of Heredia. In return for Castillo's murder, leftist thugs murdered a prominent conservative, José Calvo Sotelo.

Finally, unable to any longer restrain itself from intervening in what it saw as a nation sinking into left-wing chaos, the army reacted. On July 18, most of the military garrisons in Spain rose against the constitutional state. Many were successful in overthrowing the Republic's authority; many, including those in Madrid, Barcelona, Valencia, and Málaga, were not. As a coup d'état, the rising failed, but as the opening of civil war, it succeeded all too well. The man proposed as the rebels' overall leader, General José Sanjurjo, was killed in an aircraft accident[49] just as the rebellion got underway. Thus the man who would overwhelmingly be the most important figure in modern Spanish history elected this moment to march onto the stage of history, and within two months he would be named Generalissimo and head of the forces committed to destroying the Republic.

Francisco Franco y Bahamonde, one of the youngest[50] and brightest generals in the Spanish armed forces, commander of the Moorish troops that had crushed the Asturian miners, and the provincial governor of Spain's Canary Islands, threw his crucial support to the rebels, a group soon to style itself "Nationalists." A native of the great Spanish naval base of El Ferrol,[51] in northwestern Spain's Galicia, the forty-four-year-old general's greatest strength—beyond his considerable military skills—was an unshakable imperturbability, an extremely useful asset in the trials that would fill his next three years. After he was flown from the Canaries to Morocco, Franco's intention was to take the Spanish Foreign Legion and a contingent of Moorish troops, both groups firmly on the Nationalist side, across the Strait of Gibraltar to support the rising. The only impediment to Franco's plan was a lack of air transport with which to carry out this task.

While these events rushed headlong in the making of Spanish history, the three most powerful of Europe's dictators were studying the unfolding drama in Spain—and preparing to make foreign intervention the predominant issue in European relations in the years leading to continental war. The shaping of the Spanish struggle arising from this intervention would have a dramatic effect on the world's attitudes toward the successful neutrals when the wider war exploded three years later.

The first to actively lend assistance—to the rebels—was Adolf Hitler. Little evidence exists that in the summer of 1936 the German dictator sought or even envisioned any kind of "Grand Alliance" between Germany and Spain, and there is no certainty that at this point he foresaw a German partnership with an embryonic right-wing dictator on the Iberian Peninsula. What Hitler unquestionably did fancy, though, was a Spain unfriendly toward France. Not only would French influence in Spain be thereby weakened, but France's principal ally, Great Britain, would as a result find its own influence in Spain commensurately diminished.[52] There was one other consideration in Hitler's decision to help Franco's insurrection. The German leader expected that a Spanish government brought to power with German help would in a broader

European war be grateful enough to provide naval, particularly submarine, bases as well as the raw materials the Wehrmacht would need to
keep its war machine in tone.

The initial offering Hitler rendered the Spanish dissidents was to give
life itself to their rebellion. When most of Spain's military garrisons rose
against the Republic on July 18, enraged Loyalists were able to crush
them in the most important cities, thereby destroying an important segment of the coup makers and leaving vital areas of the country still under
government control. But at Hitler's orders, on July 29 Germany military
aircraft began Operation *Feuerzauber* (Fire Magic). This insurrection-
saving operation ferried the first of 13,523 of Franco's Foreign Legion-
naires and Moors across the Strait of Gibraltar to the mainland, providing
the extra armed weight the rebellion desperately needed to stay alive. The
ferocity of those troops—particularly the Moors—in support of the rebel
army grew into a legend, eventually becoming a nexus of bitter hatred by
the Loyalists. Ironically, Britain's policy of nonintervention in the Spanish uprising contributed notably to the rebel cause—inadvertently perhaps—by denying the Republican navy refueling facilities at Gibraltar,
thus helping cripple the small fleet's ability to effectively patrol the Mediterranean.

In November, Hitler upped the ante considerably by contributing to
the Nationalists his famous Condor Legion, a combination of five skilled
flying units. It eventually reached a strength of 5,600 men and participated in thirty battles after the Gibraltar airlift. [53] The Condor Legion's
importance to the eventual Franco victory is little disputed, but what *is*
disputed is Hitler's motivation in sending the cream of his Luftwaffe pilots
and aircraft to Spain. The German leader certainly desired the victory of
an insurgency he considered firmly in the fascist camp, but he very likely
didn't want that victory to come any too soon. Keeping the West in
turmoil over the Spanish conflict met Hitler's specific needs. Many of the
most articulate voices in the democracies considered the war a black-
and-white conflict between good and evil, good being the Republic, evil
being the rebels. As long as they fussed and worried themselves sick over
Spain, political conditions were made all that much easier for Germany
to quietly build itself into a military machine capable of eventually destroying such democratic nonsense.

Benito Mussolini, the second-ranking of the fascist dictators though
the first to have come to power, also saw opportunity in Spain's internecine war. Mussolini's government had been generally supportive of Britain and France in the early years of Italian fascism, regarding them as a
kind of hedge against a too powerful Germany. Even in Hitler's first years

as chancellor, Mussolini kept a figurative distance from Berlin. When the pro-Nazi coup against Austrian chancellor Engelbert Dollfuss appeared to threaten Italy's Alpine buffer with Germany, the Duce even went so far as to send troops to the Austro-Italian frontier, a feisty gesture in the circumstances.

The advancement of Italian glory out of Spain's tribulations was motivated in greatest part by the troubled Italian campaign in Ethiopia. The megalomaniac Duce wanted to divert the world's eyes from his nearly Pyrrhic African victory, and militarily underwriting Franco seemed a good place to start. Though the Ethiopian war had finally been disposed of (largely to Mussolini's satisfaction) by the time the Spanish struggle got underway, the disagreeable time he had snatching victory from Haile Selassie had tarred the Duce's military with an aura of incompetence. But with his ideological affinity with Germany's National Socialist brand of fascism, his fears of Germany were alleviated when Hitler began to support Italy's African aspirations.[54]

A further inducement to Mussolini to take up Franco's cause was the Italian attraction to Spanish-style fascism in the guise of José Antonio's Falange Party. Though José Antonio was captured and imprisoned by the Popular Front in March 1936,[55] other rightist leaders kept Mussolini apprised of plans for a rebellion against the Popular Front government. When the Italian dictator did finally decide to help Franco, because his treasury was bled white from his African profligacy he demanded cash from the rebels for that help—a condition the far richer Germany would not impose.

Italian aid to Franco's crusade would eventually exceed that sent by Germany—though with the cash-on-the-barrelhead price tag. But where Hitler's largess primarily focused on the Luftwaffe units of the Condor Legion, Mussolini's assistance came mainly in the form of infantry. Eighty thousand Italian soldiers fought in the Spanish Civil War, of whom nearly 4,000 were killed.[56] Mussolini did make an effort to match the German air donation: 729 aircraft of the Royal Italian Air Force, though inferior to the German models, were to prove a boon to Franco's rebels in destroying their Republican opponents.

The third of the grand dictators to involve himself in the Spanish rebellion—on the Republican side—was Joseph Stalin, the Soviet Union the only *government* providing direct aid to Madrid in the war. In the years immediately preceding the rising in Spain, Stalin concentrated his foreign policy energies on the protection of the Soviet Union's frontiers—in the west from the Nazis' salivating for *Lebensraum*, in the Soviet Pacific from an increasingly aggressive Japan. His backing for Communist movements in countries other than his own mainly took the form of exhortations to local Communists to support Popular Front governments, such as those established in both France and Spain in 1936. The fear of Communism on the part of the right in Spain was, of course, a major inducement to their rebellion.

After the Popular Front's electoral victory in February, the far left pressed hard for reforms, with labor strikes becoming endemic and rabid anti-clericalism—the burning of convents, a gruesome example—a specter haunting the right of what the Popular Front would eventually sink to.[57] Though the rightist reactionary parties—the Falangists and others— were also responsible for the unrest in Spain in the months preceding the rebellion, it was a leftist government that was in power, and *appearances* led all parties right of center to the conclusion that Spain was on the verge of a social revolution, one that would officially and irreversibly establish a Communist tyranny. Though the Spanish Communist Party received only 3 percent of the vote that year—fifteen of its candidates were elected to the Cortes—the Popular Front government was all too eager to accept whatever help Stalin offered.[58] And like Mussolini's aid to the rebels, Stalin's too came with a hard-cash price tag.

Stalin could not easily send large numbers of troops to the Republic, if only for reasons of geography. But the dictator preferred any struggle be waged as far from his own frontiers as possible, even—perhaps especially—when success or failure for a Communist insurgency was involved. Technical specialists from the Soviet Union soon began to flow into what was left of the Republic, though, as did, unfortunately, political "advisers," among whose Moscow-assigned tasks was the indoctrination of the International Brigade members. Russian help came later than did that of the fascist powers, arriving only in October, three months after the war erupted. But the aid the Soviet dictator gave would transform the whole tone of the Republic into something very like a Communist state—a different Republic from that which had entered the Civil War. Franco would be far more successful in keeping Axis help from turning his insurgency into a Nazi facsimile.[59]

By far the best-known aid either side in the Spanish struggle attracted came to the Republic. The International Brigades of volunteers from a dozen countries represented the very essence of romantic war making. Imbued with a profound desire to defeat an insurgency they equated with fascism, its members were convinced that that insurgency's destruction would also somehow eliminate the fascist scourges in Germany and Italy. Most of the young idealists obviously were of liberal or leftist sympathies, and this fact made them highly suspect in the democratic but conservative countries they came from. Nonetheless it was widely taken as an article of faith in 1936 that the supposedly fascist attempt to overthrow the Republic was another move in a fascist game of dominoes: first a remilitarized Rhineland, then Ethiopia down and Spain going, and God only knows what's next. The fact that Spaniards—Republican or rebel—were too proud, independent, and just plain contrary to be pawns in anyone's game was universally overlooked.

In the furtherance of their cause, some 20,000 of these volunteers died. The addition of Ernest Hemingway to the 2,700 members of the Brigades' American Lincoln Battalion produced some of the best and most influential literature of the twentieth century. Hemingway's and other writers' works were instrumental in creating the legend of a beleaguered but pure Republic fighting with nearly the whole of the Spanish people behind it. The legend would bear strongly on the West's attitude toward Franco's state in the larger conflict to come.

It should be noted that the other Iberian nation, one with a powerful interest in the outcome of the Spanish struggle, gave itself unremittingly over to the Nationalist camp. The Portugal of General Antonio Salazar was governed along much the same lines as fascist Italy, although its willingness, indeed its determination, to stay out of international headlines rendered it somewhat less objectionable. From the beginning, Salazar made Portugal's roads and telecommunications systems available to Franco and his rebels. It wasn't the Republican ambassador in Lisbon who was treated as the legitimate representative of Spain, but rather Franco's younger brother Nicolás, who established a quasi-official diplomatic and financial headquarters in Lisbon in 1938 (in 1936 Lisbon broke relations with the Republic, but it would be two years before it officially recognized Franco's regime). When the Republic embargoed German supply ships, preventing them from entering Spanish ports, Salazar permitted the ships to use Portuguese ports and allowed the subsequent transport of these goods over his country's roads to the Spanish border.[60]

These three major dictatorships—and one minor one—were not the only nations to ponder the degree to which they should become involved in Spain's Civil War. Many would have it that republican Spain's greatest supporters were the Western democracies. But with one devastating act on the part of Britain and France, the victory of the Nationalists was almost assured from the beginning of the rebellion. It was the democracies' policy of "nonintervention" that most grievously wounded the Republic. As historian A. J. P. Taylor viewed it, "British and French policy, or lack of it, not the policy of Hitler and Mussolini, decided the outcome of the Spanish civil war."[61]

Léon Blum, head of the French Popular Front Government, at first decided to honor the legitimate Spanish government's urgent request for sale of French arms to ward off the rebellion. But Britain, France's principal ally, convinced its neighbor to cancel the already promised weaponry.[62] London reasoned that a policy of maintaining a rigid system of keeping the Spanish government from purchasing arms on the international market would stop the war from spreading, this in spite of clear evidence that Germany and Italy were perfectly willing to supply the Nationalist rebels with all the weapons they needed or could afford—not to mention evidence that matériel from the Soviet Union to help the legitimate government would come only at a cash price. Their joint decision in 1936 to embargo aid to the rebel insurgency against the constitutional but left-wing Spanish government, a decision taken at Britain's urging, served also to intensify the closeness of the Anglo-French relationship, with ramifications that would soon become evident. In the end, twenty-seven nations, including Germany and Italy, signed the Non-Intervention Agreement, to be effective August 8, 1936. Britain and France meant to stick to it; Germany and Italy enjoyed a good laugh.

It is often assumed that London and Paris's effort to keep arms out of Spain and thus contain the war, to keep the conflict from becoming a general European war, was a well-intentioned effort, directed primarily (though one wonders exactly how) at helping the legitimate Spanish government. In fact, a considerable body of influential governmental leaders and their advisers viewed the Non-Intervention Agreement as an instrument to help Franco come to power and thus keep the specter of radical socialism—perhaps even Communism—from spilling over Spanish borders and infecting all of Western Europe. Though Paris turned a blind eye to nonofficial and semi-clandestine shipments of arms to Madrid and Barcelona, France's official policy nonetheless remained adherence to the Non-Intervention Agreement. The decision on the part of the Blum government, a policy that essentially crippled its sister Popular Front government across the Pyrenees, had the unintended effect of irreversibly pulling the carpet out from under its own ideological position. The Madrid government was further wounded by Washington's decision to extend America's own neutrality legislation to cover civil wars, and despite the pleas of thousands who sympathized with the Republic's plight, the United States refused to export arms to the Loyalists.

The majority of Frenchmen probably favored the Republic, fearing that a Franco victory in Spain would automatically mean a third frontier to contend with in a war with the fascist dictators: Italian forces in the Mediterranean in a co-effort with Franco's potential navy might well cut France's vital lines of communications with its troops and matériel in Africa. But Blum's government feared loss of power—even a civil war—if it militarily supported a Spanish administration even partially composed of Communists.[63] Finally, a section of French opinion—and a powerful section—found itself in sympathy with the Spanish rebels because of class affinity.[64]

Britain's position wasn't far different. London worried about a loss of Gibraltar to Franco's substantial military capability, thus jeopardizing its own lines of communications through the Mediterranean. But subtly overriding that worry were the class ties between Britain's governing caste and the Nationalists, ties based on privilege and property, and that went hand in hand with British fears of spreading Communism that seemed dangerously likely with the Bolshevik-tainted Republican government in Madrid. Though no British government could publicly voice support for the Nazi-supported Francoist insurgency, the Non-Intervention Agreement agreeably served the interests of vested power in the United Kingdom.

As to the burgeoning Civil War itself, Franco's insurgents got off to a strong military start, although their failure to capture the capital with their initial coup would mean a war protracted far beyond what any of the conspiracy participants foresaw earlier in the summer. The uniting of the often mortally fractious parties of the left—republicans, socialists, syndicalists, anarchists, Communists—in their reaction to the insurgency meant the Republic would have almost three more years to exist. But those three years would be deadly, fratricidal, and expensive.

The rebels' initially successful summer offensive against the capital—by August they had begun to form their lines around Madrid—might have succeeded had Franco not been sidetracked in Toledo. Besieged Nationalists in that city's Alcazar led the Caudillo to disregard sensible military considerations for what he deemed overriding political logic. Charged with centuries of Spanish history, Toledo was a symbolic prize that had to be retaken, and breaking the seventy-day siege of the rebel-held fortress delayed Franco until the end of September. Moorish troops at Toledo upheld their reputation for brutality: when entering the fallen city, the 600 Loyalists wounded in the central hospital were immediately murdered with a spray of hand grenades tossed through the wards.[65]

The weeks spent in taking Toledo gave the government precious days to strengthen Madrid's defenses, an added bounty of rainy weather arriving in time to further bog down the Nationalist army. When Franco finally attacked the city, the result was some of the war's fiercest fighting—and the Republic's most brilliant defense. Stirred by the invocations of Dolores Ibarrurri—soon to become world-famous as La Pasionaria (the Passionate One)—for her vow that the enemy "shall not pass"—the besieged Loyalists stopped Franco's forces literally at the city's gates.

But on all fronts, the Republic and its will and ability to resist crumbled inexorably in a hail of cruelties from every sector of the quickening insurgency. In a world still capable of experiencing deep shock at wanton savagery, the Condor Legion's terror bombing (with the help of the Italian Air Force) of Guernica captured international attention in June 1937 as did no other single incident in the war. Guernica, the symbolic spiritual capital of the Basques, found itself singled out for special attention from the Nationalists primarily because of Basque support for the Republic. The devoutly Catholic Basques, a non-Spanish-speaking group whose lands spilled over the Pyrenees into France, abhorred the Republic's repression of the church. But they believed their sole prospect for any kind of autonomy within the Spanish state could come only from the Republic, and they thus threw their fortunes in with the Loyalists.[66]

The terror bombing of Guernica, a town of 7,000 swollen by 3,000 refugees, was the first time in history the population of an entire city, noncombatants along with defending soldiers, would be massacred by aerial bombardment. Franco's effort to classify it as a legitimate military target was a sham: its sole work site manufacturing war matériel lay outside the city, and that factory wasn't even touched in the bombardment. For generations born since the war, the tragedy of Guernica has been kept uniquely alive in Pablo Picasso's extraordinary painting of the city's passion. It was that passion that helped change public opinion in the West away from the policy of appeasement of the fascist powers. It did not, however, sway the democracies to change their nonintervention policy, to the contrary steadying their will to avoid the kind of confrontation with the dictators that might lead to a Guernica-like episode in their own countries.

Nineteen thirty-eight was for the Republic a year of few victories and many losses. Offensives and counteroffensives, retreats and miraculous escapes filled the year for both sides, but the rebels began 1939 with nearly the whole of Spain under their control. Stalin withdrew his support for the Republic after Britain and France caved in to Hitler at Munich. The International Brigades were demobilized, the government hoping *all* foreign troops would thereby be obliged by international sentiment to leave. Mussolini responded by withdrawing a token 10,000 of his soldiers. By the beginning of 1939, little other than Madrid (the government itself had long since fled the city) and Barcelona, Spain's two great metropolises, remained under Loyalist control. After being terror-bombed by Franco's air force, Barcelona finally surrendered on January 25, with the insurgents rapidly racing up to the northeastern corner of the country to cut off the Loyalists' last land escape route from Spain. London and Paris recognized Franco's regime as Spain's legitimate government a month later: both countries reasoned that Franco, clearly on the verge of victory, should not be totally isolated and thus forced to ally with his chief military supporters in the war.

All that remained between Franco and final victory was Madrid. Unlike the ferocious battle that saved the city for the Republic in 1936, this time there would be no deliverance. In hopes of negotiating with Franco, a military coup, directed against the Communist-controlled Republican government, unseated President Juan Negrín, and the short-lived Council of National Defense, as the coup makers represented themselves, sued for peace. Franco did not negotiate. He accepted the surrender unconditionally.

·   ·   ·

After almost three years, the war ended. Spain lay in desolation. Some 600,000 of its citizens (out of a prewar total of 24 million) had been killed, perhaps 100,000 of that number by murder or execution. The fighting had been sickeningly vicious, with the left indiscriminately slaughtering priests, nuns, landowners, middle-class bourgeoisie, the right butchering anyone with a union card or record of having voted for a leftist party. The national treasury was depleted by 30 billion pesetas (about $14.5 billion at 1937 exchange rates). Agriculture was in ruins, a third of the livestock gone as well as much of the farm machinery. So was its industrial plant devastated. The transport system was running at a fraction of its prewar capacity, with 67 percent of the passenger cars gone, 27 percent of the locomotives destroyed.[67] Perhaps most thoroughly shattered was the nation's spirit.

There would be on the part of the victor toward the vanquished no mercy, no clemency, no tolerance, no lenience. Franco intended that his enemies should not live to rise again. He regarded his victory as full license to change Spain as he saw fit, and the fact that he was able to achieve a kind of enforced unity out of the tragically disparate factions of prewar Spain seemed to him to be his moral justification for doing so.

For months after the fighting ended, executions—judicial murders would be a more accurate description—were carried out in astonishing numbers. Anyone who had been an official of the Republic or an officer of its armed forces, anyone whose politics constituted even a nominal threat to the new order, anyone who resisted the new regime in any way was shot. Perhaps a million were thrown into the prisons and concentration camps that spattered the country like bacteria. The class struggle-cum-war that was the Spanish Civil War raged over a country in which the majority of the people were perhaps only helpless bystanders, but the levels of viciousness *on both sides* clearly bespoke a deep disturbance in the Spanish psyche.

The effect of the Spanish Civil War on the Western European democracies was disastrous in light of the coming totalitarian avalanche. Britain's appeasement policy toward Hitler and Mussolini was in no small measure shaped by fear engendered at the ferocity of the Spanish war. To prevent such a thing from coming to the island kingdom, Conservative cabinets found themselves giving in to the fascists in an appallingly cowardly fashion. Prepared or not for war, to answer the advocates of appeasement with the abandonment of decent and principled Czechoslovakia in the face of Hitlerian aggression was inexcusable, and was much a result of the horrors of Spain.

France's fear was based more on its proximity to Spain. Seeing itself with the victory of the Spanish insurgents now nearly encircled by totalitarian governments, and now too its lines of communications with its African possessions threatened, France's foreign policy degenerated into one of fear-driven cowardice. The complicity of Daladier in Chamberlain's shameful episode at Munich came just as much from the Spanish experience as did Britain's behavior.[68]

Not only did the western half of the anti-Hitler coalition falter in part because of the Spanish war, but so was Stalin partially dissuaded by that conflict from joining the democracies in doing anything to save Czechoslovakia in 1938.[69] What had started as a purely civil war in 1936 had by 1939 the international effect of seriously weakening any chance of an Anglo-French-Soviet alliance that might have stood up against Germany.

Germany got what it wanted out of the war. Many historians have observed that the Iberian adventure was secondary, at most, to Hitler, that his only real interest in Spain was to keep up tensions in Europe, to keep Britain and (especially) France at odds with Italy, to draw Mussolini closer to Berlin and ensure Italy's partnership in a future continental war. But Hitler surely *thought* about and appreciated Germany's enormous strategic advantages that would come from an alliance with Franco's similar-minded government. The best way to dislodge the Royal Navy from Gibraltar, and thus from the western Mediterranean, was in alliance with a friendly, even a helpful, Spain. The war in that theater may have been too far off to see from Berlin in 1936, but it certainly wasn't in 1939. Not only was the Gibraltar factor important to Germany, but so were Spain's rich mineral deposits, especially of wolfram, the critical ingredient in the sort of high-grade steel that Germany needed for its growing war machine. The mineral rights that Franco gave the Reich in 1938 were instrumental in Germany's delivering the war matériel necessary for Franco's final series of offensives.

By appreciating the Spanish Civil War, especially the violence of emotions that arose from it all over Europe, one can better understand Spain's Byzantine behavior in the greater conflict just over the horizon.

Lisbon

One of the minor consequences of the continent's new war would be the rendering of this languid nation into more than simply a bit player on the international stage, its first really juicy role since Portuguese caravels found themselves overtaken by more powerful ships of more powerful nations four centuries earlier.

At the outbreak of European war, Portugal's capital served as the seat of a dictatorship where, in the pithy triplet of one observer, "football, fado, and Fatima" were the officially blessed pastimes that kept 7 million minds off politics. But the attention of Portugal's dictator on the dawning war was primarily focused on the relationship with his fellow dictatorship next door on the peninsula, and only more distantly on his country's centuries-old friendship with England. The latter, stretching back to an alliance first formulated in the fourteenth century, had proven a generally worthwhile association. Still, the overriding reality of Franco's blood debt to the Third Reich meant that Spain's success or failure as a neutral in a European war would decide its Iberian neighbor's fate as well as its own. Beyond these considerations, the underlying compass heading by which Portugal would steer through the conflict ahead was its detestation of Communism and the closely held perception that fascist totalitarianism was Portugal's only alternative.

What has been for eight hundred years the nation-state of Portugal traces its historical origins to a province the Romans called Lusitania. Its native people were a splinter from a larger group that had already inhabited the Iberian Peninsula for at least three thousand years before the

Romans claimed it as their westernmost bastion. From those early proto-Portuguese sprang a second-century-B.C. chieftain whose name—Viriatus—and reputation as a military leader would 2,100 years later be invoked in the service of a new European war.

True "Portuguese" history as connected to an identifiable state began at the end of the eleventh century. Alfonso VI of Castile married off his illegitimate daughter to a French noble, Henry of Burgundy, the Spanish king granting the newlyweds their own little fiefdom-county centered on the town of Porto, whose Latin title, Portus Cale (Warm Harbor), warped into a new designation of "Portugal." Henry's son, Alfonso I, turned the infant county into an infant kingdom, quickly earning the recognition of the neighboring Castilian court. Foiled in his initial northward drive, the king turned about-face, headed south, and captured the town of Lisbon. Helped in his enterprise by English Crusaders, Alfonso was thus involved in the first recorded mating of the intertwined Anglo-Portuguese relationship that would last into the mid-twentieth century.

The foundation stones of the alliance with England, first laid by the Crusaders, were strengthened when the island kingdom rallied to Portugal's support in defeating Spaniards bent on merging the two peninsular nations under the latter's throne. Portugal's present land borders were set by the mid-thirteenth century, giving the country what ranks today as the continent's oldest essentially unchanged political configuration. In 1373, another story was added to the friendship's structure when Ferdinand I sought and obtained an alliance with England. Since that date, the two countries have never been at war, an extraordinary feat in the blood-soaked history of Europe. The capstone of the relationship was set in 1386 with the Treaty of Windsor, a concord concluding in the marriage of Philippa, daughter of England's John of Gaunt, to Portugal's John I.[70] Almost six hundred years later the treaty would be key to Portugal's unneutral tilt toward Britain when the second world war of the twentieth century got underway.

Portugal preened at the center of the world's cultural and economic stage in the fifteenth century, its one million people recovering from the ravages of the Black Death and standing on the threshold of their own world-changing discoveries. Portugal was spared the debilitating religious wars and battle with Islam its neighbors were enduring, and the nation's relative serenity and abundance allowed it to seize the lead in the great voyages of exploration that opened the planet both to Europe's culture and to its tyranny. It was now that Portuguese navigators discovered the unpopulated Azores and the Madeira Islands, archipelagoes that soon became magnets of settlement from the mainland and provided all manner of delights for the tables and purses of Portugal's wealthy.

Portuguese mastery of the sea continued with new ship designs, revolutionary navigational technology, and wealth flowing into the country from the spice trade—especially from the fabulous cloves that could magically preserve meat and were even reputed to cure the plague—and whatever other profitable merchandise the Portuguese sailors happened onto. It was in this era that Portugal established its great colonies of Angola and Mozambique on African shores, as well as city-states on the perimeter of the Indian subcontinent and, in the southwestern Pacific, domains from Vietnam to the Spice Islands. In 1500, Pedro Alvares Cabral took possession of the greatest neo-Portugal of all, Brazil.

This "Manuelina" era, named for the then King Emanuel I, saw Portugal at the zenith of its power, in reflection of which its king proudly styled himself "Lord of India." Camoëns, the towering Portuguese poet, commented on his nation's erstwhile glory: "Did the world stretch farther, they would have gone there too." But it was a glory even then slipping from its grasp like sand from a child's fist. The nation's very much larger peninsular neighbor was turning its avaricious grasp to Portugal and to Portugal's empire.

Eighty years after Portuguese mariners claimed Brazil, Spain forced Portugal, its royal line as dry as the nation's creative juices, into a dynastic merger of their thrones. Even Pope Alexander's 1493 splitting of the world into Spanish and Portuguese halves was twisted against Portugal, when it was decided through a bit of creative geography that the Spice Islands were really in the Spanish sphere. The next sixty years, spent as what was essentially a semi-autonomous province of Spain, was a period of bitter resentment for all Portuguese. They were forced to watch as Spain dragooned Portugal's ports into its service for the marshaling of the armada against old friend England. Portugal's primacy of the seas had come to an end, and in a not too distant future it would be Dutch and English seamen who would successfully vie for supremacy on the far sides of the horizon.

The last Portuguese dynasty, the Braganzas, captured the crown in 1640. The duke of that family (distantly related to the prior dynasty) took advantage of Spain's preoccupation in foreign wars and domestic rebellions and seized the throne as the new King John IV, ending the unhappy years of Spanish dominion over the nation's affairs. Spanish military efforts to resume the merger failed, and Portuguese independence was bolstered when one of its princesses, Catherine of Braganza, was maritally merged to England's Charles II, bringing to her new homeland the immensely valuable dowry not only of two million cruzados but also of an entire Indian city, Bombay—England's first connection with India. Most of Portugal's Pacific empire was lost during its Spanish period, but still Brazil and its lucrative sugar trade brought riches to the mother country—just as did the continuing West African slave trade.

In 1703, one more diplomatic link was forged with Britain, this one an economic covenant called the Methuen Treaty. The effect of the accord was that Portugal would increasingly become the economic vassal of its old ally. The Methuen Treaty had Britain agreeing to buy Portuguese wine in preference to the French variety, in return for which the Portuguese allowed British merchants to open textile markets, a commodity whose far greater importance meant Britain was getting much the better part of the deal. Britain told Lisbon that the accord ensured that Portugal would be the recipient of "a greater trading balance than any other country whatsoever."[71] Others more accurately pointed out that the accord effectively turned Portugal into Britain's economic satellite, the riches flowing northward helping to create the capital accumulation from which England's industrial revolution was born.[72]

After the country survived—by grit and luck—the 1755 earthquake that all but destroyed Lisbon, its next crisis sprang from the turmoil caused by the troublemaking successor to the French Bourbons, Napoleon Bonaparte. Napoleon's hostility to Portugal primarily came from the fact that the country's ports remained open—and immensely valuable—to France's principal enemy, Great Britain. France invaded in 1807, causing the regent John VI (standing in for his mad mother, Maria I) to flee to Brazil, Portugal's chief and most comfortable colony. With lots of British help, particularly from the Duke of Wellington, the French were ejected from metropolitan Portugal (which, by the way, brought considerable esteem for Britain in Portuguese eyes), but John decided he still preferred the serenity of Rio to the insecurities of Lisbon. In any event, Portugal's economy had already been torched by the French, its industry ruined and its rural development arrested. John declared his heretofore Brazilian province an independent kingdom, with himself its new king. The grant to Britain of equal trading rights in Brazilian ports was to be the beginning of Portugal's economic decline, one that would lead the country by the twentieth century into disaster. When mother Maria died in 1816, John was forced to return home to take over the throne—and, in 1822, made to accept a distastefully liberal constitution.

For a good part of the nineteenth century, the thrones and monarchs of Portugal and Brazil were traded back and forth in a sort of royal musical chairs. Not that it did Portugal any good. The 1822 constitution was ignored, the economy was sinking, and the population was slipping ever deeper into poverty. By the end of the century, the court was fighting an unquenchable tide of republicanism, which its proponents associated nobly with "liberalism" but not with any specific program that might actually lift the Portuguese out of their thickening morass. Capping the era's woes was a potentially nasty 1891 contretemps with its British benefactor. Portugal wanted to link up its colony of Angola, in West Africa, with its colony of Mozambique, in East Africa. The space between was British, however, and London issued an ultimatum to Lisbon warning it to discard any such ideas, on the legal basis that Portugal had no right to claim territory over which it had no physical control. Portugal backed off. Eight years later, when Britain wanted Portuguese help in its war against the Boers, its again friendly attitude toward its old ally led to a pledge to defend Portugal against all enemies, both present and future, the final and most specific element in what had by now become a fairly sturdy structure of Anglo-Portuguese ties.

The Braganza dynasty's end came quickly and ignominiously. The first act saw the murders on January 31, 1908, of the unpopular Charles I and his heir, the crown prince Louis Philip; their assassins, two disgruntled republicans, were responsible for the first instance of regicide in the nation's 800-year monarchial history. An ominous portent for the throne's future was the fact that while 200,000 people showed up for the killers' funeral, hardly anyone attended the concurrent services for the departed royals.

Charles's second son, the woefully unprepared eighteen-year-old Manuel, ascended the throne as the last of his house. With the government unable to stem a republican onslaught demanding an end to the repressive measures associated with the monarchy, a revolution broke out two years later—the second and final act in the drama of the throne's demise (a demise abetted by the young monarch's inability to behave sensibly with regard to his French bonbon, dancer Gaby Deslys). The royal family sought and received refuge in England. But the British Foreign Office informed the royal Portuguese government that the alliance was between nations, not regimes, and thus refused to send any military help to prop up the old dynasty—and in the summer of 1911 a republic was finally proclaimed, with Manuel de Arriaga its first president. Sadly, as in all too many similar cases, the liberal revolution was, in historian Hugh Kay's words, unable to "take root in soil unprepared to receive it."[73]

The next decade and a half were tempestuous years for Portugal, years marked most notably by bad government and its mistress, a worse economy. A lack of leadership and of experience with democratic government resulted in a government in deep trouble. A new constitution produced a strong parliament and a weak executive, meaning cabinets fell quickly over petty issues in a rudderless, top-heavy legislative system. Though it stayed out of the Great War for two years, by 1916 Portugal was finally sucked into that cataclysm because of both British pressure and a fear its colonies might without its direct participation become bargaining chips among the Great Powers. In December 1917, domestic inflation and food shortages led to a military-backed coup, putting Sidônio Bernardino Paes in power as Europe's first modern republican dictator. He lasted for a year, until an assassin shot him in Lisbon.

Something resembling unfettered chaos followed. The Portuguese voters massively ignored elections, a sign that the parliamentary system itself was beginning to implode. The middle class was still so small that no kind of fascist opposition to parliamentary liberalism was able to find ground deep enough to take root. Many people yearned for a return to premodern clericalism to provide the leadership missing in the nation's squalid political life. The country was so atrociously governed, so corrupt and mismanaged that the League of Nations coined a word to describe the absolute low in national welfare: "Portuguesé."[74] Patience with the status quo was fast beginning to run out. Finally Portugal's experiment with liberalism ended in 1926, in a military coup under the not very able leadership of one Marshal Manuel Gomes da Costa.

Gomes and his officers weren't able to make much more out of the hash of Portuguese politics than the republic had. What was most seriously missing was a leader strong enough to pull the country together and overcome the factional rivalries that had been so disastrous in the experiment with parliamentarianism. Six days after he took over the government, Gomes da Costa brought to Lisbon a relatively obscure young economist from Coimbra University[75] named Antonio de Oliveira Salazar.[76] The academic with a reputation for brilliance was to assume office as minister of finance. The astonished Salazar put up with the new government's bumbling incompetence for only a few weeks before getting on a train and returning to Coimbra.

A year later, it was obvious the military government was all but finished. Rioting broke out all over the country, with a hundred dead in Lisbon, another eighty killed in Oporto. The government's managers looked to Salazar again, but *this* time the economics professor demanded guarantees that he could put his own agenda into effect—immediately. What his agenda came to was a program of austerity and fiscal responsibility such as Portugal had never experienced in modern times. A budget was to be rigidly regularized, with expenditures to come out of current revenue. Department heads exceeding their budgets would be subject to civil and criminal penalties. The metropolitan (the mainland, the Azores, and the Madeira Islands) budget would be defended from colonial money demands. And there would be absolutely no state financing of private enterprise.

Assured of such powers, Salazar came back into government, and his scheme quickly began to show the success of sound economic rules scrupulously followed. "Excess" public employees were fired. Greater efficiency in collecting taxes began to fill the treasury. The budget was balanced—at least on paper—and the national floating debt funded. Business was taxed to the hilt while struggling landowners were helped as much as possible.

To make sure things went the way he wanted them to go, Salazar would employ highly unorthodox means. Once when bothersome delays in the customs office were reported to the minister, Salazar disguised himself as a minor clerk, went to work along with the baggage handlers, and finally discovered and corrected the inefficiencies causing the problems.[77] The Portuguese bureaucracy may have been nettled by his direct methods, but the results caused a great deal of attention to be focused on the efficient young Salazar.

By 1930, the generals' four-year-old coup was coming to be more and more centralized under the control of its remarkable finance minister. Not only was Salazar's the final word on matters financial; his vision of the nation's future political orientation was now earning the unquestioning backing of the revolution's makers. In an era when the continent would experience a variety of radical political systems—Italy's corporative state, Germany's National Socialist system—1930 saw the birth of Portugal's revolutionary version of the future, the Estado Novo, or New State. And squarely behind this vision stood Salazar, just as he would for the next four decades.

In July 1932, finance minister finally became prime minister. Salazar's promotion spelled the official end of military rule, and his position was now one of unqualified dictatorial leadership of the state. On a salary of $208 a month,[78] the dictator led an unremarkable and chaste personal life. He became a sort of foster father to two young girls, Micas and Maria Antônia, both brought up by a housekeeper—a woman everyone in Portugal knew simply as Dona Maria. The son of a farmer, Salazar had once fallen in love with a landowner's daughter, who was—according to legend—denied him because of his inferior birth. The same legend has it that he took a vow of chastity and remained a bachelor forever thereafter, and, in fact, Salazar never married. His personal justification for his marital status after coming to power was that a national leader should consecrate himself to the "public welfare," evidently a family being a distraction to such a calling. The reasoning was borne out when, after one of the girls became ill and he stayed up all night to comfort her, he said the next morning, "You see, I was right about a family. Today I am too tired to do good work."[79] The story has the air of the apocryphal, but it is entirely in character with a man who lived solely for his country.

Salazar's New State was his personal answer to what he saw as Portugal's long-term need for a strong state, one in which authoritarianism could be justified by memories of the chaos parliamentary government had brought the country since the downfall of the monarchy. Inherent in his new order were an abolition of trade unions and political parties (the latter replaced by a single quasi-party called the National Union), a regimentation of society,[80] near-total censorship of the press, political power centralized in a tiny executive, and mass indoctrination in the supreme virtues of Deus, Pátria, e Família (God, Country, and Family).[81]

It was a state supported by the church, but one in which theocracy found infertile soil. It was a state deeply monarchist in sentiment, but one in which the Braganzas were offered no hope of royalist restoration. It was a state fervently supported by large landowners, industrialists, bankers, military officers—but one in which none of those interest groups was able to control Salazar or the direction of government. Men from these callings staffed the regime's political agencies, but did not form mini-empires unto themselves. Class was undeniably important, but sons of shepherds and policemen were able to become cabinet ministers. Elements from the extreme right to the moderate left expected to benefit from the new regime.[82]

Salazar was little attracted to the icon role so many dictators savor. A military general, Antonio Oscar Fragoso de Carmona, had since 1926 been the president and mainly ceremonial head of state (a man who, incidentally, had a taste for the more luxurious trappings of a head of state, and who indulged—and was allowed by Salazar to indulge—them). The dictator kept himself deliberately below Carmona, but no doubt existed as to where supreme power resided in the new Portugal. What distinguished the nation's strongman government from the more malevolent variety in Europe was the comparatively benign nature of Salazar's rule. Activist democrats never had an easy time in the Estado Novo, but neither did its citizens have to contend with a homegrown version of the

Gestapo making life an exercise in terror. As a result, the Portuguese public, weary of two decades of domestic strife, was remarkably inert in its acceptance of the new order.

At first admired internationally, the methods and policies of Salazar and his New State began to attract the label of fascism at the beginning of the Spanish Civil War. In the idiom of the time, an authoritarian government was either "fascist" or "Communist." With some irony Salazar himself ascribed to this view, his pro-Franco course in the Spanish conflict being dictated by, at bottom, a belief that Communism was the only indisputably *mortal* threat Western European civilization confronted. After centuries of reliance on Britain as its primary international protection, the gathering war clouds in Europe and the virulent battle in Spain led Salazar to turn to his neighbor's Nationalist insurgency. Although it was British and French policy that in large measure made the Republic's cause in the Spanish war hopeless (Lisbon adhered to the nonintervention policy), Portugal and Salazar nevertheless interpreted Britain's official abhorrence of Iberian fascism and Franco's insurgency as representing the true voice of British sentiment. In consequence, Portugal began to carefully shift itself away from the British orbit, gaining greater sympathy from Madrid and probably also burnishing its image in Berlin. It was by no means clear as early as 1936 that Hitler's fortune would be the triumphant one, but it *was* apparent that Britain (and France too, for that matter) was making little effort to deter the increasingly balance-of-power-upsetting rise of Nazi Germany.

Salazar's policy in siding with the Spanish rebels from the beginning had several causes. Foremost was his ideological and religious affinity with the Francoist side. The realization from early in the war that Franco would be the likely victor also undoubtedly led Salazar to want to support a winner. Of some significance was the fear that a Republican victory would result in a Spanish invasion of Portugal—some thought that Iberia was ripe pickings for international Communism, and a victory in both countries would have, according to historian Hugh Kay, "been of the utmost value to Communist world strategy." Salazar further worried about the "Balkanization" of Spain, should the Republican penchant for allowing greater regional autonomy prevail, and believed semi-independent Catalonian and Basque areas would contain the seeds of disunity, a disunity eventually resulting in a Communist invasion of Portugal.

Of no small importance in Salazar's actions was a desire to move Portugal from its lopsided domination by Britain, a wish to make his nation less dependent on one country and more on several.[83] Irrespective of his hope that Franco would eventually succeed in Spain, Salazar never entertained the notion of actually entering the Spanish fray. But of all the relevant players except the Soviet Union and Germany, only Portugal made it absolutely clear virtually from the war's beginning which side it favored to win.

During the Spanish Civil War, Portugal's support for Franco's Nationalists was never less than transparent.[84] Correct relations were maintained with the Republic until broken off in October 1936—the embassy in Lisbon was not disturbed, though its ambassador received scant official attention from Salazar's government—but it was the rebels' mission that became the focal point of Spanish affairs in Portugal from the beginning of the insurgency. After the break with the Republic, an unofficial mission, under the direction of Franco's brother Nicolás, became the de facto embassy in Portugal.[85] "Portugal and Spain are like two brothers, each possessing his own home in the peninsula" was Salazar's publicly voiced sentiment, but the Spanish brother was purely Nationalist. Throughout the war, Portuguese policy was directed solely at assisting the rebels.[86] In battles near the frontier, Republicans who escaped into Portugal were almost invariably sent back across the border, where many faced summary execution. Salazar permitted a private Spanish broadcasting company to be set up on Portuguese soil, where it was able to supply the insurgents with a wide variety of militarily useful information. Portugal even severed diplomatic relations with Czechoslovakia when that country's government demanded that the weapons it sold to Lisbon not be resold to the Spanish rebels.

One of the most tangible expressions of Portuguese assistance to the Nationalist cause was the formation of a legion of Portuguese fascist professional officers and volunteers called the Viriatos to serve alongside their Spanish rebel co-ideologists. Named for the second-century-B.C. warrior Viriatus, a man who had played an important part in the establishment of a strong Portuguese presence on the peninsula, the estimated 18,000 to 20,000 Portuguese who joined Franco suffered some 6,000 to 8,000 dead in the war.

In March 1939, as Spain's battlefield agony was drawing to an end, Salazar and Franco met to establish a working arrangement between their two regimes. The Treaty of Friendship and Nonaggression, or *Pacto Iberico*, making up what was somewhat overly grandly called the Iberian Bloc, largely represented Franco's hope to show an even hand between the European alliances then squaring off. The pact required that the two countries protect each other's territory and frontiers, and that they not enter into a treaty or alliance that under any possible circumstances would require aggression against the other. The Iberian Pact did not end the special treaty status between Portugal and Britain, but it certainly made London uneasy about the political and ideological course on which its heretofore client state was embarking. The Anti-Comintern Pact, the loose association by which Spain (for whom this pact had very few tangible obligations) allied with Germany, Italy, and Japan in a partnership against international Communism, was not joined by Salazar.

Thus on the eve of general European war, Portugal's course was in some ways a self-contradiction: a continuation of the British alliance and a strong Iberian solidarity. The former reflected the realization that the Royal Navy remained the primary barrier against its independence of action, the latter its best hope to influence the Spanish dictator in resisting joining the Germans in their war, a path that Salazar saw leading squarely to Portugal's transformation into a German vassal.

CHAPTER II

THE WAR BEGINS

September 1939–April 1940

Bern

Shortly before the outbreak of World War I, the German emperor, Wilhelm II, was paying a visit to Switzerland, where he was invited to the annual military maneuvers. Proud of his imperial army, the condescending Kaiser stopped to question one of the Swiss soldiers. "You are five hundred thousand men and you shoot well, but if we attack with a million men, what will you do?" Unhesitatingly, the soldier answered, "We will fire twice." The Kaiser sent his army through Belgium instead. [1]

In September 1939, Switzerland wasn't so sure it would get spared a second time.

• • •

Bern that September was much like what it is today—about as physically perfect a city as humankind has yet been able to devise. Drawn as tight as a driving glove to the thumb-shaped peninsula around and below which flows the river Aare, the small metropolis was the very essence of middle-class prosperity and Swiss notions of shipshape. Perhaps more auspiciously, it also manifested the happiest traditions of European civilization and social progress.

From the hills surrounding the city, many of the residences of the embassies accredited to the confederation looked across the Aare's deep ravine to the massive Bundespalast, Switzerland's domed and crenellated Florentine Renaissance-style capitol building. In this symbol of Swiss unity, legislators from each of the nation's twenty-two cantons speculated through the first hours and days of the war on the belligerents' next moves. Those politicians worried not only about German armies short-cutting through Switzerland to outflank French armies but also about the possibility that the French armies might try the same maneuver to out-flank the Germans. In either case, Switzerland would be the sure loser. Though the government clearly and unequivocally reiterated the confed-eration's unqualified neutrality the moment the war broke out in Poland, it made certain both sides understood that such neutrality would be backed to the utmost with the nation's army ready to defend against an invader from *any* direction.

In the interwar years, the Social Democratic Party and left-wing groups opposed the government's increases in military spending, the ef-fect of such opposition being a weakening of the nation's defense struc-ture in the standard socialist furtherance of "peace." Only after Hitler became German chancellor in 1933 did Switzerland begin a serious shaping-up regimen for the flabby state of its post-1918 defense network. The quickening pitch of Berlin's aggressiveness sent shudders down the collective Swiss back, leading the government to pass the first of the decade's several significant increases in defense spending. In the mid-1930s, newly levied appropriations pointed most directly at beefing up the national system of fortifications. In quick succession, basic military train-ing was lengthened, measures were passed to extend call-ups for units undergoing advanced training, the maximum age for compulsory service was raised from forty-eight to sixty, and the Federal Council was given the power to mobilize reserves in an "immediate emergency" without waiting for formal parliamentary approval. Promptly after the frightening Munich crisis in the fall of 1938, roads, bridges, and tunnels were mined, and Swiss industry was set to developing new weapons, with the 47-millimeter antitank gun quickly reputed to be the equal of any antitank weapon in the world. When six months later Germany threatened the forced annexation of Liechtenstein—the tiny principality wedged be-tween Switzerland's eastern border and Austria—the Federal Council authorized the first emergency call-up to strengthen the Frontier Guards. By the end of 1939, more than a billion francs (about a quarter of a billion 1939 dollars) had been spent turning Switzerland into an armed hedgehog.

In the tension-filled weeks preceding the attack on Poland, many Swiss understood that this military buildup could be neutralized by a domestic danger as potentially deadly as any Wehrmacht division. Though the vast majority of the Swiss found the Nazis, their philosophy, and their methods almost farcically repugnant, a vocal minority continued to openly agitate for Swiss merger with the Reich, and, as is the nature of a democracy, Switzerland freely allowed such political expression. Such incitement was fervently acclaimed in Germany, where mapmakers had since the inception of the Nazi state shown the German-speaking parts of Switzerland included in the "future" Reich and where such expression was predictably acclaimed as the "real" will of the Swiss people. Most of these Swiss in sympathy with the Nazi cause probably were so out of ideological considerations, though some were subsidized in their activities by the German treasury. But not only did Bern have to face the fact that some of its own citizens—albeit merely a noisy minority—were undermining national resolve to withstand Nazi pressure; a significant fifth column of German nationals also resided in Switzerland with the view to supporting a network of agents dedicated to sabotaging the confederation after German columns marched into the country.

Fears about Switzerland's psychological capacity to withstand the German threat found particular currency in Western intellectual circles among those who remembered the Swiss reaction—abruptly banning the Communist Party—to the perceived Comintern threat at the time of the Spanish Civil War, and reasoned that the right-wing threat would be treated as less dangerous. Americans were particularly worried Switzerland might come under some kind of semi-*Anschluss* with Germany to stave off the real or imagined Communist menace. Bern's wish not to provoke Berlin or Rome furthered such fears, though more sympathetic circles in America and the West understood the government's correctness toward Berlin as justifiable *Realpolitik*. Nonetheless, these perceptions would soon affect Switzerland's relationship with the Allies when the Western press began to criticize the country for what was perceived as unseemly licking of fascist boots.[2]

As it happened, the concerns both domestic and foreign about Switzerland's incapacity to withstand German pressure appear to have been overdrawn. In spite of Germany's obvious potency, the overwhelming majority of the Swiss continued to reject the Reich's overtures for either union or anything like Nazification of Swiss institutions. This rejection was made clear despite government concessions to Berlin in such matters as the importation of propaganda material, or even the far more important issue of silencing its press criticism of Germany for fear of offending its threatening neighbor.

One highly consequential Swiss viewed these equivocations toward the Reich from his government with such misgivings that all of the nation's costly and politically hard-won defense buildup might in the end, he feared, count for nothing. Henri Guisan would be the sole indisputable Swiss hero to come out of World War II, indeed the first such Swiss hero since William Tell. A French-speaking[3] gentleman farmer from the canton of Vaud, the sixty-five-year-old corps commander had in 1939 been a professional, full-time officer for only nine years.[4] But Guisan's reputation for decisiveness and firmness—two qualities that would be much needed in light of Bern's flaccidity—had immediately after the Munich crisis led to an agreement between parliament and government to his appointment as the commander-in-chief of the Swiss armed forces, and two days before the German attack on Poland to his official promotion to the rank of general—the nation's sole officer of flag rank. Accorded sweeping powers by the terms of his appointment, Guisan quickly communicated an ominous but unavoidable message to the Swiss people: war is coming, the army must be ready to defend the nation, and life "as usual" has to end.[5]

On the first weekend in September, the Swiss finally understood both the depth of the crisis and their danger, and virtually overnight Guisan's picture and framed aphorisms began to adorn the walls of homes, offices, factories, and restaurants all over the country.

The first days of the war were spent in a flurry of diligence preparing for an assault against the confederation's borders. Though widespread panic over invasion wouldn't come until the spring of 1940, the fear of German and French armies trying to outflank each other through Swiss territory had led Guisan to ask for and receive from parliament on September 1—immediately after it was certain the German attack on Poland was carried out without a declaration of war—authorization for general mobilization. Since the nineteenth century such an act had been a near-certain overture to war itself, and predictably provoked an outraged howl from the German side of the border at what Berlin termed an act of Swiss "aggression." Guisan ignored the protest, and within two days the army was amassed at its full strength of 435,000 men divided into three army corps, ready to assume whatever stance its general would determine appropriate.

What the general determined appropriate was to concentrate his citizen-soldiery in a line along the northern tier of the country, facing both France and Greater Germany. (For a year and a half, there had been, of course, no independent Austrian frontier in the northeast, Austria having been incorporated into the Reich in 1938.) It was here that the command staff expected fighting between opposing German and French armies most likely would spill over into Swiss territory. Both antagonists' major fixed defense systems—the French Maginot Line and the German Siegfried Line—ended at Switzerland's northwestern corner, in the greater Basel area; the city itself was Switzerland's largest directly facing Germany. Guisan surmised that one country trying to outflank the other would do so by going around the southern ends of these opposing defensive lines, at the so-called Belfort Hinge, hard against Swiss territory.[6]

Guisan formed this "national shield" in the north by setting up two lines of defense. The primary line closely followed the frontier around the top half of the country, using the fortifications built over the prior five years—mainly blockhouses armed with machine guns—to slow down an initial German onslaught. Then, after this first shield was breached, as he knew it would be, the main resistance would kick in. Stretching in a shorter, shallower arc under the first line, the stronger defenses extended from the Alps in the east, across a line south of the Limmat River, and ended at the Gempen Heights overlooking Basel, the commercial entrepôt sitting at the *Dreiecke*, the three-cornered point where Switzerland, Germany, and France meet; the city itself was considered expendable. The westernmost guns of this principal defense tier lined up with the southernmost fort on the French Maginot Line, enabling the two nations' guns to cross each other's fire in case of a German attack through the *Dreiecke*; clearly it was a German invasion—not a French one—that most concerned Guisan. Zurich, Switzerland's largest city, sat in the middle of this second defense tier, virtually on the front lines, and it too would be sacrificed in the event of all-out fighting. Between the two lines of defense, Guisan placed six divisions; a mountain division and a mountain brigade were held in reserve to try to plug breaks in the main line. If this second line broke, for Switzerland the war would be lost.

But here fate—Hitlerian strategy—stepped in. Instead of a blazing continuation in the West of the success he had in the East, Hitler stopped his Wehrmacht divisions after crushing Poland. The pact with the Soviets had translated into a splitting of Eastern Europe into German and Russian spheres, with the Red Army pouring into Poland from the east and meeting the Germans at the line predetermined in the secret Moscow protocols between the two foreign ministers; that the Soviet Union was on Hitler's list of victims-to-be was, of course, unknown. The German leader hoped to persuade Britain and France to give up their war against Germany, the Wehrmacht's victory in the East already a fact which the democracies could do nothing to change. But confounding this line of reasoning, the latter had had their line in the sand breached, and, cognizant of the stakes, refused to negotiate. What came of this standoff was *Sitzkrieg*—the so-called Phony War—with ground forces sitting nose to nose against each other on the Western front, doing little other than verbally taunting their foe across the fortified lines.

For Switzerland, this period of declared but dormant war[7] came as a relief, though one with potentially disastrous effects on the national treasury. With nearly half a million men on active duty out of a total population of only a little over 4 million, keeping the country running with anything resembling normality proved a formidable, not to say impossible, undertaking. Soldiers' wives beseeched the government to return family breadwinners, and it wasn't long before both unions and political parties demanded the release of soldiers as the Allied-German standoff continued. In December, bending to pressure, the government finally began to demobilize troops, so many that by the last day of 1939 only 175,000 men remained under arms. For those still serving, a system of rotation permitted home visits so necessary chores could get done.

In the early months of the war, while he worked on the strategy he hoped would protect the nation from the Wehrmacht, General Guisan labored under an additional weight, one which if discovered by Berlin would very likely have given Germany the meager diplomatic pretext it wanted to justify any future invasion of Switzerland. Since 1938, the Swiss military had been engaged in highly secret joint defense discussions with its French counterparts, the talks aimed at devising a strategy on how the two countries could ward off a German invasion of Swiss territory.

Though neutrality still ranked uppermost in the Swiss pantheon of national principles, these "discussions" with the French were not the first time such military exploration—even that aimed at offensive operations— had been conducted with various neighbors. When the great liberal insurrections of 1848 and 1849 swept the continent, some Swiss militarists pondered with their French counterparts intervening on the side of the liberal insurgents in Italy. Another instance, in 1914, saw detailed plans jointly drawn up to attack Italy, with the Austrian Army to recover the lost territories of the Valtellina. Neither of these operations came even close to fruition, but clearly the army planners in Bern hadn't always been entirely mute on the subject of military operations on foreign soil.[8]

The initial substantive contacts between Guisan and French military officials were made nearly a year before the Wehrmacht crossed the Polish frontier (though Guisan, as commander of the 1st Corps, had held personal talks with the French Army earlier in the decade). Those discussions were initiated at the request of Rudolf Minger, then Swiss minister of defense. Since the German military buildup got underway in earnest in the mid-1930s, the Swiss took as a ground rule of defense planning that any German attack in the West would have to somehow breach the Maginot Line, France's billion-dollar chain of underground forts extending from the Belgian border in the north to the Swiss frontier in the south. Further, if that breach were directed at the line's southern end, the attack would very likely spill over on the northwest corner of Switzerland. In October 1938, with Minger's specific authorization, Guisan visited the French general Jean-Marie de Lattre de Tassigny, the purpose of the visit a secret inspection of the Maginot's fortification arrangements. Guisan knew the danger inherent in the visit, that Hitler would view any such contact as a lessening of Switzerland's pledge of neutrality, regardless of the clearly defensive Swiss motivation for the talks.

After the war started, Guisan, now commander-in-chief, could no longer risk personally continuing with these contacts. Appointed to stand in for him was Bernard Barbey, a novelist and a reserve cavalry officer on the Swiss general staff who prior to the war's outbreak had been living in Paris. Given his natural reasons for traveling in France—he was also literary director for the French publishing firm of Bayard—as well as his useful contacts in the French capital, Barbey seemed the perfect choice to take over the discussions, and was appointed to serve under Colonel Roger Masson, head of the Swiss intelligence service.

In December 1939, with the tension of the Phony War at its full height on the facing Maginot and Siegfried lines, Major Barbey paid a visit to the commander-in-chief of French armies on the eastern front, General Besson. Besson laid out to Barbey the plan he had devised to occupy, should the Swiss government so request, the Gempen Heights south of Basel—the area in which a presumed German attack would try to outflank the southern end of the Maginot Line. There the joined French and Swiss armies would together try to halt the advancing German invasion of Switzerland, even if such invasion was clearly aimed only at outflanking the Maginot Line, and not at a general invasion of Switzerland itself. The French officials conceded that no such operation could ever be mounted without a request from the Swiss general staff, Bern's fundamental condition for even considering such talks.

Meanwhile, the Swiss high command decided that in case the Germans got wind of these talks with the French, they had better cover themselves by initiating the same sorts of discussions with the Germans,

Berlin's indignation over Franco-Swiss joint defense discussions thereby nipped, so it was hoped, if the Swiss could respond that it was merely the same sort of thing they had been talking about with the Wehrmacht. For these counter-talks, Bern sent a trusted envoy, Hans Berli, a major with the experience of having attended staff courses in Germany and thus known to ranking Wehrmacht officers. Berli's mission was, like Barbey's, top secret, and no documentation of its results has ever been uncovered.[9]

As the closing days of the decade unfolded, Switzerland's fears of German invasion waned. The Phony War between the Reich and the Western democracies seemed—at least on its Western European land front—to amount to little more than a war of mutual intimidation, and hopes began to rise that the belligerents might even find a peaceful resolution to their not yet catastrophic dispute.

· · ·

If the barrage of rhetoric was louder than the clash of arms that first season of war, the average Swiss citizen was nonetheless beginning to feel war's economic sting. To a country whose existence is a tribute to the nobility of free trade, the sudden reality of embargoes and other restrictions on that trade arrived as a shock. What such restraints led to within weeks of the war's onset was a kind of state-mandated preemptive rationing that would by the end of the war alter virtually every Swiss citizen's occupation, diet, and way of life.

Foreseeing the likelihood of war, by 1937 the Swiss government had started planning for the inevitable turbulence with the disruption of the nation's normal trade. Within a year, Bern moved to protect the importation of supplies deemed vital to the nation's economic survival, granting special import permits to firms which undertook to bring in supplies guaranteed to last for at least half a year. Six months before hostilities broke out, every household in the country was directed to lay in a two months' supply of staple foods, the government extending credit to those families too poor to meet the requirement. Rationing began within weeks after the war began. At the end of October, the sale of a few essential items began to be restricted, with the first ration cards being distributed nationwide the first of November. Volunteer citizen "militias" were recruited from private enterprise to control the use of raw materials and to ensure equity in distribution. At the same time these procedures were established for consumers, farmers were ordered to treble their wheat planting, a requirement which could obviously only be met at a cost to other, less vital, crops.

On a larger scale, landlocked Switzerland had to ensure that neutral ports would remain open through which the annual 1.2 million tons of goods bought overseas could be received, as well as see to the availability of the ships to carry these goods. To prepare for the time when neutral cargo vessels would be preempted by other countries, the government secured a freighter fleet that included fifteen small Greek steamers. Bern set up a general agent in London authorized to oversee the flotilla's operations, and port commissioners were appointed in Genoa, Lisbon, and Marseille both to make sure that ships bearing goods destined for Switzerland weren't held up by bureaucratic red tape and to organize the transport of the goods from the ports overland to the Swiss borders.

What they could import into the country wasn't entirely up to the Swiss to determine. On the day Britain and France declared war, the Allies instituted a blockade against Germany. The procedures the Allies set up to control neutral states' imports of foreign goods were based on a system of permits called "navicerts." The coercion used by the Allies to enforce their economic blockade against the neutrals lay in their navies, but it was navicerts rather than guns that became the navies' most powerful weapon. Both Britain and, later, the United States employed the system, the latter initiating it many months before its own official belligerency began.

The navicert proved to be an early and rousing success. The way it worked was straightforward. If a given country wished to sell goods to a European neutral, such as Argentina marketing meat to Switzerland, or Venezuela oil to Portugal, the vending country's agent was required to consult with the local British or American consul to determine whether the particular consignment was within the Allies' predetermined ration for that commodity for the receiving nation. (Occasionally navicerts were applied for in the neutral country, rather than in the country of the goods' origin.) If everything jibed, the consul would issue the navicert, allowing the goods to pass through the Allied naval blockade guarding the sea lanes to the neutral country. If they didn't jibe, no navicert was issued, and if the consignment was sent anyway, it would be subject to interception and seizure by patrol boats of the Allied navies. Should any suspicion arise as to a given cargo, a search could go on for days, with the cargo being off-loaded and probed with unsympathetic thoroughness. Being caught with unauthorized goods meant virtual ostracization in international ports for the ship, its crew, and its owners.

The navicert's upside was that it provided assurances to the shipowners that their vessels and cargoes wouldn't be seized as contraband as long as the navicert conditions were adhered to, though random checks of the ships were still conducted to ensure such adherence. British and American shipping agents around the world were instructed to cable home if any ship left for a blockade port without a navicert, with naval patrols stopping those vessels; very few captains attempted such a maneuver during the war.[10]

Setting the amount of goods that would be allowed through the blockade was arrived at after painstaking negotiations between the neutral and the Allies, who had for economic purposes become, in effect, the neutrals' adversaries. The Allies worked out accords with each of the neutrals called War Trade Agreements, formulas to which each country was obliged to agree or else watch as Allied warships cut off all goods within their naval reach. The whole point of the exercise was to try to ensure that the neutrals had only enough for their own use, that they wouldn't be tempted to transfer excess goods on to the Axis or its allies in order to profit from sale or trade of such excess. Because Switzerland shared a direct border with Germany, no Allied blockade of its frontiers could, of course, be seamless, but the policy served nonetheless as a severe restriction on Swiss economic sovereignty.

Switzerland found out early on that it would be painfully tried by the war's economic consequences. Dependent on coal and iron for its industries,[11] the country also imported a considerable proportion of its food, both for humans and for livestock. To pay for these imports, the Swiss manufactured high-technology goods, products that had achieved hard-won international repute for their quality and reliability. For this system to remain successful, a success that had made the country one of the world's most important workshops, Switzerland was forced—if, that is, it wished to maintain its high standard of living—to face the blockade restrictions as imaginatively as the talent of its people could contrive.

On the reverse side of the Allied blockade, the Swiss were confronted with—as were all the neutrals—a German counter-blockade, one forming a sort of second seal around Switzerland, with the Allied sea and land (the latter until France fell the following year) blockade facing down the German counter-blockade. Neither was designed specifically to harm Switzerland or any of the other neutrals. Instead, each side's enemies were the targets, the economic measures taken, as we've seen, to ensure that the neutrals weren't used either to directly transship goods through their territories to the enforcers' foes or to craft imported raw materials into finished goods which would then be transshipped. Though the neutral mightn't be the direct target in what unequivocally amounted to economic warfare, a manufacturing and exporting nation like Switzerland ended up with its markets diminished for its precision wares with military or strategic applications.

The conundrum for the Allies in their blockades was the flip side of the coin: how to circumvent the German counter-blockade and get Swiss exports into Britain or its allies. Many of the traditional Swiss imports to the United Kingdom, those such as watches, were classified by the blockade authorities as nonessential, and were thus suppressed in the interests of Britain's nearly empty treasury. On the other hand, while watches weren't needed in Britain, chronographs—stopwatches—were of tremendous value to the Royal Air Force in its bombing operations. The Germans were naturally aware of this application, and banned their export to Britain. To circumvent Berlin's intentions and get them through the German blockade anyway, Swiss watchmakers put chronograph movements into ordinary watch cases. When the phony watches arrived in Britain they were reassembled to serve the purpose for which they had been built. [12]

. . .

An endlessly repeated axiom about wartime Switzerland is that if such a neutral island in the middle of Europe hadn't existed, it would have had to be invented. That observation symbolizes many functions the Swiss performed for both sides in the conflict, but it has always primarily referred to the country's role as *the* international espionage center. Embassies and legations, as well as the cafés that were their informal outbuildings, acted as the principal venues of espionage, but diplomatically protected consular officials in the cities near the frontiers—Basel and Geneva two prime examples—were equally active in the art and science of spying both on each other and on the Swiss. In late 1939, it was the Germans who far outdistanced their adversaries in the sophistication of these espionage efforts.

A primary function of the three German intelligence services operating in Bern—the Wehrmacht, or armed forces, network; the apparatus of the Gestapo, or the Secret State Police controlled by the SS; and the Nazi Party's own spy setup—involved assessing Swiss defense capabilities. Aided by a network of domestic spies, a fifth column eager to turn their country into another Nazi *Gau*, Berlin was anxious to be able to accurately evaluate the probable Swiss military reaction to a German invasion.

Germany recruited its Swiss spies primarily from the pro-National

Socialist and pro-German parties that had sprouted like poisonous weeds in Switzerland after Hitler's capture of power in 1933. An important mission of all the Reich's intelligence services operating in the confederation was to find weak places in the Swiss resolve, vulnerable points to poke into in order to seek out ways to weaken the country's will to resist the "inevitable"—the overwhelming Nazi surge that would eventually incorporate all of German-speaking Europe into Hitler's super-state. More concrete missions—the condition of Swiss armaments, Bern's state of rapport with the Allies, how to overcome the country's formidable defenses—were also carried out. But inexorably, Switzerland's own counterespionage capabilities grew, from the military intelligence service's ten agents who served the country on September 1, 1939 (plus one agent each in Berlin, Rome, and Paris), to eventually 120 on the staff of Colonel Roger Masson, as well as a number of clandestine agents in the service's pay. Colonel Masson's agents worked not only at home but in Germany: knowing the fluctuations in German troop concentrations along the Reich's Swiss frontier zone allowed Bern to more accurately gauge the probability of a German attack.

By virtue of its neutrality—and its internationally accepted stance of official impartiality as to the affairs of the warring states—Switzerland assumed the function of "protecting power" for the belligerents in each other's capitals, the agent by which Germany was still able to talk—albeit unofficially—with Britain, and vice versa. The Geneva Conventions had in 1929 first established the legal framework for protecting powers, foremost being the protection of prisoners of war. Even though at war, the enemies still had legitimate reasons to continue a dialogue: the exchange of diplomatic representatives trapped when war was declared, inspections of each other's prisoner-of-war camps, questions of property belonging to each other. By the end of the war, 35 Swiss diplomatic missions around the world shared 219 mandates as protecting power, in many instances for countries at war with each other.[13]

. . .

Almost immediately after Hitler came to power, one of the first dilemmas Germany presented its southern neighbor was that of *Flüchtlinge*—refugees, the unwanted, hounded, and reviled enemies and rejects of the Nazi state. Starting as a small sore in 1933, six years later the tragedy of escapees from Nazi tyranny had grown into a cancer. Nearly half a century after the end of World War II, its treatment of these refugees is still the issue most associated with Switzerland's behavior during the six years of war. The associations have, assessed with the greatest charity, been ambiguous, an irony in light of Switzerland's centuries-long tradition of receiving those unfortunates badgered by its neighbors.[14] Ironically, the *Germans* considered the Swiss attitude toward refugees, particularly Jewish refugees, irksome in the extreme. Nazi criticism of the Swiss safe harbor for the Reich's enemies gravely jeopardized Switzerland's policy of neutrality. An article in the January 1939 issue of the German periodical *Nationalsozialistische Monatshefte* unequivocally threatened that Germany would be forced to ignore Swiss neutrality "in all circumstances" unless it stopped the harboring of its enemies.[15]

With the almost immediate onset of persecution of their political opponents and the only slightly more measured brutalization of German Jews, it was not surprising that many such unfortunates tried to use Switzerland as an avenue by which to escape the Nazis. But after *Kristallnacht* and the worries it brought of "inundation" by Germany's Jews, both countries made the process agonizingly slow and difficult. Still, the majority of German émigrés used Swiss sanctuary only as a way station, a temporary safe haven until completing the difficult process of obtaining visas for settlement in the few countries willing to accept them. Celebrities like the brothers Thomas and Heinrich Mann encountered relatively little difficulty in completing the process, aided generously by humanitarian organizations in Switzerland;[16] some refugees of this stature were even allowed to remain in Switzerland. But those who were not illustrious, or were without illustrious connections, found the process heartbreakingly intimidating.

At the outbreak of war, some 7,000 refugees from Germany were in Switzerland, most of whom—about 5,000—were Jews waiting for papers to leave the country for other destinations. Five days after the attack on Poland, the Federal Council decreed that only persons with visas would in the future be allowed to enter the country, a calamitous decision in light of the urgency facing many of those trying to flee Germany and areas under German control. At first, the visa requirement was loosely applied, but after mid-October the border authorities were ordered to turn back persons trying to get into the country without the requisite papers.

In an apparent effort to distinguish between "economic" refugees and those fleeing from mortal danger, Bern established the category of "émigrés" for the former, "refugees" for the latter. Emigrés were required to leave Switzerland with especial haste, and while they were in the country the national police were instructed by their chief, Heinrich Rothmund, to keep them under close control. Both categories of unfortunates were subject to internment, and sometimes the place in which they were interned was, for lack of other facilities, a prison.

The rationale behind measures that in later years seemed shockingly inhumane (despite worse records for other "democratic" nations in their refugee policies) was ambiguous. A wariness existed on the part of the government and the bureaucracy that such elements represented a danger, not only in overcrowding the "little Swiss boat"—a phrase current in Switzerland in those years—but in injecting a foreign virus that the Swiss leadership had for centuries made strenuous efforts to keep out. Another factor barring permanent settlement for more than a handful of refugees and émigrés was the omnipresent fear on the part of the Swiss that jobs would be taken by the foreigners, tossing natives onto the dole. For this reason, trade unions stood foursquare behind the government policy. As historian Michael Marrus points out, the Swiss saw the refugees only as a threat rather than as a potential source of workers to strengthen Swiss industry and agriculture.[17] Though humanitarian considerations made little difference in its xenophobia, Switzerland of the war years can't be said to have reacted very differently from virtually every other country in the world in the matter of refugees—especially Jewish refugees. In fact, the Swiss record, in terms of the nation's size, was considerably better than that of most countries.

Private Swiss citizens often went to dangerous lengths to negate the worst effects of their government's attitude toward those trying to escape arrest—and often death—at the hands of the Germans. Even members of parliament criticized the fearfulness of the authorities, the local variety of which was often more zealous in implementing the letter of the visa rules than were the federal police. But it was clear in the early months of the war to all Swiss—private citizens as well as responsible members of the government—that the refugee/émigré problem would get worse. At the end of 1939, Hitler and his state didn't seem in danger from any quarter, and those the Nazis were determined to persecute would grow steadily in number as Hitler's dominion spread inexorably across the continent.

· · ·

On December 29, with only two days left in an awful decade that was going to be followed by a far worse one, an announcement gratifying to most Swiss appeared in Zurich. The last two daily newspapers of the Swiss Nazi Party, the *Front* and the *Grenzbote*, stated that they had been forced, for lack of subscribers, to amalgamate, and would henceforth appear as one paper—a weekly.

Stockholm

Godchild to the old Queen Désirée and born at a time when some forty kings governed Europe, King Gustav V of Sweden and of the Goths and the Wends[18] occupied a throne that would have been unrecognizable to Désirée's husband.[19] By 1939, the eighty-one-year-old sovereign had long been an institution in the life of Sweden, though an unreservedly constitutional institution in a kingdom where the king influenced rather than commanded. Gustav's late German queen, Victoria,[20] an arch-reactionary princess from Baden who, when her husband's throne was undergoing its early-twentieth century change to modern constitutionalism, opposed the process every step of the way. But so did a large cross section of Sweden's military, which had received an important part of its officer training in Germany, the country from which also sprang a sizable segment of its aristocratic classes.

The king and his family—despite their French petit bourgeois origins—were as much a part of the warp and weft of their country's life as smorgasbord. Crown Prince Gustav Adolf was the eldest of Gustav and Victoria's three sons. Gustav had since the death of his first wife—Princess Margaret, a granddaughter of England's Queen Victoria—been married to Lady Louise Mountbatten,[21] sister of the rising star in the British Admiralty, Lord Louis Mountbatten.[22] Rare for an heir to the throne, Gustav Adolf had gained for himself a measure of international academic respect as a professional archaeologist. Wilhelm, the king's second son, married beneath his rank, had his status ratcheted down from royal prince to Duke of Södermanland for having done so, and became an author, an even more novel enterprise than archaeology for a member of a European royal family. Erik, the youngest son, died young.

The imposingly tall king, thin to the point of gaunt and aristocratic in appearance, had made his own reputation as a skilled sportsman and dedicated bon vivant, his graceful dexterity on the tennis courts exceeded only by an assiduity in the gaming rooms of the French Riviera. Until 1939, Gustav's proudest claim was to have kept his nation out of World War I. With the start of another war, he was equally determined to make it two for two.

In 1939, despite the diminution of his political authority, Swedes continued to refer to their king as "First Power of the State," a recognition that the monarch embodied the total of the nation's political sovereignty. The still current 1809 constitution did in fact grant Gustav enormous theoretical powers, but 130 years of gradual democratization of the Swedish government had left Gustav only a minor voice in the workings of the state. What he did possess in abundance, and what would play a crucial role in Sweden's tightrope minuet with Nazi Germany for the next five and a half years, was his prestige.

The sole cloud shadowing the royal family was its conspicuous partiality toward Germany—though a proclivity that did not include the present German government. Sweden's upper classes shared this pro-German predilection with the royal family, so much so that if economic circumstances had forced the country to enter the 1914–18 war, it likely would have done so on the German side. Though sympathy for the powerful neighbor across the Baltic was now nowhere near so strong as it had been a generation earlier, the royal family nonetheless continued to maintain close ties with its German kin and contacts. None of this was to imply that Gustav was himself anti-British or anti-French, the king's only real antipathy being for the Russians, the thieves in the not too distant past of his predecessors' Finnish territories.

Had the octogenarian Gustav not occupied the throne in 1939, his heir, Crown Prince Gustav Adolf—who filled in as regent for his father every winter when the king made the rounds of the pleasure palaces and tennis courts of the French Riviera—might presumptively have brought a more pro-British, anti-German bent to the court and, by extension, to royal influence in national affairs. That the prince's first wife was the daughter of Queen Victoria's third son, and his present wife the granddaughter of the same English queen's youngest daughter, helped ensure that the crown prince's ties were as strong in Britain as were his father's in Germany. Though Gustav Adolf was regarded as the most pro-British member of the royal family, *his* son—the hereditary prince Gustav Adolf—was married to a German princess whose father was one of the earliest and most aristocratic backers of the Nazi movement, and Princess Sybilla herself was widely characterized in Sweden as a Nazi sympathizer. Another minor member of the royal family, Prince Carl, was circuitously related to Baroness Carin Fock, the late wife of the Nazi air force head who was soon to be Germany's first and only *Reichsmarschall*, Hermann Göring.

From the opening days of the war, the prestige of the monarchy was used to clearly enunciate Sweden's attitude toward the conflict, and here family ties were ignored. Speaking from the throne on September 9, King Gustav emotionally expressed his government's determination to stay out of the war—and, to back up this determination, to substantially expand the country's armed forces through far higher defense spending. For the duration, this attitude, realistically tempered with the pragmatism to bend to the demands that would be placed on its sovereignty, would guide Sweden through the minefield of world war.

Since 1932, Per Albin Hansson had, except for a 100-day break in the summer of 1936, been the king's first minister. The son of a mason, Hansson was born in Malmö in 1885. Working fifteen-hour days as a twelve-year-old, when he left school, he helped found the Social Democratic youth movement six years later, the memory of those long days of apprenticeship a likely motivating factor in the depth of his political bearings. Hansson soon attracted national attention as a convinced opponent of army service; rumor had it that he himself tried to avoid the rigidly class-stratified military service by making himself sick on cigars and black coffee before submitting to the medical examination with appropriately attenuated vital signs. He was, nonetheless, accepted, and went on to gain a reputation as the strictest corporal in his regiment.[23]

By 1925, Hansson rose to the Social Democratic Party's leadership, succeeding the first Social Democratic prime minister, Hjalmar Branting, whom Hansson had served—with some irony—as defense minister. In 1932, he himself became premier, succeeding the Popular-Liberal Carl Gustaf Ekman. The Swedes acquired a brilliant parliamentarian in their new prime minister, a man who soon demonstrated a statesmanlike readiness to bargain and compromise to secure as many to the party's labor-oriented goals as possible. Hansson was also a convinced prohibitionist, storming against the evils of drink while quoting Aristotle's admonition: "Those who go to bed drunk beget only daughters."[24]

Following the lead set by Branting, Hansson too cast off the doctrinaire Marxism that had characterized the Social Democrats as an opposition party. Though championing the welfare state, the party abandoned ideas of nationalizing all Swedish industry, settling instead simply for greater central control of the economy. And though a workers' party to its core, the Social Democrats as led by Hansson were able to function courteously and effectively with big business, a principal factor enabling the country to meet the challenges presented by the gathering war clouds in a relatively strong economic position. By 1939, Hansson had become—as had his predecessor—a politician of stature, enjoying widespread popularity throughout virtually all levels of Swedish society. Even his personal relationship with his sovereign was close, so close that the two men often sat up together at the palace until early morning, playing bridge.

With the onset of the war, Hansson's Social Democratic administration took in all other parties, except the Communists, to form in December 1939 a "National Government," much like the British fusion of Conservative, Labor, and Liberal that became Winston Churchill's governing wartime coalition. The National Government might, though, have been more accurately named the "Government of the Maintenance of Neutrality," for that was at bottom its program and, throughout the war, the principal reason for its existence.

· · ·

The first consequences of the new war faced by Sweden were demands from both Allies and Germans that it trim its trade and commerce to suit each's needs. The commodity at the core of the issue was iron ore. This treasure from Sweden's soil was so vital to Germany's ability to wage war that it would dominate the kingdom's policy in the war as did no other economic issue. While the existence of the mineral on Swedish soil made the country a ripe prize for an aggressor, that same factor was likely the preserver of Sweden's independence. But for almost six years both sides would bring intense and unending pressure on Sweden, coercion in large measure related to this indispensable mineral.[25]

If neutrality was the heart of the government's program in 1939, iron ore was the heart of the nation's economy. The mineral was coveted by all the powers forming the ring controlling Sweden's paths to the rest of the world. Mined above the Arctic Circle, in the barrens of Sweden's far north inhabited primarily by the reindeer-herding Lapps, the ore was crucial to Germany's military standing. Containing twice as much iron as the French ore of the Lorraine fields—two-thirds as against one-third—and relatively easily accessible, the kingdom's deposits were estimated at more than two billion tons. The arms producers of the Ruhr basin as well as others in German-controlled Europe depended on the Swedish ore in the manufacture of their high-quality, weapon-grade steel.

Most of the ore was exported from the producing centers of Kiruna and Gällivare and exited Sweden through the Norwegian port of Narvik, across the Scandinavian peninsula's far northern neck shared by the two countries, and a hundred miles north of the Arctic Circle. Narvik, ice-free year-round thanks to the Gulf Stream, had been developed as a port for this express purpose in 1902, while Norway was still a part of Sweden. When in 1905 the countries dissolved their union, Stockholm tried to switch the whole operation to its own port of Luleå, at the head of the Gulf of Bothnia. But with that body of water closed by ice for a third of the year, the effort proved impractical, and Narvik retained its supremacy.

The world's most northerly railroad traverses the hard land between the Lapland fields and Narvik, and over this line nearly seven million tons of iron ore were carried in 1938.[26] Upon reaching the town's wharves, the Swedish ore was dumped into special vessels for transport to America, Britain, and the continent. Before the invasion of Poland, the Swedish Iron Ore Trust employed about a thousand freighters to export the mineral, with about two-thirds of the exports going to Germany; in 1938, nearly ten million tons arrived in German ports, which the Reich paid for essentially in barter—by shipping its coal and coke to Sweden. The latter, vital to the Swedes, heated their country, moved its transport system, and stoked the fires that transformed much of the Swedish ore into Swedish steel. The ore Stockholm sold to Britain paid for vast quantities of British coal, contributing to the economic framework by which Sweden would continue to maintain itself during the Phony War.

The price it paid Germany to allow this system to remain unmolested was its government's undertaking of absolute neutrality, as well as its promise to resist Allied pressure to compromise ore shipments to Germany. With Denmark still free and passage through the Skagerrak relatively unrestrained by German naval control, Swedish ships were thus able to maintain trade ties outside the Baltic. But even during the Phony War the conflict's dangers couldn't be ignored: forty Swedish freighters were sunk by German U-boats (and by a few Allied subs as well), their captains quicker to loose torpedoes than to accurately identify the nationality of ships framed in their periscopes.[27]

The British government was not so appreciative of Sweden's economic realities that it was willing to leave the iron ore traffic from Narvik to Germany totally unimpeded. In early January 1940, Whitehall addressed a memorandum to Norway protesting the use of the port for the Swedish transshipment of the ore to the Reich. Oslo rejected the rebuff as an infringement on its own neutrality, a rejection Sweden quickly echoed. The British government put off—for the time—plans to try to physically prevent the ore reaching German ports.

A few days later, Britain's foreign minister, Lord Halifax, confronted Björn Prytz, the Swedish minister in London. Halifax wanted to know if Stockholm planned any measures to at least reduce the ore traffic to Germany, warning that unless such reduction occurred, the Royal Navy intended to blockade Narvik harbor. The Swedes, given notice by the Reich Chancellery not to cut down on the ore shipments from their 1938 levels, officially ignored the British threat;[28] the mines were, in fact, now working twenty-four hours a day, with the ore output substantially increased as a result. To Britain, Stockholm argued that Sweden was dependent on the coke and coal it was receiving from Germany in return for the iron ore, and at the same time tried to minimize the importance of their ore to the German war machine. Further, Stockholm reminded London that Swedish goods bound for Britain were *also* passing through these waters off Norway, and that if the North became a theater of war, a grave risk loomed that such trade would be stopped, or at least severely hindered, by the German Navy; the British would be, according to Stockholm's logic, risking trade worth ten times as much as that which they wanted to stop by military action.[29] Here matters stood, but very soon the Narvik issue would be dealt with in a manner far more violent than exchanges of intimidating diplomatic protests.

· · ·

Because of the failure of the League of Nations in providing small nations any real safety from the aggression of stronger neighbors, Sweden had already concluded it would find security only in its own defenses. Furthermore, it judged that its capacity to assure the rest of Scandinavia's deliverance from harm, a central principle of its foreign policy, depended as well on its own armed might. Though its military preparedness lacked international standards of depth in 1939, Sweden still stood far ahead of most of Europe in the quality of its armed forces. The nation's first line of defense was, of course, profound expressions of neutrality voiced to the belligerents, but most Swedes all too clearly sensed the danger that such protestations would be ignored by the dictators. The resulting reality of Sweden's vulnerability left the country with little choice but to turn itself into a military foe no aggressor would—in the absence of overriding considerations—choose to take on. In his September 9 speech from the throne, Gustav vowed Sweden's neutrality while also emphasizing his government's determination to substantially increase the nation's military spending. Given Berlin's contempt for neutral "rights," the government's decision seemed entirely prudent.

Strengthening of Sweden's military defenses, long neglected in the lotus years following the Great War, began to accelerate in a serious way after the *Anschluss* and Munich, the latter event branding appeasement with the opprobrium it deserved. With Denmark's decision to spend the bulk of its national treasure on welfare rather than armaments, and Norway's unwillingness to significantly increase its defense spending—Norway was perfectly content to sit behind the shield it expected the Swedes to erect—Sweden more than ever shouldered the responsibility for the security of the nations of the North. From its pre-1936 levels, defense spending nearly doubled for 1938–39, to almost $60 million. Even at this increased level, the Swedish defense shield remained profoundly inadequate to seriously address a concerted German threat.

Sweden's first line of security lay, of course, in its three services: an army and a navy and a fully independent air force, plus a home guard reserve. Universal conscription formed the basis for the bulk of the services' recruitment,[30] with a cadre of voluntary enlistees forming the professional training corps. Men faced the draft at sixteen, their active and reserve military obligation lasting until their seventy-first birthday. At the outbreak of the war, the army was relatively small—about 130,000 men—but foreign observers rated highly the quality of its officer corps. The army's best weapons were its antitank and antiaircraft guns, products of Sweden's world-famous Bofors works, a firm whose high-class armaments formed part of the American Navy's arsenal.

Nearly 200 aircraft made up the Swedish Air Force, organized into flotillas emulating those of the German Luftwaffe. Its principal strength came from torpedo-bomber squadrons designed to strike at an invasion force's support units. Saab, Sweden's own prestigious aircraft manufacturer, widely recognized for the quality of its planes,[31] was a primary factor making the Swedish Air Force the most muscular defender of Sweden's neutrality.

At the heart of the Royal Swedish Navy, by far Scandinavia's most powerful, was a fleet of unique coast defense ships, specially designed to patrol and defend the shallow-water shoals that characterize much of Sweden's coastline. With names like *Gustaf V* and *Drottning* (*Queen*) *Victoria*, *Sverigae*, and *Oscar II*, the ships carried the same 15-inch batteries as the battleships of its rival navies, but displaced only two-thirds the tonnage of Germany's famed pocket battleships. Fifteen submarines had, like the coast defense ships, been specially engineered for patrolling of the shallow, 1,400-mile-long Swedish coastline. A chain of coastal forts, under the control of the Royal Coast Artillery and attached to the navy, guarded Stockholm, Gothenburg, Härnösand, and Karlskrona.

Since before the war the services had prepared themselves for the start of hostilities with joint military and naval exercises designed to practice warding off an invader. The successful German tactic of using aircraft to carry both bombs and torpedoes, employed brilliantly in the Luftwaffe's blitzkrieg tactics, had been thoroughly studied by the navy and air force working in harmony (a harmony, incidentally, still foreign to the American military). Since being set up as a separate service in 1936, the air force had undertaken a crash training program for pilots, with its skills at dive-bombing and instrument flying—the latter a new concept at the time—bringing the Swedish Air Force the respect of many other national air arms, including, importantly, Germany's.

With the start of the war, Swedes other than active-duty members of the forces were trained to specifically check any invasion. Government-aided rifle clubs, long a tradition in the country, saw their membership triple to 300,000. The volunteer air raid watcher organization began its schooling of what would eventually total 600,000 men and women, and a volunteer airplane spotter corps enlisted 45,000 members. Beginning in 1940, 800,000 women volunteered for defense-related duties—catering, office work, telephone service, nursing—in the "Lotta" movement, an organization that was set up in the other Scandinavian countries as well; in the event of German invasion, the Lottas were to be incorporated into the quasi-military home guard. This last line of defense was one in which a huge proportion of Sweden's citizenry received part-time training designed to harass an invasion once the enemy got past the nation's first line of defenses.

Despite all these defenses and expenditures, Swedes fully understood they couldn't hope to beat off a concerted German invasion. But what they did hope their defenses would do was convince Hitler that Sweden's 6.5 million people were prepared to wage an all-out struggle if he moved to extinguish their independence. Hansson's government did all it could to make clear to Berlin that its measures were not designed to threaten the Reich, but simply to keep Sweden neutral. The implied threat nonetheless remained that its military capacity *would* be called upon to the fullest measure possible. As foreign minister Christian Günther expressed Sweden's purpose: "to make ourselves as indigestible as possible."[32]

As with virtually all the European states, so too did Sweden face the menace of internal subversion emanating from the Reich. A major part of Nazi policy was to establish fifth columns, bodies of resident Nazi sympathizers, or paid stooges, willing to corrupt the independence of their own countries, or their hosts' in the case of German nationals, to advance the eventual victory of Hitler's Reich. So it was in Sweden that a well-organized fifth column was planted soon after the Nazis came to power, one that it was hoped would grow into a fraternity eventually able to deliver an intact Sweden into the German lap.

The most visible manifestation of this German poison in Sweden was the domestic Nazi Party. *Parties*, actually, as a welter of Nazi-style clones existed in prewar Sweden, though none ever grew into prominence or attracted many members. Most significantly, and despite their leaders' best efforts, no one associated with such a party ever got himself elected to the nation's parliament. The fact was that Sweden offered barren ground for National Socialism. Economic conditions in the country were, despite the depression, not nearly as desperate as those in much of Europe (despite the financial tumult that followed the Krueger crash); nor was there a lost war to be avenged, Bolshevism to be rooted out, or an anciently despised minority available for hounding or to act as a scapegoat for what relatively few ills the country did suffer.

Nonetheless, a handful of disgruntled malcontents roiled waters to the degree their talents allowed. In 1930, Birger Furugård, veterinarian and rabble-rouser, founded a Nazi-style association called the Swedish National Socialist Party, its byword, logically enough, "Heil Furugård!" After limping along for six years, it merged with the equally moribund National Socialist Workers' Party, founded in 1933 by Olov Lindblom, who, according to *Time* magazine, looked like an "intelligent football player." Lindblom squeezed out Furugård for the leadership, and then, in an effort to make the new organization less laughable, eliminated most Nazi rubrics from the party's catechism. He was left with little except a tendency to brag about his putative friendship with Hermann Göring.

More dangerous because they were, in the main, smarter were the members of the German colony in Sweden. Not counting the refugees from the Reich, the "loyal" German contingent consisted of not only two to three thousand German nationals living in the capital but many more scattered across the country. As with the Nazi penchant for close organization at home, so was Sweden tightly organized into the *Landesgruppe Schweden der NSDAP*, headquartered in a large office building on the Sveavägen, one of downtown Stockholm's main thoroughfares. The head of the Landesgruppen was *Landesgruppenleiter* Heinz Bartels, who considered that his post in Sweden rated him chief of all Scandinavian Landesgruppenleiters.[33]

After it came to light in 1936 that money publicly collected for the ubiquitous *Winterhilfe*, the Nazi relief fund, had actually been used to finance German propaganda in Sweden, the Swedish government threw Bartels and two of his associates out of the country. Not surprisingly, Berlin retaliated by throwing three Swedish businessmen out of the Reich. Because of the deep commercial ties between Germany and Sweden (especially between the upper classes of the two countries, for whom German was generally the preferred language of intercourse), the greatest danger from the indigenous Nazis lay in their capacity to influence and even compromise major industrial and commercial enterprises in Sweden. In December 1941, Germans in Sweden would be able to establish what was virtually a German newspaper, published in Swedish, called the *Dagsposten*, with nearly every advertisement purchased by a German business concern.

One of the most bizarre manifestations of the Nazi infection in Swedish society involved the internationally famous writer and Himalayan explorer Sven Hedin. So beloved to Hitler was Hedin for spreading the Nazi gospel in Sweden that the German leader had a street in Berlin named after him. Hedin did, in fact, perform a noteworthy public service for his own countrymen, though likely an unwitting one. Hitler so trusted Hedin that he listened to the Swede's insistence that the Swedish government would eventually bring the country into the Axis of its own free will without its having to be driven in at the point of Wehrmacht's bayonet. There is no certainty of Hitler's credence in this counsel, but the explorer was so adulated in the Reich Chancellery—he wore a chestful of Nazi medals—that the advice may have played some part in Hitler's eventual decision to spare the country an invasion.[34]

German fifth column activities in Sweden caused the government comparatively little concern mainly because no outstanding individual existed around whom a nationwide organization could be built. Hedin was the only internationally famous pro-Nazi Swede, but as an octogenarian little fear existed he might become any kind of local Quisling. Furthermore, Swedish Nazis tended to work openly in the open society in which they found themselves, and thus were amenable to close observation by a police force quick to pounce on miscreants of any political persuasion.

• • •

Though Swedish policy in respect to the struggle between the powers was to make the country as quiet and as figuratively small as possible, the attack on a neighboring Scandinavian democracy in the late autumn of 1939 severely strained this effort. On November 30, Finland fell victim to an onslaught of more than a million Soviet troops. The attack launched what has come down in history as the Winter War, one of the most murderous of all the local struggles that coalesced into World War II. The world's largest country had brutally invaded a small neighbor, the latter an independent nation only since 1918. Finland's 3.5 million people remained far beyond the helping reach of any Western power. The only neighbor to whom it could turn for help was Sweden. Hansson's government knew that the manner of its response to Finland's crisis would prove critical to Sweden's own course through World War II.

The source of the 105-day Finno-Russian war lay, most immediately, in the stunning pact Germany concluded with the Soviet Union only hours before the Wehrmacht's lightning invasion of Poland. This collusion between dictators blessed not only the gang rape of Poland; it also provided for the broader division of all Eastern Europe between the continent's two totalitarian superpowers.

For Soviet Russia, the end goal was essentially to reestablish the borders that had defined tsarist Russia until the losses brought about by World War I. The Soviets' principal problem with Finland was that the Finno-Russian border was too close to Leningrad for Moscow's own perceived security needs—at twenty miles, the city wasn't much more than a cannon shot away from the frontier. Since after World War I the Finns had emerged as a distinctly pro-German and anti-Communist state, with the rise of the Nazis it dawned on Stalin that some real dangers for Russia were inherent in the Finnish situation. By late 1939, he decided to do something to rectify it.

Seventeen days after World War II began, the Russians advanced into "their" half of Poland, as prearranged in the pact, reattaching 75,000 Polish square miles to the country to which they had belonged until 1917. Days later, Molotov summoned to Moscow the foreign ministers of the three Baltic states—Latvia, Lithuania, and Estonia—to sign, or else, treaties of "mutual assistance." The pacts would officially give the Soviets the right to march into the three sovereign nations, all with overwhelmingly non-Russian populations though belonging to the Russian empire before 1918, the pretext to "protect them from aggression." Powerless to thwart the Soviet Union, all three gave way, and the following year Stalin snuffed out the independence each had known in modern times for but a single generation.

To complete this near-resurrection of his tsarist predecessors' European empire, only Finland stood in Stalin's way. On October 5, the very day the Kremlin strong-armed Latvia into signing away its freedom, Moscow demanded the Finnish government dispatch a delegation to discuss "concrete political questions which have become urgent through the outbreak of war."[35] What Stalin required of the Finns was that they hand over a sizable portion of their country to Soviet control, or face outright annexation. Stalin's demands were not unimpressive: they included a lease on the Hangö Peninsula—the tip of southwestern Finland jutting into the Baltic and commanding the Gulf of Finland—on which to build a Soviet naval base; the cession of 750 square miles of the Karelian Peninsula, the isthmus joining the two countries between the Gulf of Finland and Lake Ladoga, which in 1939 was Finnish territory almost all the way to the city of Leningrad; relinquishment of several strategically situated islands in the gulf; and the handing over of the western half of the Rybachi Peninsula, west of Murmansk on the Barents Sea. In return, Stalin offered the Finns 2,135 square miles of eastern Karelia, an area mostly made up of woods, lakes, and swamps. The net effect on Finland would amount to the crippling of its economy and its defense capabilities, the latter disproportionately situated in the areas Moscow demanded Helsinki cede.

The Soviets admittedly possessed a certain logic fueling their demands. When Finland was detached from Russian control and given its independence following the Great War and its own small but vicious civil war in 1918, the border of the new state was indeed placed incredibly close to Petrograd, the struggling Soviet Union's second city and its "window on the west." Clearly, such proximity could be fatal if Finland were to come under the control of a Russian enemy. Early in 1939, when the initial growls of Soviet "requirements" in the area were first raised diplomatically, Field Marshal Gustav Mannerheim, the militarily brilliant head of the Finnish armed forces, suggested to his government that Finland voluntarily move its borders back a few miles from Leningrad. Mannerheim well understood that the geographic proximity of the small and decidedly democratic state to the gigantic and decidedly undemocratic Union of Soviet Socialist Republics was going to cause difficulties in the future, probably in the very near future.

Mannerheim's government wouldn't even consider the suggestion, the idea of a government voluntarily giving up an important part of its national territory then as now beyond the pale of the politically possible. Stalin had understood from the outset, of course, that his pact with Hitler would be a temporary thing, that eventually the German leader would expand—eastward. With the southern approaches to the Gulf of Finland covered with his stranglehold over the Baltic states, to protect the gulf from the north he needed Finland's acquiescence to the border "rectification." To the Finns, he flatly (and he thought quite logically) stated that "we must be able to bar the entrance to the Gulf of Finland" for Russia's safety, adding that "we cannot move Leningrad, so we must move the border."

Faced with these concrete demands in October, Mannerheim again urged concessions—to give Russia the islands it wanted in the gulf as well as the Karelian territory, but not to permit the lease of Hangö, which would bar Finland's ability to wage any kind of successful defense against attacking Russians at their back. The Finnish cabinet could not accede as Mannerheim urged; the fact was that to do so would have brought the government down, irrespective of the military considerations or the hopelessness of fighting the Red Army. Mannerheim's chief concern was for the future of an independent Finland, a country he knew the Russians had the power to swat like a fly. The Finnish government's chief concern was, sadly, for the short run. Discussion of the question between Helsinki and Moscow reached an unbridgeable impasse, the two sides' mistrust of each other negating any chance of finding a way to avoid war.

Finland's president, Kyösti Kallio, hoped that some sort of statement of Scandinavian unity might help his country in its standoff with the Russians. Though neither Denmark nor Norway was in a position to offer any substantial help to the Finns, Sweden was, as Kallio knew, a different matter. But at a meeting with the kings of Sweden, Denmark, and Norway, what he got was little more than sincere but largely useless incantations for peace.

Swedish public opinion did stand strongly in favor of coming to the Finns' rescue.[36] Swedes felt closer to the country across the Gulf of Bothnia than even to their fellow Germanic-speaking Scandinavians. Centuries of ties between them, as well as their mutual distrust and fear of Russians, had drawn the two into a remarkable unity of spirit. Much of Finland remained Swedish-speaking, its upper classes heavily ethnically Swedish, and the Åland Islands between them (at the bottom of the Gulf of Bothnia) were—though Finnish territory—virtually a condominium, with Swedish the islanders' primary and official tongue.

But Hansson's government couldn't even consider the possibility of militarily taking Finland's side. The Soviet Union and Germany were allies, and the Swedes feared Berlin would consider such a move an act of aggression against its Soviet "ally." Furthermore, Stockholm was in no position to expend its still dangerously limited military capability on Finland when it might well need that capability to turn back a German invasion on its own territory.

On November 30, at the stroke of 8 A.M., without a declaration of war, the Red Army fell on Finland along a ninety-mile-long front, the Red Air Force bombing Helsinki in the bargain. To justify its actions, Stalin simply copied the so-called Big Lie technique that Hitler had brought to the peak of sanctimonious perfection in assigning blame for his own attack on Poland on the Poles' "aggression."

Stalin fully expected the exercise to amount to a walkover (Krushchev later said the Soviet leadership thought "we could fire one shot and the Finns would put their hands up and surrender"[37]), but his expectations hadn't reckoned with Finnish determination. Finland's 135,000 troops, organized into nine divisions, a tiny fraction the size of the army the

Soviets could muster, did at first fall back from the border. But in contravention of what the world expected to be a replay of Hitler's Polish blitzkrieg, the Finnish lines held. As virtually its dying gasp, the League of Nations took the opportunity to read the Soviets out of the organization (while impotently ignoring the larger European war), writing an end to the valiant but fatally flawed collective security system installed in the wake of World War I. The League's moral gesture did not, however, lead to any effort to rescue Finland.

Though Sweden refused to intervene militarily, Hansson's government went as far as it could in supplying the Finns with matériel as well as humanitarian and moral assistance. Included in the first category were 80,000 rifles, 50 million cartridges, 112 field guns and howitzers, 300,000 artillery shells, 25 planes, and considerable quantities of oil.[38] Most important were the 8,000 Swedish volunteers allowed by their government to go to Finland as the vanguard of a kind of International Brigade that would eventually number some 11,500 men. Ultimately, volunteers from many Western nations joined the Swedes, including 300 men of the Finnish-American Legion. The United States loaned the Finns $30 million for civilian goods, but—in the name of its neutrality policy—placed an embargo on strategic materials.

The Swedish public remained dispirited over its government's seemingly token and heartless response to the Finnish cries for help. Hansson felt constrained to enlist the king to publicly explain his country's rationale for its actions. "With sorrow in our hearts, we have come to the conclusion that if Sweden now intervened in Finland we would run the gravest risk of being involved not only in the war with Russia but also in the war between Great Britain and Germany." Gustav added sadly, "I cannot take that responsibility upon myself."[39]

The war was fought in the deadly cold of the subarctic, as characterized by its name—the Winter War. That winter of 1939–40 was the fourth coldest in the 150 years such records had been kept. At first the cold—temperatures as low as 70° below zero were reached—would prove the Finns' most helpful ally, though eventually the advantage would be turned and help the Russians defeat the Finns. The most successful of the Finnish tactics was the hit-and-run harassment of the clumsy and unprepared Soviet forces. The Red Army, its leadership all but destroyed by Stalin's purges two years earlier, couldn't even find the white-clad Finns in the blizzard conditions at the front, and Finnish knowledge of the terrain and the ability to quickly traverse the battle zones on skis kept the larger but hapless Russian force on the defensive.

Under improved generalship—Stalin replaced Voroshilov with Timoshenko—the Soviets eventually got the measure of their foe, turning the tide of war with it. The freezing over of both Lake Ladoga and the Gulf of Finland allowed the Red Army to get its larger tank corps over the ice to attack the Finnish rear. On February 22, the desperate Mannerheim urged his government to try to reach a compromise with the Russians. Though still leader of an intact fighting force, the aristocratic Finnish marshal saw that the Soviet juggernaut would have to soon overwhelm his army simply by virtue of its inescapable numerical advantage. Mannerheim hoped Finland might get reasonable terms from the Russians while it still fielded an effective force, and further reasoned that even the Kremlin was worried about Russia's huge losses, this when the Soviet leadership was becoming increasingly fearful of Germany's intentions.

Sweden's cruelest dilemma in responding to its neighbor's agony came when the British and French governments offered on February 5, 1940, to send an expeditionary force to Finland. The offer hinged on a formal request for such help from the Finns, as well as the approval of the Norwegian and Swedish governments for the Allies to cross their territory to get to Finland—no Allied force could have gotten intact through a German naval blockade of the Baltic. Not until the last hours of their battle with the Russians did the Finns formally request such assistance. Helsinki knew that the Germans would probably consider such permission an unneutral act on Stockholm's part in respect to the wider war and that it was more likely Sweden could get away with helping the Finns if no Allied incursion of their territory was involved. Berlin reasoned, probably correctly, that Britain and France's principal interest in the offer was not Finland's rescue, but of taking physical control of Sweden's ore fields and the Norwegian port through which that ore could be exported.

It was this German consideration that was most responsible for Sweden at first temporizing and then categorically vetoing any plan for an expeditionary force across its territory. Furthermore, though the Germans had no desire to see Finland destroyed by the Soviets, neither did they wish at the time to mar the appearances of harmony with the Kremlin. If the Allies were unhappy about Sweden's (and Norway's) refusal to allow its territory to be used to get Allied aid to Finland, it was the Swedes who were vulnerable to Germany's displeasure and the consequences of that displeasure. Neither Britain nor France was in any position to help Sweden should it face a German invasion. Sweden came quickly to resent and fear the spotlight the issue had thrown on the country.

Stockholm foresaw that the Soviet-German "friendship" was ephemeral, at best, and that Germany might indeed permit more substantial Swedish help—even to becoming a co-belligerent with Finland against

Russia. Most Swedes certainly hoped Russia could somehow be bested—or at least humiliated—in its David and Goliath standoff with Finland; the last thing Sweden wanted or needed was a Soviet-occupied Finland sitting across the Gulf of Bothnia from its major population centers, not to mention the long mutual border across which it would confront the Red Army if Finland were occupied. Swedish policymakers could in the event of a German attack on Sweden envision a Soviet drive to come to Sweden's "rescue"—with little hope of the Russian colossus ever being ejected once it had settled in.

While Stockholm mulled over the courses of action open to it— especially the consequences of those actions—it continued to allow quiet measures of assistance to be sent to the despairing Finns. Sweden allowed Allied technical missions to pass through Sweden, and private contributions from Swedish citizens proved helpful to the Finns. In fact, the quantities of Swedish material sent to Finland were so great that Britain was seriously concerned lest Stockholm dangerously compromise the country's capacity to defend itself from German attack.

In the end, Sweden's policy was to do everything in its power to convince the Finns their cause was hopeless, that the war had to end— even on the onerous terms demanded by Moscow. Stalin's terms had become considerably harder in the meantime. On March 8 a peace delegation from Finland arrived in Moscow and found the Russian ante had gone a long way up. Ironically, had Finland accepted the proposals Molotov first offered the prior October, in its final position would have been far superior. Stalin demanded—and would get: the gulf islands, a thirty-year lease on Hangö, an enormous slice of Karelia (from which the Finnish population was given fourteen days to evacuate—or else become Soviet citizens), the Rybachi Peninsula, the shores of Lake Ladoga, the strategic heights of Salla, the loss of Finland's second-largest city, Viipuri, and a Finnish pledge to build a railroad from Soviet Murmansk to the Gulf of Bothnia. Altogether, Finland relinquished 22,000 square miles to the Soviets, including a tenth of its cultivable land. In a country with half the population of New York City, 24,923 were dead, 43,557 wounded. On the other side, the Russians suffered a million dead, an astonishing figure later confirmed by Khrushchev.[40] (At the time, Mannerheim estimated Soviet losses at 200,000.) Russia also lost nearly 1,000 planes, 2,300 tanks and armored cars, and vast quantities of other assorted war matériel, losses which in the following year would prove nearly fatal.

On March 11, 1940, the Treaty of Moscow ended the war. Mannerheim's last Order of the Day on March 13 addressed the nation:

We are proud in the consciousness of a historic mission which we will continue to fulfill, which is the defense of that Western civilization which has for centuries been our heritage. But we have also paid to the Western countries the debt of this heritage.to the utmost farthing.

What Mannerheim might have added was that in spite of Finland's horrendous wounds, it could claim what Poland and Latvia and Lithuania and Estonia could not. Against all the odds, it—most of it—was still a free country, still unoccupied by the Red Army.

Sweden skillfully managed to come out of the Winter War firmly neutral—and more determined than ever to stay that way. Its resources were severely depleted by the generosity of its aid to the Finns, but that fact moved the government to redouble its defense measures, and prompted the Swedish people to more seriously recognize the dangers that would have to be overcome if they wished to emerge unscathed from a world war.

The Treaty of Moscow would be merely a respite, the war between Finland and its Soviet tormentor not nearly over. In little more than a year, it would continue, under a new name, with new players, and with even more disastrous repercussions for Finland.

· · ·

One consequence of the Winter War had unmeasurable effects on the history of World War II. There was the widespread perception in Berlin that the Soviets' military capabilities were laughably poor, an understandable perception in light of the drubbing the Red Army took at the hands of the bantam Finnish forces. What is known of the German decision to invade Russia in 1941 is that the Nazi commanders expected the Soviet Union to be a walkover, in much the same way Moscow thought that Finland would be a walkover. Berlin possessed little concrete intelligence on which to judge Soviet military capabilities, and was anxious to believe the Red Army's performance in its war against the Finns would foreshadow its performance against the Wehrmacht. Had the Germans reason to think differently, the history of World War II—and of the world— might have been very much different from what it was.

Dublin

The memorable remark "Who are we neutral against?" asked by some unknown Irishman at the war's outset,[41] found its way into the international press and during World War II became a kind of epigrammatic symbol of Eire's moral dilemma. Because the island was almost entirely dependent on Britain for its overseas trade, many Irish found it a source of considerable economic anxiety that their government was opting out of Britain's fight with Germany. But few found moral shame in the Taoiseach's position, for this was the same Britain that had engendered almost bottomless Irish hatred for so many wounds inflicted over so many centuries.

That Eire intended to remain neutral was, conversely, to most Britons bewildering and offensive—and to no Briton was it more offensive than to Winston Churchill. Three weeks after hostilities broke out in Poland, he wrote a minute summarizing his notional perception of the Irish situation: three-quarters of the Irish people, he commented, "are with us, but the implacable, malignant minority can make so much trouble that De Valera dare not do anything to offend them."[42] In few instances in the war was Churchill more wrong.

Newly installed as First Lord of the Admiralty in Chamberlain's war cabinet, Churchill had to bear the results of Chamberlain's "folly" of appeasing the Taoiseach by handing over the Treaty Ports to Irish sovereignty. On the first night of world war—September 3—a German U-boat torpedoed the British passenger liner *Athenia* off the northwest Donegal coast. The ship carried 1,400 people, of whom 112 died. The First Lord was convinced that more such disasters to Empire shipping would occur in Irish waters as the Kriegsmarine became increasingly aware of British weakness in the area. Churchill attributed a great part of this weakness to the loss of the Treaty Ports, and he would not—he believed he *could* not, as First Lord—accept that incapacitation as a done thing.

Churchill maintained that Chamberlain's gesture—the prime minister's "heart-to-heart settlement,"[43] as he put it—would unremittingly and in increasing degrees damage Britain. Deeply distrustful of de Valera, the First Lord—an acknowledged expert on wartime administration, having headed the Admiralty in the Great War—warned whoever would listen that the price to Britain for full Irish participation in the war, or for *any* kind of aid, was going to be the handing over of Ulster to the south. More ominous, Churchill even began to realize that without the Treaty Ports in the hands of the Royal Navy the Taoiseach could and undoubtedly would be successful in his avowed policy of Irish neutrality in the fight between Britain and Germany. With Britain out of Eire, and with Germany therefore bereft of an excuse to violate the south's neutrality, Hitler could simply wait until he finished off Britain before taking defenseless Ireland like a piece of fruit ripe for the picking.

Contrary to Churchill's fears, a number of influential British voices—most notably that of dominions secretary Anthony Eden—reasoned that Eire's neutrality might indeed prove the best course for both countries. This faction thought that defending the dominion as a co-belligerent would dangerously overextend Britain's already thinly stretched capabilities. Two weeks after the war began, Eden summed up his views of the dilemma of Irish neutrality in a memorandum to the cabinet.

> On the constitutional side the question of any formal recognition by this country of the neutrality of Eire presents a serious difficulty. We do not want formally to recognise Eire as a neutral while Eire remains a member of the British Commonwealth. To do this would be to surrender the hitherto accepted constitutional theory of the indivisibility of the Crown. Equally we do not want to take the line that Eire is no longer a member of the British Commonwealth. This would involve the rejection of the policy followed with the assent of the other Dominions since the establishment of the new constitution of Eire in 1937 and would moreover have serious repercussions in many directions, e.g. the status under United Kingdom law of individual Irishmen.[44]

Still, it seemed at the war's outset that to risk a German occupation of an undefeated Eire might prove a foolish gamble, the island's strategic position in relation to British supplies and communications obvious from a glance at the map. Only a few dozen miles west of Britain, Ireland lies directly at the point of convergence of the sea lanes on which three-quarters of the raw materials for Britain's industries passed. The ships carrying these vital supplies meet in the seas directly west of Ireland as they approach the larger island, and if Germany controlled Ireland, it would also be controlling this critical bottleneck.

De Valera's government rationalized the Treaty Ports' denial to the Royal Navy and to Britain's increasingly de facto American ally in a way that received the full support of the Irish parliament and people. The prime minister declared that the ports had been returned by the British people at a time (1938) "when war was evidently imminent and after consideration of the political and strategic factors involved . . . there was, therefore, no constitutional or political claim which the United Kingdom could advance for their return."[45] Further, during the first months of the war neither de Valera nor the Irish people were challenged by an enemy seen as overwhelmingly dangerous. Not only Britain and its empire stood between Eire and the fascist menace, but France's military might remained very much undefeated; the French, judged by Western military analysts to possess the strongest army on earth, were still protected behind their impregnable Maginot Line. Germany was far away, Britain was close, and memories of English transgressions in Ireland over the prior seven hundred years loomed considerably larger than the Wehrmacht.

In the event, Churchill continued to let Irish neutrality rankle him personally as did few other issues in the war. He adamantly refused to accept the status quo as regarded Irish neutrality. In a memo dated September 5, he demanded:

A special report should be drawn up . . . upon the questions arising from the so-called neutrality of the so-called Eire. Various considerations arise: (1) What does Intelligence say about possible succouring of U-boats by Irish malcontents in West of Ireland inlets? If they throw bombs in London,[46] why should they not supply fuel to U-boats? Extreme vigilance should be practised.

Secondly, a study is required of the addition to the radius of our destroyers through not having the use of Berehaven or other South Irish submarine bases; showing also the advantage to be gained by our having these facilities.

The Board [of Admiralty] must realise that we may not be able to obtain satisfaction, as the question of Irish neutrality raises political issues which have not yet been faced, and which the First Lord is not certain he can solve.[47]

The generally dogmatic view Churchill harbored of Irish neutrality was that it represented more a matter of assertion of the Twenty-six Counties' sovereignty than of Dublin's considered assessment of the military situation. In mid-October, when a German sub sank the British battleship *Royal Oak* in home waters, Churchill demanded the cabinet take action, warning that "the time has come to make it clear to the Eire government that we must have use of these harbors and that we intend in any case to use them." Had the cabinet not restrained the First Lord, a state of war between Eire and Britain might well have been the end product of such high emotions.

Eden summarized for the cabinet where matters stood on the Irish dilemma by outlining three courses Britain could take. First, although Britain might argue the benefits of belligerence with de Valera, he believed little would be accomplished by doing so. Second, Eden noted that Britain could, by dint of its military strength (though it would have taken a Gallipoli-size operation to do it), forcibly take the ports. The skilled diplomatist counseled that such a move would probably not lead to Eire's defending itself, but backed by nearly the whole of the Irish people, de Valera could "indict" Britain before the world, causing especial damage to the British position in the still neutral United States, a country with a large Irish-American minority. Further, Dublin might under these circumstances even provide facilities for Germany on Irish soil.

The third option and the one Eden advised his colleagues to take was to acquiesce in Eire's decision to adopt neutrality, hoping—though not hoping very much—that Dublin would eventually grant Britain concessions in the furtherance of the Allies' war on fascism. As for Churchill, the First Lord still urged the cabinet to challenge the constitutionality of Eire's neutrality, presumably by military means with the Treaty Ports as the target, but Chamberlain and the rest of the cabinet disagreed. Though in postwar years it has been posited that Britain "nearly" invaded Ireland at this juncture, the limits of British aggression in fact stopped with Churchill's words.

In truth, Britain's reach into the Atlantic sea lanes would unquestionably have been greater had it enjoyed the use of the Irish ports, with the increased search-and-rescue range of seaplanes one of the most obvious benefits. Churchill believed, with justice, that Eire's security depended on British arms, not Irish capabilities, that the danger to the dominion came not from its former British master, but from an avaricious Reich anxious for plunder gained with as little energy expended as possible. Furthermore, those ships most in danger from German submarines were the freighters delivering cargoes an appreciable part of which would eventually reach Irish markets. For all this, the First Lord of the Admiralty judged Eire's gratitude to be slim indeed—and its rationale for neutrality equally slim.

De Valera believed, just as strongly, otherwise. In the first place, it was hard to fault his reasoning that Germany would have every legal excuse to regard Eire as a belligerent if it permitted Britain access to three ports strung around its coastline. Would not Britain have claimed the same right to strike at any self-claimed neutral state if that state leased Germany such facilities? The Taoiseach further held that his all but independent country's economic dependence on Britain nonetheless rested on trade—that, in other words, Eire *paid* in full measure for what it received from Britain.

That left the issue that British arms were the ultimate factor keeping Eire safe from German invasion. But to stake everything on those arms and join Britain in a formal, substantive way in its war would open the country to German attack—an observation that would soon be borne out by Ulster's experience. Further, the overwhelming majority of the Irish people were, de Valera knew (as did Britain's policymakers), fully behind their government's decision to remain neutral. In the Dáil, only one member advocated co-belligerence with the Allies, the remainder of the

Twenty-six Counties' elected parliamentarians supporting de Valera. The popular feeling of the Irish people toward the British was acidly remarked upon by Maurice Walsh in the January 13, 1940, edition of *The Saturday Evening Post*: the author wrote of the widespread feeling that Britain had tried, and was still trying, to maintain Ireland as a kind of "colonial cattle ranch, a place where there was the best food for England, good sport, a simple standard of living for the aborigine—a place to visit in summer and forget in winter." The words were bitter, but would have met with much Irish agreement in the emotional climate of the time.

It is true that Eire's military capacities were not enough to give a determined aggressor pause, though it is not disputed that Irish defenders would have fought hard for their country. What in fact would have given Germany pause were the enormous difficulties the Wehrmacht would have found in a joint amphibious and air-supported invasion of the island. But granted a strong, thoroughly committed German determination to undertake such an invasion, Eire's military capacity—or the state of its defensive preparations—would, beyond question, not have been able to thwart it.

Such thwarting could only have fallen to the Royal Navy, and that was the reasoning behind Churchill's argument that ultimately Irish protection from German aggression depended on Britain. Though Hitler would have been overjoyed with the prospect of easily gaining a platform from which to throttle Allied shipping as well as from which to launch a westerly attack against Britain, Berlin understood that Britain would never have permitted such a scenario. The British would have fought to defend all Ireland, not just its province of Ulster. Not to have done so would have allowed itself to be put in the extreme, perhaps mortal, danger of encirclement.

De Valera concluded, likely because of the horrendous nature of Britain's enemy, that Eire could afford to make a few gestures in the Allies' direction. The principal such benefice consisted of joint planning with a small British staff of officers as to how best to defend the south in case of invasion, either from a German force in Ulster or from a general island-wide landing. The agreed strategy for the latter, code-named Plan W, called for British troops in Ulster to enter Eire in case of an attack, where the combined British and Irish armies would attempt to hold a line north of Dublin. Moreover, Dublin agreed to institute a system for alerting the Royal Navy to the presence of German ships and submarines off the Irish coast; the Irish coast guard would signal, in plain language, the location of such ships, and the Royal Navy could use such open-language transmissions for their "own purposes." When the British requested that

Royal Navy craft be allowed to enter Irish waters in pursuit of U-boats, de Valera made no response, with the assumption that the British would accept such silence as assent; very much the same thing happened when the Taoiseach was asked to allow British seaplanes to overfly Irish territory on their way to the aid of Allied shipping in distress or to spot German submarines.[48]

Perhaps, at the most fundamental level, more even than the memories of the hideously wasteful loss of Irish life in the Great War, it was the island's partition that most acutely fired de Valera's determination to remain clear of Britain's war. The Taoiseach thundered ("thundering" was a rarity for de Valera) at the British diplomatic representative sent to Dublin in September 1939 that the "real source of all our troubles" was Ulster, that as long as Britain remained in the north, the south would not cooperate in any way with its former master, though he would later soften his position. But it was that very partition that allowed Eire to be neutral, partition that kept Britain from absolutely *having* to invade the south. That de Valera enjoyed the overwhelming support of his people in his neutrality policy speaks to a democratic foundation for the course Eire took. Beyond all other considerations for neutrality, the idea remained that the Irish leader might jettison the policy and make common cause with Britain had the latter offered to withdraw from Ulster. This idea, that partition drove de Valera's policy, hung most heavily on the minds of Britain's leaders, and within the year London would make a gesture to test those murky waters.

• • •

Throughout World War II, the Allies, which by the end of 1941 would finally come to officially include the United States, continued to manifest the bitterest resentment at the presence in Ireland of diplomatic missions from the Axis—particularly from Hitler's Reich. Such diplomats were automatically accounted as espionage agents, spies who could prize the Allies' military secrets in the setting of a relatively open country lying across a few miles of Irish Sea from Britain. Though Germany's diplomats in Dublin undoubtedly reported to Berlin whatever useful information they uncovered, Eire could find no legitimate grounds on which to deny Germany a diplomatic mission in its capital.

With one highly consequential exception, wartime diplomatic representation in Dublin from the major belligerents was skillful and professional. Where Germany might have accredited to the de Valera government a Ribbentrop-like Nazi, the envoy it actually got was far better than it should have been able to hope for from a Foreign Ministry noted more for its National Socialist ideology than for diplomatic excellence. Eduard Hempel, the Reich's Envoy Extraordinary and Minister Plenipotentiary in Dublin since 1937, was an envoy trained in the days before Hitler and Ribbentrop turned Germany's foreign service into a corps of true believers. He was an old school conciliatory diplomat who, though conscientiously furthering Germany's objectives, nonetheless counseled his ministry against precipitous actions, conduct that could drive Eire into Allied hands or the Allies into Eire. Though the rest of his staff were Nazi Party members, Hempel was not, a positive sign in de Valera's view; the Catholic Irish government had let Berlin know it would not look with favor upon Dublin's mission being led by a Nazi, a wish Ribbentrop's ministry evidently acceded to. Notwithstanding Hempel's relative moderation—if such a term can describe *any* diplomatic representative of Nazi Germany—when war was declared Britain still expected Eire to expel or intern Hempel and his staff, along with all other non-diplomatic German nationals in the country.

From the conflict's onset, Hempel was allowed to express approval for the Irish policy of neutrality—a policy that came as no surprise to the envoy. Hempel reported to Ribbentrop that Germany should be extremely chary of providing Britain any excuse for a preemptive invasion of Eire, that it would be Britain that would gain immeasurably from the use of the country's facilities—its airfields and ports and its material resources. A memo dated October 8, 1939, is quoted at length for being instructive of the tone of the minister's advice, and of the kind of information one of the Reich's most perceptive envoys was sending to Berlin:

> The declaration of Irish neutrality and, according to past observation, the careful, consistent adherence to it, have the support of the great majority of the Irish population, despite the undermining efforts of certain pro-English circles. It has visibly strengthened Irish national self-consciousness. It has also caused the Irish Republican Army, without basically changing its attitude, to recognize the danger of premature activity and to stand by inactive for the time being, although supposedly determined to intervene if the neutral attitude is abandoned. The IRA is said to be continuing acts of sabotage in England, but otherwise to be confining its cooperation exclusively to the Irish in America. The arrest of nearly 100 of its members in Ireland went off without incident. The Irish Army is supposedly ready to defend neutrality in all directions, in spite of the presence of pro-British elements. . . . The Irish press is strictly controlled, but the British press gets through. The Catholic Church is obeying the Government's appeal for a neutral stand. The personal attitude of the Government toward me is definitely friendly.

The leading British statesmen and officials, probably Eden too, are said not to have any objections to Irish neutrality; other British groups with a certain amount of influence do object, however, so that the position of the Irish Government has become somewhat more difficult in London. Previous bad experience on the part of the British in British-Irish conflicts, as well as regard for America and the Dominions, may impede the consideration of possible steps against Ireland. However, there is fear of British demands for Irish harbors and airports—especially if the war situation should become more acute—although there do not appear to be any concrete indications of that effect so far. . . . Irish neutrality is said to be watched very closely in the United States of America; conversely, a possible abandoning of American neutrality would constitute a threat to Irish neutrality. We should continue to support consolidation of Irish neutrality and independence on a broad national basis, which is also important in its effect on the Dominions, India, and America as symptoms of the loosening of the ties of Empire. . . . It should be kept in mind that Ireland strictly rejects [words garbled] belonging to the Empire and recognizes only a loose connection with it in matters of foreign policy.

Hempel[49]

In addition to the insightful observations and knowing advice (with the main exception being a partial misreading of the IRA—primarily its supposed endorsement of neutrality), Hempel was clearly alive to the fact, one which might have been beyond the ken of a more doctrinaire and less perceptive representative, that only de Valera enjoyed the national stature needed to control the country. He also saw that the Irish were in overwhelming numbers behind their leader, that the policy of neutrality bolstered a national self-consciousness. He advised Berlin that it would be to the Reich's advantage not to forget these facts. And—critically—in spite of his government's view that the IRA was Germany's natural ally in Ireland, Hempel distrusted the organization, convinced it presented a potential danger to de Valera's government and thus to Ireland's neutrality.

By 1940, when Berlin began to fear that the IRA-German connection would give Britain an excuse to invade its dominion, Hempel counseled that the eventuality would first lead the Irish to seek aid from the still neutral United States, and only if unsuccessful would they turn to Germany. But he warned Berlin that *any* violation of neutrality by Germany (especially attempting to forcibly gain a port for U-boat repairs) would cause de Valera to make good on his promise to defend the country's neutrality—as the Taoiseach put it: "if we must die for this then we will die for it."[50]

Britain enjoyed equally professional representation in Eire, a situation that worked to both countries' strong advantage during the coming contentious years. At the war's outset Anglo-Irish diplomatic relations floated, however, in a kind of limbo. Because of the fundamental disagreement between Dublin and London over their legal relationship, no British diplomatic mission existed in Dublin in September 1939. London had consistently demanded that any diplomatic representation be headed by a high commissioner, the standard envoy in its other dominions—Australia, New Zealand, Canada, and South Africa. De Valera, intent on discarding what he considered outmoded "imperial trappings," insisted on a full minister in what was in reality far more a republic than a "dominion."

But the British cabinet refused to send such a representative to Eire, judging that such a deviation from the usage in the other dominions would imply Britain's recognition of full independence, an independence which at the time did not legally exist. The solution London finally came up with was "United Kingdom Representative in Eire," a compromise sent to the Taoiseach for his approval. After briefly considering the proffer, de Valera crossed out the "in" and substituted "to"—a subtle but significant semantic modification. Whitehall quietly let it pass.

In September 1939, Sir John Maffey (to be ennobled in 1947 as Lord Rugby) thus became Britain's "United Kingdom Representative to Eire,"[51] charged by Chamberlain's government with working out what both knew was going to be a difficult wartime relationship between the two longtime adversaries. A product of Rugby and Oxford, Maffey was, like Hempel, a diplomat of the pre-World War I school honed in colonial service, a well-mannered aristocrat whose practiced negotiating skills would immediately be called into play upon his appointment. This former Colonial Office head and public servant of spotless reputation would play an influential role in keeping the two countries from each other's necks during the next six years.[52]

Maffey well understood the nature and force of Eire's neutrality, an understanding that helped bridge the wide chasm in views that would so badly impair the relationship between de Valera and Churchill. The advice Maffey gave his government was among the best diplomatic counsel Britain received during the war. An example, an October 1939 report, attests to the envoy's insight:

> The creed of Ireland today was neutrality. No Government could exist that departed from that principle. The question of the ports was at the very nerve centre of public interest in that matter, and the public mood would react with intense violence to any action invalidating their integrity. If a demand were made—he fully realized that no demand was

being made [in reference to de Valera]—he would be forced at whatever cost to treat such a situation as a challenge, and his Parliament would endorse his measures. If, on the other hand, facilities were voluntarily afforded in breach of neutrality, his Government could not live. No other Government which might endeavour to meet our request could survive for twenty-four hours.[53]

Maffey noted importantly that the policy of neutrality enjoyed widespread approval among "all classes" and interests in Eire, advice that likely weighed heavily in the decisions the British cabinet would in the following days make regarding Eire.[54]

Two controversial diplomatic missions in Dublin throughout the war were those of Japan and Italy, whose representation in the neutral capital was a kind of "proof" to many among the Allies of the Axis's sway in Eire. Vincenzo Berardis acted as Italian minister; Japan was represented by a consul, Satsuya Beppu. Neither of these men was notably colorful or controversial; rather it was the fact of the countries they represented that lent them a kind of notoriety among the Allies.

The single substantial exception noted above to the major diplomatic representation in Dublin was the American minister, David Gray. One historian wrote that Gray's performance in the Irish capital during the war made "the activities of the weakest of the Irish diplomatic corps look inspired."[55] An uncle, by marriage, to Eleanor Roosevelt, and thus a long-distance relation to the president of the United States, Gray would during the course of his tenure in Dublin come to a mutual hatred with the Taoiseach, a situation guaranteed to ill serve their two countries. Replacing John Cudahy, in Dublin since 1937, Gray would exemplify the damage that could be caused between nations when a diplomat is incompetent. Roosevelt, who liked personal liaison with his advisers, perhaps believed that his kinsman would feel freer than would a career diplomat to personally report events in Dublin, but the effect of Gray's tenure was generally to alienate from each other the leaders of the American and Irish governments. Another historian viewing Gray said his biggest mistake was "allowing his social connections to influence his political judgements"[56]—by becoming attached to the upper-class, Anglo-ascendancy world and losing touch with the more representative world in which de Valera and his government operated.

·   ·   ·

As with all the other successful neutrals except Switzerland, Ireland's concerns centered not only on the threat of German invasion but also on the very real possibility of preemptive Allied incursions—or even outright invasion—to beat the Axis to the use of its territory, a scenario held early in the war to be entirely within the range of London's plausible options. Even though the German record for integrity was a joke, the German minister in Dublin had, on the day war broke out, given assurances to de Valera's government that Germany would respect Eire's neutrality, its problematic dominion status notwithstanding. London, it was gravely noted, gave Dublin no such assurances that Britain would respect Eire's neutrality.

In spite of this disparity, de Valera subtly warned Hempel that Eire would be forced to show "a certain consideration"[57] for Britain. He added that any German violation of Ireland's neutrality—especially any attempt to co-opt "anti-British radical nationalist groups"[58] (the IRA) to carry out espionage against Britain anywhere on the island, *including* Ulster— would inevitably lead Eire into closer cooperation with Britain. That "certain consideration" for Britain would be eventually carried to manifestly unneutral lengths in favor of the Allied cause, the breadth of which Hempel couldn't have foreseen in 1939.

To back his warning, de Valera's strongest weapon—aside from British force—was the Irish Army. That army's capacity in September 1939 was, in terms of its ability to carry out any real defense, negligible. Besides the smallness and poorness of the Twenty-six Counties, no clear defense policy had been adhered to since the end of the civil war. The regular army was purposely kept at least 10 percent below its constitutionally mandated size, the total of which fell in March 1930 to an extraordinary 5,299 officers and men, the unspoken understanding then being that Britain would come to Ireland's defense in any serious emergency. When the 1930s began, Britain was in fact responsible, by treaty, for the country's coastal defense; it was only after Chamberlain's return of the ports in 1938 that this mandated protection was allowed to lapse.

Eire's neglect of its military establishment in the 1930s was by no means unique—in 1932, Americans were protected by only the sixteenth-largest army in the world, putting them behind Czechs, Turks, Spaniards, Poles, and Rumanians—among others. Dublin's military strategy, such as it was, involved a small and hardened permanent training cadre backed by a relatively large reserve. Its operational plan to thwart an invasion was to conduct a series of delaying tactics and guerrilla operations meant to hold off an enemy, while putting together a larger force from its reserves.

The total *authorized* armed strength amounted to 37,560 men. As to an enemy against which it would be directed, the minister for finance stated shortly before war broke out that it is highly improbable that Britain would attack us; if [it] did, an army of 37,000 would be of little use; and "attack" by another country is also improbable considering the strength of the Royal Navy. If Britain was defeated, resistance to her conquerors would probably be futile on our part.[59]

Such an assessment accurately condensed the realities of Eire's military situation—as well as its political position at the start of the war. Others, however, noted that buoyant morale in the Irish services outweighed mere physical constraints, that it was guerrilla tactics that carried the day in the War of Independence.

After hostilities broke out, the total strength of Ireland's army would reach only a little over half of the authorized levels. Nineteen thousand men—or two divisions—would be in uniform within days of the Emergency's beginning; this compared to the 136 divisions the Germans fielded in the Battle of France. Nearly every Irish unit was understrength. Of the eight authorized rifle battalions, none was yet organized. The cyclist squadrons—known as the "Piddling Panzers"—would have posed precious little threat to real panzers. The army had at its disposal two "serviceable" tanks and 21 armored vehicles, most of the latter of which were already in 1939 antiques—1920, and earlier, Rolls-Royces. The air force, a branch of the army, was equally toothless, with only 24 craft, of which 10 might be called modern. There was no navy other than a small coast guard unit. Prior to May 1940, no strike force capable of resisting any invader existed. Few commands had reserves. Armaments, ammunition, and vehicles were extremely scarce.

But so quickly did the land war turn into Phony War that the army's General Headquarters announced on September 21 that "the present Emergency does not constitute a war situation and it would not be justified in maintaining its Establishment and that the strength should be reduced."[60] By Christmas, most of the army personnel who could manage the journey had gone home for the holiday. Only an IRA raid on the central army munitions magazine in Dublin's Phoenix Park, in which the raiders escaped with large quantities of arms and ammunition, caused headquarters to order troops back to their duty stations.[61]

During these early months of the war, Irish soldiers weren't even sure of receiving a uniform. That was perhaps as well. With some irony, and undisguised distaste on the other side of the Irish Sea, the soldier of the Twenty-six Counties looked uncannily like his counterpart in the Wehrmacht—most notably so in the same "iron scuttle" steel helmet both forces wore. It was likely this unfortunate symbolism rather than the uniform's scratchy uncomfortableness that caused the Army Department to scrap it in 1940. In its place came a new uniform little distinguishable from the British pattern, soup-plate helmet and all (the latter being the same style helmet worn by American GIs until replaced in 1942 with the familiar rounded, nearly brimless model).

Not only were the soldiers dressed poorly; they were housed poorly as well. Most of the barracks remained as leftovers from the British regime, with little new military shelter built since. Many derelict country houses had been fixed up to provide minimal standards, and farmboys turned soldiers suddenly found themselves living in once grand but now sadly dilapidated mansions.

Privates earned 14 shillings a week—about one dollar in contemporary terms, but then with strikingly greater purchasing power, of course. The income wasn't entirely discretionary, though. A forced haircut deduction of two pence was taken out of each pay packet, as was six pence for laundry and another tuppence for "social welfare." In theory the Irish soldier was fed better than his civilian compatriots—supposedly a daily three-quarters of a pound of "best home-fed beef," a quarter pound of fresh vegetables, a "liberal" quantity of butter, cheese, jam, eggs, sausages, bacon, etc. In fact, his diet consisted of the usual monotonous regime of many armies: oatmeal, brown stew, jam rolls, bread and butter, and tea.

To meet the costs of their new defense requirements, the government forced the Irish taxpayer to pay taxes higher than any ever known. The first increase predated the outbreak of war: in the spring of 1939, the new £ 5.5 million defense appropriation meant jumping the income-tax rate by a half shilling to a shilling on the pound—5 percent. Along with this income-tax increase came new surtaxes, as well as additional taxes on the richest ratepayers. Two months after Germany attacked Poland, the income tax went up another shilling on the pound, together with higher increments in estate duties and new levies on beer and whiskey. Through the next two years, tax increases on income would rise until the Irish citizen was paying on average 37.5 percent of his income to the government. Though the Twenty-six Counties remained at peace, their government was assessing tax levies as onerous as those of most of the countries at war.[62]

·   ·   ·

If the island was not yet threatened by a Wehrmacht held in its traces, it *was* threatened by the ruthless and bomb-prone activities of the IRA. The Irish Republican Army's raison d'être was to end British control of Ulster by whatever means necessary, however appalling or murderous. The terrorist organization's position was, simply stated, that "England's difficulty is Ireland's opportunity." To achieve its goal, the organization maintained a complete, albeit underground, government, a constitution, and some 7,500 mostly youthful members—plus perhaps 15,000 more or less dedicated supporters (the figures are from *Time* magazine).

What *popular* support the IRA received in the south during the Emergency was given almost entirely in token of the perceived injustice of the island's partitioned status. As to the organization's relationship with the Dublin government, its policy provided that no terrorist activities would be carried out against Eire, as long as the IRA was free to carry out from southern bases operations against Ulster and that province's British targets. De Valera refused such a concession, understanding full well the danger of British retaliation against Eire.[63]

Some months before the outbreak of war, the IRA had undertaken to traumatize the British people into demanding that their government leave Ulster. The shock was carried to Britain itself in the form of a series of terror bombings. In January 1939, young Irishmen recruited in Britain set off explosions in what were, with war approaching, the kingdom's most vulnerable sites: factories, power stations, and telephone exchanges.[64] At the time, even a few well-placed blows against British defense facilities were enormously crippling to the catch-up effort to match Germany's industry. The campaign reached its moral nadir back home with a bombing of the Irish country hotel where Prime Minister Neville Chamberlain's son Francis was spending a hunting holiday, the fortunately ineffectual assault an apparent attempt to sour the personally cordial relationship between Chamberlain and de Valera. Britain endured over a hundred more explosions in July alone, with blast sites including Piccadilly Circus and Madame Tussaud's waxworks. Harried police waded through crowds arresting anyone with a brogue. The IRA's outrages culminated in an act that finally crystallized public opinion and marshaled concrete action against the outlaw organization.

On August 25, a package-laden bicyclist made his way through the crowded streets of Coventry, an ancient and, by 1939, heavily industrialized Midlands city. The rider left his parcel—a pre-fused bomb—at a café in crowded Broadgate, in the center of the city. To hide the device's origins, its makers had assembled it in one place and brought it carefully to another, where the last man in the deadly chain put it in his cycle's carrier basket. Delayed by traffic and worried that the bomb would blow him up along with the innocent bystanders who were its intended victims, the anxious IRA terrorist hurriedly threw his bicycle against the wall of the café and left. The explosion a few moments later blew off the front of the building, along with the windows of the neighboring shops. Ankle-deep debris settled over a wide area. Five people lay dead, including an eighty-one-year-old man and a small boy. Seventy more were injured.

Recognizing the threat this and the earlier outrages represented to an Anglo-Irish accord, the authorities reacted by searching every Irish home in Coventry, jailing hundreds of activists, and ending with the apprehension of three members of the city's IRA unit. Two others were later arrested for complicity in the terror attack. The dragnet resulted in an immediate and sharp decline in IRA terror activities in Britain for the rest of the war.[65] But among Eire's citizenry who deplored the IRA's methods, so deep was the vein of antipathy for Britain that when two of the accused were hanged in Birmingham in February 1940, almost the entire country mourned them, with flags dropping to half staff, theaters closed, and masses offered for the repose of the executed men's souls.

Hitler understandably regarded people who could commit such acts against Britain as his natural allies. In fact, Germany had been trying to cement a relationship with the terrorist organization since at least 1937. The military intelligence agency, the Abwehr, directed by Admiral Wilhelm Canaris, initiated planning in November and December of 1939 to send its agents into Ireland by submarine to establish contacts with the IRA, with German agents instructed to tell prospective recruits among the Irish that Germany strongly desired a united Ireland and that the best course for the IRA would be to join efforts with the Reich in destroying "England," the sooner both their goals being fulfilled.

But Hempel warned his superiors in November 1939 that Germany had best not rely too heavily on playing the IRA card. On the fourteenth, he wrote to Berlin that "the I.R.A. is hardly strong enough for action with promise of success or involving appreciable damage to England and is also probably lacking in a leader of any stature." He pointedly cautioned the Foreign Ministry that open cooperation with the IRA would very likely lead the more moderate sections of the Irish public into blaming the organization for making the country's national interests dependent on Germany, which "in view of the widespread aversion to present-day Germany, especially for religious reasons, could rob the I.R.A. of all chances of future success."[66] Hempel also noted, again, that such a course would give Britain an excuse to intervene militarily in solving its own outstanding problems with Eire.

Because of the IRA's potential to damage Eire's neutrality policy more than any other group in Irish politics, the organization's British atrocities had in June 1939 given de Valera a good excuse to outlaw it. The move enabled him to marshal the resources of the state in chasing down its members and generally branding it a menace to Eire's survival in the Emergency. But by the end of the year, the IRA openly declared its sympathies lay in a Germany victory in the war, evidently on the amazing deduction that such an outcome would, by Britain's defeat, mean the end of partition.[67] The perhaps more likely possibility that Hitler would occupy Ireland—the *whole* of the island—apparently didn't occur to the IRA leaders. Though Nazi Germany's most scorching depravities and betrayals lay in the future, its many double crosses up to this point should certainly have put the IRA off any hope that it or the nation for which it purported to fight would be treated with respect by Adolf Hitler.

On December 23, 1939, the organization carried off one of its grandest coups—though one of its last—against the Dublin government. When the IRA stole more than a million rounds of ammunition and cases of guns from the Phoenix Park arsenal, it looked as though the phantom army might turn itself into a real army and attempt a coup d'état, or even try to start another civil war. Dáil member James M. Dillon warned of the raid: "I believe the ultimate end of the activities of these gentlemen [the IRA] must be assassination. God knows how many of us may be victims!"[68]

The reaction of the government was to arrest every member of the IRA who could be rounded up, sending 5,000 Special Police armed with rifles to seal the frontier with Northern Ireland and hunt down the clandestine terrorists. To further the search-and-destroy operation's success, the government rushed through Parliament a bill suspending the constitutional guarantee against holding suspects for more than forty-eight hours without evidence. With the sweeping of this safeguard under the rug in the name of overriding security considerations, de Valera's powers to run the government unchecked by constitutional niceties approached those of martial law. But the Taoiseach's fears of IRA-bred mischief were real. If Britain judged the legitimate government of Eire to be falling to IRA control, it would almost certainly send an expeditionary force to the island. And just as certainly, any such British action would be exploited by the IRA in an appeal to all "patriotic" Irishmen to join them in throwing back the hated invaders. It was a scenario whose avoidance was devoutly—and rigorously—sought.

Madrid

When foreign correspondent Frank Gervasi returned to Spain in the early spring of 1940 after a six-year absence, what he found stunned him:

"When I left Spain in the winter of 1934, the country was still a republic, its democratic institutions intact. But the Spain I saw on my return was politically as Fascist as Italy or Germany and physically a hollow shell of its former self. In Madrid, I saw Madrileños living like rodents in the bombed and shelled houses they were too poor or too weary to repair."[69] In a time when Europe north of the Pyrenees was locked in the tension of the Phony War, Spain was equally locked in a misery born of its own war.

During those queasy months when Europe waited for Hitler's next move, the 25 million Spaniards endured a suffering as great as their country had ever known. The two-thirds of a million killed in the Civil War—about 4 percent of the population—were, at least, spared the Spain their countrymen inherited from the conflict. So too, for a while, were the half million who had managed to escape, mostly to France, from Franco's vision of the moral state. Another million sat desiccating in the Caudillo's jails, each aware that every week thousands were being pushed in front of firing squads after "trials" that made the worst of the Republic's excesses seem tame in comparison; eyewitness Gervasi called this legalized butchery "a twentieth-century reenactment of England's seventeenth-century Bloody Assizes."[70]

Probably half the population still harbored Republican sympathies,[71] a fact disturbing enough to the Franco regime to scare it into ever more draconian reaction. A grim story told in Madrid turned Spain's misery into a commentary on the country's situation: The spirit of José Antonio, the murdered Falange founder, was visited by Franco. The ghost asked the Caudillo how his revolution was going. Franco replied, "All the people are with me." "Perhaps," José Antonio responded, "if you don't find some means of feeding them soon, they'll all be with me."[72] While the firing squads attended to Franco's enemies, famine would be even less discriminating in its selection of victims.

Francisco Franco was the cynosure of Spanish existence and the fount of its pain. Likenesses of the pudgy, hooded-eyed, ever uniformed Caudillo embellished countless walls, his name celebrated in the repetitive Avenidas del Generalisimo Franco coursing through many Spanish cities. In mid-October 1939, the nation's new autarch abandoned his provisional seat at Burgos for the symbolic authority as well as the greater splendors of the traditional capital, Madrid. Choosing not to occupy the cadaverous royal palace—workers nonetheless kept its salons dusted for grand state ceremonial occasions—he instead settled in the palace of El Pardo, located in the ilex-covered hills sixteen miles north of the city. Built by Charles V and inhabited by Philip II before he gave it up for the

Escorial, El Pardo nicely suited Franco's style of contained self-grandeur.

At the center of his new state, Franco's political strength grew at a rate echoed by the spreading apathy of the Spanish people, but his personal life had settled into an orgy of praise to God—the God that apparently guided him and his corporate state along a road of retribution to its enemies, both imagined and real. From his palace, he and his wife, Doña Carmen, led strictly apportioned lives mimicking the rigidity of royalty: mass schedules and confession hours assiduously adhered to, horseback rides and tennis and hunting, and, for the Caudillo, attendance at the Friday cabinet meetings that often extended into the early hours of Saturday. He was protected principally by the highly competent Guardia Civil, but at close range his security came from a personal guard made up of Moors. These ever-at-hand Africans, alien but picturesque in their blue, white, and red burnooses, owed their position of honor so near to Franco to the Caudillo's appreciation for the sanguinary service they had so effectively provided the Nationalist cause in the Civil War.[73]

· · ·

Spain's position at the start of the European war was basically that of a pauper, outcast in the eyes of the Allies, cut off economically from its heavily extended German and Italian creditors. But however much the Western democracies held the Franco state in contempt, their treatment of Spain during World War II centered on a single inflexible foundation: that Spain's neutrality was imperative, and to maintain it they were willing to overlook a very great deal that was distasteful about its regime.

Though, because of their stand against the "disorder" of Western parliamentary democracy, Franco's fundamental sympathies lay staunchly with Hitler and Mussolini,[74] the Caudillo was acutely sensitive to the dangers his still vulnerable regime would face by participating in an international war. During the lull of the Phony War, Spain's intentions remained opaque, though Franco clearly coveted wresting Gibraltar from Britain and gaining new possessions for Spain in North and West Africa. During this period Berlin neglected few opportunities to demonstrate its goodwill to the new Spanish government. Madrid hedged its bets by maintaining good relations with at least the British half of the Allied partnership, but on December 22, 1939, it signed a German-Spanish commercial accord agreeing to export a variety of goods to Germany, unless such goods were needed for home consumption or to earn foreign exchange in other countries. Franco further saw to it that the German embassy in Madrid was kept updated on information from diplomatic reports, and he permitted German propaganda to almost totally override Allied propaganda in the fascist-dominated Spanish press. Perhaps most dangerous from the Allied standpoint was the Spanish concession that allowed Iberia Airlines to use German pilots, even on routes from which Allied shipping could be observed.[75]

Another important accommodation Franco allowed Germany was the reprovisioning and refueling of its submarines in Spanish ports, requiring only that the Reich do so in secret so the British wouldn't launch reprisals against Spain. Among the ports thus used were Vigo, on the Atlantic,[76] Las Palmas in the Canary Islands, and Cartagena on the Mediterranean coastline, the latter base supplied with a stock of U-boat spare parts. On January 3, 1940, the first submarine to make use of the new gift was the U-25, when it floated into Cádiz harbor to tie up alongside the German freighter Thalia. After four hours of taking supplies off the merchant ship, the U-25 glided back out to sea, doubtless grateful for Spain's favor.[77] Berlin made sure its U-boat captains exempted Spanish carriers from its otherwise nearly indiscriminate sinking of shipping to Allied ports. In justification for these concessions—concessions seen as not much more than lukewarm from the German perspective—the Nazis contended it was their help that had allowed Franco to come to power in the first place.

Franco continued to believe the real enemy to Spain—to all of Western civilization in fact—was Soviet Russia. When the Red Army attacked Finland in November 1939, Spanish sympathy and, more usefully, even a small supply of Spanish arms were quickly dispatched to the Finns. Simultaneously, the press unleashed a noisy and intemperate campaign against the "Reds." Along with the commiseration with Finland was an open annoyance with Germany for allowing the Soviets into Eastern Europe in the first place, a situation Madrid held to be a direct result of the Molotov-Ribbentrop pact.[78] The following month, Franco strenuously denounced the Soviet Union as "the common enemy"[79]—in spite of its alliance with Germany.

Franco's chariness of the very strong Germany was matched by his closeness to a conversely weak Italy. It was Mussolini's regime with which the Spanish caudillo felt the greatest affinity, two Mediterranean "corporate" states roughly equal in both their degree of authoritarianism and their instinctive loathing of the Soviet Union. Mussolini, still free of the choke chain Hitler would have on him within a few months, even suggested he and Franco take the lead in setting up a kind of Mediterranean "axis" of the region's authoritarian states. The Duce thought it might include Portugal and perhaps some of the Balkan states. Franco understood the idea of an "axis without strength" wouldn't make much sense, but allowed his diplomats in Rome to toss the idea around. In the event, Mussolini soon dropped it altogether.[80]

•   •   •

Spain was manifestly an authoritarian state in 1939, but whether authoritarianism would be able to effectively control the many still competing forces in the country—fascism, monarchism, clericalism, Carlism—was still an unresolved question. In his *Report from Spain*, correspondent Emmet John Hughes characterized the sort of confusion that the still unconsolidated regime faced:

> While sympathetic Foreign Office officials in Madrid might be striving earnestly to meet the demands of Allied diplomats, Falangists in Barcelona might be distributing Nazi propaganda on the street corners; *Seguridad* police in a jail in Irún might be torturing a French refugee; and ex-Blue Legionnaires, enrolled in the service of German espionage, might be invading the American Consulate in Valencia to smash furniture and scream their hatred of the *yanquis*.[81]

These contradictions painted a more accurate portrait of the early Franco regime than did those accounts in the Western press reporting a cohesive, centralized state. The confusion inferred from Hughes's account of the domestic scene was mirrored by the regime's contradictions on the foreign policy front. When immediately after the start of war Franco wired assurances to Hitler that he would "tilt Spanish neutrality in favor of Germany whenever he could,"[82] such assurances were cheap. As long as Franco was able to count on the unlikelihood of Spanish soldiers fighting in Western Europe alongside the Wehrmacht, he could promise Hitler almost anything without being called to redeem the pledge. Later, after the attack on France, he would hedge such promises by making them wholly dependent on German largess, a card his Italian fellow dictator played—albeit less well—in Italy's relations with the Reich.

Falangist hopes at the end of the Civil War for revolutionary "reforms"—a phobia for the archconservative Franco—were, in the main, not to be fulfilled. Though Franco put on a great show that the victory belonged to the Falange, control of the government would not be turned over to the loyal ranks of José Antonio's party, but rather remain firmly in the hands of the small clique of like-minded ultraconservative officers who had surrounded Franco from the beginning of his revolution. The excuse Franco offered to the Falangists for failure to implement the program they wanted—most importantly a broadening of social programs and greater nationalization—was that the revolution remained too weak and faced too many dangers, and furthermore that such innovations would offend the right, the faction that had been vital in the Nationalist victory. Franco also knew that there wasn't money for new Falange-proposed programs, that the limited money available to the state had to be reserved for defense in light of the enormous external dangers of the brewing world war.

If the old Falangists felt betrayed by Franco's victory, which historian Stanley Payne termed more a victory of reaction than of fascism, there was very little their exhausted ranks, massively depleted in the Civil War, could do about it. What was growing in the still warm ashes of the Republic was not the new Spain they envisioned, but something much more like the political and financial structure of the old kingdom. In Payne's words: "The outwardly imposing edifice that had been created for the Falange was indeed to be used as a 'totalitarian instrument'—not for 'the nation' but merely for the regime."[83] What Franco's state would become was not an ideologically pure or rigorous Spain-cum-Third Reich, but one in which the Caudillo's brand of authoritarianism would be the guiding spirit of the new state. Payne concluded that Franco's "formula was a conservative syndicalism, bounded by all sorts of state economic controls, spiritually tied to Catholicism, ready for any kind of practical compromise, and always backed by the Army."[84]

· · ·

Though the vast majority of the Spanish people lived materially miserable lives in the winter of 1939–40, a semblance of restrained glamour was still available for the rich and for the foreign in the capital and tony watering places. Madrid's high society, such as it was in the aftermath of the Civil War, disproportionately concentrated on the diplomatic colony and the few Madrileños rich enough, noble enough, or well connected enough to associate with this segment of foreigners in Spain. An element of peril existed for Spaniards in their contacts with such foreigners, though, and discriminating officials avoided particularly the British, French, and American embassies' functions, as did most Spaniards who valued their political reputation.

Through all levels of society in the country, a new censoriousness had set in. In Madrid, the state's moral expurgators kept busy assessing the suitability of public entertainments, their efforts presumably directed at protecting the morals of the few sufficiently well off to afford any kind of frolicking at all. The most "mass" of available distractions remained the *corrida*, but the Bullfight Division of the Entertainments Syndicate, the Francoist watchdog on such goings-on, dampened the bullfights' spontaneity by politically classifying the matadors. At least the ring regained much of its pre-Civil War physical grandeur, with the glamorous young bullfighter Manolete of Córdoba acclaimed by crowds hungry to forget the dourness of the new Spain.

In San Sebastián, the old royal summer capital and that desperate winter still the country's smartest retreat, bathing costume regulations took a considerable step backward in the spirit of Francoist Grundyism. Men were now required to wear tops again, and women's costumes returned to the black dresses and stockings typical of a generation earlier. Even such garb was deemed adequate coverage only when the body was actually in the water: once back on the beach, a full-length dressing gown was required. The German ambassador's wife was arrested on the beach for taking off too many clothes, the offender carted off to the police station screaming that Hitler himself would punish such disrespect.[85]

By its nature an instrument of nonconformity, the theater was constantly hamstrung by official meddling. The Spanish version of Clare Boothe Luce's *The Women*, playing that winter in the capital, was "altered" by the authorities, turning what was a witty comedy into a somber diatribe against divorce.[86] Even though a large part of the Spanish population would have thronged to American films, to keep such moral dangers off the market the state raised barriers against them, including a black list of Hollywood film stars who had supported the Republic. (Even though *The Story of Louis Pasteur* was shown, Paul Muni's name was kept off the posters for this reason.) Preferential treatment was generally given German and Italian films, but the Spanish moviegoing public still clearly preferred the Marx Brothers (when their films were put on) over the Italo-Spanish blockbuster *Frente de Madrid*, a politically correct but dramatically deadening saga of the Civil War.

A notch up on the gaiety scale were the capital's still thriving nightclubs, one of the principal pastimes for Madrid's foreign colony. Perhaps the preeminent fun-making, though, was found in the ubiquitous cocktail parties, gatherings where the guests could be marginally less concerned about their jokes and grousing being overheard by Franco's police. A topic of constant interest at the diplomatic colony's parties was the state of the relationship between Madame Franco and Madame Serrano Suñer, siblings married to the two most powerful men in the state. The two women's relative intimacy bore importantly on the political situation:

when the sisters stopped speaking, the colony assumed Franco was on the verge of clipping his vocally pro-Berlin brother-in-law's wings.[87]

One by-product of the Civil War was the reaction against "un-Spanish" customs associated with the Republic—divorce, civil marriage, other newfangled and/or immoral ideas. The teaching of contraception came to an abrupt halt. The reestablishment of the church in Spanish life after its brutalization and official repudiation at the hands of the Republic meant that widespread lip service was now paid it, though Franco's officials paid it little else, as much of that class never managed to attend mass.

In June 1940, anticipating the French collapse, the footloose Duke and Duchess of Windsor found themselves in Madrid; for the royally well-heeled couple, one luxurious refuge in the maelstrom of war was about as good as another, even that found in the actively anti-British atmosphere of Madrid. Staying at the Ritz, the very epicenter of the country's high society, the Windsors gave a cocktail party in the dining room for a group of highborn Spaniards, which the observer Gervasi recorded:

> I . . . saw the headwaiter bring in a trayload of hors d'oeuvres. The duchess inspected the appetizers and imperiously waved them away as evidently unfit for human consumption. The waiter passed me on the way back to the kitchen, and I saw that what the duchess had rejected were tiny squares of toasted bread topped with bits of *jamón de serrano*, snow-cured mountain ham. The duchess wanted caviar, which was unavailable. I didn't stay to see how the matter was resolved . . .[88]

Very few others were similarly able to dicker over caviar and *jamón*. Spain was on the verge of mass starvation, and would become the only nation in Europe in World War II in which a significant part of the population was to actually starve to death. The country, caught in a natural drought cycle, saw a bad harvest in 1939 followed by two more such disastrous harvests in 1940 and 1941.[89] Civil War-induced transportation dislocations magnified these crop shortfalls into a nationwide cataclysm, thus by early 1940 making starvation a part of the country's life. Not only was the country short of at least a quarter of its normal wheat ration, but such staples as oil and rice were scarce as well. For countless Spaniards, breakfast was a glass of warm water, dinner a mash of turnips, a crust of bread a special treat. Catalonian breadlines were longer than those that had formed during the Civil War. In Valencia, famed for its *arroz* dishes, rice—the main ingredient—was in extreme shortage. Adding more pain to the deficiencies was the 20 percent tax on everything, two-thirds of which went to government relief, the other third to the army. Besides food, metal currency was in short supply, and for change of sums less than one peseta, postage stamps were used. Anyone daring to protest these dismal conditions faced the figurative whip of the Guardia Civil, the black-hatted thugs who stood armed with rifles on street corners all over the nation. Such conditions, combined with the fact of half a million Spaniards out of work and millions of others underemployed, augured grimly for the Caudillo's new order.

· · ·

Gibraltar. The mention of that three-mile-long comma dangling from Iberia's underside sends a flood of adrenaline surging through the Spanish psyche. Though Spain hadn't owned the rock for more than two and a half centuries, not an insignificant part of Franco's hopes for an Axis victory was the vision of regaining this deeply humiliating symbol of Spain's imperial emasculation.

Together with the African promontory it faced across the fourteen-mile-wide strait, Gibraltar had been known to antiquity as one of the Pillars of Hercules, the entrance to the great unknown ocean that lay beyond the pillars' safe embrace. From the earliest Phoenician settlement at the flat base of the great 1,400-foot-high limestone rock, the singularity of this place has assured it importance in the affairs of each civilization that has touched it.

In 711 A.D., Târik ibn Sijâd, a Berber of Ceuta, landed near present-day Algeciras and established a fortress on the rock in the name of the Caliph of Damascus; from this Berber it took its modern name, a contracted form of *Gebel Târik,* or Hill of Târik. The fortress remained under Muslim control until 1309, when Castile captured it; it was taken again by the Moors in 1333, then finally in 1462 the Duke of Medina-Sidonia claimed it and it passed permanently into the power of Castile. Its modern provenance as a British crown jewel came in 1704, when during the War of the Spanish Succession the British fleet overpowered its Spanish garrison. The following year a combined siege of French and Spanish forces failed to wrest the Rock from British control, and four years later it was ceded in perpetuity to Great Britain as a crown colony. Another combined attack of some 40,000 French and Spanish troops begun in 1779 was held off for almost four years; during that siege, military engineers began the Rock's defensive system of tunnels and gunports. Spaniards have had to stomach the Rock in British hands ever since.

By 1939, the cramped quarters at the foot of the monolith sheltered some 21,000 souls, mostly civilians, and mostly descendants of Spanish and Italian settlers. The administration was headed by a governor—then Lieutenant General Sir Clive Liddell—who was also commander-in-chief of the 3,500 or so army and naval personnel in whose defense the colony lay. The town huddling in the Rock's shadow exuded charm, a not unusual attribute for the gubernatorial seats of Britain's colonial possessions. The garrison was free to amuse itself in the cafés on Commercial Square, or take exercise at the golf links at Campomento. Officers joined the colony's Calpe Hunt, practiced their strokes at the Lawn Tennis Club, batted at the Cricket Club. For the British military—for that matter, for the civilians too—Gibraltar was likely far more agreeable than wherever they came from.

But Gibraltar was a great deal more than agreeable. Its position gave it an importance far exceeding that of most of Britain's mini-colonies. In 1939, Gibraltar was a relatively minor naval base, but its control of its strait was a fact of immense strategic importance to the well-being of Britain and its empire—and, by extension, of Britain's democratic allies. During World War II, it would keep the German Navy out of the Mediterranean, keep the Italian Navy in, and keep both from any idea of using Spain as a shortcut to northwestern Africa.[90]

Lines of communication and commerce between Britain and its Far Eastern empire wound inescapably through the Mediterranean and its passages at either end, Gibraltar and the Suez Canal. Plug either passage, and users of those lines would be forced to make the far greater journey around the tip of Africa.[91] Serving as the choke point of the western entrance of the Mediterranean Sea, British batteries on the Rock could effectively control surface shipping through that strait. Furthermore, the fortress was virtually impregnable from the sea, its only weak point the narrow isthmus that connected it to the Spanish mainland at La Línea de la Concepción. (A concerted and prolonged German or Spanish air bombardment would have made the Rock fairly useless as a naval base, but the permanent garrison would nonetheless have been able to keep the strait closed to enemy traffic.)

As much as Franco relished the *idea* of reincorporating Gibraltar into the Spanish state, the actual carrying out of such a vision was not the Caudillo's intention. The British press played up stories of increased Spanish military preparedness in the vicinity of the Rock as a prelude to an attack on it. But British intelligence knew the increased military presence in Andalusia—the province to which the fortress is attached—was primarily designed to thwart die-hard Republicans still harassing Franco's troops in the area. Official British worries devolved on the incomparably more dangerous German threat to the base, either in alliance with Spain or after having invaded Spain and placated or gotten rid of Franco. These threats forced Britain to draw up contingency plans to occupy Gibraltar's hinterland, the areas from which a land-based attack could be launched. Franco, for his part, worried that the British might make some kind of preemptive strike against Spain in fear Germany might beat them to it. Thus in the spring of 1940 Spain began to build a twenty-mile-wide defense perimeter around Gibraltar, planting concrete machine-gun posts, gun emplacements, and a landing strip.

As long as the European land war remained confined to Germany and the Allies glowered at each across the double threads of the Siegfried and Maginot lines, Gibraltar continued relatively tranquil. But within weeks, a stunned Britain would be forced to evacuate a large part of Gibraltar's population, and even consider abandoning the fortress itself.

Lisbon

Among the least understood players on the New European war stage was Antonio Salazar. Prime minister and dictator, professor, economist, orthodox financier, even more orthodox Roman Catholic. In eleven years he had transformed his invitation to govern into an ordination to rule, along the way delivering Portugal from bankruptcy and giving the Portuguese people—the politically quiescent among them—the first taste of social tranquillity in decades. And while underscoring the failure of parliamentary democracy, he frankly made authoritarianism the fundament on which his *Estado Novo* stood. Portugal at the beginning of World War II was neither a Nazi Germany nor a fascist Italy, and certainly no brutalitarian state in the mold of the Soviet persuasion. For those of its citizens willing to accommodate to Salazar's stern work-oriented, church-centered formula, this sunny corner of the continent wasn't a bad place to be in 1939, at least not in the context of much of Europe.

Genuine contradictions differentiated the Hitler-Mussolini ideology from that adopted by Salazar. The former represented, in theory, a progressive movement fostering the interests of the many and replacing old principles that had provided grossly disproportionate privileges for the few; Germany and Italy both negated, of course, any good in such theoretical rationalization by giving themselves wholly over to force. On the other hand, Salazar's New State made no pretense of progressivism, frankly and proudly hailing back to the order of the old, pre-technological age, an order its proponents regarded as "natural." The state's betterment lay in its guarantee of the welfare of its law-abiding citizens. Brute terror, race-baiting, the mystical worship of national "blood" had little, if any, place in Salazar's Portugal. But that it was a "police state" is undeniable—the fracturing of its rules led to midnight knocks on doors by security men with discretionary power to handle offenders as they thought best. Police power represented a natural element of Salazar's political landscape, and the dictator saw to it that its representatives pounced on whatever was considered subversive.

Though a minority, there were many in Portugal highly responsive to the Nazi clarion; such people were most likely found among the upper classes and the organized youth movement that supported the new Germany's "social discipline." Though rarely praising Hitler's over-the-top methods, a worrisome tendency existed in Portugal's upper social strata to favorably compare Germany's orderly society and strong economy with the poverty and social discord out of which Salazar had steadily brought the country.[92]

At the apex of the nation's power structure, Salazar the man was as much enigma as flesh and blood. He was not personally avaricious, but his financial astuteness was such that he turned a bankrupt country into one fully solvent and even mildly prosperous. He shunned display, allowing his constitutional superior, President Carmona, to enjoy unaccompanied whatever glories were inherent in the nation's highest office. The fifty-year-old dictator expressed his greatest pride in his peasant origins; took his greatest pleasure in spending a few days at "home"—the cottage at Santa Comba Dão where he had been born; and looked forward most earnestly and with no apparent insincerity to a long career of service to his country. But now everything he wanted for Portugal was threatened by the dangers undermining the entire continent's future. *His* Portugal— his tidy vision of its future—would rest on how well he negotiated his country's path through that peril.[93]

· · ·

Salazar's preoccupation at the outbreak of war came down most pointedly to the safety of both metropolitan Portugal and its empire.[94] Keeping the two well clear of Europe's conflicts would, he believed, give both the nation and his authoritarian revolution their best hope of survival. Welcoming President Carmona back from an empire tour in early October, the autocrat took the opportunity to address the National Assembly, defining the course Portugal would take through what lay ahead:

Germany has made it known to us that she is prepared to respect the integrity of Portugal and its overseas possessions should we keep neutral; England has asked us nothing in the name of the centuries-old Alliance and friendship which would oblige us to enter the conflict; and, apart from common interests which link us with European nations, we have no direct interests of our own to defend in the conflict.[95]

But Salazar knew Portugal's future would be as much controlled from Madrid as from Lisbon, and that the cunning Caudillo next door was still assessing Spain's interests in the European conflict. Aside from the Spanish question, other external considerations remained to be weighed—most prominently Britain, its navy, and the centuries-old alliance between this still quiescent corner of Europe and that now embattled island.

With its declaration of war, the British cabinet decided against any attempt to use the two countries' special relationship to bring Portugal into active co-belligerency, a sizable part of the cabinet even judging Portugal's neutrality to be an unvarnished plus for the Allies. Had Salazar jeopardized his neutral status by an unfriendly attitude toward Germany, Whitehall foresaw the possibility of such a move provoking a German invasion, in turn giving Salazar leave to invoke the alliance's provisions that would require Britain's help in rescuing its treaty partner.

As it happened, Hitler seems not to have given much thought to Portugal—at least, not Portugal by itself, as separate from its larger peninsular neighbor. However—a big however—Berlin gave a great deal of thought to the Azores, Portugal's island chain lying a thousand miles out in the Atlantic. The islands, not a colony but formally an integral and integrated political district like any other on mainland Portugal, dominated not only a substantial part of the Atlantic but also the air lanes converging on the western entrance to the Mediterranean. What would stay Berlin's hands in taking the islands was its recognition of the difficulty of holding the islands if the United States were to enter the war.[96] Yet Hitler continued to dream of them as a launching pad for long-range aircraft capable of bombing New York, ensuring that these tiny mid-ocean stepping-stones would be heard of a great deal more in the war to come, and remain firmly at the center of Portugal's wartime tribulations.

·   ·   ·

Shortly before hostilities broke out in September, it was Franco who was advising Salazar that Portugal's position in the upcoming conflict should be one of neutrality, the Caudillo's concern now focusing on the possibility of Lisbon coming to favor Britain's cause. But strict neutrality was, of course, a position the Portuguese dictator had already arrived at on his own.

Through his capable network of agents, it hadn't taken the German chargé d'affaires in Lisbon long to learn of the Caudillo's advice. The envoy had cabled the Foreign Ministry in Berlin on August 25:

> I learn from a most reliable source that the Spanish ambassador [the Caudillo's brother, Nicolás, who wasn't really the ambassador] inquired of Minister President [Prime Minister] Salazar yesterday whether Portugal would remain neutral in a general conflict. Salazar gave him to understand that he would do everything to ensure that Portugal remains neutral, but did not give him any binding declaration. Thereupon Franco's Ambassador gave him to understand that Spain would be compelled to revise her policy towards Portugal, if Portugal did not maintain her neutrality.[97]

Five days after the German chargé's cabled analysis, the same official again reported to his ministry on Iberia's coming moves. On the very eve of war, he disclosed that Salazar's ambassador in Madrid told him he had been instructed to inform the Spanish government that Portugal "would try to remain neutral as long as possible, but would probably not be able to withstand excessive British pressure in the long run, especially in view of her [Portugal's] colonies." The following day Ribbentrop wired the Lisbon legation. "Germany was," he said

> determined, should hostilities break out, to refrain from any aggressive act toward Portugal . . . and to respect Portuguese possessions, *if* Portugal maintains an impeccable neutrality towards us in any future conflict. Only if this condition should, contrary to our expectation, not be fulfilled, would we naturally be compelled . . . to protect our interests in the sphere of warfare in such a way as the situation then prevailing might dictate.[98]

In fact, Lisbon did now find itself having to consider British interests, since British protection safeguarded Portugal's colonial empire, most of which was in close proximity to substantially stronger British possessions and nearly all of which was strategically important to Britain's war effort. There was in the equation the unvoiced but unignorable threat of loss to the mother country if Portuguese possessions remained off-limits in that effort.[99]

Salazar had already found reason, stemming from an incident in the late 1930s, to mistrust Britain. He had learned—from the Portuguese ambassador in London, Armindo Monteiro—that leading far-right-wing members of the Chamberlain government had, in that time of frantic attempts to contain the burgeoning Nazi behemoth, proposed appeasing Germany by giving it economic and settlement rights carved out of Portuguese Angola and the Belgian Congo. The proposal, clearly a crackpot idea, was not heard of again after Hitler began his conquests in earnest, but it had been enough to worry Salazar. Now, with the onset of war, he believed a British loss would likely mean a German takeover of Portugal's African possessions, and thus the end of the prestige and the potentially enormous financial advantages its African empire brought to metropolitan Portugal. If he allied Portugal with Spain in a military partnership with Germany, one designed to finesse Hitler into letting Portugal's African possessions remain Portuguese, the result would have been, in Salazar's judgment, an eventual British invasion of Iberia and the collapse of his—as well as Franco's—regime.[100] It was from such deadly and serpentine considerations that Salazar would ever increasingly urge Franco to keep his country out of the war.

CHAPTER III

WAR IN THE WEST

Spring 1940–Summer 1941

The Northern War—Copenhagen-Oslo

On April 9, 1940, the Phony War *passed into history, and with it the radical purging of Europe's neutrals finally began. The second general European conflict of the twentieth century was unambiguously underway, and nearly every state on the continent would shortly find itself either a belligerent or occupied by a belligerent.*

Five weeks earlier, Germany's warlord signed a formal directive for the conquest of Denmark and Norway. "This operation should prevent British encroachment on Scandinavia and the Baltic [and] it should guarantee our ore base in Sweden and give our Navy and the Air Force a wider starting line against Britain. . . . The numerical weakness [of our force] will be balanced by daring actions and surprise execution."[1] In exceptionally clear phrases, Adolf Hitler summed up the justification for the invasion of two neutral and peaceable kingdoms, and set out for his commanders the approach by which he meant to guarantee its success.

In the soberest terms, it was geography that doomed Denmark and Norway. Further, economic and naval necessities, abetted by Hitler's wounded national pride, tipped the scale against their immunity from the century's second continent-wide conflict. Though both had managed to get through World War I with their neutrality and territory untouched, the *factors which in 1940 made them—especially Norway—so attractive to the belligerents had been greatly magnified.*

Freighters brought their cargoes of Swedish iron vital to Germany's war-making capacity down the Norwegian Sea, mostly sailing through protected passages called the Leads that ran between Norway's mainland and a 1,200-mile-long series of offshore islands and reefs. If the Royal Navy were to interdict the shipping through these sovereign Norwegian waters, it would, perforce, be committing an act of war against that neutral state. But so important was the Swedish ore to Germany's capacity to carry out its aggression that for months First Lord of the Admiralty Winston Churchill had been urging that the Leads be sown with mines, the idea being to force the ore-laden freighters out into the open sea, waters in which Britain's powerful navy could destroy much of the vital traffic. The First Lord pressed his provocative plan on the cabinet with the justification that "small nations must not tie our hands when we are fighting for their rights and freedoms."[2]

Though the cabinet overruled the scheme, Churchill's proposal was quickly followed by another course, albeit one that would just as gravely violate Norway's neutrality. Now he urged a landing at Narvik, where an Allied expeditionary force, ostensibly meant for beleaguered Finland's rescue in its war with Russia, would be put ashore. In reality, Churchill simply intended to capture Narvik and with it access to the Swedish ore, and in so doing preempt the Germans from what he believed they themselves intended to do. There was even a hint in the plan that Britain hoped the operation would lead to a general German attack on Scandinavia, giving the Allies the justifiable pretext they needed to "rescue" the ore fields rather than simply appropriate them. Though reluctant to abandon the moral high road by agreeing to violate Norway, Prime Minister Neville Chamberlain's cabinet finally accepted Churchill's proposal, justifying its decision with the tenuous logic that Norway had already given up its immunity as a neutral by allowing German traffic in the Leads.

As for Germany, it was Britain's fleet that powerfully influenced Hitler's decisions to strike at the North. Whereas the Royal Navy operated in the North Sea as though it were a British lake, Hitler's armada was new and unproven, only a fraction the size of its opponent, and easily confinable in its narrow home waters. Even in open seas it had trouble fueling and provisioning and repairing its damage. Grand Admiral Erich Raeder, commander-in-chief of the Kriegsmarine, was fully conscious of the fact that his country's surface fleet stood no chance against Britain's. On the September day Britain and France declared war, he admitted in writing that "our surface forces can do no more than show that they know how to die gallantly."[3]

When Germany lost its colonial empire in 1918 it also lost the capacity for a worldwide navy. Conversely, Britain maintained its empire after the Great War, and with that empire it retained its ability to control the world's oceans. But with command of Norway's ports, the German fleet would be able to powerfully counterpoise its British enemy in the Western Ocean, maneuvering around the top of the British Isles in greater safety, and more readily able to break into the open Atlantic (with a far greater portion of its fuel and supplies intact as well), where ships of the Reich could tear at the lifelines connecting Britain with the New World.

The Admiral Graf Spee, sleek as a greyhound and deadly as an adder, exemplified the new Wehrmacht as did few other symbols. Its designers specially built the vessel to raid the commercial shipping that kept Britain alive. The pocket battleship[4] had been launched in the mid-1930s. Only a handful of Allied naval vessels were able to counter the Nazi threat posed by the Graf Spee and its two sisters, the Admiral Scheer and the Deutschland. When war with Britain came, Raeder ordered the killer, then on station in the North Atlantic, to the South Atlantic and Indian oceans to destroy Allied commercial shipping.[5] From those seas in the following weeks, it sent nine merchantmen to the bottom, though its captain, the forty-nine-year-old Hans Langsdorff, was so solicitous of fellow seamen's lives that not a single Allied sailor was killed in the sinkings.

In December, Captain Langsdorff turned the Graf Spee toward the River Plate, the wide estuary separating Argentina from Uruguay. There he planned to attack a five-ship convoy leaving Montevideo, having learned of the British ships' movements from papers recovered from the pocket battleship's last victim. Upsetting this neat agenda, Langsdorff instead ran straight into a squadron of enemy cruisers, Britain's Ajax and Exeter and New Zealand's Achilles. In the ensuing battle, Allied craft damaged the Graf Spee so badly that Langsdorff was forced to run for the Uruguayan capital. Denied sanctuary long enough to make repairs—the Uruguayans were fearful of jeopardizing their status as neutrals—and knowing any attempt to make for the open sea would end in destruction by enemy guns, its captain chose to scuttle the ship, shortly after which the chivalrous and non-Nazi Langsdorff put a bullet through his head.

The incident generated an enormous uplift in British morale, but for Hitler the humiliation of the episode was overwhelming. When within weeks the Royal Navy violated neutral Norwegian waters to rescue British prisoners from a German merchant ship—the celebrated Altmark incident *of February 16—the German dictator went wild with anger. Hitler's fury spelled the end of any reluctance about invading Scandinavia, an ambivalence founded in his belief that such an invasion would dissipate the attack in the West slated for the spring.*

Plans went forward at full throttle for the attack. Designated Weserübung, or Operation Weser, it was named for the German river flowing into the Baltic where the invasion fleet lay marshaled. Its objectives were Norway and—tragically—Denmark. The Danes had proclaimed early and loudly their neutrality in the fight between the powers, but the tiny kingdom's fatal attraction—its location—it could do nothing to change. Denmark is a small finger of a peninsula jutting up from Germany which with its adjacent islands separate the Reich's North Sea coastline from that on the Baltic. Between Denmark and Sweden is a waterway which at its narrowest point is not much wider than a good-sized river. By controlling Denmark's airfields and harbors, this waterway would become an extremely effective German choke point—a Gibraltar-like bottleneck at which the Baltic could be effectively stoppered. As for Sweden, these straits, the Kattegat and the Skagerrak, were the conduit through which that nation's shipping reached the open seas.

Germany's lightning storm against its two northern neighbors broke in the predawn of April 9. Denmark was a walkover.[6] Its king, Christian X, surrendered his country to avert a senseless bloodbath he and his government knew would result from Hitler's threatened bombardment of Copenhagen. In any case, the kingdom's tiny army wouldn't have lasted more than a day or two against the overwhelming force Hitler gathered to make sure the operations went without a hitch.[7]

In fact, they went disastrously in the considerably more formidable Norwegian phase of the undertaking. The invasion got off to a calamitous start for the ships assigned to take troops to capture the capital region. In the Oslo Fjord, a Norwegian torpedo battery at Oscarsborg—so antiquated as to have been tactically discounted by the Germans—fired on the Blücher, disabling the heavy cruiser's steering gear and allowing it to become a sitting duck for the Norwegian torpedoes. When the brand-new ship rapidly sank in the narrow passageway's frigid waters, more than a thousand heavily equipped shock troops disappeared with it. The incident gave the Norwegian government and royal family precious additional hours to escape northward in advance of the paratroopers who took the city that night, scotching Hitler's plans to capture King Haakon and use him to legitimate the new German order. The head of the local Nazi-style party, Vidkun Quisling, proclaimed himself prime minister in a puppet government, an act which would lead to his name becoming a new internationally understood synonym for treachery.

German landings planned for Norway's Atlantic seaports met with even greater disaster. The Germans readily captured the towns of Christiansand, Egersund, Bergen, and Trondheim from the defending Norwegian forces, but at Narvik the plan went further awry than it had in the Oslo Fjord.[8] The British fleet designed to carry out Churchill's plans to capture Narvik and strike at Bergen and Trondheim (and, for good measure, mine the Leads) had departed its British bases on April 4. Though neither side knew it, it turned out to be a race between the Royal Navy and the Kriegsmarine to reach their common prize—Norway's Atlantic coast.

Hitler's preventive invasion beat Britain's preventive invasion to Norway. By April 20, when the Anglo-French expeditionary force arrived to try to dislodge the German landings, it was already too late, and the attempt to mine Norway's territorial waters was abandoned. Within another ten days, the 15,000-man Norwegian Army and the 13,000-man British, French, and Polish relief force were compelled to give up the southern and central parts of the country after Allied forces failed to oust the Germans from Åndalsnes, Namsos, and Trondheim. A major part of this Allied failure had resulted from delays caused by Anglo-French wrangling over tactics, as well as by French political changes—then supposedly more energetic Paul Reynaud succeeded the obstructive Edouard Daladier as prime minister on March 21.

Only around Narvik, farther north on the coast, with its vital rail connection with the Swedish ore supplies, was the enormous prize still being contested between the opposing forces;[9] there the Royal Navy's superior strength was slowly outweighing the German advantage of first occupation. The German Navy, with its warships doubling as troop carriers, suffered two serious defeats in this area, when a superior British naval force caught it and sank a number of such troopships. Resistance continued in Narvik for a month, only ending on June 4, when London and Paris withdrew their forces—ironically, the Germans had by then withdrawn inland to the Swedish border[10]—because of the desperate need for their presence in the closing days of what had become the Battle of France. When withdrawing south, the Kriegsmarine seriously damaged the fleeing Allies, with the loss of six British vessels; the cruiser carrying King Haakon and his government narrowly escaped in sea lanes now under German control from bases in the Norwegian ports.

Britain's failed attempts to dislodge the Germans from Norway had *been a valiant but near-total loss, the disaster's only saving grace that it led to the fall of the Chamberlain government and the subsequent ascent of Winston Churchill to prime minister. Chamberlain's admission that his government had known of planning for the German attack for weeks appeared to make it guilty of gross neglect in forfeiting such an important sector in the Anglo-German standoff, dredging up memories of another such disaster: Gallipoli—the very symbol of a feasible plan's failure for lack of commitment in men and matériel needed to ensure success.*

Germany didn't emerge from the campaign without grievous injury of its own, primarily to its navy and merchant marine, forces which suffered enormous losses: the Kriegsmarine saw three cruisers sunk, in addition to losing ten destroyers, eleven transports, and various other ships, while a battleship and three more cruisers were badly damaged. Historian Ronald Lewin concluded that for the sake of a "flashy success" in Norway, Hitler threw away his fleet and with it any hope of a successful cross-Channel invasion.[11] Still, the campaign ended up a net gain for the Reich, bringing to an end any further problems in transporting Swedish ore to Germany. What was more, their new Norwegian bases enabled the German fleet to operate with far greater freedom against Atlantic shipping, and— equally ominously—would within a year serve as marshaling ports for German convoys bound for the Soviet Union.

Stockholm

To the Swedes, it seemed the risk of war on their soil had with Weserübung been transformed from merely a threat to what now appeared a virtual certainty. In fact, Hitler had no intention of invading Sweden in his assault on the North. Though fully within Germany's capacities, Hitler put a Swedish invasion in the category of an unnecessary diversion, one that because of Sweden's strength might well have disastrous consequences by upsetting his plans for France. If the kingdom's occupation were to be meaningfully contested by the Swedes, and Hitler fully expected it would be, thousands of troops might well be bogged down in the North, troops needed for the coming enterprise in the West. Furthermore, a surprise was no longer possible after the Weserübung attacks on its neighbors. Accurately assessing Swedish resolve and its still weak but growing military defenses, Berlin reasoned it could get what it wanted from Sweden by means much less burdensome than a military invasion and costly occupation. And by keeping Sweden in a state of apprehension, it added considerably to a German arsenal in which such fearful anticipation had become a formidable weapon.

Three days after Germany descended upon the North and in expectation of a German request to use Sweden to get to Narvik, Prime Minister Hansson took to the radio to confirm to his countrymen their government's continuing policy in regards to its warring neighbors. Hansson's unambiguous words took no one by surprise:

> Sweden is firmly determined to follow the line of strict neutrality. That implies that we must reserve for ourselves independence of judgment and independence of action in every direction. It is not consistent with strict neutrality to permit any belligerent to make use of Swedish territory for its activity. Fortunately no demands in such a direction have been made to us. Should any such demands be made they must be refused.[12]

In fact, Berlin's most nagging, if somewhat farfetched, worry in regards to Sweden in the immediate wake of Weserübung was that the country might, out of loyalty to its Scandinavian neighbors, attack the invading German forces in their rear. But promptly after the assault began, Germany made its conditions for Swedish safety exhaustively clear: Sweden must not depart in any way from conforming to the most exacting neutrality, Berlin warning Stockholm that to do so would result in instant revocation of its neutral status—that it would "suffer the consequences" should that happen. Berlin additionally cautioned that under no circumstances could the ore shipments to Germany be diminished, and further that Stockholm was responsible for ensuring that no British-inspired harm came to the mines supplying that ore, though it is difficult to imagine how Sweden might have stopped a concerted Allied bombing effort to damage the ore fields' production and transportation facilities. For Swedish popular consumption, the Danish and Norwegian invasions were painted in the usual Nazi blather, that they were carried out to make sure that Scandinavia did not become a theater of war, thus making Sweden a "net beneficiary" of German goodwill.

But these first admonitions and shocks would be as nothing compared to the demands Berlin addressed to Stockholm after the Scandinavian campaign became fully engaged: if Hansson's government were to accede to Germany's new ultimata, it would, simply put, mean the transformation of Sweden into little more than a Nazi client state. Berlin's central demand required Sweden to permit German troops to transit Swedish territory so Wehrmacht garrisons in northern Norway—most importantly at Narvik—could be supplied without resort to air or sea transport directly from Germany. The resolution of this astonishing ultimatum led to a standoff between Stockholm and Berlin that threatened to end in the Wehrmacht's overrunning Sweden itself.[13]

From Germany's standpoint, the need for the Swedish concessions was both clear and crucial. Keeping the Narvik-centered force supplied by sea would have been extremely costly to the already overstretched German surface fleet capacity—and might, in fact, have proved impossible. German control of the Baltic and its western approaches was assured by its occupation of Denmark and that country's airfields and ports, and thus permitted relatively safe access to *southern* Norway. But northern Norway was another matter, for getting there by ship meant taking head-on the still vastly superior Royal Navy and its ability to monitor the North Sea. No land connection, by rail or road, existed beyond Trondheim to Narvik in Norway itself, and the military high command in Berlin calculated that the generally nasty weather in the area made air transport too unreliable a method of getting troops and matériel to Narvik.[14] Nonetheless, Hansson's response to the German demands was quick and to the point, and didn't shift an inch from his previous position. "Sweden is firmly determined to follow the line of strict neutrality. . . . It is not consistent with strict neutrality to permit any belligerent to make use of Swedish territory for its activity."[15]

But the reality of near-encirclement by the Wehrmacht soon forced the government to reassess its stand. Having, of course, been expecting the demands,[16] in late April Stockholm concluded that it had no realistic alternative but to give in, if only a fraction. That fraction was that it now stipulated that any German shipments it allowed to cross its territory must be strictly limited to medical supplies until *after* the capitulation of the legitimate Norwegian government, at which time the Swedes could at least justify their actions with the rationale that nothing more could then be done to help the Norwegians in their fight against the Nazis.[17]

This desire not to injure its neighbors led to agonizing self-recriminations in Sweden—though recriminations ameliorated by noting that while Swedish taxpayers had been paying to arm themselves, Norway had followed a pacifist and much less expensive course, one leaving the country with no credible barrier to the German threat. Further, Swedish arsenals were now seriously depleted following the just-ended Finnish war. And perhaps most important, Swedes knew that their country was geographically even more vulnerable than Norway. Once Norway was defeated—which was held to be inevitable, with or without Swedish assistance—no appreciable Allied help could be gotten directly to Sweden except by a long and dangerous trip around the northern tip of Scandinavia and through Finland, a country with which Germany was now virtually allied.

Convincing Hitler of Sweden's neutrality would clearly require measures that would be deeply hurtful to a people who held the neighboring Norwegians as a part of their own extended family. But in light of its expectations of German invasion, Stockholm concluded that it had to exhibit a measure of ruthlessness in regard to the Norwegian struggle. First of all, it informed Oslo that its actions had to be judged as a response to a world war, a very different situation from the open help it gave Finland in its brutal struggle against Russia. Accordingly, the Swedes refused to allow any recruitment of volunteers for the Norwegian war, even though it had freely allowed the departure of those who wished to go to Finland. It forbade the passage of supplies classifiable as war matériel to be sent from one place in Norway to another over the more direct Swedish routes. Norwegian soldiers escaping into Sweden were interned, though their incarceration would be of short duration.[18] Norway, expecting concessions and "compassion" rather than what it viewed as rigid legalisms from the Swedes, expressed deep offense at Stockholm's actions.[19]

Hansson's government contrived a narrowly technical subterfuge which, at least technically, seemed to get around the matter of violating its own neutrality: even though Norway had not yet conceded to the Germans, Stockholm would allow "Red Cross" trains, operating as regular commercial freight carriers, to transit its territory carrying "nonmilitary" goods—mainly food and clothing—for the Narvik defenders. As might have been foreseen, the Germans quickly made a mockery of this mockery. The "medical personnel" the Wehrmacht put on the trains would in reality be critically needed military specialists, the "nonmilitary" goods mostly food but also snowshoes and skis, medical supplies, radio equipment, and oil and coal.

For its part, Sweden extracted critical rewards for its unneutral concession: from the Reich it demanded and received substantial arms shipments for its own defense buildup,[20] a strengthening it hoped would help it resist what it now sober-mindedly anticipated would be ever increased pressure with ever increased transit demands. The issue was still far from settled with this Swedish capitulation to the reality of Germany's superior position, though Stockholm bravely and staunchly pledged to resist any further German demands.

The ante quickly went up, though. Berlin now demanded that Sweden effectively surrender its rights as a neutral in what to the Reich had become the critically important matter of protecting its far northern Atlantic flank. Pleas from the beleaguered commander at Narvik, General Edouard Dietl, for more men and supplies grew increasingly fevered as Allied pressure increased, and those pleas were translated by Berlin into ever nastier demands. Germany now flatly wanted war matériel itself transported—undisguised and unlimited weaponry, ammunition, artillery. The Swedes refused point-blank. At first, Berlin extended the carrot of sweet reward, but increasingly the Reich turned to the cudgel of threatened retaliation to bend the Swedish government's uncooperative attitude. Before April 9, Swedish shipping still possessed some freedom of movement in the northern waters, a freedom allowing its own international trade to be carried on with a measure of independence. But in the new circumstances, Germany possessed the power to throttle this Swedish shipping, thanks to its control of the shipping lanes around Swedish ports. Now, Berlin warned that if Stockholm refused to acquiesce to German demands for transit rights to Narvik and other Norwegian ports, the Kriegsmarine would take measures to "restrict" Swedish shipping to a level Stockholm knew would crush the Swedish economy.

In a constitutional monarchy, the monarch is expected—is indeed required—to remain aloof from politics and governance, to leave the state's functioning to responsible ministers and government. But on April 19, King Gustav concluded that the situation had become so perilous, and so great was the danger of a German invasion, that he personally entered the transit dispute—his motivation clearly to impress the ex-corporal with the gravity of a monarch's pledge. In a letter written to Hitler that day, the king assured the leader of the German Reich that Sweden was determined with all the power at its disposal to defend its neutrality against attack—against attack from *any* quarter. He added that he had assured London and Paris of these facts and this determination. To underline the point, Gustav's government conspicuously placed the bulk of its army in the north to guard the ore fields against Allied attack, assuring the Germans they were "strengthening their neutrality guard" in accordance with Berlin's wishes. Gustav believed Hitler might be less concerned about his military position in Norway if he received solemn assurances Sweden would neither make common cause with the Allied effort to help Norway nor stand by if Britain made a grab for the Swedish ore fields in order to cripple the German war effort.[21]

Stockholm also hoped Berlin would read the subtler message in the placement of its troops: its ace in the hole remained its ability to destroy the ore fields before any armed forces could capture them. Soldiers stationed around the mining facilities would see rapidly to that destruction, and it wanted Berlin to be aware of that fact now and throughout the rest of the war.

Berlin hoped that Gustav, whom it (mistakenly) gauged a better friend of Germany than of Britain or France, would be able to convince his cabinet of the necessity of cooperation with Germany. But Prince Viktor zu Wied, the elderly and purportedly anti-Nazi head of the German mission in Stockholm, had to inform his Foreign Ministry that in his opinion not too much hope should ride on the eighty-one-year-old monarch's being able to alter established Swedish policy in the Reich's favor. In a wire dated April 24, Wied advised:

> The Swedish Government regards the question of transit traffic as an essential part of its neutrality policy and has, obviously as a precautionary policy, declared its point of view. . . . In these circumstances there is little likelihood that the King . . . can adopt an attitude other than that already declared by the Government.[22]

Even promises of more military aid to bolster its defense needs wouldn't move Hansson's government from its refusal to go beyond the seriously compromising concessions it had already made. On April 27, Wied reported to his Foreign Ministry that "an expeditious way to take up the question of transit to Narvik . . . without danger of an official rejection . . . is receiving those deliveries of arms [Germany was even prepared to give the Swedes heavy antiaircraft guns "should it absolutely insist on them"] to which we have already committed ourselves."[23] But three days later he was forced to report to Berlin that "the impressions of our negotiators is that offers of further German deliveries of arms are not regarded by the Swedish Government as compensation for [further] modification of its neutrality policy,"[24] and that "the German suggestion that transit of arms and ammunition to German troops in Norway be permitted in conjunction with the German supplies of arms to Sweden was rejected in these discussions."[25]

Addressing a May Day rally, Prime Minister Hansson pronounced again Sweden's resolve to assert and defend its neutrality "with all the means in our power." Speaking to an emotional gathering in Stockholm, he maintained that "this neutrality implies that we demand our independence and our freedom be left unmolested." He went on to plead for the solidarity and the loyalty of the crowd, and beyond, of the nation, ending with the hope that "the sun will shine again over the north, and that its peoples can continue their peaceful work."[26]

Minister Wied contemptuously referred to the government's determination as the Swedish "neutrality complex,"[27] and within days, the snarls from Berlin grew more menacing. German policy now moved to full-fledged economic force to budge Stockholm from its obstinacy. First came an embargo on the weaponry that Sweden paradoxically needed to protect itself from Berlin. Concessions on overseas Swedish shipping—shipping controlled now by Germany[28]—were canceled. While Dietl was anticipating a concerted British drive on Narvik at any moment, and frantically wiring Berlin with urgent pleas for artillery—he estimated he would be able to hold out against an Allied assault for only ten to fourteen days without it—Sweden remained steadfast in refusing to allow rail shipments to be expanded to meet Germany's "needs." Neither, though, did the Allies make their move against Narvik, which meant Germany still had time to tighten the screws against Sweden without the need to invade the obstinate country.

The Western War—Amsterdam-Brussels-Paris

On May 10, the second shoe dropped. Postponed twenty-nine times since he announced the plan to his generals on the day six months earlier when Poland surrendered, Hitler's offensive against the West struck the Western democracies like an avalanche. With it went the last pretenses of the efficacy of neutrality as a barrier to Nazi aggression. Though the offensive was meant to knock out the French and force the British to a negotiated armistice, Hitler's ulterior purpose was to eliminate the West so his full attention could be turned to the Soviet Union and the destruction of Communism. The first kill in his Operation Yellow was the Netherlands,[29] a nation which hadn't fought since 1830, which had sat out World War I, and which expected its declaration of neutrality to get it through this one. It was mistaken.

At 4:30 in the morning of the tenth, German airborne units began landing near The Hague and Leyden in one end of a concerted attack that included the Netherlands, Belgium, and Luxembourg and that stretched from the North Sea to the Moselle River. The ability of the Dutch to defend themselves was, at best, slight. Half the 125 aircraft of their air force were destroyed on the ground by the Luftwaffe in the opening hours of the onslaught. Their army of ten divisions, in what was clearly intended only as delaying tactics, withdrew into the watery country around Amsterdam and Rotterdam, there hoping to slow the invaders by using the network of rivers and canals as a kind of human tank trap. The tactic had worked well against the Spanish and the French three centuries earlier;

*against the Wehrmacht—especially Göring's Luftwaffe—it was patheti-
cally insufficient.*

*German airborne troops dispersed over broad stretches of the flat na-
tion, where they awaited the arrival of supporting tank forces. On the
morning of the thirteenth, a German bomber squadron destroyed Rotterdam, wiping out the antique heart of the city and killing 814 people, the
attack presaging the carpet bombings that would later turn scores of Europe's venerable cities into rubble. Not only signaling a new and malevolent character in the war, Rotterdam's travails also effectively put an end
to the four-day-long Dutch resistance. On board a Royal Navy destroyer
together with her government, Queen Wilhelmina fled to Britain on the
same day (after begging King George VI personally for more British help
and though she protested she would rather go to one of the overseas Dutch
colonies). The Dutch began what would be among the most terrible of the
German occupations in Western Europe.*

*Though it took the Wehrmacht a mere ninety-six hours to eliminate the
neutral Netherlands, neutral Belgium proved slightly tougher to bring to
heel. Having endured the most brutal of imperial Germany's occupation
behavior between 1914 and 1918, Belgium nonetheless placed enormous
faith in its status of neutrality and the expectation that in this war
Germany would respect that status. But to defeat France, Hitler's army
had to be directed straight through Belgium, the German leader having no
intention of trying to breach France's Maginot Line head-on. Instead, his
highly mobile armored tank divisions, the creation of the brilliant General
Heinz Guderian, would simply flank the northern end of that barrier.*

*In the 1930s, both France and Belgium placed an almost sophomoric
faith in the notion that the northern end of the Maginot Line could not be
successfully skirted because of the geographical fact that it ended in the
Belgian Ardennes, a dense forest thought of as impenetrable to invading
tank-led armies. And, this line of thinking continued, even if it were
breached, beyond the Ardennes the Belgian fortifications were expected to
be sufficiently powerful to hold off invaders while the French armies—the
"best in the world"—could mass and drive the invader (the Wehrmacht,
of course) back.*

*But just about everything in this hopeful scenario that could go wrong
went wrong. For one thing, Belgium's most fundamental strategy after
Hitler remilitarized the Rhineland in 1936 lay in neutrality, not in continuing its post-World War I alliance with France. The country had
prudently spent enormous sums on its key fortresses, with the "impregnable" Fort Eben Emael guarding the road to Brussels and the key point in*

Belgium's defense, one of the strongest forts in the world. But its government decided that absolute neutrality would best counter the German threat, and refused to compromise that neutrality by coordinating defense plans with France, whose confused Socialist foreign policies further strengthened the Belgian resolve to go it alone. Hitler munificently granted the little kingdom a solemn guarantee that the Reich would respect its neutrality. When the reneging Führer struck from the east, it was far too late for Brussels to coordinate an effective strategy with its French neighbor, and the deadly nature of its chosen course quickly became apparent.

Not that any amount of joint planning with France would have made all that much difference. The fact was that in 1940 the French Army so much of the world regarded as invincible was an antiquated relic, physically and spiritually unfit to effectively challenge the Wehrmacht. The failing wasn't so much in the character of the soldiers who made up its 101 divisions, or even its immobile nature—it had nothing to compare with Guderian's superb ten panzer divisions. Instead, the rot was at the head, in the mind-set of its generals and above them, of the government. Mired in the appeasement mode, the French governments of the 1930s served European peace fully as badly as those of Britain served that country. Now hiding behind the "inviolability" of the Maginot Line, the French commanders—men who a generation earlier had been the staff officers of the generals who ran the Great War with such deadly stolidity—were utterly crushed by that barrier's irrelevancy. And at the top, the government exerted no leadership worth the price the soldiers would have to pay to withstand the Germans.

Eben Emael stood for one day before a sophisticated team of German paratroopers captured the massive hedgehog of a fortress on the Meuse. On the twelfth, the Germans entered France at Sedan, the small city where Frenchmen's unhappiest memories—the defeat in 1870 by the armies of Bismarck—gave the event particular poignancy. The entire German strategy was now clear to its victims: pierce the Ardennes to outflank the Maginot, then a dash to the Channel ports, and finally a lightning drive for Paris and the seizing of the befuddled French Army, government, and nation.

Belgium was, of course, a secondary objective in Germany's grand drive westward. But the attack on this small country worked brilliantly. The combined forces of the seven divisions of General Lord Gort's British Expeditionary Force, the French Army, and King Leopold's army were blown across the Belgian lowlands like so much chaff in the wind. Understanding that further resistance would result in the annihilation of his kingdom, on May 27 Leopold ordered his forces to lay down their arms, having concluded that his army could retreat no further west in its support of the BEF, which was fast becoming entrapped in what would become the Dunkirk perimeter. Against the wishes of the Allies, and contrary to counsel from his own advisers, Leopold remained in Belgium to share his people's fortunes rather than flee to Britain to form a government-in-exile.[30]

With the BEF backed up to the Channel, Hitler's single-minded aspiration to see his armies reach Paris—and thus avoid a possible replay of the arrested German drive on the French capital in World War I—gave Britain the miraculous chance to evacuate its expeditionary force.[31] The chance was managed with brilliance: while the pursuing German armies held back forty-eight hours, the all-but-written-off British executed the greatest rescue in history. From the beaches of Dunkirk, virtually every operable craft available in southern England—887 vessels ranging from dinghies to destroyers—spirited 199,129 British soldiers and 139,097 French troops[32] back to Britain. All their equipment was left behind and thus forfeited, but the nucleus of the Allied fighting force survived to engage the Germans another day. The British press characterized the operation as "the greatest feat of arms in history." Churchill more accurately saw it for what it was, telling parliament that "wars are not won by evacuations."

The defeat of France produced few other miracles—except perhaps for Hitler's reputation as a modern Feldherr of genius. Seven panzer divisions, totaling 2,270 tanks, self-propelled guns, and armored vehicles, rolled around the northern end of the Maginot Line, blazing forward unopposed through neutral Luxembourg and the Belgian Ardennes. The unimaginably rapid German destruction of France's military capacity was a blow as stunning as any the Western democracies had ever suffered.

Dunkirk's fall signaled France's final agony. Momentous events happened so fast that little sense could be made of the catastrophe by countries now aware that Hitler was determined on the conquest of Europe, and possibly even beyond. France abandoned all resistance plans: gone was the intended massed stand south of Paris, gone a "redoubt" in Brittany, gone even the evacuation of the government to continue the fight from the nation's still substantial colonial empire.

Instead, defeatism spread like a shroud over the nation and its leadership. The government of Paul Reynaud fled from Paris to Tours on June 10, leading a biblical multitude of terrified refugees. The following day, Mussolini entered the war with his attack on the defending French armies in the southern Alps—"the hand that held the dagger has struck it into the back of his neighbor," as Franklin Roosevelt characterized the tragically *foolish action of the Italian dictator. Mussolini called it "a chance which comes only once in five thousand years." The principal effect of Italy's entry into the war would be to jeopardize British contacts with its Middle Eastern oil fields and make the Allied position in the Mediterranean more difficult generally.*

The end came on June 16 with Premier Reynaud's resignation and succession by the vice premier, World War I hero Marshal Henri-Philippe Pétain. Possessed of enormous moral authority in France as one of the last of the great leaders of that war, Pétain saw Communism as a greater menace than Nazism and believed further resistance to Germany futile. France's army was in rout, its air force more than half destroyed in the defense of Belgium. At de Gaulle's urging,[33] Churchill proposed an "indissoluble union" of Britain and France in a symbolic gesture to try to keep the French in the fight, but the appeasers in the cabinet rejected the notion as unrealistic; one French government official spoke for many when he said he "did not want France to become a dominion [of the British Empire]."[34]

The following day, newly installed as head of the French state, the marshal sued for an armistice. The Germans were already in possession of more than half of France, with their armies steamrollering over the French countryside virtually unchecked. Concerned that the nation would fall into leftist-led disorder, Pétain seemed almost to relish the prospect of surrender to the Germans, as though it were a way to demonstrate to his fellow Frenchmen the evil of their post-Great War self-indulgence. The onetime hero even characterized as "desertion" an exodus to the colonies to continue the fight. Pétain was convinced that Britain wouldn't be able to long withstand the Germans, and would itself soon demand an end to the fight.

The aftermath was pitiful. In a gesture designed to delimit the already overstretched Wehrmacht's occupation duties, the southern part of France was created a nominally free state, the zone libre, with its seat of government the old spa of Vichy, in the beautiful valley of the Allier. Occupied France was essentially the nation above the Loire, plus the entirety of the Atlantic coast (with its rail access into Spain) and the Alpine frontier; Alsace and Lorraine, the two provinces that had seesawed between Germany and France for centuries, were incorporated into the Reich proper, as Elsass and Lothringen. "Vichy France," as the unoccupied zone soon became universally known, remained technically sovereign, with Pétain its "head of state" and commander-in-chief of a 100,000-man "armistice army." In reality, the new state was a dictatorship pure and simple, its governors' desires to placate Germany taking it into a shameful collabo-

ration in the Nazi racial trauma that would quickly stain France's soul. Though the government could have allowed the fleet—a formidable surface force, the fourth largest in the world—to escape to Britain or the colonies, it chose instead to intern it in its North African and Mediterranean ports, firmly under Vichy control. That navy now became one of Britain's principal concerns, leading the British within weeks to attack it in its new bases.

The finale was played out in a rail coach in the forest of Compiègne, a gesture of wrenching humiliation. In the same coach, on the same spot, France had twenty-two years earlier exacted the armistice from a shaken and demoralized German government, ending the Great War. What was done that eleventh day of November 1918—which was essentially to make Germany accept the responsibility for a war that had come about because of the actions and policies of all the European powers—led directly to what was happening on this twenty-second day of June 1940.

Gathered in the car awaiting the French delegation were the major Nazi satraps: Göring, Ribbentrop, Hess, Keitel, Raeder. Their Leader, in his first visit to his new conquest, reveled in a state of barely concealed glee.[35] France was now down, Britain quickly would beg for terms, and Russia was soon to be taken to slaughter.

The countries that had gotten in his way on the road to this moment were swept aside as remnants of the old, soft, discredited order. The neutrality of Denmark and Norway, of Luxembourg and Belgium and the Netherlands, had been ignored by a state that had no need and no impetus to recognize it. The reality of that fact was one the remaining neutrals would study very closely.

Bern

When the Wehrmacht's massed divisions pounced on the West, the beginning of Switzerland's own real danger was also being signaled. The jeopardy to the Swiss came primarily from the fact that the Maginot Line had two ends. On the south, the great barrier terminated where France, Germany, and Switzerland all touch on each other, the exact point of convergence of the *Dreiecke*, or "Three Corners," lying in the middle of the Rhine. Switzerland's potential peril resulted from the obvious conclusion that all the Wehrmacht had to do to sidestep the bottom of the Three Corners was to invade a bit of the surrounding Swiss territory. Berlin's temptation to do just that must have been great, so great the Swiss thought they might very well yield to that temptation.

But as had been the case with Sweden, Berlin had decided against invading Switzerland, largely because the Wehrmacht's assault on France was going so smoothly there was no need to do so. Bern didn't know Berlin's intentions, of course, and it remained crucial to German plans that its opponents continue to believe it might do as the Swiss feared—namely, that an end run around the Maginot through Swiss territory was still very much a possibility. The reason for the stratagem was uncomplicated. Tying up French defensive forces opposite the area of the *Dreiecke* meant there would be fewer soldiers available to oppose the real invasion. Though plans for a genuine incursion through Switzerland—code-named *Tannenbaum*—had indeed been formulated by the German general staff, the sense of peril among the Swiss in mid-May had been only the result of a German-engineered deception designed to keep French forces badly needed in the north instead pinned down in the south.

But the panic that swept through the Basel region in that season of terror represented an all too real threat to Swiss efforts to defend their country. As late as mid-June, as scores of thousands of French troops streamed across the border into Swiss territory to escape the Wehrmacht, they encountered fully equipped Swiss soldiers, in whose lee shuffled the flood of civilians from the cities in the path of the expected Wehrmacht. Though France was clearly defeated at this point—the Maginot Line had already been taken from the rear by Guderian's panzers—thousands of Swiss continued to believe the Germans would seize the momentum of their French invasion and march right on into Switzerland.

Not only did this civilian hegira impede a military defense effort against the Germans, but the masses of directionless people brought with them a broad swath of panic everywhere they went. Attempting to put some order in a situation threatening to quickly get out of control, Bern closed the country's borders to all rail and highway traffic, and even ordered foreigners to surrender their firearms to the police. The fear of sabotage grew so great that identity checks became an annoying but inescapable part of everyday life, the dozen checkpoints on the sixty-mile highway between Bern and Zurich typical of the intense levels of surveillance. As the French exodus from Paris and the north was reaching its own apogee, so too were the Swiss highways congealed with Citroëns and Renaults and Fiats, their roofs topped with mattresses as evanescent shields drivers hoped might protect the occupants against Luftwaffe strafing.

Ironically, these Swiss refugees disproportionately represented the better-off, more mobile classes. In the fall of 1939, many well-to-do Swiss took out leases on chalets in the west of the country, particularly in the area around Lake Geneva, thought to be out of the way of greatest danger. So too did Swiss corporations rent similar facilities in which to store irreplaceable records and corporate archives, and urban museums and churches removed priceless artifacts and stained-glass windows and packed them off to similar remote places of safety.

Although the Swiss exodus never reached anything like the human tidal wave in those Western nations actually attacked by the Germans, it isn't difficult to understand the panic overtaking Switzerland that spring. With virtually every country on their periphery at war, and with the reminders of the bombing of Warsaw, and even more of Rotterdam, vast numbers of Swiss were convinced it was only a matter of time before the German behemoth similarly engulfed their own country.[36] The stunning collapse of the vaunted French military was received with profound shock by the Swiss, especially the Francophones in the western part of the country close in thinking to France, who had been indoctrinated in the invincibility of the Maginot Line and the French Army—for such Swiss, if the war was over for the French, it must just about be over for them too. The worst of this panic would subside only when General Guisan ordered, with the near-dictatorial but providential authority given him by parliament, that everyone stay put unless specifically directed otherwise by explicit military command.[37]

Switzerland's more fundamental dilemma came after France collapsed, while the Wehrmacht was still securing the French heartland. Most Swiss stood united in resolve to defend their own territory. An army again fully mobilized and led by a military leader cognizant of the consequences of defeat, as well as a German-language press whose editors constantly reminded their readers what it would mean to Switzerland to be merged into the New European Order, kept high a fearful people's will to resist. But when France's ignominious end came at Compiègne, a wave of pessimism began to vitiate the nation that suddenly found itself surrounded by forces—including Hitler's ally, Stalin—inimical to democracy and to almost everything for which the Swiss Confederation stood.[38] What was more, France's downfall markedly increased Switzerland's economic dependence on Germany—especially for food and energy—leading influential voices to question the wisdom of further resistance, either physical or moral, to the "inevitable" Nazi triumph in Europe.

It was now, in this turbulent summer of 1940, with the Swiss at their lowest spiritual ebb, that two seminal events for their nation took place. A radio broadcast and then a gathering of the army's officer corps on a near-sacred meadow called the Rütli set the tone for the rest of Switzerland's course through World War II.

In the unique rota system among the Federal Councillors from which the country's heads of state emerged, Marcel Pilet-Golaz became president of the confederation in 1940.[39] Since this virtually anonymous civil servant would also serve concurrently as head of foreign affairs in 1940, his capacity to dominate Swiss federal policy was portentous in what was his country's most critical year since the destruction of Napoleon's empire.

Pilet-Golaz was, like Guisan, a native Vaudois and a Francophone, but there just about all similarity between the two men ended.[40] The president perceived his duty to Switzerland as one of literally saving the country. But whereas Guisan knew accommodation to Germany would eventually prove fatal to Switzerland's independence, Pilet-Golaz believed—as did Chamberlain and Pétain and many like-minded European statesmen of the era—that appeasement embodied his nation's only salvation. A man of intellectual power, he unfortunately saw the future through the blinkered eyes of his day rather than through a vision that might evaluate what Nazism would truly mean to his country or to European civilization.

Pilet-Golaz's was, of course, no lone voice counseling his country's accommodation to the German colossus next door. Joining him was a select and influential cross section of Swiss society: the majority of the Federal Council, many ranking army officers, the country's principal diplomats to the German or German-occupied countries, and senior officials in the Political Department, Switzerland's equivalent of the Foreign Office.

The motivation for appeasement can only be truly appreciated in light of the dangers and pressures that Switzerland faced between the fall of France and the attack on the Soviet Union. Germany was winning—both militarily and diplomatically—on every front and in every campaign. From negating the Soviet threat by the brilliance of the Molotov-Ribbentrop pact to destroying resistance in Poland and Norway, in Belgium and the Netherlands and, finally, France, and thus appearing to be on the verge of what most observers believed would be a successful invasion of Britain, in mid-1940 there was little reason to doubt Germany's invincibility. And to a country nearly surrounded by the victorious Reich and its allies or its conquered territory, Germany seemed not only indomitable but terrifying as well. Many Swiss—not traitors or even necessarily the faint of heart—believed the confederation's only course was to acquiesce to the Reich and its policies while such support could still be interpreted as voluntary. These Swiss concluded that after Germany finished off Britain, it would crush too an antagonistic and still democratic Switzerland. So sure was the Pilet-Golaz faction that a show of Swiss arms would only precipitate the Germans into such action that on June 7 the president stood down two-thirds of the nation's forces.[41]

In spite of all this, the majority of the Swiss people still opposed the Pilet-Golaz line of thinking. These men and women were backed by the German-language press, a large proportion of the top military leadership, and a part—albeit a minority—of the Federal Council. But far the most important was the confederation's military commander, Henri Guisan, the driving force behind the notion that Swiss neutrality was meaningless unless the nation could protect its independence. And that independence, Guisan knew, could itself only be guaranteed by military means.

It was the general's complex plan to establish a national "redoubt" that most concerned Pilet-Golaz and those who shared his views. As Guisan envisioned it, this redoubt was to be that part of the nation to be defended to the last man, the mountainous center turned into a fortress designed to hold out against a German invasion even as the rest of the country was put to the torch in a scorched-earth policy presenting an invader with as little as possible of value.

On June 25, an ill-devised action of the federal president brought the tensions between the two camps to a head. Apprehensive that the Swiss people were confused as to the government's basic orientation regarding the war and the belligerents, Pilet-Golaz decided to set matters straight. His forum would be an address to the country over nationwide radio. Speaking in the French of his native Vaud province,[42] the president issued an amazingly undisguised call to the Swiss to get used to the idea that Europe's future was a German one—that if Switzerland indeed was to have a future, its people had best make their peace with that fact.

The address has been called "an odd mixture of egocentricity, derision, and boastfulness."[43] In what amounted to a personal harangue, Pilet-Golaz characterized the Swiss way of life as indolent, comfortable, and snug, adding that that condition was going to have to change. Using the vocabulary of Nazi Germany and Vichy France, the president sounded like a petit Pétain with his dicta exhorting the Swiss people to "discuss not, but work; enjoy not, but produce; demand not, but give." Parroting the exact phrases of Nazi jargon, he called for the *Erneuerung* (renewal) and *Anpassung* (adaptation) of Swiss institutions and policies. Going on to demand that everyone get rid of his "old personality," he appealed for unquestioning support for the government. The broadcast's finale was a reprise of the Pétain-type exhortation; referring to the government, he enjoined: "Be calm as it is calm. Stay firm as it is firm. Have confidence as it has confidence." There wasn't a word of praise for the nation's soldiers, certainly not for the work Guisan had undertaken to strengthen Swiss defenses. Nor was a word spoken about resisting an invasion should one come. It seemed that the president viewed Guisan as a greater danger than Hitler.

The speech was a body blow to most Swiss, though Berlin predictably applauded it as a "sensible" coming to terms with the reality of a Nazi Europe. (The Nazis had, however, expected a follow-up from Bern by cashiering Guisan.) For those army commanders who had used the breather of the Phony War to strengthen the country's defenses against the expected German attack, it caused sheer incredulity. Most Swiss listeners believed that in the broadcast the president was condemning their way of life, and to many Pilet-Golaz overnight turned into a near-collaborator by apparently easing the way for a Nazi takeover. Many believed that if their traditional—that is to say, thrifty and frugal—way of life was now to be branded "snug and selfish," the fault might be more with the man making the judgment than with the people being judged. Though Pilet-Golaz's role as a high official of a small country trying to chart its way through the threats from the Nazi barbarians would have inevitably brought criticism of his methods and goals, more than a few Swiss thereafter regarded Pilet-Golaz—who would continue as a Federal Councillor and foreign minister until 1944—as the country's leading symbol of appeasement.

Guisan's reaction was swift. He believed the president's speech cast doubt on the authority and direction the Federal Council had bestowed on him—namely, to protect the country militarily. Though Bern's paring down of men under arms proceeded drastically while the government assured its commanding general that his mission was not in any way diminished, the undaunted Guisan immediately began planning the next phase in the defense of Switzerland against the Nazi hurricane. Guisan's actions were sure and expeditious, and they won for the general what would become a near-mythical place in his country's small pantheon of heroes.

Exactly 649 years earlier, the Swiss Confederation was born on the shores of the Lake of Lucerne, one of the loveliest of the chain of Alpine basins ornamenting the center of the country. At the top of the fjordlike banks that ring the lake, a small meadow called the Rütli, where the nation's authors met to seal the federation's foundation, had over many centuries become in the collective Swiss psyche something of a shrine commemorating those ancient events. On July 25, exactly one month after the presidential speech, Guisan commanded that a gathering take place on this Rütli meadow. He assembled his top 650 army commanders, from corps level down through battalion. Framed in a protective cordon of Alpine infantry, the speech Guisan gave that July day crystallized Switzerland's resolve. As he enjoined his officers to save their nation from the German-oriented future envisioned by the propitiatory Pilet-Golaz, the general's dramatic words and their symbolic setting etched a deep impression on those gathered to hear him. Guisan invoked the *Bundesbrief*—the 650-year-old federal constitution—in warning his officers that Switzerland should make no compromises with the Powers, or as the *Bundesbrief* termed them, *die Arglist der Welt*—"the cunning of the world."

Though no verbatim record of Guisan's address exists, a later official reconstruction of his remarks reveals the tone so at variance with the appeasement-minded:

> In 1939 the Federal Council entrusted the army with the task of protecting our centuries-old independence. This independence has been respected, until now, by our neighbors, and we will see to it that it will be respected to the end. As long as in Europe millions stand under arms, and as long as important forces are able to attack us at any time, this army has to remain at its post.
>
> Come what may, the fortifications you have built preserve all their value. Our efforts have not been in vain, since we still hold our destiny in our own hands. Don't listen to those who, out of ignorance or evil intention, spread negative news and doubt. Let us trust not only in our right but also in our strength, which enables us, if everybody is possessed of an iron will, to defend ourselves successfully.[44]

If the president and his supporters were shocked at the general's actions—and they were—Berlin was furious. The German yelp at the news of the Rütli address came right to the point. Otto Köcher, German minister in Bern, wired the Foreign Ministry in Berlin:

> The Army Staff reveals through the local morning press that on July 25 General Guisan, on Mt. [sic] Rütli, personally gave the order of the day to his troop commanders down to battalion commanders. In his orders General Guisan states that Switzerland is at a turning point in her history, that it is a matter of the preservation of Switzerland. . . . I suggest considering whether joint or separate demarches of similar content by the Axis Powers would not be in order, expressing our surprise at renewed incitement of Swiss public opinion against Germany and Italy; if anything could make the allied Axis Powers vacillate in their resolve

to maintain their previous attitude toward Switzerland, it is such an inopportune demonstration as that of the General.[45]

For all its air of distress, Köcher's telegram occasioned no substantive demarche with either of the Axis members' diplomatic policies in respect to the Swiss. But what had seemed like a docile Switzerland reconciled to the death of democracy in the New Europe now had shown itself capable of following a very different course, a loosened genie that the timid Federal Council in Bern wouldn't be able to put back in its bottle.

When the prior August 31 Guisan had been given overall command authority for Switzerland's defense, it hadn't been foreseen that the general's vision of a neutral Switzerland would come to differ so radically from that of the government. But as opposed to those who had constitutional authority over him, Guisan saw neutrality as meaningless without the military wherewithal to enforce it. Merely declaring that Switzerland would be neutral in Europe's struggle was, he knew, insufficient to persuade Hitler that Switzerland meant to maintain not only its independence but its democratic way of life as well.

The course Guisan outlined to his officers on July 25 was essentially the "redoubt"—or fortified central stronghold—plan he had envisioned the prior autumn. The formula became an affirmation of Guisan's determination to ensure Swiss independence, an independence the redoubt was designed to safeguard. The government had felt obliged to approve the commander-in-chief's overall strategy before the Rütli gathering, though quite likely unappreciative at the time of its cost or that the policy would come to shape and dominate Swiss political and strategic thinking for the remainder of the war.

For the year following the outbreak of European war, Pilet-Golaz's and Guisan's mutual antagonism led to a schizophrenic situation in Switzerland, one in which the federal president and the military commander-in-chief were determined to lead the country along opposing courses. Guisan unquestionably possessed the authority to group his military forces in the pattern required by his redoubt policy. But guided by both conviction and economic imperatives, Pilet-Golaz still tried to steer—despite his and the Federal Council's approval of the redoubt program—national policy and opinion in the direction of demobilization and accommodation to German demands. The president found, though, that to push for demobilization was tantamount to abandoning the redoubt policy. Ironically, the redoubt plan thus gained its first success in that it was effectively keeping Bern from disarming the country.

Since Pilet-Golaz knew Guisan was too powerful and popular a target to squash, the appeasers changed their tactics and went on the attack against the general's strong supporters, the German-language newspapers, a force that in that pre-television age wielded enormous influence. The relatively uncensored tone of the Swiss press represented a major cause of friction between Berlin and Bern. Berlin was easily affronted by the anti-Nazi remarks in many Swiss papers, and one German official in early 1940 threatened the Swiss president (Henri Vallotton at the time) that there would be "retaliation" unless the situation were "rectified"; the official gloatingly reported to Berlin that he had "impressed upon the federal president how necessary it was for the Swiss press to adopt a different attitude than that heretofore taken."[46] This would be followed by many more German demands that Switzerland and its press recognize the futility of clinging to Europe's old order. When the German press attaché in Bern insisted that *Der Bund*, one of the country's principal anti-German newspapers, dismiss its editor, the Swiss government did almost nothing to protest such impudence, in effect giving leave to the German legation to keep up its pressure.

When the Germans produced a petition signed by two hundred prominent Swiss supporting a drive to have an editor fired, it became painfully apparent to what degree influential elements of Swiss society were willing to go to reach an "understanding" with Berlin,[47] an understanding that would have at its core the merging of the Swiss economy into that of the Reich. Not only did this "Petition of the Two Hundred" propose what amounted to silencing a free press; it also called for such sundry side demands as the revocation of court sentences against criminals convicted of treasonable acts committed in favor of Germany. Ironically, the Two Hundred were energetically supported in their efforts to muzzle their own press by the Swiss minister in Berlin, who tirelessly urged Bern to force all Swiss newspapers to delete any negative or unfriendly references to Germany; the realistic accounts of the Wehrmacht's difficulties in waging the Battle of Britain were particularly unwelcome to the Germans. Bern initially rejected the petition, and even began to look into the activities of those who had signed the document, but the investigations were soon dropped.

Meanwhile, Pilet-Golaz was making his inclination to appeasement ominously ever more concrete. German aircrews and aircraft landing in Switzerland (as well as those forced down by Swiss fighters[48]) were freed to return to Germany. Bern sent a delegation to Berlin to inquire as to how the Swiss economy might be made to interact more fruitfully with that of the Reich. Perhaps most startling in its pro-German toadying, the ban on importing Nazi newspapers into Switzerland was lifted, though it goes without saying that no free Swiss papers were ever allowed into Germany.

•   •   •

While this political struggle between the pro- and anti-German forces in the higher reaches of Swiss society went on, Guisan drew on his military authority to forge ahead with the redoubt. Since he was firmly in possession of the confidence of the overwhelming majority of the Swiss people, the difficult realities in his redoubt policy would fortunately be accepted as a warranted conclusion of what had to be done to save Switzerland were it invaded by Germany.

The essential idea of the redoubt was that it would serve as a truncated stronghold, a symbol of both national survival and sovereignty in the event of German invasion. Part of the inspiration for the plan came from the Belgian experience in World War I, when King Albert and his government held out against the Germans in the northwest corner of the country from 1914 until the war's end in 1918. The original plan for a larger Swiss redoubt envisioned holding a line in the north, from the end of the Maginot fortifications in the west to the (former) Austrian border in the east. With circumstances changed by Italy's entry into the war in the spring of 1940, the concept of the redoubt was geographically refigured south, to the Swiss center, between areas of a potential joint German-Italian invasion on both north and south margins of the country.

Guisan's working plan for the redoubt had been in the hands of his commanders within a month of the Compiègne armistice. Its basics weren't kept from the Germans, who were meant to be influenced in their own planning by the military strength inherent in it, and many of the redoubt's particulars were openly discussed in the press in an effort to raise Swiss morale.

As to its chief attributes, the redoubt was to be an elliptical circle enclosing the whole central Alpine area of Switzerland. The strongpoints were the Fortress St. Maurice in the west, near the east end of Lake Geneva, and the Fortress Sargans in the east, just west of the southern tip of Liechtenstein. In the center the Fortress St. Gotthard protected the St. Gotthard tunnel, a fundamental element in the concept's success as a deterrent to German invasion. The equally critical Simplon tunnel lay on the southern edge of the redoubt. This southern edge followed the high mountain chain, the Matterhorn most prominent, that formed the frontier with Mussolini's Italy. Though a number of small industrial cities lay within the perimeter of the redoubt, the strategy of necessity required that the country's largest cities, all located on relatively flat plains, be abandoned to invaders.

Guisan's concept was designed to be as flexible as possible. As had been the defense plan since the war's beginning, the actual national frontiers were still set with elasticized forward-defense measures to take up the brunt of an invasion, while giving the main armed force time to fall back into second and third lines of defense based on the heavily fortified ring of the redoubt itself. It was envisioned that if the army was forced to retreat into the redoubt, it would be virtually unreachable by an invading force. From such safety, Swiss defenders could harass their pursuers indefinitely. An additional plus in Guisan's logic was the knowledge that Berlin's calculations could not take surprise into account in attacking Switzerland, as it had done, for example, with Norway and the Netherlands.

About one-quarter of the Swiss population lived within the roughly 400-mile perimeter of the redoubt, leaving the inescapable fact that about three-quarters did not. From this emanated significant political and psychological reverberations.[49] Not only were the major cities, including the federal capital, left out of what was meant to be unoccupied post-invasion Switzerland, but there was no chance whatsoever that anything like the majority of the Swiss people could be saved—no plans were ever envisioned that would move everyone to the redoubt. Amazingly, the great majority of the Swiss people, in part influenced by the patriotic tone of the press, accepted the necessity and moral logic of the national redoubt as the pro-Guisan forces rationalized it. Rather than lose all, most Swiss reasoned, it was preferable to save the core of the nation as a nucleus which would carry on the struggle.[50]

In this massively fortified center, the nation's identity would be preserved whatever might come. Most vitally, the two supremely important Alpine tunnels, the St. Gotthard and the Simplon, would be held as Guisan's ultimate strategic nest egg, ready to be instantly blown to bits should German forces break through the redoubt's protective barriers. Chiseled into the mountains that formed the essence of the redoubt would be a chain of fortresslike communities, each supplied with power plants, dormitories, stores of all kinds stocked with necessities calculated to last the defenders three years, hospitals, even a gymnasium in which the inhabitants—both defending soldiers and managing bureaucrats—could keep themselves fit.

• • •

Because the country's economy unavoidably depended on German sufferance for imports of raw materials and exports of finished products, Switzerland had lost a sizable part of its economic sovereignty. And because it now found itself surrounded by German, or German-controlled, or German-allied territory, the September 1, 1940, Nazi decree that placed all Swiss imports under Axis control became an unalterable obstacle to its former free trade. Every day the Swiss business community was forced to deal with the burden of securing German permits for nearly everything coming into and going out of the country. Conversely, trade with the Allies virtually ended. The 17 percent of the confederation's prewar exports shipped to Britain, for example, was cut to almost nothing by 1940.[51] Paradoxically, some of the products that the Germans would have permitted Switzerland to receive from the Allied countries—primarily bulk foodstuffs—were denied entry by the Allies themselves, who withheld navicerts (for shipment into Genoa, landlocked Switzerland's leased "home port") for fear they would be resold or transshipped to Germany.

In the war's opening months, the initial German blockade forced Switzerland to switch from civilian export production to military production, goods bought by all the belligerents and which brought back 1938 export levels by the spring of 1940. But with the fall of France in June of that year, exports again dropped dramatically, though within another twelve months purchases by the Axis partners and their allies again returned the nation's export total to the 1938 figures. With the blocs now unable to bid against each other, Germany effectively set prices after June 1940, cutting Switzerland's profits and in some cases forcing the Swiss to sell armaments below cost.[52] Bern defended the loss policy on the basis that it at least kept Swiss factories in production, thereby enabling the country to produce weapons for its own defense, the Swiss Army's sting depending in large part on its own domestically produced armaments.

Among the gravest wartime shortages Switzerland endured was gasoline, the last dribble of free access being cut off in the spring of 1941 after Germany arrogated the Balkan oil fields. Of the 120,000 automobiles registered in the country in August 1939, within two years only 15,000 would be in normal daily operation. The army maintained its own gasoline reserve, but was able to avoid drawing down on it by tapping civilian stockpiles the government had astutely set aside in September 1939. Private motorists had only their private stocks to use, and then only in rationed amounts; car owners without reserves—the great majority, of course—were forced to put their vehicles in storage.[53]

One of the lessons Switzerland learned from World War I was that the mobilization of so much of the nation's manpower would disastrously skew the economy if measures weren't taken to mitigate the consequences. Hence, one difference between the two wars was that this time activated reservists collected an amount comparable to their civilian salaries out of a national compensation fund, a fund to which employers and employees, as well as the cantons and the federal government, contributed. This enlightened compensatory policy spread the nation's economic difficulties relatively evenly across the population.[54]

* * *

As though Guisan weren't troubled enough trying to divine German intentions, the nagging matter of the secret joint-defense planning with France since the prior summer continued to haunt him. With France now out of the war, the issue itself had, of course, become a dead letter. But Guisan felt constrained to conceal from Germany knowledge that the two countries had ever gotten together to work out a joint defense against a Wehrmacht attack on Switzerland. Either the secret notes on the negotiations and planning or the formal agreements between Paris and Bern would, if discovered by Berlin, embarrass, not to say endanger, Switzerland. Guisan wanted no smoking guns for the Nazis to use in one of their weird justifications to attack a free country.

The Swiss copies of the secret documents were safely locked away at Guisan's headquarters. The French copies, though, were another matter. After Compiègne, they had been evacuated from Paris and stored in a railway car at La Charité-sur-Loire, a town north of Vichy named for its ancient Cluniac priory; there on June 16 invading Germans unfortunately found them. Though many Frenchmen were privy to the plans for a military move into Switzerland and such information would have certainly reached German ears after the French capitulation, with the actual agreements in hand Bern would face a very difficult time denying the cooperation between the two countries that had the Reich as its objective.

As it happened, German interest in the matter was considerable. A special study group set up in Berlin under Hans Adolf von Moltke found that the Reich had gained itself a very sharp knife to hold to Switzerland's throat. As Berlin saw it, the papers clearly compromised Bern's stance of "absolute" neutrality, and Switzerland could be construed as having consorted in a warlike way with Germany's enemy. One of the most vocal of the high-ranking Nazis wishing to exploit the find as an excuse to invade Switzerland was Foreign Minister Joachim von Ribbentrop. Ribbentrop and like-thinking SS leaders believed the papers could, at the very least, be used to blackmail Pilet-Golaz into firing Guisan, the peskiest Swiss nettle under the Nazi saddle.

In the end, Berlin decided to keep the papers under wraps, waiting for a more opportune time to use them. The Reich's Foreign Ministry hoped that eventually publication of the documents would scare the Swiss government and people so badly as to prime the country for a domestic National Socialist takeover, the first but necessary step to the eventual easy subsumation of at least the German-speaking parts of the country into the Greater Reich.

Guisan, whose Berlin moles informed him of the La Charité-sur-Loire find, understood the advantage it had handed Germany. When in late 1942 and early 1943 the German high command came to believe an Allied attack on the Axis might be driven through Switzerland, more than ever because of the papers Guisan would be forced to convince Berlin that his army would fight such a move with its full efforts.[55]

. . .

Still another aggravation came to the beleaguered little country, this time from its neighbor to the south. The Italian citizenry couldn't learn from their own fettered press how bad things were going for Mussolini's bungling army, but they *could* find out all about it from the Swiss newspapers. The Italian government thus banned the import of several offending papers, including the *Tribune de Genève*, with a snarling warning to the Swiss press to stop printing what it characterized as "unneutral" war news. The Italian press predictably took up the cry, with the *Popolo de Brescia* vowing:

> We will place the name of Switzerland, which for months has allowed air violation by enemy aircraft, side by side with that of our detested enemy. The fate of Greece and Turkey already is sealed, so is the fate of the little mercantile, intellectually dull, anti-Italian and anti-German Swiss.[56]

There is little evidence that the Italian threats had much effect on their intended targets.

Stockholm

The German attack in the West stunned Europe's remaining neutral governments. With the sovereignty of Luxembourg, Belgium, and the Netherlands trampled for having gotten in Hitler's path to Compiègne, it became finally, unmistakably clear to the remaining nonbelligerents that mere declarations of neutrality were worthless. And nowhere was the danger to neutrality now heightened so explosively as in Sweden. The peril no longer centered on iron ore—Germany had gained enormous supplies of that valuable commodity in Lorraine and Luxembourg. Rather it was the question of German military transit rights over Swedish territory, a matter Berlin treated with the highest gravity, and one that still stood a good chance of sparking a war in Scandinavia's sole remaining haven of peace.

. . .

Herman Göring's association with Sweden long predated the Nazi era. In the winter of 1920, while in Sweden toiling as an air-taxi operator, the rakish and then still trim Great War air hero was introduced by his friend Count Eric von Rosen to the nobleman's sister, Carin von Kantzow. Born Baroness Fock, the attractive aristocrat, prominent in Swedish society but bored by an uncongenial marriage to an army officer, saw in the German the romance and excitement her life was missing. Göring seemed to be just the ticket to such exhilaration: a man who had been the last commander of the Richthofen squadron and holder of the Pour le Mérite, imperial Germany's highest military distinction, he was also agreeably and ardently charming. The flier and the noblewoman fell in love, the dissolution of her own marriage to marry Göring begetting one of Sweden's most celebrated society scandals of the day.

The newlyweds made their home in Munich. There the epileptic Carin contracted tuberculosis, causing her return to Sweden in 1927. Her husband, having remained in Germany, was in those years enjoying a nimble rise in the new National Socialist Party and becoming a political figure of substance, though his own ills—morphine addition and the traumatic "cures" employed to overcome it—made his personal life painful even as his public position skyrocketed. For a time the drug struggle jeopardized his career in the growing Nazi Party, but by the end of the 1920s Göring had sublimated his addiction enough to rise to a position as principal underling of his party's Führer.

In October 1931, three years after rejoining her husband in Germany and ravaged by debilitating heart and lung disease, Carin Göring died. Deeply grieved by his wife's death, the future *Reichsmarschall* lost what one biographer called the only person—or thing—he would ever truly love. But through Carin von Kantzow, Herman Göring had established deep contacts with Sweden's upper class, and he had inexorably come, in his characteristically egotistical way, to think of himself as Sweden's most important friend in the new Germany.

· · ·

On May 6, 1940, Swedish businessman Birger Dahlerus arrived at Karinhall, the pleasure palace belonging to his old friend Göring. The lavish estate, set in the dense woods of northern Brandenburg, had been named by the marshal for the wife who had given Göring what he held to be the singular credentials to manage the transit stalemate between Sweden and the Reich. On this specially bidden visit, Dahlerus didn't find himself in the presence of the jolly Hermann whom he had known before the outbreak of the war. Instead, Göring greeted the Swede with a bitter harangue against Sweden and Sweden's "attitude" toward Germany, declaring that Dahlerus's countrymen "had to learn that Europe had entered a new era"[57] in which the Great Powers expected small countries to do exactly as they were told—or else suffer the consequences. The substance of the ensuing audience was that Göring wanted the influential Dahlerus to impress on the Swedish cabinet Germany's seriousness in forwarding its demands for transit across Swedish territory.

Nazidom's chief paladin began the meeting stormily enough, but soon appeared to cool his temper and in a pleasanter guise offered Dahlerus two plans by which he "suggested" Sweden might comply without mortally compromising its neutrality, and thereby overcome Stockholm's "formalistic" objections. The options were to disguise the German traffic in sealed railroad cars under Red Cross auspices, or else contrive to make it appear Sweden had been "duped" by Germany, and would thus not be held responsible by the Allies for allowing German artillery to be delivered to Narvik. As to Swedish objections that either choice would end up hurting its Norwegian neighbor, Göring dismissed Dahlerus's concerns with the Nazi view that the battle in Narvik was between Germany and the Allies—that Norwegian troops were not themselves involved. (Norwegian troops were in fact serving alongside the Allies in the Narvik campaign.) The Swede responded that he himself wasn't empowered to make such a decision for the Swedish government, at which Göring told him to send back someone who was.

When after returning to Stockholm Dahlerus informed the cabinet of Göring's demands, Hansson quickly assessed the situation and decided to send a deputation to Berlin to "say some kind words but repeat our decision regarding weapons and ammunition." And in case Germany lashed out at Sweden for having received a reply it didn't want to hear, the cabinet authorized the transfer of an army division from Skåne, in the south, to Värmland, on the Norwegian border, where it surmised a Wehrmacht attack or invasion would most likely take place.

The new negotiating party included Gunnar Hägglöf, head of the Foreign Affairs Ministry commercial department, Admiral Fabian Tamm, and Dahlerus. Their meeting with Göring took place on May 11, one day after the Wehrmacht descended on the West. The trio of Swedes opened the interview by informing the *Reichsmarschall* that the objections Dahlerus had outlined to Göring at Karinhall still stood: Sweden would not permit its neutrality to be jeopardized by acceding to German transit demands beyond what they had already allowed. Furious, Göring blasted the Swedes about their lack of faith in the forthcoming German victory, after which he taunted the only professional envoy present, who had just confirmed the inflexibility of the Swedish refusal: "You, Herr Hägglöff, are a hidebound jurist and diplomatist; you understand nothing about the fate of nations." Undaunted, Hägglöf responded that to do Germany's bidding in this matter would be an unforgivable and unchivalrous breach of trust to Norway. After muttering about "a few bombing attacks" perhaps changing Swedish minds, Göring dismissed his "guests." At this juncture, with its military intelligence revealing that German occupation troops in Norway were starting to mass on its border, Sweden put its military forces in a state of highest military readiness.

Next up to bat for the Reich (for the second time) in the increasingly grave matter was its icy and utterly humorless foreign minister, Joachim von Ribbentrop. Summoning Arvid Richert, the Swedish minister in Berlin, to Bad Godesberg, where Hitler had established his Western command post, Ribbentrop again put forth the Reich's case for the transit rights. After the foreign minister archly informed the diplomat that international law actually did not prevent a neutral country allowing a belligerent to transship war material on its territory, Ribbentrop came to the heart of the matter by pointing out the "factors of *Realpolitik*" that were involved. Should Sweden continue in its refusal, so Ribbentrop went, the chances of its becoming involved in the war would be greatly heightened if Britain and France were not driven out of Narvik and the struggle were to spread across the whole of the North.

The next day, Ribbentrop's "request" was clarified for Richert by Ernst von Weizsäcker, the principal German state secretary and the real brains in a Foreign Ministry titularly headed by the agonizingly arrogant Ribbentrop. Weizsäcker, precisely spelled out what Germany would require: a total of three trains, each with thirty to forty sealed carriages containing artillery, antiaircraft guns, and ammunition, as well as clothing and sundry communications and engineering equipment. Though the *Staatssekretär* downplayed Narvik's strategic importance, he let it be known that the Führer "expected" Sweden's compliance and would be "disappointed" if it were not forthcoming. Richert left for Stockholm immediately to present the demands to the cabinet.

There the prime minister, unanimously supported by his cabinet, declared that to assent to the demands was "unthinkable." Hansson knew that the shipments Berlin wanted would represent only a fraction of Narvik's long-term needs and that caving in would unquestionably lead to further German demands.

But the voices for accommodation to the Reich were powerful. The king's emissary in Berlin urged Hansson and his fellow ministers to accede to the German demands, warning that a refusal to do so would result in a Nazi attack on Sweden. Besides Richert, the military commander-in-chief, Olof Thörnell, advised acceptance, cautioning that the nation's state of military preparedness was hardly in a position to take on the Wehrmacht. Thörnell's readiness to comply was based on the simple logic that avoidance of war with Germany outweighed every other factor.

Throughout Hansson's government's deliberations on the transit question, Britain's interest in Sweden's decision constituted another critical element in the dilemma. Through diplomatic channels London made it clear to Stockholm that if Sweden became "considered as completely dependent" on Germany, His Majesty's government would take it as its right to prevent the export of iron ore to the Reich by whatever means would be required, even at the risk of Sweden's defending itself by joining the German side in the war. Britain had even issued "preparatory orders" for mining the Swedish ore-shipment port of Luleå at the head of the Gulf of Bothnia, though they were canceled on the rationale that the political repercussions would outweigh the advantage of such a course.

When Richert returned to Berlin on the eighteenth to inform Weizsäcker of his government's decision (the Swedish military was still on the highest state of alert—*givakt*, or "attention"—with all leaves canceled), the diplomat explained the decision primarily as a matter of honor, that to do otherwise would be an unforgivable act of treason against the Nordic sense of community. Richert knew Hitler tended to disregard his Foreign Ministry bureaucrats, so the relatively "friendly" manner in which the state secretary took the news was itself, he later assured Stockholm, no guarantee that Sweden's decision wouldn't lead to a German invasion. Richert, who had already counseled acquiescence to the Reich, wrote his government that

> I am deeply and seriously anxious about the future for our country if the government intends to hold unyieldingly to the course. . . . The devastation of the country and the definitive loss of our people's freedom can be the consequences of this policy, which soon enough can show itself to be a policy of sheer suicide.[58]

During the last critical days of the Allied-German military standoff in Narvik, a desperate Swedish diplomatic proposal may have played a part in keeping the Germans negotiating with Stockholm rather than taking more direct military actions to get what they wanted. Hansson proposed that Narvik and the surrounding area of northern Norway be neutralized under Swedish protection. All belligerent forces—Allied and Axis— would be withdrawn, with Sweden guaranteeing that the northern Norwegian coastal area would not be used by naval forces of either side to further their ends in the North Sea. Little chance existed that a triumphant Reich would accept such a proposal, regardless of the difficulties in keeping Narvik supplied. But while the cabinet promoted the idea, it may have had some utility for the feint it provided at the height of the crisis, giving Sweden critical additional days to plan for the German invasion it now expected at any moment.[59] Meanwhile, the nearly solid opposition in the cabinet to accepting the transit demands was weakening, not only because of Richert's continued urging but because King Gustav made it known he did not wish to risk war with Germany by continuing to refuse its demands. Still, though, Hansson stood firm.

When the Allied assault on Narvik finally began on May 28, the crisis reached its climax for Sweden. A combination of Britons, French, Poles, and Norwegians pushed the Germans back from Narvik into the mountainous region bordering Sweden. It was at this point that Hitler ordered his commanding officer in Narvik, General Dietl, to retreat into Sweden and have his forces interned rather than risk capture at the hands of the Allies. But just as Dietl reached the end of his resources, fate intervened to resolve the crisis. London and Paris made the hard decision to withdraw their forces to the collapsing Western front, where it was judged they were needed more critically than in Norway. This act effectively ended the Norwegian campaign—and, with it, perhaps the threat to Sweden of German invasion.

Though Hitler wanted to avoid taking on Sweden at this juncture, one at which the victorious Wehrmacht was about to finish off France, there is little question that a concerted effort by the Wehrmacht would have succeeded in subduing the kingdom if the Narvik force appeared about to succumb. The loss of Swedish ore—blown up by its owners— would have been a serious consequence, but to a Reich on the verge of complete victory, and with new access to French ore, such a short-term loss (the ore fields would have been repairable, after all) might well have been judged an acceptable price to pay for a completely neutralized Sweden. Finally, Hitler's personal inclinations remained relevant in the face-off: Hägglöf was told in Berlin that Hitler would never permit his "heroes of Narvik" to succumb because of Stockholm's stubbornness on the transit question.[60]

The withdrawal of the British and French expeditionary forces from their Norwegian venture on June 8, and the subsequent collapse of Norway's resistance, changed Germany's immediate stakes in the issue of supplying Narvik. But Berlin would continue to regard the presence of its troops in the Scandinavian Far North as vital. The capacity to safely and relatively easily rotate and supply those troops remained dependent on crossing Swedish territory connecting Narvik with the Gulf of Bothnia. And though the Allies had given up in Norway itself, the Royal Navy still made the Norwegian North Sea coast a risky place for German transport ships.

The Allied collapse in Norway, and soon in France, portended wider consequences for Sweden, in that it now became completely isolated and removed from any possibility of Western help. Further, the Swedes' economic dependence on the Reich for vital supplies went from substantial to nearly total. Now that it was squeezed between these two unpalatable realities, the Swedish government's reckoning of what constituted neutrality would almost certainly have to be reweighed. The Norwegian fight was over, and for Sweden to allow German access to Narvik across its territory would not, in its view newly calculated by necessity, be prejudicial to Norway's own interests.

Berlin was now equally aware that Sweden's principal argument in refusing the transit rights—the unwillingness to injure the still fighting Norway—had been eliminated. The chief of the Wehrmacht's general staff, General Wilhelm Keitel, told Ribbentrop that the issue must now be settled with Stockholm, adding that the need was as acute as ever to reprovision not only the Narvik area but Norway in general. With the force of Hitler's approval of Keitel's logic, Ribbentrop hurriedly summoned Richert to Hitler's headquarters in occupied Belgium, there to reiterate the transit demands. Germany now "expected" Sweden to comply to the transport through Sweden of an *unlimited* amount of all kinds of war matériel, and of German troops, particularly those going to and returning from leave. Richert was instructed to report to his government that a refusal would be considered a "plainly unfriendly action,"[61] a not inconsiderable threat in the circumstances of the day.

Though the stakes were no longer as high for Germany, Richert still couched his report to the cabinet in terms of the disastrous consequences of a negative response. Such a reaction "would in my opinion lead to the most far-reaching, perhaps catastrophic consequences for our country. . . ."[62] Richert's views were clearly shaped by events in France, where the magnitude of the German victory was overwhelming. The diplomat reasoned that now that the Wehrmacht had mopped up one of its two principal Allied enemies, finishing off the other would only be a matter of time. Berlin would then have little reason not to do as it wished with Sweden too.

Further muddying these muddy waters was a related incident that has since become a footnote in history: the so-called Prytz telegram. This cable was sent on June 18 from Björn Prytz, the Swedish minister in Britain, to the cabinet in Stockholm as a warning about Britain's proposed course now that its French ally was beaten. The message's central postulation was that the British government was looking for a way out of the war—a "reasonable" accommodation with Germany—and that in the effort to achieve these ends Churchill stood in danger of being replaced by his foreign minister, the infinitely less defiant Lord Halifax.[63] The Swedes would correctly assume that should such a development come to pass, it would represent the final isolation of Sweden, leaving it vulnerable to Nazi retribution if it continued in its attempt at evenhandedness toward the belligerents. For many years after the war, London denied the telegram's existence and, by extension, that such measures were under consideration. But the information from its London mission did influence, as did the other indications that further resistance was no longer in the country's interests, the decision Sweden would soon take to succumb to the pressure from the Reich.

On June 18, in the face of a renewed German threat that rejection of its transit demands would result in "coercive measures"[64] against Sweden, Hansson's cabinet agreed to German requirements, and the Riksdag was formally informed in secret session three days later.[65] The pressure on Sweden had simply become too great for it to any longer hew to the neutrality it had up to this time sought to follow with near-judicial scrupulousness.

Though the Swedes wanted to hold German transit demands to the lowest level possible, Berlin's "requirements" soon turned out to be far more extensive than Stockholm had hoped. Hansson's government anticipated keeping the traffic at two trains per week, but in the end the German demand for a daily train was acceded to. Most of the Wehrmacht personnel transported could be categorized as "on leave" (and weaponless except for officers' sidearms), with total numbers theoretically balanced between those going in each direction; the Swedish railway was not, according to the agreement, supposed to be used for a *buildup* of German personnel in the Norwegian north. The "horseshoe traffic"—in which troops and war matériel could be moved from one point in Norway to another via Sweden—was also approved by Hansson. A final concession to the Reich—not revealed until 1946—was permission for Germany to lay submarine nets in Swedish waters in the Öresund, the narrow, riverlike strait separating Sweden from Denmark at their closest points.[66]

To the Swedish people, Premier Hansson justified his government's compromise with the observation that "we in our country cannot disregard the course of events which has seen seven European countries wholly or partially occupied . . ."[67] As unpalatable as the consequences of the government's decision were to the vast majority of the Swedish people, and as widely criticized as they were at the time, the relief that an excuse for imminent invasion of the country had been removed was unmistakable.

Though Sweden withdrew its legations (but not its consular officials) from German-occupied countries, it refused to grant official recognition to the Norwegian government-in-exile in London. Hansson reasoned that to do so would give Germany grounds to demand the withdrawal of the Swedish consul general in Oslo, which if acceded to would have in turn frustrated Stockholm's ability to give Norway what help it could during its occupation. The Swedish government did maintain unofficial contact with the Norwegians in London through its mission to the Court of St. James's.[68]

Britain realistically held the transit agreement to be something forced on the Swedes by a very much more powerful adversary, and refused to condemn the country as the equivalent of a belligerent for doing so. But Sweden's relations with the still neutral American government were altered by the transit agreement. In October, the State Department informed Stockholm that the United States would henceforth bar export licenses for war matériel to Sweden, and 110 airplanes already ordered by the Swedes from American manufacturers would not be shipped as they were now needed for "training purposes."[69]

In one respect, the Swedish isolation confirmed by the collapse in the West brought some benefit to the Allies. Swedish shipping had been harassed and in some cases destroyed by German naval attacks since the war began the prior September; by the time Germany invaded Russia in mid-1941, Swedish merchant marine losses to German fire would amount to 400,000 tons, a level that caused serious shortage of necessary imports. The German blockade, initiated in the spring of 1940, meant the cessation of half the country's overseas shipping (the half not going to the Axis). But when that blockade began, about half of the Swedish merchant fleet was caught in waters west of the Baltic, their captains seeking asylum in Allied, mainly British, ports. Sweden formally leased these ships to the Allies, an act of certainly questionable neutrality, accruing heavily to the West's favor, and which is frequently overlooked in the often negative light in which Sweden was seen by the victors during the immediate postwar years. Granted the ships were unable to return to Swedish ports, but some or all of them could have been sailed to neutral ports to avoid German ire. The action taken by the Swedish government represented the basic anti-Nazi, pro-Allied sentiments that bubbled just below the surface of much of wartime Sweden.

The near-term domestic consequences of Sweden's actions were reflected mainly as a kind of self-disgust, not only for the damage the agreement was seen to do to the Norwegians but for the sustenance it gave a regime close to unanimously regarded by Swedes as odious. Though it was its active trade with Germany that the world would longer remember as the principal criticism of that neutral nation's actions during the war, it was the transit issue that the Swedes themselves came to look upon in the bleak war years as most repugnant. This breach of neutrality affected not only Sweden but in the larger sense Norway, a neighbor and as close a cousin as one nation can be to another, that became a real and personal victim of the moving of German soldiers and matériel via the rails of a neutral. In response to the official Norwegian protest against Sweden's actions, Hansson replied that the Norwegian government-in-exile "is certainly aware that any neutrality policy has its limits in the means available to the neutral state in the assertion of this policy." Though this skewing of its foreign policy in the direction of the Reich was highly unpalatable to most Swedes, in retrospect it was probably the only realistic course the nation could have taken. Lamentably, events would shortly transpire that would require an even greater compromising of the nation's sovereignty to the Nazi colossus.

· · ·

In its new relationship with the Reich came other reminders of Sweden's diminished dominion over its own affairs. Press freedom, already compromised at the Reich's insistence by a government anxious to keep anti-German and pro-Allied views out of the country's newspapers, soon grew increasingly strict. The Gothenburg *Handelstidningen* found the government suppressing a number of its editions after that paper reported too thoroughly and in too anti-Nazi a tone the transit question. Zeth Höglund, editor of the *Social-Demokraten*, wrote on April 9, 1940:

> With the exception of a few isolated newspapers that still uphold their independence, there no longer is a really free press in this country. The public must keep this fact in mind when reading comments upon this or that international event. There is still liberty of expression on issues of municipal interest, and such things as the theater or sports. Foreign policy, by contrast, is taboo. Step by step the Swedish press has been regimented and muzzled . . .[70]

One of the tools used by the government to enforce its suppression of the nation's newspapers and magazines was an old press law making it a criminal offense to insult the head of a foreign state or to "endanger the good relations between Sweden and foreign powers." The editors' arguments that these provisions had not been enforced for more than a century and thus effectively abrogated by time were ignored by Hansson's press overseers. Warnings, seizures, and indictments would eventually be meted out against more than a hundred newspapers and magazines. In the face of such actions and to their credit, some editors remained willing to risk having their papers shut down, to keep both their editorial principles unsullied and their readers apprised of the finer points of Nazi behavior.

Though the government framed its restrictions in a cloak of impartiality to both sides, it was, understandably, only Germany's ire that worried Hansson's government. More specifically, it was a fear that the Nazi threats of "reprisal" would in some way be carried out. The government's lopsided accommodations were rationalized as a "reasonable adjustment" to the realities of the country's imperiled situation, one of many such "reasonable adjustments" the Swedes would make to get through the war unscathed. A circular jointly issued by the private Press Council and the government Information Board illustrates some of the "guidelines" editors were expected to obey to keep their papers from confiscation: "If communiqués from the belligerent powers regarding one and the same matter do not correspond, it is inadvisable to adopt an attitude which supports one side or the other" . . . "As far as the material received permits, attempts should be made not to give prominence to the reports of one side at the expense of the other" . . . "Derogatory statements which cast a slur on the actions of foreign armed forces, unless fully confirmed, must be carefully avoided" . . . "Headlines, whether on the billboards or in the newspapers, should be worded in such a way as to avoid favoring one side or the other" . . . "Editorials and surveys, as well as articles discussing military events or the military situation, should be strictly objective."[71] These rules were difficult to follow and easy to transgress, and the outcome was that many newspapers simply avoided substantive reporting on the war.

One Stockholm paper's German sympathies were eventually reversed. The *Aftonbladet* was a daily of considerable circulation and not merely one of the relatively crude sheets that characterized much of the pro-German press. When hard facts about Nazi frightfulness became widely known outside Germany, the *Aftonbladet*'s editorial board printed some sharply worded columns condemning the Reich's behavior. This led the offended local Nazis to buy a newspaper of their own in Stockholm, the *Dagposten*. The *Dagposten* never achieved as large a circulation as the *Aftonbladet*, but its commercial space was always filled with advertising from Germany companies, evidence of the ongoing funding the local keepers of the Nazi flame received from their tutors across the Baltic.

Few of the Swedish Nazis were prominent. Sven Hedin, the nationally respected arctic explorer whose bent toward German intellectualism degenerated into apologism for the Nazi regime, and whom we've already discussed, was best known both at home and abroad. Other than Hedin, Torsten Krueger earned the worst reputation for forwarding Berlin's cause in neutral Sweden. Brother of the late Ivar Krueger, who was the principal in one of Europe's most notorious financial scandals a decade earlier, Torsten sprang from a family of local social prominence. Publisher of two Stockholm dailies, including the aforementioned *Aftonbladet*, he too got himself involved in a financial scandal, specifically misrepresenting his financial situation to enhance the salability of securities. He went to prison for several months, an experience that perhaps accounts for his resentment toward the government and subsequent willingness to take up the cause of a regime threatening to that government's existence. Torsten Krueger's morning paper, the *Stockholm-Tidningen*, managed a less outspokenly pro-German tone than the *Aftonbladet*.

The summer of 1940 witnessed the high-water mark of German influence in Sweden, and by autumn the tide began to change as it became apparent that Britain was not going to collapse in spite of France's fall. The realization resulted in a newfound courage that prompted popular anti-Nazi demonstrations among Swedes disgusted with the Reich's bullying. As more reports came into the country of German brutalities—particularly those against Norwegians—the general Swedish attitude toward Nazi Germany hardened. Though such popular sentiment didn't affect the government's accommodation to German transit demands, at least the overwhelming fear of Germany now began to subside.[72]

Even while Swedes continued to steel themselves to face down the Reich, Germany persevered in flooding the country with spies whose mission was to "study the possibilities" for an attack on Sweden should the country renege on its trade or transit agreements.[73] In the two months preceding the Nazi attack on the Soviet Union, more than a thousand Germans entered Sweden, including a group of thirty-one architects who roamed the country to inspect the "architecture of farmhouses and rural electrification systems," a subject that could have been of little interest to a Germany on the verge of launching the greatest military attack in history. When the Berlin Philharmonic Society visited Sweden, its delegation included, in addition to its 102 members, an extra thirty "non-musician" observers. Perhaps most ominous were the countless tourists of military age whom the Reich unaccountably allowed to take wartime "vacations" on the islands scattered around the Swedish coastline.

Sometimes the Swedish government was able to actually catch a Nazi spy red-handed. As he traveled about the country making "geographical movies," the Gothenburg police arrested one H. Torin, of Cuban nationality. Head of a film company that purportedly made educational films, Torin was detained by the Gothenburg authorities for showing unwarranted curiosity in areas held to be of more military than geographical interest. On questioning, Señor Torin confessed his true German nationality, and the fact that he was under orders from the Reich's general staff to get as much firsthand information on Swedish defenses as possible.[74] For every Torin, though, many more spies were able to elude a Swedish police force still bound by the civilized rules of evidence that no longer applied to its counterpart in the Reich.

In addition to the press censorship carried out because of the government's desire to placate a snarling Reich, writers also found their work suppressed, with some arrested for their pro-Allied or anti-German out-spokenness. Works like *I Saw It Happen in Norway* by Storting president Carl Joachim Hambro and *Hitler Speaks* by Herman Rauschning were examples of books the authorities believed might give dangerous offense to the Reich.[75]

The same censorship applied to virtually every field of entertainment or artistic endeavor in wartime Sweden. Radio, theater, and the film industry were all subjected to official scrutiny for content that might be considered slanted against the Reich. Not only were anti-Nazi remarks taboo in any of these branches of the media; the artist himself could be subjected to economic hardship if he continued to express views contrary to official policy.

The popular stage actor Karl-Gerhard, called the "Swedish Aristophanes" for his multi-layered activities in the theatrical world, was victim of one example of suppression. His satiric piece *That Notorious Trojan Horse* lasted a single night before complaints from the German mission caused the police to close the actor's show and issue him a severe warning not to repeat his mistake.[76] Another artist, writer Joachim Joesten, concluded that his country had sunk "to the level of a Nazi province."

But by the late summer of 1940, the indigenous Swedish Nazis were having a hard time getting their message heard. With the ominous reports trickling into the country disclosing Nazi treatment of captive peoples, most Swedes—including even former adherents of the Nazi siren—came to regard National Socialism as irretrievably repugnant. When domestic Nazis tried to share a Conservative Party meeting in Dalarne in order to disseminate their own propaganda, the angry Conservatives physically attacked them, and only police intervention kept the situation from escalating into violence. In another outburst, Swedish Nazis attempting to stage a demonstration in Trelleborg infuriated the local residents so much that police intercession was again necessary to keep the groups from each other's necks. Little question exists as to official Sweden's compromising its honor under the threat confronting the kingdom, but ordinary Swedish citizens had by this point in the war come to understand the moral depths to which their Nordic cousins had descended.

Dublin

The prospect of being invaded by Britain dominated Irish thinking in the year after the fall of France. Indeed, by December 1940, the probability of British invasion of Eire to secure air and, especially, naval bases was considered so great that the government placed Eire's army on the highest state of alert. De Valera calculated an attack would come not only at Dublin but also in Donegal, the far northwestern county in which lay burrowed the Treaty Port and naval base of Lough Swilly. The widely separated positions of the expected penetrations forced the Taoiseach into the hazardous splitting of the island's still puny armed forces, a situation de Valera's military commanders viewed with trepidation.

An expanding list of warning signs led Dublin to anticipate a British move against Eire. For one thing, the British press's attitude toward Irish neutrality reached new heights of vituperation. De Valera held that the campaign was directed at the Irish people, a population Fleet Street wished to believe disagreed with its leaders on the question of the Twenty-six Counties remaining out of the war. Dublin in turn supposed White-hall was directing Fleet Street, with the campaign a likely prelude to military action against the island.

To make a grim situation worse, it wasn't only the prospect of British invasion worrying Dublin that summer. On July 16, the Dominions Office in London informed de Valera that it had information that a German invasion of Ireland was to have taken place six days before, though it offered no explanation why the planned attack hadn't occurred. Four days later, London again notified Dublin of imminent danger from Germany, that in fact it believed an invasion was scheduled for the following day. In the absence of any more detailed intelligence to confirm the likelihood of what would have been an enormous undertaking on the part of the Wehrmacht, de Valera might have been justified in a suspicion Britain was fielding such rumors to serve as an excuse to enter Eire to "protect" it from such aggression. The government could do little other than to re-avow its determination to thwart any attack, from any quarter, by any belligerent. Whatever the British motive in informing Eire of its danger from a German attack—whether it believed such to be imminent or whether it was indeed setting up a foundation on which to intervene—nothing more was heard of a Wehrmacht landing in the dominion.

In any case, the weakness of Eire's military position rendered its bravado essentially hollow. In the first place, the government, hopeful that Britain and Germany would overcome their differences, had squandered the opportunity offered by the Phony War to shore up its utterly inadequate armed forces. In consequence, after the attack on France, Dublin began desperately appealing to the United States for weapons. London concurred in the necessity for these weapons, but only on the understandable condition that any arms sent to Eire not take precedence over those already committed to Britain.[77] Though it is difficult to accept that Britain would approve *any* military aid to Eire while it continued to hector de Valera's government over the ports, it serves to manifest London's realization that a German invasion of an Ireland utterly incapable of defending itself would equally imperil Britain.

Despite British approval, Washington waffled on Dublin's appeals. It finally went London one better and informed de Valera that any arms would have to come out of the weaponry earmarked for Britain, *and* at Britain's discretion, in what was apparently Roosevelt's way of expressing his own growing displeasure at Irish neutrality. He told his emissary David Gray that Ireland was going to "have to fish or cut bait"[78]—yield to Britain in the matter of the ports or go without American help. Gray and Roosevelt were of a mind about Eire.

The fall of France transformed Eire's predicament. The Allied shield against a German invasion of the island had now been weakened immeasurably, while the Axis naval menace in the seas surrounding the island was now substantially increased. This meant yet a new concern for Dublin: Germany's magnified capacity to fetter the Irish economy by controlling what came into and went out of a country dependent on trade for its national well-being.

Though Germany set up an absolute blockade around the British Isles, an area incorporating the entirety of Ireland, Hempel made a proposal to the Dublin government that might lessen Eire's difficulties. Berlin propounded that the Twenty-six Counties would be exempt from the blockade provided Eire clearly marked its shipping and the government promised not to transship any goods to Britain, presumably including Ulster.

The motivation for the offer was, of course, more for whatever propaganda mileage it could derive from Dublin's grateful acceptance of German "magnanimity" than concern for the well-being of the Irish people. Berlin knew a German blockade would only serve to stress the ties Eire still maintained with Britain, that the two islands remained linked "for better or for worse."[79] Whatever its future plans for Ireland, the Reich had no desire to drive de Valera's dominion into Britain's camp before Britain itself was finally subdued—after which the testy Emerald Isle could be Germanized at Berlin's leisure.

Fearing London's wrath if he entered into an agreement of any kind with Germany, de Valera stalled on Hempel's offer. Though the British could well have regarded such an arrangement as a hostile act on Eire's part, the United Kingdom might also have benefited from such a concession: a German agreement to allow unrestricted amounts of animal feedstuffs into Eire could have translated into greater livestock exports to Britain, assuming the cargoes could be gotten safely across the mine-strewn Irish Sea. In any case, Dublin simply let the proposal sit unanswered. Berlin didn't push for a response, evidently being too pressed with other matters to worry much about concluding even a "prestige" agreement with a neutral government.[80]

In days already permeated with fears of invasion, evidence found in an IRA safe house disclosed German plans for the occupation of Northern Ireland. On June 27, a forty-three-year-old Dubliner with IRA connections, Stephen Held, was found guilty of aiding and abetting the dissemination of information "likely to prejudice the safety of the State" by having in his possession a wireless transmitting set. To de Valera, such incidents signaled a link between the IRA and its German co-conspirators,[81] a view resulting in his approval of talks between the Irish and British armies to take mutual measures to thwart an island-wide German landing. They indicated as well the Taoiseach's dissipating fears of a British takeover. Britain believed such talks and joint planning would be useful, but predictably held that an abandonment of Dublin's neutrality policy would have a very much better outcome for the overall defense of the British Isles.[82]

When Hitler finally scrapped a cross-Channel grab at Britain, widespread questioning began of how Hitler, having failed to cross the few miles between Calais and Dover, could then have his armies negotiate the 300 miles of open sea to reach Eire. But then between the Wehrmacht and England had stood a combined British air, land, and sea force among the toughest and best in the world (though admittedly then extended to the uttermost), while the Wehrmacht and Ireland were separated by only a handful of troops, a few coastal boats, and a minute air force. As writer Donald W. Mitchell wrote at the time of the danger to Britain:

> In enemy hands Ireland would . . . threaten the very existence of the British empire. Germany would have bases within close bombing distance of every point in England, bases which would so dominate shipping lines to the west that convoys would be a prey to submarines and planes of all types. Protecting British planes would have to operate farther from their bases than planes of the attacker. The life line across the Atlantic would be cut. Finally, Ireland is not to be despised as a possible land base from which Great Britain could be invaded by way of relatively unprepared Scotland and Wales.[83]

The assessment bore potently on Britain's strategic outlook in the dangerous days of 1940, particularly on its relationship with de Valera's troublesome domain.

As for Eire's outlook, de Valera always remained cynically aware that if Hitler were to make a move against his country, it would be the British—not his insubstantial army—who would have to repel it. We now know that Eire never stood in any substantive danger of a German invasion separate from a landing in Britain. But had such an assault on the larger island been successful, Northern Ireland would almost beyond question also have been occupied. And with nearly equal certainty, in that scenario the Twenty-six Counties would have eventually come under a more or less integrated German domination with Ulster. But Hitler decided early on in the war against an invasion of Ireland, probably at the same time he realized that taking Britain required a great deal more effort than he was willing to put into it—and which effort he would rather assign to the forthcoming Barbarossa. Instead, the German leader counted on neutral Eire to give him considerable advantages in the Battle of the Atlantic while allaying the certainty—to him—that an attack on Ireland would inevitably bring the United States and its not yet fully exploited but nonetheless vast resources into the war against the Axis. What was more, Hitler must have taken pleasure knowing the mere threat of a Wehrmacht invasion of Eire kept an entire motorized British division in Ulster, a division that might have been put to lethal effect in the Mediterranean campaign.

In spite of France's defeat and Eire's impotence, the perception of a German threat to Ireland slowly receded in both Dublin and London in the latter months of 1940, largely because it was becoming more evident in the two capitals that the British were neither going to go down in military defeat nor about to see their island invaded. With a still quick Britain on his hands, it was increasingly less likely that Hitler would launch his massive *Plan Seelöwe*—Operation Sealion—against that island, much less go on to invade Ireland.[84] Ireland itself as an invasion target was most cogently argued against by the German Navy, which reasoned that as long as Britain remained supreme in naval strength it could still check any German invasion. In fact, Britain's fleet superiority *was* overwhelming in relation to Germany's, with ratios of two to one in battleships, twenty to three in cruisers. Furthermore, any hope of employing surprise was out of the question because of Ireland's location. Equally out of the question was the prospect of developing secure supply lines, again because of Britain's superior naval standing. Even air support from its theoretically stronger air force was judged doubtful in its efficacy, primarily because Ireland's notoriously difficult weather could at almost any moment render air offense, defense, or supply unreliable.

But the peril to his island's neutrality did not in de Valera's view recede altogether. Instead, it reverted to renewed fears of a British invasion. Dublin continued to calculate that violation of Eire's neutral status would be far less worrisome to London than the specter—then, it must be remembered, still deadly real—of losing the supply war at sea.[85] For his part, Churchill did nothing to assuage these fears. In a rebuke in Britain's House of Commons on November 5, the prime minister disparaged the state he regarded as virtually the enemy:

> The fact that we cannot use the south and west coasts of Ireland to refuel our flotillas and aircraft and thus protect the trade by which Ireland as well as Great Britain lives, is a most heavy and grievous burden, and one which should never have been placed on our shoulders, broad though they be . . .[86]

Rejoining the barely concealed threat in Churchill's blunt words, the angered but controlled de Valera spoke to his own parliament with equal toughness. "Any attempt to bring pressure to bear on us by any side—by any of the belligerents—by Britain—could only lead to bloodshed. . . . Certainly, as long as this Government remains in office, we shall defend our rights in regard to these ports against whoever shall attack them, as we shall defend our rights in regard to every other part of our territory."[87] To underline the seriousness of his implied return threat, de Valera sent half of Eire's army to the Eire–Northern Ireland border to be ready for any incursion by the British.

Considering the enormous pressure Churchill and his islanders endured in the last half of 1940, de Valera was perhaps justified in his fear that the British prime minister's anxieties about the U-boat menace would lead to a grab for the Treaty Ports and an ensuing German response of treating Eire as a belligerent. But instead of force, Britain was about to employ a fresh tactic in its tug-of-war with de Valera, a stratagem resulting from a conversation between Sir John Maffey and the Taoiseach.

In a May 10 meeting, Maffey posed a pointed question to de Valera. "If the Partition question were solved today would you automatically be our active ally?" The prime minister's response—"I feel convinced that that would probably be the consequence"[88]—was taken by the hopeful Englishman as a signal of co-belligerency. Whether or not de Valera meant that he would abandon neutrality—and no evidence suggests he would have been free to jettison the immensely popular policy—Maffey sent the tidings to London, leading to a new plan being quickly formulated. Britain would offer the reunification of Ireland to get Eire into the war.

So great were Churchill's wartime concerns and so important was Eire to those concerns that they led to a remarkable proposition from a man whose imperial vision of Britain could not concede the moral legitimacy of Irish independence. A formal British offer, under the signature of the Lord President of the Council, the just-jettisoned prime minister, Neville Chamberlain,[89] was on June 28, 1940, conveyed to the Taoiseach:

> A declaration to be made by the United Kingdom government accepting the principle of a United Ireland. This declaration would take the form of a solemn undertaking that the Union is to become at an early date an accomplished fact from which there shall be no turning back. . . . A joint Defence Council representative of Eire and Northern Ireland to be set up immediately. . . . *Eire to enter the war on the side of the United Kingdom and her allies forthwith* . . . the Government of Eire to invite British naval vessels to have the use of ports in Eire, and British troops and aeroplanes to cooperate with the Eire forces and to be stationed in such positions in Eire as may be agreed between the two Governments. . . . The Government of Eire to intern all German and Italian aliens in the country and to take any further steps necessary to suppress Fifth Column activities.[90]

The proposal met, as might be expected, with little enthusiasm in Ulster. Lord Craigavon, Northern Ireland's prime minister, lobbied vigorously against it from the viewpoint of Ulster's Protestant majority. To even consider such a notion, Craigavon demanded that Eire first abandon its neutrality, throw out its Axis diplomats, and leave the issue of partition to be decided only after the war ended.[91] But London told the provincial leader that, in effect, the sensibilities of Ulster could not be allowed to stand in the way of the vital interests of Britain and its allies. For his part, Churchill asserted he had no wish to be "a party to the coercion of Ulster," but had "no objection to Ulster being persuaded."[92] But the insightful Chamberlain saw little hope the Taoiseach would acquiesce in a plan by which Britain meant to bring Ireland, root and branch, into the war regardless of what he had told Maffey about becoming an "active ally" of Britain; he wrote that he feared de Valera "won't be moved till the Germans are in Dublin."[93]

Realizing de Valera wouldn't be swayed, London modified its offer, deleting the requirement that the Twenty-six Counties enter the war. Instead it stated the United Kingdom would be content if the south were to "cooperate" with British forces, and that troops be stationed only in such positions as would be acceptable to both governments "for the purpose of increasing the security of Eire . . ."[94] On the part of Ulster, Craigavon, furious at the treachery he saw in the talks between Dublin and London, refused to consider any such arrangement.

In the end, the proposal died an early death. On July 4, de Valera wrote Chamberlain that his cabinet rejected the plan on the grounds that while London virtually required Eire's co-belligerency, Britain could not in the final accounting *guarantee* the island's unity. In a statement published the next day in *The Times* of London, the Taoiseach reiterated: "I desire to repeat that [my] Government has no intention of departing from the policy of neutrality as adopted last September . . . [and is] resolved to maintain and defend the country's neutrality in all circumstances."[95]

In an interview with the American press in late November, de Valera spoke of the relationship between reunification of his island and the issue of neutrality. To the question as to whether Eire would relinquish its neutrality if the British agreed to end partition, he responded:

> That is to ask shall we barter our right to unity. The Irish nation is entitled to both these rights and ought not to be asked to sacrifice one to secure the other. We are entitled to freedom as well as to unity, and there is no more important matter in which that freedom can be exercised than in the choice of peace and war.[96]

Asked under what circumstances Eire *would* forsake neutrality, the Taoiseach unhesitatingly answered, "If attacked we are at war with whosoever attacks us."

With these troubles between Dublin and London, Berlin thought it an opportune time to focus new attention on Ireland. Under instructions from Ribbentrop, Hempel offered the Twenty-six Counties part of the abandoned British arsenal that had fallen into the Reich's lap at Dunkirk. The envoy also indicated his mission was to be expanded by new military attachés, including an officer whose speciality was "military reconnaissance"—a proposition the Germans evidently believed the Irish would appreciate for the additional protection it might offer against an expected British invasion. It was a conversation de Valera could have done without. As to the matter of the weapons, the Taoiseach recognized that if such weaponry were to show up in Ireland, Britain would be mortally offended. Further, he foresaw that any expansion of the German diplomatic mission, particularly by military personnel, would be taken as a grave sign in London—possibly as an omen of already seen German tactics preceding an invasion. And, once again, all of Eire's armed forces were ordered to a state of highest alert to defend against any offensive action from either belligerent.

· · ·

In a long letter to Franklin Roosevelt dated December 8, 1940, a letter that represented, as it were, a shopping list of Britain's needs,[97] Churchill reiterated the proposal for the united Ireland that has since become one of the historical icons of the lamentable Anglo-Irish relationship:

> . . . The prime need is to check or limit the loss of tonnage on the Atlantic approaches to our island. . . . We should . . . then need the good offices of the United States and the whole influence of its Government, continually exerted, to procure for Great Britain the necessary facilities upon the southern and western shores of Eire for our flotillas, and still the more important, for our aircraft, working to the westward into the Atlantic. If it were proclaimed an American interest that the resistance of Great Britain should be prolonged and the Atlantic route kept open for the important armaments now being prepared for Great Britain in North America, the Irish in the United States might be willing to point out to the Government of Eire the dangers which its present policy is creating for the United States itself.
>
> His Majesty's Government would, of course, take the most effective measures beforehand to protect Ireland if Irish action exposed it to German attack. It is not possible for us to compel the people of Northern Ireland against their will to leave the United Kingdom and join Southern Ireland. But I do not doubt that if the Government of Eire would show its solidarity with the democracies of the English-speaking world at this crisis, *a Council for Defence of all Ireland could be set up out of which the unity of the island would probably in some form or other emerge after the war.*[98]

Had the British proposal come into fruition, the history of Anglo-Irish relations in the second half of the twentieth century would, of course, have been transformed. But for important reasons, it did not. For one, the Protestants of Ulster believed that an integration into the south would represent a desertion of the United Kingdom at a time when Britain and its commonwealth were exposed to enormous peril. Neither did Britain really wish to risk a postwar neutralized Ulster, the bases in that province providing its merchant shipping with forward protection it had lost in the return of the ports. Furthermore, Dublin believed the United States would not abandon its neutrality, and without America's protection Eire's course through a war as a British co-belligerent could be a disaster.

Perhaps most important, even if willing to trade neutrality for Ulster, de Valera understood there could be no *absolute* guarantee that Britain would honor its pledge of a united Ireland in the event it won the war.[99] And even if it tried, a maddened and bellicose Protestant majority in Ulster could well beget a new civil war on the island—and with it unforeseen but very likely disastrous consequences for the Irish future.

· · ·

In yet another letter on the Irish question to Roosevelt a few days later, Churchill continued his tack on Eire. Informing the president of his intention to stop the shipment of any more food and fertilizer to Eire, he ended with the observation that "our merchant seamen as well as public opinion generally take it much amiss that we should have to carry Irish supplies through air and U-boat attacks and subsidise them handsomely when de Valera is quite content to sit happy and see us strangled."[100]

Though Churchill's avowed aim was to make the Irish "more ready to consider common interests," the effect of it on de Valera's basic policy would be nil. Churchill did in the end carry out his threats, and by Christmas the shortages in Eire were starting to hurt. When at the beginning of 1941 London confirmed the trade cutoff with Eire, de Valera warned in a Dáil address that rationing was now inevitable, and on the morrow of the speech a ration card system was set up which would soon drastically cut goods both basic and luxe. The consumption of tea, *the* vital fluid of Ireland, quickly dropped to 25 percent of normal, which meant each Irish citizen got about a half ounce of it each week. Many other necessities also went into short supply, with oil being cut to a trickle and wheat imports ending entirely. After Irish ships began being assigned to the more dangerous outside positions in convoys, Churchill remarked that the measures might lead the Irish to more readily "consider common interests."[101] The British prime minister continued, too, to scold about the ports.[102]

Another part of the price Eire would pay for its disengagement from the war came on New Year's Day 1941. Hempel warned de Valera that his spurning of Ribbentrop's offer of weapons and permission for extra embassy staff in Dublin would be taken very hard in Berlin, a sign that Eire wasn't willing to meet Germany even partway in achieving true "friendship." On the first of January, and again the next day, German raiders dropped a small number of bombs on Dublin and four southern counties. Twenty-four people were injured, three others died. The German envoy counseled his superiors that such actions—if indeed deliberate—would only serve to drive the Irish into the British camp, and (again, if deliberate) apparently led Berlin to reject a return engagement. Berlin denied responsibility for the attack, stating the British were the culprits. Nonetheless, several officers in Eire's army believed the attack was the result of German displeasure with de Valera's unwillingness to allow the German mission's personnel to be increased.[103] At any rate, Hempel's warnings seemed to have reached ears attuned to their logic, reflected in the fact that the Germans thereafter evidently turned their back, militarily speaking, on the Twenty-six Counties.

Britain, however, kept up its own attacks on Eire, though they remained merely verbal and economic. Through the winter and spring of 1941, Eire continued to be the target of the British prime minister's wrath. On February 19, Maffey dropped a verbal bombshell on the Irish. Though tensions had somewhat eased, Churchill nonetheless told the envoy that he should give Eire no absolute assurances that Britain wouldn't invade Ireland. The Taoiseach had boldly asked London to pledge that the United Kingdom would not invade the island, but in a temper well justified by the Nazi pressure he was under Churchill instructed Maffey that his task was not simply to "mollify de Valera and make everything, including our ruin, pass off pleasantly."[104] In subsequent response to de Valera, Maffey said he could not give the assurances Eire wanted to hear "without a mental reservation." That reservation amounted to Britain's wish to be free to take any measures necessary to save itself. In a parting shot, Maffey noted that Irish neutrality accrued not to the Allies' advantage but only to that of the Axis.

With some irony, most of the Irish people were never fully aware that Churchill and the British government were trying to squeeze Eire into co-belligerency. To forestall public acrimony, the shipping cutoffs were attributed to the U-boat struggle, the Taoiseach never letting his people in on the real warfare between London and Dublin. The Irish government decided it would be to the country's best interests to let the censorship of the facts of the matter continue insofar as possible.[105]

However hurtful Britain's economic warfare against Eire became, the Twenty-six Counties were still far better off than the British—or, for that matter, their fellow Irishmen in Ulster, where rationing was producing enormous deprivation. The Dublin government ordered a million extra acres put under the plow, a tactic that would produce major increases in wheat and vegetable production. To keep homes heated and businesses in operation, the large-scale production of peat from Ireland's famed bogs was underwritten by the government with a vengeance. Before the war was over, the streets of Eire's cities would be converted into drying racks for the tons of peat cut from the island's marshes, peat that would end up in the fireplaces of Ireland to replace the fuels Britain ensured didn't reach the island.

An additional government concern in these dyspeptic days was to see to it that the country's petty neutrality directives were rigidly and even-handedly enforced, a preoccupation often resulting in ludicrous measures. In the spring of 1940 a Dundalk factory hand was hauled into court for assaulting a county councillor who had played a recording of the RAF song "Lords of the Air" at a hockey match. The judge let the worker walk, suggesting that the record be burned as "some restitution to the people." The county councillor was let off with the stern admonition that "this is a neutral state and we don't want any British jingoism here!"[106]

One more excitement for the Irish emanated out of the Reich's propaganda ministry's troublemaking. "Britain is to invade Eire through Ulster," the German *Rundfunk* continuously broadcast that winter. "In such event, Berlin is determined to react in the same manner as in the case of Norway and Belgium." Churchill was certainly militarily able, with a third of a million troops in the north, to march into Eire, but would not until being provoked into doing so by a serious German threat.

• • •

The waxing animosity between the governments of neutral America and neutral Eire had acted as a virus menacing the de Valera government since the onset of the Emergency. In the spring of 1941, it erupted into an almost full-scale hatred, albeit mostly one-sided, with Franklin Roosevelt openly vilifying Eire's determination to remain neutral. The spark lighting the president's ire came during a tour of the United States by de Valera's minister for Coordination of Defensive Affairs, Frank Aiken. Sent to the United States to try to elicit both sympathy and supplies from a hostile America that had already all but declared co-belligerency with Britain, Aiken proved to be the wrong choice for what could only have been a task for a consummate diplomat.

Kinsman correspondent David Gray had already maliciously advised Roosevelt that Aiken was "pro-German" in his sympathies, the envoy having concluded that Nazi Germany could be the only possible benefactor of Eire's neutrality. In fact, Aiken did carry out his domestic duties with a somewhat heavy hand. Anxious to make Irishmen neutral in thought as well as deed, a determination he shared with the Taoiseach, he committed a series of niggling blunders which seemed *too* tilted toward Germany. For example, Aiken saw to it that Irish soldiers killed in

Allied service were not so credited in their press obituaries. And censorship in the nation's cinemas reached a level approaching absurdity. The *Daily Herald* reported on January 7 that Charlie Chaplin's antiwar comedy *The Great Dictator* was banned for "motives of neutrality," though the film was being freely shown in Belfast, where many citizens of the Twenty-six Counties traveled to see it.[107] For Aiken, though, any cinematic comments directed at the Axis leaders violated Eire's prohibition against belittling the belligerents, including those belligerents doing their best to destroy the kind of democratic principles Eire professed to uphold.

On April 7, Aiken received a White House appointment to meet Roosevelt. The president was already in his seriously negative mind-set, fostered by Churchill and Gray, about both Aiken and the dominion for which he was coming to plead. Roosevelt got the interview off to a contentious start by accusing the Irish minister of having reportedly remarked that "the Irish had nothing to fear from a German victory." Aiken vehemently denied the accuracy of Roosevelt's information, and the president was unable to produce evidence for the charge. When Aiken tried to get Roosevelt to agree with Eire's "stand against aggression," the American commander-in-chief immediately corrected with "German aggression." The Irishman shot back "*or* British aggression," to which Roosevelt snorted "nonsense." But when asked why Churchill's government would not give Ireland a guarantee against invasion, the president—though obviously not believing such a promise was necessary or that Britain intended to invade its island neighbor—promised he would "look into" eliciting such a promise. No such promise would ever reach Dublin from Great Britain,[108] and about all that did come of Aiken's presidential talk was a general hardening of the American view of Eire's neutrality that for the remainder of the Emergency clouded dealings between Washington and Dublin.

· · ·

In early April 1941, de Valera finally got the chance to clearly demonstrate Eire's fundamental sympathies. The occasion was, however, a tragic one. On the eighth of that month, as Frank Aiken was pressing his failing case in Washington, Germany launched the first large air raid on British Ireland: Belfast, the island's second city and the capital of Northern Ireland, came under a brutal attack from a fleet of Göring's bombers. To people of the south, that city and its people were an integral part of the national territory and national community, their division from Eire a temporary and artificial sundering. The south's shock was profound, as the realization sank in that the Germans cared not a whit for the integrity of the island as Dublin viewed that integrity.[109]

Though the first raid, really only a practice run, killed 13 people and injured 81, it was mild compared to the horror that came the following weekend, the Easter holidays of April 15–16. An estimated one hundred Luftwaffe bombers roared out of the Irish Sea toward the largely defenseless city. This time, 745 Belfasters were killed and more than 1,500 injured.[110] Large tracts of the center of the cultivated city were torn apart, the raid clearly directed at the important British shipbuilding industry—exemplified by the massive Harland and Wolff works, in which the *Titanic* had been built—that had flourished in Belfast since the nineteenth century. But typical of the Luftwaffe's aerial carnage in its attacks on British life and industry, the raid extended far beyond the city's docklands.[111]

After being so requested by the Northern Ireland minister of public security, de Valera instantly authorized the sending of large-scale fire-fighting and first-aid support to Belfast from the Dublin area; the equipment included thirteen appliances from Dun Laoghaire, Drogheda, and Dundalk, as well as many more from the capital itself—Dublin was emptied of all its fire engines save one. Though the succor given Ulster in its agony unquestionably represented a breach of neutrality, the Taoiseach believed rendering assistance to fellow Irishmen superseded such considerations.

Two more raids were to strike Belfast, on May 5 and 6. Both were primarily incendiary assaults, confirming Germany's resolution that Ulster was to be militarily thrown in with the rest of the British Commonwealth. Joseph Cardinal MacRory, Ireland's cardinal-primate, did intervene with Hempel to try to thwart a possible German air strike on the Ulster city of Armagh, seat of the island's single archbishopric. As it turned out, the May 5–6 raids were the last of the war over Northern Ireland.

Once more that spring Ireland would be bombed—but this time it was Dublin that was the victim of Nazi raiders. On May 31, Luftwaffe bombers—Berlin would say they were "off course"—killed 34 people, wounded 90, and destroyed or damaged some 300 houses. Dubliners were shocked that their city had been so attacked by Germany, and Eire's envoy registered a sharp diplomatic protest in Berlin. Though the raid may have been meant as a further scare to the de Valera government, or even retaliation for the aid Eire gave Ulster the previous month, the best evidence indicates this attack was truly unintentional; after the war, Churchill wrote that the likeliest explanation for the bombing was that the German navigators had been thrown off course by the interference from the radio beams Britain used to confuse enemy fliers.[112]

. . .

Yet another crisis—this time merely *politically* explosive—came for neutral Ireland in what were in retrospect the most dangerous months of the war for that island. In echoes of 1918, the British government resolved, on the advice of Northern Ireland's new prime minister, John Miller Andrews (Lord Craigavon had died in November 1940), to extend conscription to Ulster, the one part of the United Kingdom that had so far in the war been excluded from the draft of its young men.[113]

De Valera was informed on May 20 that the question was before the cabinet in Downing Street. The Taoiseach immediately instructed John W. Dulanty, Eire's high commissioner in London, to see the dominions secretary, Lord Cranbourne. Demanding that the decision be reversed, the commissioner pointed out that a draft forcing the Catholic population of Northern Ireland—about a third of the whole—to fight a war for freedoms they themselves did not enjoy would be an outrage. When Cranbourne explained the matter was out of his hands, Dulanty requested an interview with Churchill himself.

Two days after de Valera first heard of the edict, Dulanty was ushered into the prime minister's office in Downing Street. The two men had been friends for decades, since Churchill's 1906 candidature for parliament from Manchester. Nevertheless, when the high commissioner explained that conscription in Ulster would provoke a crisis of the first order all over Ireland, Churchill's anger was unmistakable. The Irishman didn't flinch, but went on to explain that such an action would give the IRA—an organization the southern authorities had managed of late to stymie—a first-class point of sympathy in increasing converts to its cause. According to Dulanty, nothing less than the peace of the whole island was at stake.

Churchill's icy response was that the request for inclusion in the kingdom's generalized conscription had come from Ulster itself. The prime minister inferred that to continue to exclude Northern Ireland from conscription would be "unfair" to the rest of the kingdom—but that if "anyone wished to run away," no one would make any effort to stop him. Churchill's fury became almost corporeal, that he should be so disturbed over so "unimportant" a matter when the British people were very nearly *in extremis* in their war with totalitarianism. To the contrary, to Dulanty the matter was of the utmost importance, and the prime minister had to be made to see what damage the decision could cause.

Dulanty's fears were, in retrospect, manifestly justifiable. Conscription in Ulster was decried from one end of the island to the other. Even Ulster's Unionists, of all people, objected to it, on the novel grounds that they didn't want to see the Nationalists armed. Cardinal MacRory, echoing all the bishops, said it would create "indignation and resistance" among Irishmen everywhere,[114] that it would be "an outrage on the national feeling and an aggression upon our national rights."[115] Even Ambassador Gray, normally a man who wouldn't hesitate to do whatever he could to damage the interests of neutral Eire, advised (presumably to whoever would listen) that unless Nationalists in Ulster were excluded from Britain's forced conscription, American interests in Ireland would be hurt by the popular reaction in both parts of the island. He further predicted draft riots and the reception of fleeing draft dodgers in the south as "hero-martyrs."[116]

If, in fact, conscription were to meet with widespread resistance in the north, the resistance would inevitably be headed by the IRA. And in such a case de Valera would be forced to show solidarity with that resistance, in effect teaming him and his government with its sworn enemy. In such a scenario, the IRA would stand to gain new prestige, and undoubtedly new converts, in the Twenty-six Counties.

De Valera wouldn't accept a resolution to the crisis merely involving the exempting from the Ulster draft of Nationalists—that is, the province's Catholics. On May 26, Dulanty delivered a personal message from de Valera to Churchill (though de Valera considered personally taking the message to Churchill before being dissuaded on security grounds):

> . . . Before your final decision is taken, I feel that I should again put before your government, as earnestly as I can, my view that the imposition of conscription in any form would provoke the bitterest resentment amongst Irishmen and would have the most disastrous consequences for our two peoples. . . . The Six Counties have, toward the rest of Ireland, a status and a relationship which no Act of Parliament can change. They are a part of Ireland. They have always been a part of Ireland, and their people, Catholic and Protestant, are our people. I beg of you, before you enter on a course which can so affect so profoundly the relations of our two peoples to take all these matters into the most earnest consideration.[117]

Incensed at what he considered the phoniness of the plea, as well as the implied breaking of the 1921 treaty between the two nations by which Ulster had been formed, Churchill would only consent to put the matter before the cabinet—after threatening to tell the world exactly what he thought of the Irish Taoiseach *and* his petition. The following day, to de

Valera's vast relief, the British government decided that since the total men available would only range from about 60,000 to perhaps 200,000, the imposition of conscription in Ulster represented more trouble than it was worth.

Ulster's prime minister nonetheless got in one last dig at the Taoiseach. In Belfast, Andrews made an announcement maligning de Valera for his "unwarrantable interference," archly adding that "all matters connected with Northern Ireland are completely outside the jurisdiction of the Eire government; and so they shall remain."[118]

Madrid

For Francisco Franco, a great deal had changed. On June 22, the first Wehrmacht units rolled up to the Bidassoa, the muddy little stream separating French Hendaye from the Spanish towns of Fuenterrabia and Irún. Those gray-clad soldiers represented a vastly altered game plan for the Caudillo, one that dramatically transformed the relationshp between Europe's belligerents and his still unsettled Spain. For obvious reasons, the fact that fifty idle Wehrmacht divisions now sat in conquered France would color Franco's new assessment of his options to a critical extent.

Since the world war erupted the prior September, the Caudillo had been only too happy to keep his impoverished and exhausted nation outside any actual choosing of sides in the conflict. Indebted as he was to the dictators, and equally hostile to the democracies, his propaganda machine's pro-Axis bent hardly surprised anyone. But the reality of the Royal Navy, coupled with his still fractious people's hunger and the inability of either Hitler or Mussolini to feed them, required consummate caution, a skill the preeminently prudent Franco had mastered since he first took supreme command of the Nationalist cause in 1936.

As a result of the Wehrmacht's sledgehammer drive through Western Europe, Spain now found itself connected directly to a Nazi-controlled Europe via the French land bridge.[119] Anticipating the German victory and bowing to a request from Italian foreign minister Ciano to demonstrate solidarity with the Axis, Franco had on June 12 ominously changed the status of his country, from officially "neutral" to the more menacing "nonbelligerent," a standing by which Franco believed his "freedom of action" and "options" might better be maintained.[120] The Allies (including the still neutral United States, whose government now regarded Spain as little more than a political clone of Berlin and Rome) interpreted the maneuver as Spain's dangerously nearing all-out co-belligerency with the

Axis, though the only real effect of the change itself was an increased symbolic tilt toward Berlin and Rome. In his new circumstances, the Caudillo's sense of acquisitiveness, his passion to redress past injury to Spain's dignity, his vision of a restored empire all began to shine with a new, yet still cautious intensity. For the next eighteen months, the shift in Spanish policy toward the Germano-Italian axis looked as though it would overturn Franco's precariously neutral applecart. What had not changed was the desperation, the hunger, and the political terror in which a war-wounded Spain wallowed nearly inert.

To the still hunted adherents of the former Republic, hundreds of whom continued to be shoved in front of firing squads each day, escaping the dragnets of Franco's police was the most pressing problem in Spain in the early years of World War II. To almost everyone else, it was hunger. Before the Civil War, Spain's food resources were virtually self-sustaining; ironically, after the Nationalist victory the food situation grew worse than it had been at any point during the Civil War itself. Even with the stringent rationing sternly enforced by the government, food remained unevenly distributed, and in many provinces was in desperately short supply.

Inevitably, the poor—the vast bulk of the population—suffered to a far greater degree than did those on the higher economic rungs. With smuggling and black marketeering rampant throughout the country, those with the money to pay the extortionists' inflated prices managed fairly nicely, though conspicuous consumers ran the risk of paying the piper for their more egregious indulgences. Government ration boards often cut the food allowances for the affluent, sometimes heavily fining them for grosser displays of sumptuary inequity, and occasionally even sending the worst of the offenders off to labor battalions to atone for their greediness. In April 1941, changes in the rationing system (eighty different food items were by then rationed) actually gave the poor higher daily bread allowances than the rich, presumably on the laudable logic that the poor worked harder and thus merited the extra calories. In any case, what bread there was had become all but inedible, "extended" to the point of unpalatability with rye, barley, chick-pea, and potato flours.

But even such an adulterated basic seemed luxurious to urban workers. Many were so destitute that a breakfast might be a glass of warm water, lunch pancakes made of lupine flour, dinner a kind of mush concocted from turnips. This diet was, unsurprisingly, at the root of the poor health that was emblematic of wartime Spain: in Madrid in the spring of 1941, malnourishment and bad hygiene led to an epidemic of exanthematic fever,[121] and pellagra and the effects of malnutrition during the war would in the years to come undermine an entire generation of Spaniards.

The bureaucratic managers of Franco's Spain believed the protection of public morals to be one of the state's highest responsibilities. This meant a rigid about-face from the perceived licentiousness allowed under the Republic as well as a preoccupation with controlling many petty but symbolic manifestations of civil freedom. Women were, figuratively speaking, re-veiled: dresses with short sleeves or hemlines too high or necklines too low were made to correct their improprieties, with priests given authority to chastise those women who continued to publicly show themselves so dressed. Far more seriously, so many women were destitute that in the evenings prostitutes paraded the paseos, unfortunates trying to earn enough to keep themselves and their families from starvation.

Those who offended the state's morals in such relatively minor ways were lucky compared with the more than a quarter million former Republicans who sat in jails, many awaiting the inevitable time when their captors would come to take them to the courtyard to be shot. Some managed to escape that fate, but many others still had to contend with torture and rape in the prisons of Franco's new state. When the Germans gained control of France, thousands of Republican refugees who had been existing precariously in that country were returned to face Franco's appallingly severe "justice." Lest anyone dare publicly protest such conditions, the regime sent roving complements of the Guardia Civil to patrol the streets, rifles at the ready to break up the least sign of dissent.

To help the regime maintain iron control, in October 1940 elements of the Gestapo arrived to "assist" the local police, the latter already discreetly called the "rubber syndicate" for their ubiquitous truncheons. The Nazi toughs were allowed free range of the country and granted every courtesy by local police. This gift of the Gestapo agents came directly from Heinrich Himmler, who in another gesture of solidarity between his police state and that of Franco returned to Spain the renowned Catalonian nationalist Luis Companys. Companys was shot by a firing squad virtually the moment Himmler's agents delivered him onto Spanish soil.

·   ·   ·

So far in the war, Spain had maintained a respectful posture with Britain, the two nations continuing a mutually beneficial trade while the former spat poisoned propaganda darts at the latter; Spanish spleen vented itself particularly in the matter of the country's critical food condition, which its propaganda machine blamed on the United Kingdom. From London's perspective, British economic policy toward Spain since September 1939 aimed at a middle course, neither starving it into closer cooperation with the Reich nor allowing it to build up enough supplies to tempt it into reexporting those goods to Germany.[122] London concerned itself, wisely, not with shadow but with the substance of Spain's behavior. Though Madrid's official rhetoric was pro-German, as long as the Reich's capacity or willingness to feed it was impeded and the Royal Navy could control what entered Spain, the equation brought relative safety to the Allied war effort. With the fall of France, that balance shifted.

Under his newly enhanced relationship with a Spain now connected to German-controlled territory, Hitler's attention turned to the peninsula—especially to its southern tip, Gibraltar, Britain's plug to the Mediterranean's Atlantic portal. The German leader understandably coveted this dot of real estate so crucial to British power, and he judged that the very least Franco owed him was to help him get it. That meant either a capture of Gibraltar by Spain itself or else Spain allowing the Wehrmacht to take the vitally important fortress.[123] Once in control of the Rock, Hitler planned to move his armies across the strait into Spanish Morocco, and then persuade Franco to cede one of Spain's Canary Islands to serve as a U-boat base. After rewarding the Caudillo with a southward extension of a newly drawn Spanish Morocco, Germany would further demand one of the Moroccan ports in recompense. Final plans called for making over parts of French North Africa to compensate Madrid for both the island and the Moroccan port. In its ultimate political configuration, however, Spain itself would become virtually a German dominion, with northern and middle Africa under permanent German suzerainty.[124]

For his part, the Caudillo remained pragmatic about the blood debt his own fascist state owed another fascist state, even a state for which he publicly and repeatedly professed boundless esteem; as Churchill concluded, Franco's policy throughout the war was entirely "selfish and cold-blooded. He thought only of Spain and of Spanish interests. . . . This narrow-minded tyrant only thought about keeping his blood-drained people out of another war."[125] Though a large part of the democratic world's opinion regarded the Spanish leader as a despot whose reign was held together with little more than blood, the reality of Francisco Franco is that he calculated Spain's and his regime's odds for survival with cunning, intelligence, and precision. Regardless of any visions of glory he harbored, he refused to let his country become a German satrapy. He would do everything in his power to ensure that it did not, not hesitating for an instant to lie, prevaricate, stall, or to demand rewards and bounty and bribes he knew weren't available to be given—whatever it took to keep himself and Catholic authoritarianism in power and Spain independent, to keep the dogs of war at bay and to give his nation time to recoup its strength.

Still, there were new realities that had to be considered. Germany (or its Vichy client) now controlled Spain's Pyrenean frontier, and in the summer of 1940 few in Spain—or elsewhere—would have predicted the Reich's defeat in its war against the British and their empire. Göring's Luftwaffe had been vested by the Führer with the task of breaching the British moat, a job it seemed breathlessly obvious would take but a short time. Even trade with Britain, though still vital, didn't look to be *quite* the life-or-death matter it had been up to now. With France subdued, Germany could theoretically supply its Spanish ally without incurring the risk of Britain's still potent fleet. And all the while crowds of enthusiastically pro-belligerency Spaniards demonstrated in the streets of Spain's great cities, their anti-British fervor expressed in roars of "*¡Gibraltar para España!*"

Did these changes in circumstances add up to a state of affairs in which Spain could profitably ally itself militarily with its ideological benefactor? Co-belligerency with the Axis meant a declaration of war on the United Kingdom and, by extension, on the United States, Britain's moral co-belligerent many now saw as willing to undertake serious and warlike actions to help ensure that Britain survived. Britain was so sure Spain would indeed succumb to the Axis siren that for the few weeks after the arrival of Sir Samuel Hoare, Britain's new representative to Madrid, his official aircraft remained in readiness at the airport to snatch the envoy back to London the moment the Germans marched into the peninsula.[126]

Throughout World War II, the Allies' fundamental political stance regarding the Iberian Peninsula was that they wanted, above all, a *neutral* Spain and Portugal. Neither Britain nor the United States expected anything like perfect neutrality—in thought or public expression—from either country, particularly from a dictator in Spain installed on the wings and good wishes of Nazi Germany and fascist Italy. Though the Allies' hopes for a neutral peninsula *centered* on Gibraltar—on keeping it from Axis control and on its maintenance not merely as a besieged symbol but as a functioning military and naval post[127]—they also desperately wanted to keep the entirety of the two countries from becoming a giant Axis base, as had France. As to this latter goal, the democratic alliance was less successful.[128]

Even before France collapsed in June, Franco had allowed Germany—and to a lesser and less important degree, Italy—important tactical privileges on Spanish soil and in Spanish anchorages. Principal among these was free access to the country's ports for the safe harboring, reprovisioning, and rest for the personnel of the Kriegsmarine, the branch of the Wehrmacht then constituting the gravest danger to Britain. Ports including Vigo, Santander, and Cádiz would throughout the war remain open to German surface and undersea naval forces. The Canary Island refueling and resupplying bases used by the Germans with Franco's permission represented a vital refueling point for the critically important U-boat fleet until December 1941, when Germany's "milch cow" method of resupplying submarines at sea was initiated.

Spanish assistance to the Reich went considerably beyond providing Germany with safe harbors. Spain's factories produced vast quantities of matériel that helped Germany keep its war machine in tune. Factories in Barcelona, Seville, and Valencia turned out items destined for the Reich ranging from cartridges to uniforms to submarine engines. Furthermore, as a result of an agreement signed in April 1941 Spaniards were allowed to travel to Germany to work in industry. As historian Max Gallo frankly characterized the situation, if Spain's sword wasn't at Germany's service in the war, it was certainly "an active collaborator."[129] For the democratic alliance to temper its repugnance toward the Spanish regime meant swallowing bile to keep from what it thought would tip Franco irretrievably into Hitler's arms and the far greater threat that would have brought.

* * *

The view from the Pardo Palace in the summer of 1940 was that Germany had all but won the war. After France's defeat, Britain was both materially and spiritually done in. Though the Royal Navy remained effective on the world's seas, Britain's Dunkirk-crippled army seemed incapable of successfully defending the island against the coming German storm, an onslaught clearly in the offing unless Churchill's government sued for peace. Though few doubted a defeated Britain would continue to fight Hitler from the refuge and with the resources of its imperial offspring in the Western Hemisphere and Africa, in Europe itself the New German Order appeared to have scored a bull's-eye. And, so the Pardo's master was also convinced, once a Nazi-controlled Gibraltar was achieved, Hitler would treat both him and his Catholic-and Nationalist-oriented regime with all the grace a dog accords a flea.

Despite Britain's travails Franco remained careful with the island kingdom, continuing to peaceably negotiate with London over what goods would be allowed through the Royal Navy's blockade. Of chief importance was oil, the vital component in keeping Spain's industries going, its transportation system moving and bringing food to the people, and its people from freezing in the bitter Iberian winters. Whitehall persevered in trying to balance its calculation, allowing Spain the necessities while withholding what might find its way to a Germany now connected by direct French land routes safe from the guns of the Royal Navy. To err on the side of starving the country could have the disastrous effect of pushing Franco further into Hitler's embrace if only to keep his regime from being threatened with food riots by a tired but still surly population. To err in the other direction could end up in helping the regime trying to destroy the beleaguered kingdom.

The United States cooperated with Britain in regulating Spain's vital trade flow, Washington agreeing with London's assessment that to overly restrict Spain's imports would only increase the danger of Iberian reliance on Germany. Washington also subscribed to the British conviction that Franco would stay out of the war as long as Spain knew it would pay a heavy price for joining the Reich.[130] Nonetheless, with every report of oil permitted through the Allied blockade being pumped aboard a German freighter, there were those in the democracies who bitterly decried any further trade with Spain.[131] Influential voices in Britain and, especially, in the United States continued to regard Franco's state with unbending antagonism, and denounced supplying it with sustenance, irrespective of the larger strategic considerations.[132] To a large degree, such voices found success—especially in the State Department—and shortsighted U.S. policies based on revulsion toward Spain's political regime caused Washington to occasionally lose sight of the value of the peninsula's neutrality to the anti-Nazi cause. America's politically engendered penuriousness with credit with which Spain could obtain American food surpluses reflected such policy enigmas.

Though Hitler, through his highest intermediaries—Mussolini, Ribbentrop, Himmler—would urgently press Franco to join the Reich in the war, and as sympathetic as Franco *may* have been to a vision of a fascist Europe, conditions in his country remained such that a co-belligerent Spain could have acted as little more than a very junior Axis partner. The majority of the Spanish people, stressed and underfed, remained overwhelmingly cool to German co-belligerency, a coolness even a dictator couldn't entirely ignore. The harvest that year was worse than usual—a not unexpected result of the Civil War's legacy of chaos in the countryside—with the wheat shortfall alone amounting to 1.3 million tons below the minimum needed to feed the nation. Not only foods but other essential materials came up critically short. Cotton supplies were sufficient to keep some mills in operation for just two days each week.[133] Coal, vitally needed to keep steel mills going, was also running dangerously short.

Hard-pressed for much else to do, the government engaged in some widely publicized public relations efforts to demonstrate its concern for the malnourished. For example, the civil governor of Barcelona ruled that 10,000 pesetas—about $1,000—must be paid by both the organizers of and the guests at a restaurant banquet at which gold plate was used to show honor to foreign industrialists present. The authorities held the affair to be "incongruous, unaesthetic, and unnecessarily ostentatious," and stated that in the "present circumstances" it might have disturbed public order. Further, Madrid ordered that anyone spreading rumors that the bread ration would be reduced—the ration amounted to one small roll each day—would be "severely punished" for disturbing the public peace.[134]

Here and there, a few areas of life saw a hesitant improvement. The Prado's paintings, stored in Geneva during the Civil War, were returned to their rightful home, and Madrileños of means again flocked to the Puerta de Hierro country club, though golfers were confined to the front nine holes, unexploded shells from the war still making the back nine too dangerous. The Madrid, Barcelona, and Bilbao stock exchanges reopened in the spring of 1940, having been closed for four years. Two new subways were being dug, to the annoyance of the capital's scattering of motorists, while white-helmeted traffic police tried to control the tangle of pedestrians that daily drank in the city's peace, a condition devoutly appreciated in spite of the shops' empty shelves.

Balanced against the shortages were the cries of the politically hyperventilating Falange, the party tightly under the thumb of Franco's brother-in-law, Ramón Serrano Suñer. Though Franco made it his business to keep the state's single party on a short leash, and the party's power had decreased markedly since the end of the Civil War thanks to the Caudillo's cautious balancing of contesting elements in the new Spanish state, the Falange still made a noise on the nation's stage that couldn't be ignored. Unfortunately, it was a noise heard with special acuity in the belligerent capitals. In Washington and London, the Falange represented the principal Spanish force urging that Spanish policy move toward the Axis; in Berlin, it was seen as the most useful tool in the event Franco were replaced in a German-dominated Spain, though even the Nazis credited it with more power than it actually possessed.

Serrano Suñer himself was, aside from Franco, the most politically significant Spaniard in that summer in which the Axis rode so high. A controversial character in the subsequent history of Spain and World War II, the Cuñadísimo (the word is a play on *cuñado*, brother-in-law) was, if not the rabid pro-Nazi many chroniclers of the period have since made him out to be, a man nonetheless convinced Germany was going to win the war, who believed Spain's destiny lay in tethering itself to a winner while it still seemed to be doing so voluntarily and with goodwill, and who did his utmost to bend Franco's will to that belief. Franco needed his closest collaborator in charge at what was the most difficult and dangerous period of foreign affairs in his regime's history, and both Berlin and Rome appeared satisfied with Serrano Suñer as their principal Spanish contact. So in mid-October Franco would make his brother-in-law foreign minister in place of the more and more bypassed Juan Beigbeder y Atienza, a man whose seeming pro-British sympathies increasingly embarrassed Spain in Berlin.[135] Serrano Suñer remained minister of the interior in addition to his new job; the former position meant he continued to control Spain's notoriously pro-German press.

At the same time he promoted Serrano Suñer, Franco replaced the moderate Luis Alarcón de la Lasta as industry and commerce minister with the tough pro-Axis Falangist Demetrio Carceller, the move taken in Berlin to mean that Spain would be governed by men eager "to work with, or under" Germany.[136] Carceller would, in fact, prove a success (as Franco would have defined it) in the wartime Spanish cabinet, particularly in the wake of the introduction by the British of compulsory navicerts after July 1940. The enterprising and relatively pragmatic Carceller was capable of playing one side off against the other in obtaining economic advantage from both Allies and Axis, often talking Franco into granting useful concessions to the Allies that the anti-British Serrano Suñer opposed.[137]

An element vital to comprehending Spanish actions in 1940 was the lure of imperial expansion—colonialism. As part of any price for joining Germany in its war, Franco intended to add vast stretches of Africa to Spain's puny empire—puny by the colonial standards of the early twentieth century—of which Spanish Morocco formed the only consequential part.[138] Franco saw the expansion of this empire coming at the expense of France's far greater domain then stretching right across the continent, a swath that took in both Saharan and equatorial belts. The Caudillo reasoned, naively as it turned out, that Hitler would only have to reassign French Africa from the defeated France to the now important and very much *un*defeated Spain.

When in mid-June 1940 Franco declared Spain no longer "neutral," but instead a "nonbelligerent" he also drew up a kind of territorial wish list he expected Germany to make come true as part of the price the Axis would have to pay for Spain's co-belligerency. Clearly, a Spanish Gibraltar was first among his demands, but the list went on to include the annexation of French Morocco, "that part of Algeria colonized and predominantly inhabited by Spaniards" (principally the Oran area), and a redrawing on a grander scale of the boundaries of Río de Oro and the other Spanish colonies in the Gulf of Guinea. If granted these territories, plus being supplied with its military and economic demands, the Spanish ambassador in Berlin stated "the Spanish government [is] ready, under certain conditions, to give up its position as a 'nonbelligerent' state and to enter the war on the side of Germany and Italy."[139] The problem was that Franco's vision of a proper Spanish empire conflicted sharply with the contours of France's colonial perspective.

It was this Franco-Spanish conflict of interest that put Hitler in the bind that would eventually hinder his capacity to offer Spain what it wanted. The German leader concluded that to take away so much from France—even a defeated and perhaps permanently defanged France—very well might induce its colonial governors to throw in with de Gaulle's Free French forces, and thus become a threat to the New European Order. In his quest to remain out of the war and its attendant menaces to his own regime, it is entirely possible that Franco also understood this, that by deliberately asking for more than even Hitler could deliver he was buying Spain's deliverance from the eventual war with America that would come with or without Britain's collapse. Furthermore, since the fall of France, Britain showed neither a sign of collapsing nor an inclination to sue for peace.

Franco's price for entering the war did not, of course, stop with just the territorial wish list. Equally necessary to Spain's co-belligerency was a mountain of military and civilian supplies that the Caudillo concluded was absolutely vital to Spain's ability to wage war, or, more importantly, defend itself once it entered the war. Oil and food—primarily wheat—were the most critical of these needs, and unless Germany could supply what would be lost from the supplies allowed by the Allies into Spain, Franco sensed he had little choice but to keep his country out of the war.

The Caudillo broached his thorny situation to Hitler in a cautiously politic June 1940 letter:

> At the moment when the German armies, under your leadership, are bringing the greatest battle in history to a victorious close, I would like to express to you my admiration and enthusiasm . . . when your soldiers shared with us in [our] war against the same, although concealed enemies . . . [However] the great upheavals which Spain underwent in the

three years of the war, where to our losses and wear and tear were added
the innumerable losses inflicted in Red territory, have put us in a difficult position . . . I do not need to assure you how great is my desire not
to remain aloof from your cares and how great is my satisfaction in
rendering to you at all times those services which you regard as most
valuable.[140]

In this wily prose, Franco's real purpose was clearly to erect the
underpinnings to his case for staying out of the war. But the little dictator
was playing a dangerous game with Hitler. In the last half of 1940,
Hitler's need to come to a quick or costly accommodation with Spain was
not urgent. All believed—Franco, Serrano Suñer, Hitler—that Britain
was beaten, and either invasion or a suit for peace would soon end the
fighting in Europe. Germany could comfortably wait for that to happen
and *then* see to Spain's place and position in the New Order. The Spaniards would in the meantime become even weaker, their imports from the
West decreased because of their plunging ability to pay for them (and
possibly the West's shortsighted attitude over the distastefulness of the
Spanish political order), and thus Spain's price for its cooperation lowered to a figure the Reich might more comfortably afford. Germany could
certainly not with impunity draw down on its own still limited resources—
though this was a matter the Führer intended to soon do something about
in Russia—to feed and heat the Spanish people and economy without
creating injudicious privations at home. Such privations of his own people would have caused Hitler little loss of sleep if the justification had
been great enough, but it didn't appear in the light of the war's progress
to date that they were going to be necessary.

For its own part, Germany still nursed its territorial wish list encom-
passing sovereign Spanish territory, and knowledge of this craving pushed
Franco further away from accommodation with Germany. In the Führer
Conference of July 11, 1940, Hitler informed his military chiefs that he
would still "like to acquire" one of the Canary Islands, such acquisition
to be paid for, as we've seen, with the granting of French Morocco to
Spain. Fearful that the United States might make a preemptive strike
against either the Azores or the Canaries because of the U-boat threat in
the Atlantic, Hitler reasoned it might be a good idea if Germany made
the first move to grab one of the islands.

It fell to Serrano Suñer in September to discuss these issues with
Ribbentrop. (Though formally still foreign minister, Beigbeder by this
time wasn't trusted by Franco to get his views across to the Germans.) On
July 12, the soon-to-be foreign minister left for Berlin.[141] On his arrival,
Serrano Suñer with obsequious goodwill quickly laid out to the German

foreign minister his master's "disappointment" that no German supplies had yet reached Spain, a situation thereby leaving his country unable to help share the burden of Germany's war. Without the resources to defend itself against whatever attacks would come in the wake of going into a war against Great Britain, Spain was thus powerless to help Germany. Serrano Suñer added that as to the matter of granting Germany an island in the Spanish Canaries, those islands represented sovereign and inviolable Spanish territory, and were *not* negotiable.

Clearly, neither Franco nor his lubricous emissary wished Spain to assume any risk in a war, but only to reap whatever benefits might derive therefrom, a pair of aspirations that would be exceedingly difficult to reconcile. However useful the possession of Gibraltar would have been to Germany (as invasion of Britain was rapidly receding on the horizon, the capture of Gibraltar began to take on ever greater psychic importance to Hitler), Ribbentrop—himself no slouch at deceit—probably thought his Spanish guest contemptible by this point. Nevertheless, the German believed that a Spanish partner in the new alliance Germany and Italy were about to form with Japan[142] would represent an insurmountable blow to Britain's ability to carry on the war.

But the talks clearly demonstrated how far Spain and Germany were from coming to terms. Even a second round, in which Serrano Suñer conferred with Hitler directly as Franco's "personal representative," elicited no substantive change in the basic Spanish position that it would enter the war only on its own terms and at a time of its own choosing. Though Hitler suggested how easy the conquest of Gibraltar would be —perhaps a veiled threat to take the fortress even without Spain's cooperation—the Germans got no satisfaction beyond heartfelt affirmations of eternal Spanish sympathy for the German crusade in Europe. To Serrano Suñer's expressed concerns of Britain's revenge—even a British landing in Spain—Hitler termed such a scenario a "chimera,"[143] with the Luftwaffe fully capable of turning back any such aggression.

Once again, with Franco's agreement, the Spanish foreign minister rejected absolutely the notion of the ceding of one of the Canary Islands to Germany, even though Hitler said such a transfer was necessary to enable German power to successfully protect the weaker Spain from an eventual American strike. Serrano Suñer instead threw out the suggestion that it might be possible to take Portuguese Madeira, though such largess was obviously not his to give, that island having belonged to Spain's Iberian neighbor since 1420. He told Hitler there was no "geographical justification" for Portugal's existence (Serrano Suñer's sympathies for Portugal were never deep), but it had lived an independent existence for

800 years and Spain didn't particularly want to take on the burdens that would be imposed with a forcible absorption of seven million "weeping Portuguese." Both Hitler and Serrano Suñer agreed this Portuguese "problem"—presumably meaning the issue of Madeira—would be solved not by diplomatic negotiations, but "only by a military operation."[144]

Standoff clearly well suited Franco, but it just as clearly did not suit the German dictator. Though Spain and its demands might be safely ignored until Britain had been gotten out of his hair, Hitler the military strategist still wanted all his Iberian ducks neatly lined up. It was time to talk, face to face, with the Caudillo himself.

•   •   •

The place chosen for one of the most notorious confrontations of World War II was the same town on the Bidassoa River where the Wehrmacht had sealed the Axis's possession of the Pyrenean border. Hendaye, a few miles south of the far more agreeable Biarritz, little merited the honor of so important a footnote in the history of modern European bellicosity. In 1940, it possessed a handful of resort hotels, a homemade liqueur of middling distinction, and a sanatorium kept by the city of Paris for its indigent children. At the edge of town the adjoined platforms of the two countries' rail systems abutted, the French narrow-gauge clashing with the Spanish wide-gauge.

Hendaye, the farthest populated place on the Biscayan coast of France before Spain, had last been seriously heard of nearly 300 years earlier. On the Isle of Pheasants, a minuscule punctuation point of neutral territory in the middle of the Bidassoa, the Peace of the Pyrenees had with some considerable gravity been signed in 1659, ending a tendril of the Thirty Years' War (and with it over 150 years of war between France and Spain) as well as Spanish power in Europe. The treaty stipulated that the crowns of France and Spain should never be united under one family, a condition that led to the War of the Spanish Succession, one of the many bewildering conflicts that have convulsed the continent's affairs. The Pyrenean Peace boded poorly, historically speaking, for the conference that was about to commence, except that Hitler had probably never heard of it and Franco wasn't a man to be sabotaged by ill-starred auguries.

The German leader came to the meeting—which he regarded as an opportunity to put his Spanish difficulties behind him—having recently thrashed out Axis concerns over Iberia with his Italian soul mate. At their October 4 Brenner Pass encounter, Hitler told Mussolini that he feared conceding Franco's demands for two principal reasons: the British would immediately grab the Canaries to make up for the expected loss of Gibraltar,[145] and officials in France's African empire would throw their loyalty to de Gaulle. A quick talk on October 22 with Vichy premier Pierre Laval, mainly preparing for the discussions he would be having with Pétain after meeting with Franco, encouraged Hitler in his hope that France would bend to the demands of his grand strategy. Promising Laval an "empire equivalent to its present one,"[146] Hitler knew the pledge could always be broken later, but still feared it would compromise his ability to assure the same cake to Franco if the Spaniard found out about the Laval proffer.

A German diplomatic memorandum of the time noted that "there was the danger that, if the French were explicitly told they would have to get out of certain African areas, the African possessions would perhaps desert France, even with the concurrence of the government of Vichy."[147] To mitigate such an occurrence, the Axis partners would face a considerable dilution of their activities.[148] In retrospect, it appears that it was a risk Franco correctly judged Hitler wouldn't take.

The Spaniard Hitler found at Hendaye on October 23, 1940, was no dupe in the wartime fashion of Benito Mussolini. Though Franco's physical presence would hardly seem to merit his inclusion in the ranks of Europe's leaders, his single-mindedness about his price for co-belligerency did. Franco came to Hendaye to extract *precise* guarantees that Spain's needs would be met—that it would get the military equipment it demanded, that the petroleum and food Spain needed for its economy and people would be delivered, that Spain would end up with a healthy chunk of Africa. If the German thought he was going to bully Franco into bending to his will, he would soon find out some very unpleasant facts. Though Franco continued to profess eternal devotion to Germany, to exude gratitude for its role in helping his Nationalists win the Civil War, to publicly fawn over the Führer as if he were the Second Christ, at Hendaye the diminutive dictator would not be bought cheaply.

The talks were conducted in Hitler's luxurious parlor car, the *Führerzug*, sitting in the Hendaye train station a half mile outside the town. (Hitler never set foot in Spain itself.) While the two principals discussed the broad outlines of grand strategy, their chief lieutenants—Ribbentrop and the newly promoted Serrano Suñer (the former now snidely referring to the latter as "that Jesuit Suñer")—met separately in the parlor car of the Reich Foreign Ministry, attached to the *Führerzug*, to work out the finer points of Spain's entry into the war. Serrano Suñer surprised the German with the disclosure that Spain wished to have its border with France rectified to bring "French Catalonia" under Spanish sovereignty. Ribbentrop evenly replied that such an eventuality would depend on the Reich being able to compensate France out of chunks taken from British territory.[149]

In the main carriage, the discourse between the two dictators droned on for nine hours; Hitler's interpreter, Paul Schmidt, recalled Franco's monotonous voice sounding like "an Arab praying."[150] Hitler sometimes controlled the conversation, with Franco then calmly taking his turn to expound an endless stream of reasons why Spain had to be cautious in its commitments to war. (Franco did not, be it noted, forgo his usual afternoon siesta; the company broke for the appropriate time.) Hitler remained evasive about the Caudillo's repeated claims on France's African possessions. The German's tack was meant to impress Franco: how Britain was beaten, how it failed to realize this simple fact, how Germany's final victory was as sure as the next sunrise. The Führer's only flush of excitement came during his windup, when he declared that a seized Gibraltar would mean the exclusion of the British Empire from the Mediterranean, as well as the long-overdue return of the Rock to Spanish sovereignty.

Toward the end of the day, with their foreign ministers now in attendance, Franco launched into a kind of peroration, reexplaining to Hitler the history of his struggle and the reasons for his caution. Franco even gave a lecture on how Germany's battles might be more advantageously waged, opinions his host neither solicited nor particularly appreciated. Openly yawning, the bored Hitler asked Ribbentrop to hand the Spaniards the detailed secret protocol—already worked out in Germany—in which Spain pledged adherence to the Tripartite Pact and its entry into the war when Germany considered such entry "opportune."[151] The meeting adjourned again, this time for dinner. Willard Beaulac, an American diplomat in wartime Spain and a historian of the events at Hendaye, recounted that Hitler murmured as he was leaving the dinner, "With those characters we can do nothing."[152] The assessment was, all in all, fairly accurate.

On taking leave of Hendaye and their German hosts, Franco and Serrano Suñer traveled the short distance back down the coast to San Sebastiàn, there to study the protocol's provisions. Both were anxious to return it to the Germans who waited in Hendaye (though Hitler himself left immediately after Franco's departure to meet with Pétain) to get the whole thing resolved. The document they sent back to Ribbentrop at Hendaye was properly "adjusted" to meet Spanish requirements. Franco agreed to commit his country to war, but co-belligerence could only come *after* Germany armed and supplied Spain to the degree it had been demanding for months.

Though the promises Germany made to Spain at Hendaye were generous, they were, in fact, beyond the Reich's ability to fulfill. And as for Spain, it gave very little more than it had promised Germany all along: vague promises and brave affirmations of loyalty. Further, Franco demanded the agreed protocol be kept secret until such time as Spain actually declared war on the Allies,[153] the Caudillo having no wish to see British or American goodwill evaporate before it was absolutely necessary.

Franco and Spain were a success at Hendaye. Hitler and Germany were not. Had Spain joined the Axis as a full belligerent partner, the costs to the anti-Nazi forces would have been incalculable. Germany would have gained the use of the entire Spanish coastline—its ports and its protections and the geographical dominance they would have afforded —as well as those of all the Spanish islands, both the Balearics in the Mediterranean and the Canaries in the Atlantic. All that was within the Spanish borders would be German—wolfram ore, perhaps most importantly (though, admittedly, most of this now went to Germany anyway). Gibraltar would have been gone to the British, and Britain would have been cut off from Mediterranean routes to its empire in the Far East and India, and from its Middle Eastern domains virtually altogether. Pétain, thoroughly isolated under such a scenario, would have very likely been able to scare the African French governors into cooperating with German rule.[154] It would not have been an outcome anything less than disastrous for the Allies.

* * *

The pressure on Franco was about to escalate substantially, directly emanating from an ill-judged attack on Greece by Benito Mussolini and his champing legions. But the effect of the Duce's actions would in the end be to dissuade Hitler from any notion of taking Gibraltar in the face of a hostile Spain.

On October 28, five days after Hendaye, Italy's armed forces invaded Greece. Unfulfilled by his jackal-like role in the defeat of France, the Italian dictator desperately wanted to pump up Italy's importance in Hitler's eyes as well as in the war councils of the Tripartite Pact partners. He figured a military triumph of his own might do it for him. Greece would, he calculated, be that triumph.

Using as a launching platform its recently acquired Albanian colony,

Rome publicly justified its invasion on the grounds that the Athens government was allowing the British to use Greece's ports and airfields. But with the help of seasoned British units, the Greeks quickly gained the upper hand over Mussolini's cocky but incompetently led soldiery. By November 23, the Italian invasion force had been pushed back to the Albanian border, and within a few weeks Greece's army held a quarter of Albania itself.

For Hitler, the affair was an unalloyed disaster, destroying his hopes of cheaply gaining control of southeastern Europe by diplomatic means. It also meant rescuing Mussolini as well as throwing the British out of their now expanded area of influence. To accomplish the latter meant getting his Wehrmacht to Greece, and that would require Yugoslavia's cooperation. Since a coup in Belgrade overthrew the country's pro-Nazi government and replaced it with one that unexpectedly refused Germany's transit demands, Hitler would be forced to crush Yugoslavia on the way to crushing Greece.

On April 6, 1941, five months after Mussolini precipitated the dilemma, German forces poured into Yugoslavia from bases in their Bulgarian and Rumanian ally states and from southern Germany. The republic of the South Slavs was about to endure one of the cruelest of all of the many Nazi reigns of brutality. On the first day of the attack, 17,000 Belgraders died in Luftwaffe aerial bombardments, their city pulverized by Göring's seasoned squadrons. The Führer's order—the so-called Operation Strafe (Punishment)—called frankly for the country's "destruction militarily and as a national unit . . . [and to be] carried out with pitiless harshness."[155] By the end of the war, more than one of every ten Yugoslavs would perish in the occupation, most at the hands of fellow Yugoslavs in the attendant internecine political warfare.

As Yugoslavia was scourged, so too did Greece's trial begin anew, this time with quite different results. On April 27, Athens fell to the Nazis. Three days later, the British abandoned their foothold in the Peloponnese, with it vanishing their last toehold on the continent save Gibraltar.

The Mussolini-initiated sideshow war in the Balkans and the Mediterranean threatened the entire British situation in southeastern Europe. Hitler now stood to become a power in the Levant. The British position in Egypt, with its control of the vital Suez lifeline, was gravely jeopardized. The hope ended that Turkey might soon join Britain against Germany. The only blessing, then an invisible one, was that Germany's effort in the Balkans may have been a factor in its not reaching Moscow before the first snows in the fall of 1941 would doom Barbarossa, Hitler's climactic war on the Soviet state and the Slavic people.

· · ·

When Britain went to Greece to help save that nation from the Italian Army, it clearly lent a new importance to the Mediterranean, one Hitler hadn't to that date assigned to what he hoped would be a minor theater of operations managed by Italian forces ten times larger than Britain's North African armies. While plans were being created to save the situation by striking at Yugoslavia and then supplanting Italy in Greece (Hitler initially ordered a German invasion of Greece on November 4, but it took until the following April for the Wehrmacht to get ready), the German leader would be obliged to deal with British power in the Mediterranean. The door to that power hinged, in massive proportion, on Gibraltar.

So on November 12, 1940, Hitler issued his Directive 18. Codenamed Operation Felix, the project dealt with the capture of Gibraltar and the subsequent closing of the fourteen-mile-wide strait,[156] preferably with—but otherwise without—Spanish cooperation. Directive 18 set January 10, 1941, as the approximate date for a German entry from occupied France into Spain.

Fully conceived, Felix envisioned the clearing of British influence from the entire western Mediterranean. That included making sure the Atlantic islands didn't become a British substitute for Gibraltar. The plan assigned the taking of the Rock primarily to a German assault force, the strait then to be blocked with the assistance of German land, naval, and air units; the target date for this part of Felix was February 1, or shortly after. The Germans would concentrate some 200 guns on the Rock. Luftwaffe dive-bombers would join in to support the infantry assault onto the isthmus from the Spanish town of La Línea, ending by taking the crown colony itself. Three days were allocated for ground operations, to be carried out by the same experienced and immensely skilled troops who had shocked the world when against long odds they overpowered Belgium's "impregnable" Fort Eben Emael the prior May. Plans called for the Spanish, with German help, to keep any invader out of the Canaries; Portugal's Cape Verde Islands were to be "protected" exclusively by German units. Following the assault force's attack on Gibraltar, two more German divisions—one armored, one motorized—would cross into Morocco and capture its Atlantic coast. A further three Wehrmacht divisions would enter Spain and drive toward Portugal, where they would be used to stave off the expected British attempt to gain an Iberian toehold through that country. With both Morocco and Gibraltar under Axis control, the strait would be sealed tight. When Britain collapsed, the Rock would be turned over to the Spanish government.[157] After everything was wrapped up, Germany would have been just as much the master in Spain, though perhaps in a more collegial fashion, that it was in France.

Hitler peremptorily summoned Serrano Suñer to Berchtesgaden's Berghof, his mountain sanctuary in southern Bavaria, to be apprised of Operation Felix. The first thing that was pointed out to the Spanish foreign minister was the magnitude of the honor Germany was doing Spain to allow it to participate in so important an undertaking. Because Mussolini had made a mess of things in Greece, it was necessary that this operation go forth within weeks. Though the cool Spanish foreign minister pointed out to Hitler during a break in the Führer's lava-like monologue that the Hendaye protocol allowed Spain to decide for itself when it should enter the war—Serrano Suñer was undoubtedly at that moment ruminating on the ferocity of Britain's resistance to Germany and the latter's apparent inability to force that nation into surrender—Hitler informed his guest that Spanish cooperation was absolutely vital, and that he now required assurance such cooperation would be forthcoming. A threat flickered across the table like a snake when Hitler bluntly remarked to his Spanish guest on Germany's strength and its "power to annihilate disloyal friends."[158]

Turning on the now familiar litany, Serrano Suñer begged the Führer to understand the hardships the Spanish people had so recently suffered and his government's extreme reluctance to ask them to repeat such suffering. (This when the Spanish state was executing hundreds of former Republicans every day.) He added that Spain would resist any invasion in the same way it had resisted Napoleon. By inference he meant "British" invasion, but the unspoken threat—one Hitler evidently understood—was that *any* foreigners entering Spanish territory unbidden would be opposed. Serrano Suñer added a surprise to the conversation when he informed his host that Franco did not wish to move until Suez was in German hands—Spain had no desire to get bogged down in a long war, one with which it was woefully ill equipped to deal.[159]

For four hours, the seesawing between the chancellor and the foreign minister teetered on, Serrano Suñer finally asking Hitler to send technicians to Spain to verify its needs, a ploy giving the Spaniard extra time to think how best to resist German demands that the Hendaye obligations Franco undertook be met *now*. After getting Hitler to promise to "look into" sending wheat to Spain to match the wheat promised by the American and British ambassadors—Hitler's agreement to do so was clearly painful for him in light of the almost nothing that Serrano Suñer had agreed to of *his* demands—the Cuñadissimo left to spend the night in one of the pseudo-chalet's guest rooms. The next morning he took his leave of Hitler and the Berghof.

Hitler did indeed send an "inspector" to Spain—an expert in the person of Admiral Wilhelm Canaris, the Reich's counterintelligence chief and a man well acquainted with Spain from his Civil War experiences in that country. In an early December audience with the Caudillo, Canaris told Franco that Hitler wanted to kick off Operation Felix on January 10, a little over a month away. First, the Reich would send elements of the Wehrmacht into Spain, with supplies and other economic aid accompanying them. Franco squirmed, but finally and firmly said no, going to war would be asking too much of his exhausted people; as historian Herbert Feis nicely put it, he wanted to "import a while longer rather than fight."[160] Canaris countered Franco by asking if perhaps a later date could be set. The Caudillo thought not, but did invite the Reich to send another expert—an *economic* expert—to further evaluate Spanish needs. He also asked Canaris to take his very best wishes back to the Führer.[161]

Thus on December 18, another, far grander undertaking, Operation Barbarossa, was ordered into the final planning stage, and the bright attraction of Gibraltar for the German Führer was—perforce—toned down to be reconsidered another day. In the end, Germany hadn't even gained the transit rights to send its troops through Spain to Gibraltar.[162]

A few days later—on the last night of 1940—Hitler wrote a letter to his faithful Italian ally giving his view of the general state of the war. His comments about Spain are instructive:

Duce,

. . . In examining the general situation I reach the following conclusions.

[Re: Spain] Profoundly troubled by the situation, which Franco thinks has deteriorated. Spain has refused to collaborate with the Axis Powers. I fear that Franco may be about to make the biggest mistake of his life. I think that his idea of receiving from the democracies raw materials and wheat as a sort of recompense for his abstention from the conflict is extremely naïve. The democracies will keep him in suspense until he has consumed the last grain of wheat, and then they will unloose the fight against him.

I deplore all this, for from our side we have completed our preparations for crossing the Spanish frontier on January 10, and to attack Gibraltar at the beginning of February. I think that success would have been relatively rapid. The troops picked for this operation have been specially trained and chosen. The moment that the Straits of Gibraltar fell into our hands the danger of a French change-over [to de Gaulle] in North and West Africa would be definitely eliminated.

I am, therefore, very saddened by this decision of Franco, which is so little in accord with the aid which we, you, Duce, and myself, gave him when he found himself in difficulties. I still have the hope, the slight hope, that he will realize at the last minute the catastrophic consequences of his conduct, and that even tardily he will find his way to this battle front, where our victory will decide his own destiny.[163]

· · ·

Though Spain had won reprieve from German determination to cajole or force it into joining the war, Franco knew nothing of Operation Barbarossa and was not aware that Hitler had moved Gibraltar to the Axis's back burner. It was true that the unexpected resilience and resistance of the British put the first doubts in the Caudillo's mind about Germany's final victory. But Germany was still then seen by virtually all observers as the arbiter of every continental European state's future. To flagrantly flout a Nazi invitation to become a charter member of that future was flirting with disaster. Judging Franco's actions as though he knew Hitler had now turned his eyes and his avarice eastward is missing this reality.

Hitler's top advisers meanwhile persisted in pointing out the continuing necessity for taking Gibraltar and thereby throttling Britain's access to the Mediterranean. The commander-in-chief of the German Navy, Admiral Erich Raeder, in particular still urged that the Gibraltar bottleneck be closed, noting that British control of Malta and Suez in conjunction with free passage through the strait would eventually lead to the enemy's attempt to first isolate Italy and then to attack Germany from Italian bases in concert with the Americans, who would, sooner or later, become Britain's ally.[164] Still Hitler let the January 10 deadline for entering Spain go by, and every day closer to the attack in the East meant that a resumption of Felix became correspondingly less likely for the foreseeable future. Hitler well understood what a danger it would present to the Reich to get bogged down against a hostile and immensely proud Spanish Army so soon before taking on Stalin. And he had no doubt that if the Wehrmacht attempted to enter Spain unbidden, that Spanish Army *would* be hostile.

Hitler's personal feelings about Franco sank to a kind of smoldering anger, regardless of his decision to let Spain off the hook. Correspondence sent from Berlin to Madrid over the next weeks demonstrated the magnitude of Hitler's contempt for Franco's vacillation and how much he still coveted a cheap acquisition of Gibraltar. In a letter of January 21, the Führer noted again Spain's debt to Germany for the success of the Nationalist cause: "Without the help of the Führer and the Duce there would not today be any Nationalist Spain or any Caudillo."

To the German ambassador, Eberhard von Stohrer, Franco calmly denied the validity of Hitler's pique, and again asked that some appropriate German come and see the problems Spain was having. This time, the Caudillo thought Field Marshal Wilhelm Keitel might be the right man to take a look. In a rage, Ribbentrop wired back Stohrer that he'd best drum some sense into Franco, demanding the ambassador not let the Spaniard misjudge the importance set by the Führer on an immediate Spanish entry into the war.

On receipt of the next demands from Berlin, Franco adopted a seasonal tack, replying that just now the snows were far too heavy in the Pyrenees for Germany to think of a mass crossing by its armies. At this ingenuous stall, Hitler responded that heavy snow hadn't stopped German armies yet, that on its own turf the Wehrmacht was in fact *used* to operating in such conditions. But of course, all had devolved into a fruitless exchange, the German leader's mind having now gone over to matters Russian and the Spanish leader not yet near to running out of reasons, imagined and real, why Spain should sit out the war.

Mussolini insinuated his way into the picture in an effort to heal the breach between his fellow dictators. Asking Franco for assurances of Spain's good faith, Mussolini queried the Spaniard: "Should the Germans suspect that Spain did not wish to enter the war because the German invasion of Great Britain had not come off, or because of the Italian setbacks in Libya, can I assure the Führer to the contrary?" The Caudillo replied: "Absolutely, the faith of the Spanish people in the victory of the Axis is the same as on the first day."[165] Franco added, though, that he wanted the honor of taking Gibraltar to be a Spanish one alone—and his assent to the German plan to take it in conjunction with Spain was therefore withdrawn.

Throughout this wrangling with the Axis, Spain continued to receive fuel and food from British and American sufferance, aid it clearly wished not to jeopardize by any excessively public tilt toward the Reich. For their part, the Allies continued to supply Spain in the hope that such supplies were more important to Franco than was securing his country's future in Hitler's Europe. Nonetheless, the West was pushed very far by Franco's well-publicized adoration of Germany, so far that Ambassador Weddell threatened to tie such aid to a public affirmation that Spain would not go to war on the German side. At this the viscerally anti-democratic Serrano Suñer snapped that "Spain's situation vis-à-vis Germany was identical to that of America's relationship to Britain—except that Spain had nothing to give to Germany."[166]

Spain's needs were neither imaginary nor exaggerated. Since Hitler had made the supplying of wheat to Franco dependent on his joining the war and closing Gibraltar—or allowing Germany to close it—the fact was that without Western supplies Spaniards *would* have starved in massive numbers. Since a poor harvest in 1940–41, tied with the still festering Civil War wounds, continued to prevent Spaniards from feeding themselves with anything like self-sufficiency, it was help that America supplied—or that Britain and America allowed through their blockade system—that stood between Spain and overwhelming civil disaster.

The allowance of edible vegetable oils and fats to Spain was one example that illustrates how these figures were fine-tuned according to unforeseen exigencies. When in early 1941 Britain's Ministry of Economic Warfare decided to lower the boom on oils allowed into Spain because of the evidence—accurate in this case—that Madrid was reexporting them to Germany, it found itself begged by Spain to lift the embargo when typhus broke out in April. Tallow and palm oil were desperately needed for making soap to help ward off the epidemic, and in a humanitarian gesture, London accordingly relaxed its limits.

One additional source of food from the United States to wartime Spain merits mention. In February, the American Red Cross organized relief shipments, made up primarily of milk and flour. Along with the food went trucks from Detroit to see that the supplies were distributed throughout the peninsula. As should have surprised no one, the Spanish press barely mentioned these gifts from the American people.[167]

·   ·   ·

On the second day of March 1941, Spain went into mourning—both official and real. Alfonso XIII, the last Spanish king, died in Rome, in exile from the kingdom he had ruled so imperfectly. When the news reached Madrid that night, thousands of balconies had within hours been draped in the black crepe shot through with the red and gold that symbolized the ancient arms of royal Castile. The mourning of both the tradition-minded city center and the Calle de Salamanca patrician quarter reflected the range of the Spanish people's feelings toward the defective but at least stable years of Alfonso XIII. Even in the outlying workers' suburbs of Cuatro Caminos and Carabanchel and Puerto de Toledo, where people were too poor to buy bunting and instead made do with sheets and tablecloths, miles of mourning-draped streets marked the depth of the Spanish people's sadness. The outpouring of royalist sentiment was nearly universal, excepting only among the purist-fascist elements of the Falange.

The Ritz Hotel, social nerve center of the capital and the hotel that had been built as virtually a guesthouse for visitors to the court of pre-Republican Spain, was flooded with a stream of grandees and nobles leaving their calling cards as a token of respect to the dead monarch: the Infante Don Fernando de Baviera, Alfonso's brother-in-law, solemnly received Ramón Serrano Suñer, the Falangist visiting officially to pay the Caudillo's respects to the family he refused to let re-ascend the kingdom's throne. The nation's new master ordered three days of national mourning and initiated the transfer of the royal remains to the pantheon of the monastery of the Escorial, the ancient mausoleum in whose marble vaults rested generations of the nation's kings. But the Caudillo was not about to let the discredited dynasty set up shop anew in *his* Spain. Certainly not yet, anyway.

Lisbon

If 1940 was a year of unprecedented debacle for Europe's democracies, it was a year of festive spectacle in Portugal. The nation was celebrating the eight hundredth anniversary of the founding of the royal (albeit now defunct) dynasty, and thus of the nation's birth. But more importantly, it also marked the three hundredth year of Portugal's reacquired independence from the big brother with whom it gingerly but unavoidably shared the peninsula. To mark their independence, the citizens of Portugal threw an enthusiastic welcoming gala for the observance's preeminent guest, the Duke of Kent, head of the special British mission to the celebration and youngest brother of the king of England.[168] Yet even as the nation celebrated, this so far peaceful little corner of Europe was undertaking its most critically important effort of World War II: continuing to urge neutrality on a Spain that appeared bent on war, and in so doing trying to safeguard its own vulnerable tranquillity.

The ordinary Portuguese citizen, free from responsibility for the events that might at almost any moment shatter his nation's peace, tried to forget the dangers. In their thousands, Lisboners thronged the brightly lit streets of their city, the strides of the celebrants lightened by the rhythms of marching bands. On the Tagus, flag-bedecked Portuguese gunboats made room for an American Coast Guard cutter in port to help mark this so-called Pageant of Peace and Progress. In honor of their hosts, the Americans fired off a 21-gun salute, inadvertently shattering windows in the capital's proletarian harbor district. But nothing marred the majestic *Te Deum* celebrated in Lisbon's cathedral, with the Knights of Malta, graced by the scarlet tunics of their ancient order, together with the entire diplomatic corps in attendance to join the company of Portuguese officials in marking the country's deliverance from Spain. Conspicuous in his presence was Nicolás Franco, his brother's representative to Portugal. The hum in the cathedral quieted as everyone listened to His Eminence Emmanuel Cardinal Gonçalves Cerejeira pointedly read an 800-year-old papal bull recognizing the full independence of this the continent's southwestern-most nation.

By late afternoon the city's crowded sidewalks became difficult to negotiate. By midnight, they were impossibly jammed. That was when the crowds flowed from café to restaurant to coffeehouse, venues in which topic A among the city's "temporary guests" was boats and planes and how they were going to be able to get where they wanted to go. ("My hotel porter says a Spanish freighter is in port, loading for Argentina.") Regardless of the time of day, speculators feverishly traded a dozen different currencies in what had become Europe's last truly free money exchange.

Amidst the celebrations and the celebrants, the abundant goods and the abundant gossip, this ancient capital now stood inexorably bathed in the political glare of a continent at war. It floodlit a city where statesmen and spies jostled for elbowroom, a city everyone was trying to get to and a city everyone was trying to get away from. Lisbon had become Western Europe's last major gate to freedom, the one convenient link between the belligerents, and, except for Stockholm, the last important European capital not yet immersed in war or poised on its altar. For America, it was the gateway through which its goods and people passed to leave or enter embattled Europe. For visitors from almost anyplace else on the continent, the happily animated city burst on the senses as a reminder of another, lost life.

Much of the animation was, of course, built on endlessly varying orders of tragedy. As Ernie Pyle sadly saw it, Lisbon was "a city that harbors 10,000 distresses of spirit." When at mid-1940 the number of refugees in Portugal reached twice Pyle's figure, Lisbon's housing situation attained crisis proportions. The government finally took down the welcome sign. Now to enter the country a supplicant needed both a ticket and a visa taking him . . . beyond. The trouble was, there weren't many countries "beyond"—at least there weren't many countries willing to take in the kinds of refugees Portugal harbored, specifically the Jews who in that season of racial ordeal constituted so large a share of Europe's rejects.

While their hosts celebrated, the refugees clung to hopes of getting somewhere—anywhere out of Europe. With Hitler's armies everywhere victorious, how long before their tormentors would be in Portugal itself? Many hoped for a visa to the United States, and at one point over 20,000 names filled the waiting list for the precious document. Argentina and Brazil appealed to many, while some wanted to get to a faraway colony— the Belgian Congo, the Dutch East Indies, anywhere the Gestapo, the SS, the various secret police organizations, the Wehrmacht couldn't follow. But visas to the Allied or still neutral countries were desperately difficult to obtain, and those without some kind of special influence or needed skills often waited, without hope, in the limbo of statelessness. The one relatively welcoming haven remained Britain, even when that country was suffering the worst Germany could give and its own people were rationed to near-malnutrition levels. Perhaps the luckiest ones were those willing and rich enough to be content to wait out the war in Portugal—Ignace Paderewski, the first president of Poland, and King Carol of Rumania were prominent among these privileged refugees.

The refuge of choice for these luminaries was Estoril. A few miles down the Tagus from urban Lisbon, this waterside rendezvous magnified all the factors that made Portugal such an anomaly in wartime Europe. Plenty of good food, days passed at sunny beaches untainted by barbed wire and mines, cheerful and unlimited gaming awaiting in the casino. The British journalist Hugh Muir wrote that the town's strand was "packed with beach lizards getting roasted to a fashionable brown," and "French beauties in harlequin colors" were a common sight.[169] The visitor stood a good chance of running into King Carol, often accompanied by his silky mistress, Magda Lupescu, or perhaps of spotting Don Juan of Spain, the pretender to the crown now firmly in the Caudillo's grasp. The Wonder Bar in this gambling Valhalla was sheltered by the last of the great European gambling houses still in unrestricted operation, where the bets started at one dollar.

For those who remained in the capital itself, the *crème de la crème* would likely choose the Aviz as their sanctuary. Once the town palace of a Portuguese grandee, it was preferred by the richer Allied refugees because it was usually pleasantly free of Germans, who preferred mixing with their own kind, the latter generally found at the Palacio, in Estoril. The best suite in the Aviz was permanently taken by King Carol (whose pennies didn't need pinching), having been lately vacated by the Spanish Duke of Alba. The rate—six dollars a day—made it more than even the best-heeled could easily afford, let alone the typical Portuguese, to whom that figure was more than most earned in a month. The snobby Aviz staff often disparagingly referred to their own countrymen as "just Portuguese."

Most of the refugees were persons of some means in their own country, the factor that had allowed them to get to Portugal in the first place. But confiscations of their wealth had left the lion's share in straitened circumstances, and a single small cup of coffee had to be made to do yeoman's service over an endless afternoon sitting in the sunlit sidewalk cafés of Lisbon and Estoril and Cascais. Though costs in Portugal were low by British and American standards, that relativity lost its import when one's pockets were empty, or nearly so, and to get out of Portugal often required bribing shipping agents and ship's captains to whom a large enough payoff could sometimes result in the casual bumping of another would-be escapee.

The extraordinary thing about the Portuguese themselves was the kindness which they showed the refugees, both the well-to-do and otherwise; there was little of the contempt these unfortunates faced in many of the other countries they had passed through. Nevertheless, the Portuguese were often shocked by the behavior of the army of "guests" that had flooded their country. For the natives of an ancient and sedate culture to be presented every evening with the spectacle of slacks-clad women promenading in the Rossio—the capital's Times Square—was traumatic. What was more, many foreign women went bareheaded, the age-old mark in Portugal of a prostitute. Still, all most Portuguese had to do to assuage their upset at the intrusion was to think of how much worse off their Spanish cousins were, always a thought to cheer the most depressed citizen of this small country.

Aside from the unwillingness of nearly all nations to take in Europe's refugees, transportation in and out of Portugal remained a horrendous problem. Though Britain magnanimously welcomed refugees able to get there, most simply couldn't. Ships from Lisbon to Britain were so few in greatest part because of the dangers the U-boat-infested seas presented even to vessels clearly marked as neutral. The majority of those ships sailing were in any event freighters, few capable of carrying more than a handful of paying passengers.

The shipping lines maintained registers bulging with the names of stranded Europeans willing to sell the clothes off their backs to reach a safe haven, one where they could earn a living—something the Portuguese government strictly prohibited. The American Export line ran a weekly steamer to New York, and by setting up cots in its public spaces for 200 people, it was able to clear Lisbon each week of those whose papers for the United States were completely in order. For "official" Americans in Lisbon, there was usually a U.S. Navy vessel lying at harbor charged with removing them to safety in case of a German invasion.

In a day spent at Sintra Airdrome, eighteen miles outside Lisbon, a visitor would likely witness planes carrying the national emblems of Britain, Italy, and Germany, the three biggest of the warring nations. Daily flights on London-, Rome-, and Berlin-bound aircraft were available out of the Portuguese capital; the downtown ticket offices of British Overseas Airways (where Clipper passengers from America booked for their onward flights to London) and Lufthansa stood next door to each other, the agents and passengers of each icily ignoring the others. A seeming contradiction, the belligerents much appreciated the way the airlines allowed them to get in and out of each other's sphere, not only to keep apprised of enemy actions by conveying each other's newspapers (prominently available on the city's newsstands were the *London Daily Mail*, *The New York Times*, the *Deutsche Allgemeine Zeitung*, the *Lavora Fascista*, and the Falangist *Arriba*) but to provide for the exchange of prisoners and the passage of those few civilians carrying vital messages back and forth between the warring capitals. For a long time, no one appeared willing to close this gateway by molesting the other's planes.

The great Pan American 60-passenger Clipper flying boats were far harder to book passage on than was surface transportation. The airline assigned its highest priority to mail, and maddeningly the thrice-weekly planes were so often weighed down with this cargo that only a handful of passengers could be boarded before the weight limits were reached.[170] The State Department acted as the clearinghouse for prospective passengers, with preference given to diplomats, military observers, and other government representatives; war correspondents were next on the list. Swindlers sometime sold the $425 seats on the winged boats for as much as $1,000, which bought the unsuspecting would-be passenger nothing since Pan American forbade transfer of its Clipper tickets. Factors in the unwelcome guise of Atlantic storms fairly routinely grounded the four-engine, 43-ton duralumin craft. As it was forced to make fuel stops at Bermuda and the Azores, such bad weather befuddled the already tenuous link between hemispheres. The Azores landing, made at Horta, had to be negotiated in the open sea rather than in a protected harbor. Because the plane could not set down in rough water—the limit was thirty-inch-high waves—passengers were sometimes held up for days, eastbound at Bermuda and westbound at Lisbon, while Pan Am's meteorologist kept track of Horta's waves.

Probably Lisbon's—and Portugal's—most renowned role during the war was as a focal point of European espionage. Though all the belligerents, and not a few of the more significant nonbelligerents, kept squadrons of agents in the country, it was the Germans who most outrageously offended Portuguese neutrality and hospitality in this regard. Hitler's agents included among their credits misbehavior ranging from destructive acts of sabotage to simple but vexing espionage. The Germans packed their Lisbon mission with spies, so that the establishment's total personnel eventually rose to forty, exactly four times as many "diplomats" as the British embassy housed. The Sitmar travel agency, a large German concern, employed twenty young Nazis among its staff of agents.

The feelings of most Portuguese ran overwhelmingly in favor of Britain over Germany. The manufacture of small RAF lapel buttons during the Duke of Kent's visit resulted in a thriving commerce, though when the government prohibited the traffic in the name of strict neutrality, the buttons were replaced with badges depicting a hat and a cigar—a clearly unneutral salute to Winston Churchill. The attempt to impose neutrality on the population often reached humorous heights: when war news was shown in the cinemas, a notice on the screen requested the audiences to abstain from manifestations of partiality to any of the belligerents, presumably including even smiles and frowns. A telling sign was that visitors to Lisbon found that the best way to get rid of the city's importunate street vendors was to emit a growled "*Nein, nein!*"[171]

.   .   .

While the ordinary Portuguese contended with the changes the refugees brought into the country, and the refugees struggled with getting out of the country, President Salazar was grappling with what was happening in Spain. With the fall of France and Franco's ensuing shift from "neutrality" to "nonbelligerency," Salazar more than ever foresaw Spain's joining the Axis against Britain, inexorably followed by the incorporation of Portugal into some kind of "greater" Spain. While anticipating this danger through the second half of 1940 and the early months of 1941, Salazar was also fully alive to the attractiveness to the United Kingdom of seizing the Portuguese Atlantic islands, especially the immensely valuable Azores. The hard-pressed British prime minister, strongly in favor of such a preemptive maneuver, was in the end veered away from it by his Foreign Office,[172] but the Azores matter would soon become a hot issue to an American government without the ties of a historical alliance with

Portugal and therefore far less sensitive than London to Salazar's balancing act.

To meet the most immediate of his problems—the threat of a belligerent Spain—Salazar depended on diplomacy as his militarily weak nation's only practicable weapon. Knowing that he couldn't depend on an overextended Britain to come to the rescue if attacked by Spain or Germany, through the summer of 1940 Salazar and his ambassador to Madrid, Teotónio Pereira, worked with Franco's brother Nicolás on a protocol addition to the 1939 Portuguese-Spanish Treaty. He hoped such a move would at least hold off any danger from Spanish aggression, if not from a Germany intent on controlling the whole peninsula.

The Pereira agreement signed in July contained Franco's assurances that Spain would respect Portugal's independence. For its part, Portugal promised that any obligation fulfilled in regard to its British relationship wouldn't affect Spain. If Britain were to violate Portugal's sovereignty, Spain would expect to be involved in repulsing any such incursion, which Madrid believed might bring the Wehrmacht flooding across the Pyrenees.[173] Portugal was, in short, to maintain absolute neutrality under the agreement.

Regardless of Franco's assurances, the agitation in Spain—especially within the Falange Party—to force Portugal into a single Iberian state under Spanish mastery was one of the more unpleasant realities that Salazar had to face. Though the Portuguese strongly stressed the differences between their small country and its much larger neighbor, many Spaniards tended to think of the two as a single "natural" entity, and their separation as some kind of violation of geopolitics. Even the language difference between Portuguese and Castilian Spanish was rationalized in Spain as no greater than that between Castilian and the other dialects within Spain itself. To Falangists, the two countries' "common destiny" was a politically expedient theme. *Domingo*, a Spanish paper, declared in August that the two shared a single soul, which the writer grandly called *"Hispanidad."*

This sort of thinking on the part of many powerful Spaniards understandably produced an edginess in Portugal, even a serious scare among some highly strung Portuguese. Rumors flew around Lisbon that the many Germans in the country were an "advance guard" of an invasion, the Nazis ready and willing to help Spain crush the country.[174] As a goodwill offering, Salazar sent his Iberian neighbors 16,000 tons of wheat and corn, a gift gratefully received by its hungry beneficiaries.

Franco, who had no intention of invading Portugal, himself took additional steps to damp Portuguese fears. After he bestowed on Salazar the prestigious Grand Collar of the Order of the Tower and Sword, reassuring articles on the subject began to appear in the Spanish press. The Spanish periodical *Fotos* was chastised for its comment that the will of God demanded that in the tercentenary of Portugal's reacquired independence the country's political situation should be reversed again.

Though it would be inaccurate to credit Salazar's influence as the primary factor in keeping Franco neutral, substantial acknowledgment in this regard should still be given the Portuguese dictator. His counsel that Spanish well-being depended on an uninterrupted flow of food shipments allowed by Britain, the assurances of Iberian military solidarity he proffered Franco, and the link Portugal represented between Spain and the West all helped allay Franco's fears of Portugal being used by the Allies as a site for future European landings, the factor that represented Franco's principal fear in regard to his small neighbor.

.   .   .

By the end of 1940, Salazar seems to have begun to recognize from Franco's prevaricating with Germany that the Caudillo intended, despite Hitler's pleas, to remain out of the war. The new recognition prompted Lisbon to quietly open talks with London on how it might best respond to a German attack. Salazar agreed with the British advice that after a token resistance on the mainland the Portuguese government should be moved to the Azores, islands which would then become available to the Royal Navy. The dictator undertook to double the size of his armed forces—from 40,000 to 80,000, and by way of safeguarding them to immediately station substantial elements in the Azores and Portugal's African colonies.

Through almost the entirety of World War II, Portugal was forced to deal with a bilateral threat to its Atlantic island chains. After the French collapse, Portugal's Cape Verde Islands were looked at anew by the American government for the strategic advantage they could provide. Located between the bulges of Africa and South America, the Cape Verdes[175] sat directly astride the shortest shipping routes connecting the two continents and also straddled shipping lines running from Brazil and Argentina to Britain. (At this time even the city of Dakar, in French West Africa, was seen by some Allied military planners as a legitimate target for the protection it could provide both American and British shipping interests.[176])

But the nine islands that made up the Azores archipelago represented by far the greatest concern for Salazar's government. To both Allies and Axis, these small islands—one-third of the way from Lisbon to New

York—shone as a star of extraordinary luminescence. Although gripped with the idea of using the islands as a platform from which to launch giant four-engine aircraft (which never got off the Reich's overloaded drawing board) to bomb New York City in the increasingly likely case of the United States entering the war, Hitler with greater military justification coveted an Azores base to serve his U-boat wolf packs in their attacks on Allied shipping. As for Salazar, he never seriously believed Germany would attempt to occupy any of Portugal's islands, a belief founded in his faith in the Royal Navy's ability to repel such an action. Instead, it was Britain and America's hungers that more seriously alarmed Lisbon.[177]

In the summer of 1940 the British cabinet decided that neither the Azores nor the Cape Verdes would be invaded by Britain unless either Spain or Portugal began to substantively collaborate with Germany against Commonwealth interests. A force of Royal Marines was held in readiness to seize the islands if such collaboration did occur. Since an alternative for Gibraltar occupied much of British strategic thinking in this theater of the war, permission or lack of it was to be disregarded as a factor in deciding to capture the islands. When Sir Samuel Hoare sounded out the Franco regime on the matter, he was told that any such attack would be considered a general attack against Iberia, and Spain would immediately enter the war on the side of the Axis, and would invite Germany into the peninsula, inevitably leading to an occupation of Portugal.

Bound tighter than ever to Britain by the Lend-Lease Act, through which lifesaving but novel scheme the United States delivered to Britain vast amounts of arms and ammunition, Roosevelt understandably worried about the safe delivery of these supplies. With the threat to Atlantic shipping increasingly deadly after the French ports fell to the Germans, the American president came ever more to accepting that the Azores would have to be occupied to keep the British war machine operating. Justifying his logic with the aid of the Monroe Doctrine and its provisions against Old World interference in the New, on April 18, 1941, the American government announced that the president had decided on a map configuration placing the Atlantic frontier of the Doctrine at 26° west meridian, a line west of which lay nearly all of the Azores and most of the Cape Verdes, and which thereafter became, in Churchill's reckoning, "the virtual sea frontier of the United States."[178] From a proposition that if the Germans invaded the islands the United States would counterattack to one of preemptive invasion became in mid-1941 a hot topic of American governmental debate.

In April, two potent American voices brought the Azores issues into the international spotlight, in doing so creating a crisis that Salazar realized could seriously threaten Portugal's continued neutrality. Walter Lippmann, the influential New York *Herald Tribune* columnist, wrote that Germany would have to be beaten to the Azores—with or without Portugal's permission or cooperation. Lippmann soon gained powerful adherents to this thinking. The *Christian Science Monitor* forwarded its novel observation that "the Azoreans are half Yankee,"[179] meant as a justification to just go ahead and take the islands. Then on May 6, in the course of a floor debate Senator Claude Pepper[180] advocated the immediate American seizure of the Azores to keep Hitler from beating the United States to them. Urging the government to occupy "the points of vantage from which these monsters are preparing to strike at us," he specifically included the Azores as those "points of vantage."[181]

When word of Pepper's speech reached Lisbon, the government reacted strongly. Fortunately, Salazar understood that the senator's statement did not represent official American policy, Cordell Hull having told the Portuguese ambassador in Washington that Pepper was speaking only for himself. The prior March, Salazar had already rejected the proffered visit of an American naval squadron to the Azores to bolster Portuguese resolve to defend itself. The Portuguese premier believed an Allied move in the Azores now would mortally damage any hope his country had of maintaining its neutrality and keeping German (or German *and* Spanish) troops out of his country. No one knew that in the spring of 1941 Hitler's nearly undivided attention had turned eastward. To Portugal—and to the Allies—it appeared that Iberia and the western Mediterranean could well constitute a primary target of the Reich now that it had so victoriously asserted itself in the eastern Mediterranean. Even if Franco appeared to be adhering to his own agenda of noninvolvement in the war, there was no evidence available to Salazar that Hitler wouldn't act unilaterally whenever it served his purpose to do so.

Churchill believed the islands' strategic importance overrode a breach of Portuguese sovereignty, and continued to urge Roosevelt to preempt the Germans and take, or help Britain take, the islands, warning the president that the Germans were unquestionably infiltrating the Azores with agents who could direct troop landings at a moment's notice. He added that both Lisbon and Madrid were "too intimidated" by the Germans to protest. Churchill promised Roosevelt that the action would in no way be considered to be adding to his nation's empire, that "far from wishing to add to our territory, [we wish] only to preserve our life and perhaps yours."[182] The British prime minister was willing to pledge that Portuguese sovereignty over the islands would be restored at the war's end.[183] The extent of Roosevelt's envisioned actions in mid-1941 was to plan for the possibility of an occupation of the Azores, and he would try to persuade Salazar of America's motivations and justifications before any such operation was carried out.

In a radio address on May 27, the president gave his rationale for considering the Portuguese islands so important:

> Unless the advance of Hitlerism is forcibly checked now, the Western Hemisphere will be within range of Nazi weapons of destruction. . . . Equally, the Azores and the Cape Verde Islands, if occupied or controlled by Germany, would directly endanger the freedom of the Atlantic and our own American physical safety. . . . Old-fashioned common sense calls for the use of strategy that will prevent such an enemy from gaining a foothold in the first place.[184]

At the height of the gale blowing around the issue, diplomacy intervened in the person of Secretary of State Cordell Hull, who strongly advised FDR against invading Portugal's territory. Unable to guess Hitler's next move, the Allies kept plans current to send a 25,000-man joint marine and army expeditionary force to the islands on thirty days' notice—while at the same time compelled to do the same thing in regard to Iceland, another possible target for a German invasion. It should be noted that the problems Admiral Erich Raeder pointed out to Hitler in regard to taking the Azores also were pointed out to Roosevelt by his own military strategists—namely, that the Portuguese islands would be extremely difficult to hold in light of the enemy's military capacity, especially its air power.

Germany was in fact developing its own military response to the British invasion of Iberia it feared.[185] A May 1941 directive to the army high command from General Franz Halder noted that it

> is not excluded that England in the event of the mass of the German army being tied down in the eastern theater of war in the summer of 1941 . . . will try . . . to create for herself a new continental position on the Iberian peninsula, with the aim of preventing Spain from joining the Axis Powers, compensating for the loss of prestige she has suffered, and offering the U.S.A. promising conditions for her entry into the war. . . . A landing in the Portuguese ports is to be expected primarily rather than in the ports of Northern Spain. Portugal will resign herself, under protest, to an English landing.[186]

The directive went on to outline in Operation Isabella the means by which the Wehrmacht would respond by driving out the British force.

At the same time, despite London's and especially Washington's anxiety, Salazar continued to refuse any American or British protection or involvement with the islands, convinced that to do so would dangerously, perhaps disastrously, provoke Hitler. Mortally afraid of a German reaction, Salazar reiterated his strict policy of neutrality in a note to the Allied governments. Pointing out that Portugal had done its utmost to fortify the Azores and the Cape Verdes against attack from any quarter, he said he couldn't understand why the Allies would wish to place him in a position of difficulty, apparently expecting the powers to think a Portuguese force could successfully safeguard against a German strike at the islands. Hull responded that American interest in the islands was "solely in terms of their potential value from the point of view of attack against this hemisphere."[187] For the time being, the issue stood deadlocked. Roosevelt was so certain that in a crunch Portugal would accede to a British protective occupation that he let the matter become, for the time being, a British concern.

Meanwhile, Hitler continued to hanker after the islands. Admiral Raeder wrote in May that "the Führer is still in favor of occupying the Azores. The occasion for this may arise by autumn [of 1941]."[188] Raeder's reaction, apparently respected by Hitler, was that although German force might gain one of the islands, in view of Allied naval strength keeping it would be far more difficult, not to say impossible.

Possession of the Cape Verdes remained on the German wish list too. Custody of this group would have meant the Reich's gaining greater control of Atlantic sea lanes with an advanced base from which to attack shipping bound to and from South America. But other matters took the upper hand: Italy's bumbling that required Germany's help, the disastrous Balkans adventure in the spring of 1941, French cooperation evaporating after Premier Pierre Laval's fall. However, above everything else it was Operation Barbarossa that frustrated Hitler's would-be adventure in the islands of the Western Ocean. But the Azores issue, if temporarily put on hold, was far from settled.

. . .

Besides its islands, Portugal possessed one other asset that both sides in the war came to covet: wolfram, the obscure but manifestly necessary component of modern weaponry and, by extension, of modern war.[189] One of the country's few abundant natural resources, the heavy, gray-white wolfram goes into the alloy called tungsten steel, a kind of hard, malleable, heat-resistant steel used for armor-piercing shells and armored plate as well as in high-speed cutting tools and drills—in short, the objects that went a long way in making the armed forces of World War II efficient.[190] Securing this singularly vital ore became one of the most intensely fought economic battles of the war.

In 1940, more than 95 percent of the wolfram mined in Europe was extracted from the rocky soil of Iberia, Portugal yielding ten tons to every one dug out of the less abundant Spanish veins; Sweden was responsible for the continent's remaining meager sources. The United States possessed abundant domestic supplies, much of which was shipped to Britain, and for its additional needs it bought lower-priced South American ore. Until attacking the Soviet Union in June 1941, Germany had been able to purchase Far Eastern wolfram, transported across the Eurasian landmass on the Trans-Siberian Railroad. Delivery from the South American suppliers wasn't a sure thing for the Germans because of the Royal Navy's ability to make its transatlantic shipment to Germany extremely perilous.[191] The Nazi war machine needed tungsten steel in amounts that seemed unattainable: in 1941, German steel production was almost thirty million tons, twice that of the United Kingdom, and the percentage of wolfram added to steel to turn it into precious tungsten steel ranged from about 4 percent to as much as 18 percent, translating into a lot of wolfram.

After France's surrender, Germany began getting its Iberian wolfram safely overland from Spain. The German strategy was to buy as much of the Iberian ore as it could, paying for it by bidding top price, much of this money having been filched from conquered vassal states. In the early part of the war, Britain bought wolfram from Iberia because it needed a nearby source for its own war industry. Later, Allied wolfram policy was primarily to buy the stuff on a preemptive basis, more to keep it out of Axis hands than because Britain actually needed as much as it was buying. But this wolfram would come to cost a great deal of money, money which Britain desperately needed for a million other things.

As for the ore's suppliers, Portugal and Spain would engage in markedly different patterns of wolfram production during the war. Spanish production, far less regulated by the government, was a kind of "cottage" industry, farmers collecting odd chunks from around the hardscrabble Spanish plateau. Portuguese collection, a far larger and better-organized effort, was also more tightly controlled by the government in an effort to maintain the country's ultra-precise neutrality. All Portuguese wolfram was legally required to be delivered to the Comissão Reguladora do Comércio de Metals in the Ministry of Commerce, who would then apportion it out to the lined-up buyers. But the geographical closeness of the two

Iberian neighbors and the ease with which Portuguese supplies could be smuggled into Spain meant that, in practice, both Allies and Axis treated the peninsula's wolfram as though it derived from a single political source.

By 1941, driven by Germany's vastly increased needs, Spain's unfettered production had caught up with Portugal's more controlled mining. Though Britain's needs for the ore fell off sharply after 1940, it continued to press the campaign of preemption, willing to pay almost any price just to keep wolfram out of Krupp's and the other German steel manufacturers' smelters. But German agents sidled up to all the peninsula's suppliers they could ingratiate themselves with. The result was that prices skyrocketed, from $1,144 a ton in Portugal in mid-1940 (that already several times the prewar price) to $20,000 a ton a little more than a year later. The Iberian wolfram industry became a magnet attracting anyone with a pickax and the necessary muscles to work the ore-producing outcrops peppering both countries' landscapes. In Portugal, the wolfram rush was taking away workers needed in agriculture, but to men of both countries used to earning less than a dollar a day the lure of the easy riches from scouring one's own and one's neighbors' backyards for pieces of the high-priced rock was overpowering.

Though Portugal was charging astronomical levels for its wolfram, the riches didn't come without a worry for the extremely worry-prone and ever cautious Salazar, especially where anything touching on his country's neutrality was concerned. If because of the Allies' ability to outbid the Germans, Berlin didn't get what could be reasonably seen to be a "fair" share, the dictator believed the Germans might just come and *take* what they needed.

Ore smuggled into Spain represented a booming trade, and Franco's government saw to it that the Reich got the bulk of its exported wolfram, which, because it was possible to send it overland to the Reich's steel producers and thus avoid the Royal Navy, the Allies could do relatively little to stop. Further, Franco was more sanguine than Salazar, taking the view that the Allies wouldn't seriously risk driving the peninsula into the Axis camp over the issue of wolfram. As long as the Spanish treasury was the chief beneficiary, the Caudillo was happy to let the wolfram traffic both into and out of Spain take its own head.

Until 1943, despite concerns over "neutrality," Germany remained the favored side in Salazar's more orderly disposal of his country's bounty. The Portuguese stipulation that all ore producers must channel their production through an official state sales commissariat would seriously thwart the Allied preemption effort. Salazar didn't care how much money London and Washington could throw at Portugal for the ore; to him it was more important to give each side its fairly divided share. Much of the Portuguese ore still got into Spain, and most of that ore got to Germany. But despite the fact that Spanish production had caught up with Portugal's, the latter still remained a major supplier to Germany until June 5, 1944, when Portugal finally embargoed the ore to Germany. Portuguese policies that effectively favored the Reich had lasted well into 1943, with Salazar continuing deliveries to Germany right up to the Normandy landings.

By 1943, Franco didn't have to worry very much about Hitler's retaliating against Spain, with the Wehrmacht by then in retreat in the East and in the Mediterranean. So the Spanish dictator finally acceded to Allied demands to limit sales to Germany, simultaneously cleaning up to some extent Spain's highly unfavorable image in the West. As Germany's capacity to harm Spain continued to dwindle, the American government increased the pressure on Franco to stop sending *any* wolfram to the Reich, in return for which the Allies promised to increase the amount of goods it would allow through its blockade. When Madrid then seemed about to decrease shipments to Germany, Berlin reminded Spain of its Civil War debt, and Franco—whether out of habit or some truer emotion[192]—agreed to continue to send the ore against the "debt." In retaliation, the Allies completely embargoed (at American insistence) petroleum to Spain, which soon brought Spain to its senses, economically speaking—which was, of course, Washington's goal. Finally, after the repatriation of France, when it was clear beyond any further equivocation that Germany had lost the power to punish Spain, Franco bit the bullet and halted all shipments of Spanish wolfram to the Reich. Both Britain and the United States were at last able to stop their own very expensive preemptive purchases of the now highly bothersome rocks.

The little wolfram war thus ended. Germany was forced to reduce the tungsten percentages in even critical tool tips from the normal 10–18 percent to around 2–3 percent, which necessitated slowing machinery speeds by up to 75 percent; tungsten-alloy tools in other vital industries, such as coal mining, had to be forgone. It also nearly abandoned tungsten-carbide cores in antitank ammunition, a deficiency to which German military experts attached great significance. The cessation of Iberian supplies also forced the Germans to make the ore, from whatever source, their principal cargo in running the general Allied embargo of Nazi Europe, at enormous danger to its suppliers and in lieu of the other desperately needed imports those ships could have carried.[193]

The wolfram war cost the United States and Britain about $170 million for the 6,000 tons of the ore they bought in Portugal and the approximately 9,000 tons from Spain;[194] the cost had been perhaps ten times its "normal" worth.[195] Even in light of what amounted to an astronomical sum drawn from the Allied treasuries in the early 1940s, Germany still got just about enough to meet its essential requirements up to the end of 1943. It purchased aggressively—by keeping a threat hanging over Salazar's head that not to sell to the Reich would result in retaliation against Portugal and by pressing Franco to "remember" the Civil War debt. In the final assessment of this small but inflammatory struggle, the cost the Allies paid to keep a good part of the metal from the Reich's war-making capacity was justified. Not to have done so would have undoubtedly extended Germany's capacity to make war by some period, and if that extension resulted in only a few days' extra life for the Reich, it would have added unbearably to what was already the greatest tragedy in history.

Stockholm

Though Europe's southwestern corner retained a veneer of agreeableness, in the North the disheartening effects of buckling to the Germans was turning a nation's society in on itself. Swedes may have recognized the danger and futility of resistance to Hitler's transit demands, but no amount of rationalizing could negate the fact that the nation's options were now being settled in Berlin. "It torments me that we should be forced to give way to a superior power, but I cannot see it possible to go any other way." Prime Minister Hansson's words were describing the just-signed transit agreement, and the sentiments represented an accurate expression of his nation's predicament. The agreement would stand for three years, until Germany's sword was irreversibly blunted, both a symbol and an element of Sweden's wartime tilt toward the Third Reich.[196]

The nation's modus vivendi with Germany was a sort of mutual understanding of what was expected by each of the other: Sweden would keep up the supplies of iron ore and allow its railway to be used for Germany's Norwegian purposes; Germany would not attack Sweden. The Swedes—or at least their government—thus became a kind of reluctant ally of Germany, doing what was expected of them and in the doing keeping themselves out of the war. In truth, there was little else they could have done and still maintained the constricted peace in the North. Granted Hitler was preoccupied with his various aggressions and sins elsewhere, but not to the point where Sweden would have been allowed to thwart the overriding interests of the German Reich.

Over those three years following the agreement, Sweden was forced to give way to increasingly brazen German demands, demands which required it to treat its rail facilities almost as though they existed chiefly for the benefit of the Reich. Transports grew in size during the months immediately following the accord, from one transport a week at first until finally German demands for a train a day were acceded to. What one German diplomat characterized as "the price Sweden paid for its peace" was reduced to its elemental truth by a Nazi official visiting Stockholm a few months after the agreement was reached: ". . . today 'all sides' no longer exist for Sweden."[197]

Though the country continued to be beholden to other, less loathsome German demands, including the standard Nazi pressure applied more or less successfully to all the neutrals to slant their press policy in the Reich's favor and to the Allies' detriment (in the spring of 1941, Minister Wied wired Berlin that the German effort "to reorient the Swedish press in our favor has apparently been successful"[198]), it was the transit problem that most plagued Swedish society. But in the wake of Hitler's magnum opus—Operation Barbarossa—a new contretemps would arise when Berlin baldly demanded that Stockholm permit the undisguised transit of an entire Wehrmacht division across Sweden. On the resolution of this crisis hung not only Sweden's honor but possibly even the continuation of the reign of Gustav V.

Budapest-Bucharest-Sofia

Giving in to the pressures of the spreading war, three more of Europe's rapidly expiring band of neutrals were now formally inducted into the brotherhood of the Axis. Pro-German since the mid-1930s and rabidly nationalistic since the Austrian Anschluss in 1938, Hungary floated rather than plunged into co-belligerence with the Reich. After Germany and Italy forced Rumania to cede 16,500 square miles of Transylvania to Hungary, Budapest governments understandably found themselves unable any longer to say no to Berlin. Perhaps the most conservative nation in Europe, still semi-feudal in its land ownership and society, its head of state, the regent Admiral Miklós Horthy, nonetheless took it as his duty to ensure that Hungary's contribution to the Reich's war effort was as small as possible.[199] When in November 1940 Hungary joined the Axis Pact, the kingdom[200] became little more than a German satrapy, and when the Wehrmacht needed its help in destroying Yugoslavia in the spring of 1941, its collaborationist cabinet ordered the army into active operations under the Wehrmacht. Taking advantage of Yugoslavia's tragedy, Hungary requested and received the return of territories it had lost at the end of World War I. In June, Hungary declared war on the Soviet Union, and did likewise with Britain and the United States on December 13, 1941.

Like Hungary, Bulgaria was content with its close relationship with the Reich as long as the Nazi star was in the ascendant. Also like Hungary, Bulgaria's ties with the Reich allowed it to expand at the expense of its neighbors. Bulgaria's losses in the Second Balkan War of 1913 and in World War I enormously complicated its relationships and boundary problems with its neighbors. Just as in Hungary, it too was overtaken by Nazi-style domestic politics in the 1930s and quickly slid under German domination. Though Boris III declared his kingdom neutral when Poland was attacked, by March 1941 he was "prevailed" upon to bring the country into the Axis, but as a very junior partner. The partnership brought Bulgaria chunks of Yugoslavia, Greece, and Rumania—and a tantalizing taste of the Greater Bulgaria that the nation had so hungrily envisioned in the nineteenth century.

Rumania was odd man out of the three—a nation forced into the arms of the Reich but which suffered huge losses of national territory as a result of the Machiavellian spoils system Hitler devised for his junior satellites. When it was bloated to twice its former size by the victorious and grateful Allies in 1918, Rumania's gains meant neighbors' grievances. After 1933, dominated by fascism through the notorious SA-like Iron Guard supported by Germany, politics for the remainder of the decade became a power struggle between the Guard and the flamboyant, weak-willed, but sometimes politically agile king, Carol II. The latter became titular dictator as well as monarch when in April 1938 political parties were forbidden and replaced by the Front of National Rebirth, in which the Iron Guard exercised the real power. When fear of the Soviet Union brought the country into an alliance with Germany, Hitler demanded payment from the Rumanians in the form of territory ceded to both Hungary and Bulgaria, as well as large tracts to the Soviet Union, still Hitler's theoretical ally. When Carol asked for guarantees from the Führer that no more demands would be made on Rumania, Hitler refused, making the king's position politically untenable and forcing him to abdicate (in what was essentially a bloodless coup) in favor of his son, nineteen-year-old Prince Michael. A new government headed by Marshal Ion Antonescu and backed by the Iron Guard invited German "protection" of its Ploeşti oil fields from a feared Soviet attack. The Iron Guard, jealous of the army, *then attempted an internecine coup against Antonescu's government, prompting Hitler to send troops to put it down and keep order in his new Balkan fiefdom. Rumanian independence thus expired.*

All three of the Reich's new satellites had been cynically maneuvered by Hitler's policy of divide and rule, each with new frontiers that pleased none. Rumania lost four million former inhabitants as a result of Hitler's redrawing the map, while neither Bulgaria nor Hungary achieved the territorial size each thought of as its "right." But all tried at first to be good satellites, understanding that their wartime behavior would affect how they would be treated by a victorious Reich at war's end. As historian H. Stuart Hughes put it, the Reich kept them obedient through each one's "hope of further gain and fear of further loss."[201]

CHAPTER IV

WORLD WAR

Summer 1941–Winter 1943

War in the East—Berlin-Moscow

With Hitler's assault on the Slavic East, the fast-dwindling company of Europe's neutral states lost its preeminent member. Joseph Stalin had hoped his expedient 1939 covenant with Germany would keep Russia and its congeries of fiefdoms safe for several more years from Hitler's avaricious urges. His miscalculation could not have been greater, however. The Nazi pursuit of Lebensraum began on June 22, 1941, along a 1,250-mile front, with three million men supported by 7,100 guns and 3,200 tanks covered by 2,770 airplanes and reinforced by 625,000 horses and 600,000 vehicles, all of which was assembled in 148 divisions presided over by three field marshals. Over the next four years this cataclysmic conflict would kill some twenty-seven million Soviet citizens, as well as hundreds of thousands of their German tormentors. Yet on its outbreak, the American secretary of war, Henry Stimson, called the attack "an almost providential occurrence."[1]

The campaign is seen today as a near-suicidal effort on Hitler's part, but the onslaught represented, along with racial politics, the irreducible core of Nazism. Both the Russian dictator and his German antagonist understood the cynicism that underlay the Molotov-Ribbentrop pact: that it was a breather for both dictatorships—to give Germany a free hand in the West before tackling the East, for Russia to gain time to prepare itself for the inevitable.

If the war Hitler made on the West represented an assault against democracy and Anglo-French power, a war to change Europe's fundamental political composition, the central factor in the Eastern war was racial. Integral to the collection of improbable suppositions and pseudo-Darwinian beliefs that constituted National Socialism was the notion that Germans possessed the inalienable right to use any part of the Slavic East, and its peoples, for whatever purposes it saw fit, whether it was land, or slave labor, or simply room for future expansion. While Nazism made the destruction of Jewry its golden rule, it made the destruction of Slavdom inconsequential: where Slavs could serve German needs, they would do so; if they were "used up" in this effort, German people and Aryan culture would fill the space they had vacated. For the next four years, the cold-blooded inhumanity of Hitler's war on Russia spun out on this formula.

Helsinki

In one of World War II's tragic but little-noted offshoots, a fundamentally civilized and peaceful Scandinavian people saw in Germany's war on Russia a chance to requite their own recently suffered wounds. Joining the Wehrmacht in Operation Barbarossa, but for reasons having nothing to do with the ideology that drove Germany, Finland sought frankly to overturn the humiliation and the losses of the Winter War. The fact that in seeking this goal it allied itself with infamy would make this small nation's final tragedy especially bitter.

In what was aptly termed by the Finns the "Continuation War," the genesis of Finland's military ties with Nazi Germany came in 1940. Desperately vulnerable to a Soviet threat, the Finns could see no salvation but an alliance with what they perceived as the lesser of two iniquities. After acquiring 22,000 square miles—home to 12 percent of Finland's population as well as the Finn's second-largest city—the Kremlin continued to hammer the exhausted Finns with a series of small but disabling aftershocks: the demand that the Åland Islands be demilitarized or else fortified under Soviet control, that huge quantities of Finnish industrial capacity be turned over to the Russians, that the new border be further "revised" in the Soviets' interests, and that the Red Army be permitted to transit Finnish territory from Leningrad to the former Finnish, now Soviet, base at Hangö.

Anxious to exploit the growing depth of Finland's animosity toward the Soviet Union, Germany increasingly proffered itself to Helsinki as Finland's protector against Stalinist aggression. The German military caste genuinely admired the Finns for their willingness to stand up to the Russian threat, but Berlin more sanguinely esteemed Finland both for its geography and for the mineral treasure house it represented: the Reich's arms producers coveted Finnish copper, molybdenum, and nickel deposits that were so potentially consequential to the Wehrmacht's fighting capacity.

Finland sealed its ultimately disastrous link with the Reich in the late summer of 1940, when Helsinki granted Germany the right to transport northern Norway-bound troops across its territory, from the Gulf of Bothnia ports of Vaasa and Oulu northward by rail and route march to Kirkenes on the Barents Sea. To service these shipments, the Wehrmacht stationed troops in permanent housekeeping operations along the route, the first small German foothold on Finnish territory. In response to the howls from the Kremlin, still allied to the Reich, the Germans answered that the troops were meant solely to strengthen its Norwegian garrison in case of British attack, though clearly the German troops on the Barents Sea represented a potential danger to the supply route into Murmansk. When Foreign Minister Molotov reminded Hitler in November 1940 that Finland was located in the Soviet sphere of influence as set by the spoils allotment of the 1939 pact, and further that the Kremlin demanded an unfettered hand to take whatever measures it saw fit against the nettlesome Finns, he was flatly told that the Reich would not permit any persecutions of the Finns. The Nazis couldn't wait, of course, to inform the Finns how they had thus "protected" their country, suggesting this as a basis for a much enhanced future relationship between Helsinki and Berlin.

This attachment to and dependence on a German military umbrella placed the Finnish government in an enormous moral predicament, one the Allies exerted themselves to understand. The Finns wished not to in any way appear sympathetic to the Axis war against the democracies—for they firmly placed themselves in the democratic category. Though in the months following the German link President Risto Ryti and Marshal Gustav Mannerheim foresaw the likelihood of a Nazi attack on the Soviet Union, neither man wished his country to be considered an enemy by the West. But London quietly warned the Finns that their deepening relationship with Berlin would cost Finland Western sympathy—until now still firm as a result of Finnish bravery in the Winter War—and that economic arm-twisting against Finland would be inevitable if the country showed any signs of helping Germany in an attack on Russia.

In the spring of 1941, Hitler invited Finnish military participation in "theoretical" military discussions on how to best attack the Soviet Union, all but informing Mannerheim that such an assault had already been decided. On the basis of this knowledge, the Finnish cabinet had to determine whether or not to risk the Allies' wrath by acceding to German pressure to come into the attack at the Wehrmacht's side. Finland's decision proved fateful. With faith in the invincibility of German arms and desperately wanting to restore its pre-Winter War frontiers, Finland would serve as a "co-belligerent" of the Reich, though not an "ally," and only in the war against the Soviet Union.

Three days after the June 22 attack, Finland came under fire from the Soviet Air Force. On June 25, the day Russian planes began bombing Hensinki and other towns across the southern part of the country, the Ryti cabinet, in "self-defense" (a maneuver considered politically preferable to joining the German onslaught on the twenty-second), declared war on its giant neighbor—while still carefully avoiding a formal alliance with Germany. The Finns would now exact their retribution from the Russians, who had raped the country a year and a half earlier.

The initial Finnish victories were swift. In conjunction with the Wehrmacht, then bowling over the Soviet defenses along the 1,250-mile front, the 400,000 Finnish troops proceeded to regain virtually all of the territory lost in the Winter War, most importantly western Karelia. Had Finland stopped its drive at this point, it well might have avoided the eventual British declaration of war against the country. But Ryti and Mannerheim—the two men virtually running Finland—came under incessant pressure from their German "co-belligerents" to assist in the Wehrmacht's assault on Leningrad. While with a Franco-like tactic the Finns were able to stall the Germans by promising to come into the battle for the city at the earliest possible moment, Ryti and Mannerheim declared they intended to "liberate" eastern Karelia, Finnish in ethnic makeup but which had never been a part of independent Finland. The vision of a "Greater Finland" drew the government into a far broader war than merely a return to the 1939 status quo. It was with this aggrandizement that Finland fatally overstepped itself with the West.

Through the fall of 1941, the Finnish question would constitute one of the thorniest, and most embarrassing, problems in the field of Anglo-Soviet relations. When it became clear to Britain that the Finns had no intention of stopping at the point where its Winter War losses were recouped, it found itself forced to choose between a relatively democratic soul mate and the Communist dictatorship that had violated that soul mate. The problem was that the dictatorship was now an ally in its to-the-death struggle with fascism, and that dictatorship thus had first call on Britain's amity.

So while Churchill implored Mannerheim and the Finnish government to come to an agreement with Moscow—an agreement that London had induced Moscow to offer—the Finns saw salvation only in completing their chosen course—namely, to take enough territory to ensure a protective ring around Finland in case the Russians ever again decided to attack. Field Marshal Mannerheim exhorted the nation to keep up the fight, to recognize that Finland must redraw its "old, inadequate" frontiers for the sake of its future.[2] When the British cut off Finland's food supplies, dependence on Germany, now its only substantial source of sustenance, increased daily. That dependence inexorably diminished Finland's independence of action, its ability to reach an accord with Moscow against the ominous protestations of Berlin. This was the state of affairs when on December 6, 1941, Britain declared war on the hapless little Scandinavian nation.[3] Though Finland took no part in the Battle of Leningrad, and refused to help the Germans cut the critical Murmansk railway line, the West was left with little choice but to treat the country as an out-and-out German ally. And to those who criticized him for supporting Stalin after the German invasion of the Soviet Union, Churchill responded with his classic rejoinder: "If Hitler invaded Hell, I think I would find a kind word to say about the Devil in the House of Commons."

With the American entry into the war against Germany on December 11, the Soviets' prospects of thwarting the Finns took an enormous jump. With most of the world now lined up with Finland's enemy, and with Germany at the precipice of its long decline—though that couldn't yet be clearly seen—Finland awaited the inevitable counterblow that was sure to come.

Stockholm

Whether they viewed Russia as a threat or as a shield, after June 22 the Swedes found their relationship with Germany ratcheted even tighter. Where Stockholm had so far in the war shaped its defense strategy on a balance between German and Soviet interests in the North, that balance was now destroyed. With no defender of last resort to help resist the most egregious of Berlin's demands, even a defender as distasteful as the Soviet

Union, Nazi pressure on the Swedish government came now to be exerted with a reborn vigor. Not surprisingly, the transit question was at the center of Sweden's new difficulties.

Since the transit agreement of a year earlier, the Germans had slowly jiggered the Norwegian troop balance in their favor between those going to and those leaving that Scandinavian captive state; by early 1941, troops bound for Norway far outnumbered those who were leaving, with the unavoidable conclusion that Germany was using Swedish soil and facilities to seriously reinforce its army occupying Sweden's western neighbor.

With the onset of hostilities against the Soviet Union, Berlin settled on the role it wanted Sweden to fulfill in the newly widened war: that status would be to continue without interruption its present tribute, though on an expanded, and decidedly less neutral, scale. On the morning of June 22, Foreign Minister Ribbentrop summoned Minister Richert. The Nazi loftily informed the Swedish diplomat that Germany's struggle against the Bolsheviks was equally "consistent with Sweden's old traditions" and that a German victory would contribute fully as much to Sweden's well-being as to its own, specifically by ensuring Finland's independence. Not personally pressing specific demands on Sweden, Ribbentrop only expressed a desire for "understanding" from the Reich's northern neighbor, and hoped that the Swedish press would maintain a "friendly" attitude.[4] But at the subministerial level, where Ribbentrop's generalities were rendered into specifics, German demands would prove a great deal less ephemeral and, from Stockholm's standpoint, a far greater threat to Sweden's neutrality.

Germany, Richert found out, now required a virtual catalogue of new Swedish concessions; among other humiliating demands: permission for aircraft to overfly the country unmolested by Swedish defense forces, the Swedish Navy to extend its protection to German naval vessels in Swedish waters, Sweden to help Germany lay minefields. But the bombshell was Berlin's ultimatum that the Reich expected the Swedes to permit an entire armed division from the German military district at Oslo to be carried on Swedish rails to the fighting front in Finland.

After hearing Ribbentrop's levy and then regaining its collective composure, Hansson's government immediately asked Berlin why the Kriegsmarine couldn't transport the division by sea. It was curtly told that such an expedient had been investigated and found impracticable; the Germans ominously added that refusal on the part of the Swedes of any of its demands—*especially* the matter of the troop transfer—would constitute a "dangerously unfriendly" act. Lowering its cudgel a bit, Berlin intimated that the request for the division's transfer would be a one-time thing.

Nonetheless, the Swedes were essentially told that their "neutrality," if they wanted to preserve it, must now be geared directly toward German victory.

While the Riksdag and the cabinet continued to debate whether the country should debase itself further in the face of German force majeure, an impasse within the cabinet over the issue began to threaten the government.[5] Even the abdication of the king was feared. King Gustav well understood the seriousness of Sweden's plight, the sovereign realizing that refusal on the part of his government to accede to the Reich's demands might still very well result in a German invasion of Sweden. As Gustav saw it, the very survival of his kingdom was at stake.

On the afternoon of June 24, as the Finns were preparing to go to war against Russia, the German minister wired Berlin to urge that Helsinki's envoy in Stockholm confidentially inform the Swedes of his nation's imminent intention to enter the war on the German side, adding that "the defensive character of any Finnish move, which was emphasized yesterday and today in the Swedish press, need not be affected by such a step."[6] Clearly, Berlin hoped that Sweden would wish to help its Finnish neighbors in their effort to regain the land they had lost to Stalin's armies.

Earlier that day, as the politicians continued to agonize over the problem, the king had received the German minister. Wied wired the Foreign Ministry in Berlin describing the encounter (it should be emphasized that this memo is Wied's, and the veracity of its contents was never corroborated):

> The King of Sweden summoned me this afternoon in order to inform me that Germany's principal request, for transit of one division, had just been accepted in the State Council. The King's words conveyed the joyful emotion he felt. . . . He [Gustav] . . . has gone far in giving his personal support to the matter. He added confidentially that in doing so he had found it necessary to go even so far as to mention his abdication.[7] The King then expressed the hope that Germany would make no demands on Sweden going beyond these limits.[8]

Led by the efforts of Prime Minister Hansson and Foreign Minister Günther (the king's personal role in the matter has long been debated by Swedish historians), and urged on by the Finnish government now cobelligerent with the Axis, the Riksdag agreed on June 25 to meet Germany's demands. That same night, the Engelbrecht Division, the 163rd Infantry Division,[9] began its journey across Sweden at the rate of four trainloads each day. Fifteen thousand gray-clad officers and men, along with all their weapons and supplies, traversed the neutral kingdom to the

Finnish-Soviet front. The entire operation took about two weeks. Under Swedish military command while on Swedish territory, the trains never stopped on Swedish soil.

Though Hansson's government tried to keep this massive concession to Germany secret, it inevitably leaked to the Swedish press. Norwegian and Allied condemnation was, understandably, immediate and harsh. Norwegians came to scathingly refer to Sweden as "Transitania," and Swedish journalist Torgny Segerstedt wrote that "once it was possible to be proud of being a Swede"[10]—with the unvoiced addendum that such was not now the case.

Prime Minister Hansson attempted to justify his government's decision primarily on the basis of Sweden's "special relationship" to Finland, the neighbor that had urged the Swedes to acquiesce on the question. But the average Swede was considerably less sympathetic to Finland's problems in mid-1941 than he had been during the bitter days of the Winter War. Now it seemed to many that to help Finland was tantamount to helping Germany in its war of aggression, a situation that curtailed most Swedes' strong support for Finland's struggle to right itself from Soviet belligerence. A measure of the Swedish attitude toward the Continuation War was the fact that only about a thousand Swedes volunteered to help the Finns in this second war against Russia.

Another major factor in Stockholm's decision was Germany's threat to cut off deliveries of military supplies to Sweden, supplies Sweden desperately needed to defend itself against an invader. In return for the passage of the Engelbrecht Division, the Swedes made very substantial demands on the Reich's arsenal, the nature of which is revealed in a cable from Wied to Berlin:

> Today the Swedish Government gave me a list of its wishes in regard to deliveries of German war equipment, namely: 1. Licenses for airplane engines (details are known to . . . the Reich Air Ministry). 2. Delivery of Me-110s. 3. Delivery of Twin Wasp engines from stocks in France. 4. The delivery to Sweden of tanks . . . 5. Armor for tanks . . . etc. In consideration of the great cooperation shown by the Swedish side in connection with all German military wishes . . . I consider it necessary that I be provided at this time with considerable concessions in the area of deliveries of war equipment important to Sweden. An accommodating attitude in this area will, moreover, considerably advance our political efforts here . . . [11]

The less tangible but nonetheless central issue in Sweden's decision was the sense of the utter isolation in which it now found itself. With Germans or Germany's allies on all sides, and with the Western Allies incapable of doing anything to help the Swedes stave off a German attack, Hansson believed that to frustrate the Reich might amount to national suicide—Germany, after all, looked to be invincible that summer as it attacked with apparent impunity the world's largest country. The decision to allow the Engelbrecht Division to pass through their country was the most agonized as well as the most criticized of Hansson's government's wartime acts, but it would be presumptuous to believe any other country finding itself in those perilous circumstances might have acted differently.

True to his word, Hansson saw to it that the Engelbrecht Division's passage was the last major transfer of German troops across Sweden, other than those still transported under the 1940 agreement, and Berlin's hint that such would be the case was, for once, accurate. But Germany's other demands were generally acceded to. By the end of the first week in July, Hansson's government agreed to allow Swedish rails to be used for the movement of German war supplies to Finland, a minefield was laid off Öland in conjunction with the German Navy, and orders were given that Finnish and German aircraft overflying Sweden were not to be downed, but instead merely "deterred" from Swedish airspace with warning shots. In payment for these unneutral acts, Germany began to allow Swedish shipping access to the Atlantic, such traffic having been nearly halted since March as an inducement to force Swedish cooperation. These concessions were not, as in the transport of the Engelbrecht Division, one-time matters, and Swedish historian W. M. Carlgren has concluded that they contributed materially to the Reich's military capacity in its war with the Soviet Union.[12]

The Allied governments—including that of the United States—generally looked upon Sweden's actions as those of a nation with its back against the wall rather than of a genuine German ally. The State Department approvingly noted that Sweden continued to pledge to fight an invasion from any quarter, and Whitehall mildly commented that Stockholm must beware the concessions it granted not lead to other, more dangerous compromises of its neutrality. Even Moscow was restrained in its criticisms of the Swedish action, terming the concessions an "unfriendly act," but the Soviet rebuke was seen as a merely formalistic diplomatic response and not as a serious *casus belli* between Moscow and Stockholm.[13]

In Sweden, the public attitude toward Germany plunged to new depths. Even though censored, the press was unable to keep the tone or sometimes even the substance of public opinion out of its criticisms of the Nazis, and it now reported stepped-up German brutalities against Norwegian resisters; Swedes were outraged when it was learned that two

Norwegian labor leaders had been executed in a general Nazi crackdown on the occupied country's recalcitrant labor movement. Ribbentrop upbraided the Swedish chargé in Berlin, warning him that the Swedish press had best keep these sorts of criticisms of Germany—not to mention its demeaning caricatures of Hitler and Göring—out of print.

In this atmosphere of growing hostility yet another crisis sprang up, one in which Germany threatened again to shut the tap on Sweden's precarious trade lifeline. With the 1940 fall of Norway, a significant part of that nation's merchant fleet was caught in the Swedish west coast port of Gothenburg (many of Norway's ships caught in Allied ports were by 1941 in the leased service of the British). Central to the crisis were ten Norwegian vessels preparing to sail to Britain. Fearful the ships' cargoes—or the vessels themselves—might be used against the Axis, Ribbentrop put Stockholm on notice that "if one single ship actually [slips] out and [reaches] Britain, the government of the German Reich would interpret this as an expression of a completely hostile attitude on the part of Sweden."[14]

With a total carrying capacity of 80,000 tons, the Gothenburg ships were in fact filled with goods vital to Britain's war effort. Most important was a considerable quantity of much needed ball bearings,[15] the Swedish invention of inestimable value to modern machine development; the bearings, chiefly manufactured in Gothenburg, had given rise to one of Sweden's foremost industries, responsible in 1939 for 40 million kronor (about $1,600,000) worth of exports.[16] Germany for obvious reasons wanted the bearings-laden ships to remain in Swedish ports, with the legal reasoning that Norway's London government-in-exile had no proprietary rights to the ships.[17] Britain wanted them to sail under British captains. Sweden tended to side with the former, mainly because of fear of German reprisals. The biggest reprisal would surely be the ending of any further Swedish shipping from Gothenburg, an act the German Navy was perfectly capable of carrying out. If it appeared the ships were on the verge of an attempted breakout, a situation that would unquestionably be reported by German spies, the chance that the Kriegsmarine would enter Swedish waters to prevent such breakout and in so doing lead the Swedes into actual fighting with Germany was too real and too dangerous to be ignored.

The British didn't want to see the Gothenburg traffic cut by the Germans, partly for the goods it received but also in large measure because the small but symbolically important independence Sweden's trade lifeline gave it kept it from absolute subservience to the Reich. Berlin was fully conscious of Sweden's predicament, just as was London. For its part, Germany kept up the pressure on the Swedish government, which translated into constantly escalating demands, heavily dealing with the troop traffic as well as the delivery of ever increasing amounts of Swedish iron ore.

The Gothenburg matter continued to sour the Swedish-German relationship, Ribbentrop still vowing grave consequences for Sweden if even one of the ships was allowed to escape. On March 17, 1942, the Swedish Supreme Court (prodded, some believe, by Allied pressure in the form of a threat to stop all imports into Sweden from the West) ruled that the British government had a right to dispose of the ships it had chartered from Norway as it saw fit. But Sweden would not allow the ships to hug the protective coastline; nor could they move to the more secluded fishing village of Lysekil, where a break across the North Sea would be less dangerous than from closely observed Gothenburg.

After finally deciding to move two weeks later, the ten vessels broke out of their berths in the dead of night and headed for England. The outcome was disastrous. Three were sunk by the Kriegsmarine and three were scuttled by their own crew to avoid capture by the Germans; two— the *Lionel* and the *Dicto*—were forced to return to Gothenburg, which they made safely although they were interned by Swedish naval authorities on arrival. Only the 17,000-ton tanker *B. P. Newton* and the tiny 300-ton *M. P. Lind* reached their destination, bringing with them tons of ball bearings and ball-bearing steel.

Berlin's response, surprisingly mild, consisted of a sharply worded diplomatic note delivered to Stockholm. Most important, Germany did not stop the Gothenburg trade. The Swedes, though, soon found out not only that the Norwegian ships had been armed but that the British diplomatic staff in Sweden was responsible for arming them. Stockholm was indignant, and Sir George Binney, the legation official primarily accountable, was expelled. Sweden hoped that its London minister's loud protests would convince Berlin that it had been unwitting in the violation of its neutrality, and sent written assurances to Berlin that the two ships forced back to Gothenburg harbor, the *Lionel* and the *Dicto*, would be prevented from any further attempt to depart. This melancholy saga would conclude with an unexpected coda.

·   ·   ·

By the fall of 1941, the figures revealing Swedish acquiescence to German transit demands had become truly significant in terms of Sweden's enforced contribution to the Reich's war effort: over the prior fifteen months about 670,000 German troops had been transported through Sweden, which meant about 1,400 soldiers each day; seventy German ships had been escorted through Sweden's territorial waters, all carrying troops and war matériel; every week, some threescore German aircraft were permitted to overfly Swedish territory; and the Swedish port of Luleå, at the head of the Gulf of Bothnia, had been turned into a giant German supply depot. Iron ore shipments reached 45,000 tons a day by the end of 1941, an amount previously thought beyond Sweden's physical capacity.[18]

Through the second half of 1941, the German triumphs in the East, a seeming guarantee of eventual Axis victory, were the main reason Stockholm believed it had no option except to appease the Nazi appetite. Rumors of a German invasion spread like chicken pox in these last months of 1941, with speculation in August and September that Berlin planned to attack in order to forestall any more Swedish shilly-shallying over its demands. (German Foreign Office and military records do not document such planning.[19]) In December, the Swedish envoy in Berlin was informed from home that "the air of Stockholm buzzed with rumors of an impending German move against Sweden."[20]

Sweden's stance toward the Reich underwent its first significant fluctuation when America entered the war. Japan's attack on Pearl Harbor made it hopeful and likely that the now fully belligerent United States might tip the scales against the Axis, a hope that gave Sweden the spine to refuse new credit demands from an increasingly financially hard-pressed Reich government. In a new Swedish-German agreement signed on December 19, Stockholm demanded that at least half the price of all orders to Germany be paid not in credits but in cash. What was more, Sweden refused to deliver any additional iron ore to the Reich until Berlin made up growing arrears under the expired agreement of coal, bar iron, and coke. Germany let out a stunned howl, as expected, but in the end—fighting an increasingly difficult Soviet enemy—complied with Stockholm's new, tougher line.

Nevertheless, the Germans demonstrated their pique with Swedish waywardness in a variety of petty but still ominous provocations. Accusing Sweden of being "a hotbed of spies" and "the capital of false anti-German news," Berlin warned the country that it was failing "to realize the role [it] should play in the New Europe." When the Swedish press suggested the Germans weren't finding the Russians an easy victim, the Germans called the observation an insult to the Wehrmacht.[21] Minor irritants were treated as major by Berlin, as when the Swedes refused to allow members of the indigenous German colony to send woolen garments to Wehrmacht members in Russia, Sweden asserting that such an action would contribute to the kingdom's own shortage of wool for domestic consumption. These tokens are perhaps difficult to comprehend so long after the fact, but were unquestionably frightening to a people still being prepared by their government for an invasion that might come at any moment.

In early 1942, disagreements and friction between Stockholm and Berlin were at their height and fear of invasion engulfed the country. With Germany now calculating a joint Anglo-American attack on Norway in the works, one in which the Swedes would willingly join the Allies as a co-belligerent, Hitler considered a preemptive occupation of Sweden. So alarmed was the Swedish government on learning of these plans from envoy Richert—the diplomat received his information from sources previously reliable—that an emergency session of the cabinet was immediately convened to decide how best to react. As he had (presumably) done during the transit crises, King Gustav again assumed a central role in resolving what had in the estimation of the Swedish general staff become a critical situation.

This time Gustav gave the German ambassador solemn assurances that Sweden's armed forces would totally resist any Allied incursions on Swedish territory. Hitler seems to have respected the king's word, though Sweden's increased military preparedness that had gone hand in hand with the king's message probably influenced Hitler as much as the monarch's pledge.[22] Again a crisis passed and Sweden was let off the hook. The German government even gave Stockholm assurances of the felicity of its relations with the North's last neutral, as Germany evidently understood that Sweden was more important as an economic partner than as a conquered vassal, a realization that surely underlay Germany's actions toward Sweden throughout the war.

Meanwhile, the Swedish government began pressing London to increase the supplies it allowed into Sweden under the 1939 War Trade Agreement. But Britain demanded that in return for such favors Stockholm must officially regard Finland as an enemy and assure the Allies that no supplies would be transshipped to that country. With the Americans now in the war, the British further let the Swedes know the best course it could take in regard to Berlin's demands was to start saying "no" in clear and unequivocal tones. Now that the tide of war was beginning to perceptibly turn to the Allies' favor, Churchill's government became less willing to forgive Sweden for policies seriously damaging to Britain's interests.

The weapon Britain hung most effectively over the Swedes' head was oil. Sweden was desperate for an increase in the amount of oil allowed through the British blockade, oil Stockholm still pleaded it needed in case of a German attack. But London refused to increase the allowance unless the transit traffic was throttled back to a trickle of its present level. Furthermore, the British now also wanted to be supplied with accurate statistics on the Wehrmacht traffic crossing Sweden. If Stockholm complied with both demands, it would get its oil. But Sweden hesitated to renege on its commitments to Germany, believing that the Reich's capacity to retaliate simply remained too great a threat.

Erik Boheman, chief of the chancellery of the Swedish Foreign Office, was in September 1942 sent to London to try to resolve the matter with the British. Though Whitehall remained fundamentally sympathetic to Sweden's plight, it judged now the danger from the Germans had subsided considerably from levels of 1941, and London insisted Stockholm make substantial concessions in exchange for the goods it wanted from the West.

Stockholm decided to take the matter over London's head. It was now clear to all the neutrals that Washington had quickly become the more important partner in the new Allied relationship, and, furthermore, that only the Americans could guarantee that Sweden got the supplies it pleaded for.[23] Sweden hoped that by presenting its case to the American State Department, greater understanding of its plight might be forthcoming than from Whitehall. Boheman remained the point man in this critical effort, though once in America, the Swede ran into a brick wall. Not only were the British upping the ante—London now insisted on a cessation of all escorting of German vessels by the Swedish Navy—but it had also persuaded the Americans to withhold safe-conduct passes of vessels bound for Sweden.

With no War Trade Agreement binding Sweden to the United States, playing the American card had been a gamble for Stockholm. The United States had little of Britain's understanding for Sweden's German noose. Not only did the Americans believe that it would make little real difference if Sweden were invaded; they also held that cutting off the Swedes might better serve Allied interests, a conclusion based on the notion that German interests would be hurt by withholding from the Swedes the wherewithal to maintain an economy capable of giving Germany the ball bearings and other supplies then creating havoc for the Allies. In Washington it was Treasury Secretary Henry Morgenthau and the military chiefs who were least inclined to accept Sweden's protestations, especially in the matter of ball-bearing shipments to Germany; they strongly held that Sweden's impoverishment would, ipso facto, decrease Sweden's ability to do Germany's bidding.

Stockholm promptly responded that neither London nor Washington showed "a proper understanding" of Sweden's plight. But as a result of Boheman's skillful lobbying, in December Roosevelt and his State Department advisers overrode the hard-liners and decided to treat Sweden with leniency.[24] Oil shipments, which had actually been totally embargoed for a short period, were subsequently resumed via the neutral shipping which the Germans allowed into the Baltic.

Throughout the war, American foreign policy tended to act tough with the neutrals, a toughness usually missing from the leniently disposed British—except, of course, where Eire was concerned. Boheman, later to become Swedish ambassador in Washington, told of advice Churchill gave him during an October 1942 mission to London to press for increased oil deliveries: "You want oil to defend yourselves and I think you should have it [the oil]. I advise you to arm, arm, and arm again. We don't want another German victim; all we ask is that you defend yourselves in the event of an attack, that you grant no unnecessary concessions, and that you take back those that you have made as soon as you can."[25]

But the United States declared that its primary interest in Sweden sprang from the serious breach it unquestionably represented in its strategic blockade of Nazi Europe. Fortunately for the Swedes, their country never became *critically* vital to either side—at least not critical enough for the expenditure in men and matériel an invasion would have meant to either Allies or Axis. From Germany's perspective, as long as Sweden fulfilled its trade obligations (or what Germany held to be "obligations"), no overriding reason existed to force an invasion.[26] And Sweden learned that respect for the *principles* of neutrality was far less important to the Allies than were their own interests—a maxim it found itself obligated to carry out in counterpoint.[27]

Bern

As did the Swedes, so too the Swiss still passed each day in lethal peril from their looming neighbor. After the quick victories of the summer and fall of 1941, the war in the East ever more engaged the German military machine to the point of straining the Reich's other military commitments. Many of Switzerland's citizens pragmatically concluded that the longer the Russians held out, the less chance there was that Germany would attack Switzerland. But never in 1941 did the confederation's citizenry believe that the Wehrmacht was so weakened that Switzerland could with anything like impunity flout Germany's interests. Though vast new Axis military obligations in the East and in the Balkans meant valuable orders for Swiss manufacturers, thus giving Switzerland a breathing space, Germany continued to badger the confederation, hoping to bully the Swiss into eventual incorporation into the bloated Reich.

Among Berlin's manifold demands was that Switzerland restrict its free press to report only "positive" stories about the Reich and, conversely, only "negative" pieces on the Allies. More frighteningly, Germany insisted that Bern re-legalize the banned German Nazi and Italian fascist parties, at the same time it demanded that all elements of the Swiss military be demobilized. Finally, with breathtaking effrontery, it called for the Swiss to turn over every significant Swiss industry to German "advisers," Nazi overseers who would set each enterprise's export policies.

To all of these ultimatums but one Switzerland responded with a serene refusal. That exception was the single demand Bern decided it could live with—that Switzerland rein in its press's anti-Nazi flavor. A writer for the *Basler Nachrichten* had, as an example of the kind of thing that infuriated Goebbels, only recently created an incident by impudently commenting that Germany's *"Kreuzzug* [crusade] in the Soviet Union was at best a *Hakenkreuzzug."*[28] The nation's publishers and editors were told to tone down such anti-German content in the interests of assuaging Berlin, the Federal Council viewing as reasonable prudence this relatively minor imposition on Swiss sovereignty.

One other lesser directive the government issued in the summer of 1941, not specifically demanded by Berlin but considered the better part of discretion, made the insulting of foreigners and national flags and emblems illegal. The decree, an attempt to bring a halt to the growing public ridicule of Axis leaders, was accompanied by a set of punishments for infringement, penalties that could even bring offenders prison terms.[29]

Throughout 1941, Switzerland continued to face the persistent internal threat from both resident and visiting Germans. Like hostile bacteria, the latter arrived from Germany to abet the anti-democratic, pro-Nazi activities of their countrymen. Their natural allies were those relatively few Swiss still advocating the confederation's absorption into the Reich, the collection of cantons (at least the German-speaking ones) to become another German Nazi *Gau.* Dr. Franz Riedweg, the Swiss head of the Germanische Leitstelle, the SS office dealing with these matters, instead more cunningly argued that Switzerland should become a member of a "Germanic federation" of European states, each nominally independent, but all under Berlin's tight thumb and governed by Nazi ideology.

Ironically, Riedweg's activities in establishing an SS-style paramilitary fifth column in Switzerland led to the Swiss finally taking control of the Nazi cancer in their midst. Bern's national police penetrated the pro-Nazi organization working in the Swiss militia, the so-called Friends of Germany, keeping close tabs on the group, whose members had been directed to wait for a signal from Berlin before initiating its planned campaign of internal war against the democratic government. In June 1941, the Swiss police made 131 arrests when they raided the organization, and for those who failed to escape across the border, Swiss justice culminated in swift trials in both federal and military courts. The fifth columnists not charged because of lack of evidence of treasonable activities were kept under such close watch that by the end of 1941 this German Trojan horse in Switzerland was finally rendered ineffective.[30]

Switzerland's frontiers remained open throughout the war to virtually all foreign travelers, allowing safe passage to, among others, German "visitors" sent by the Reich to whip up pro-Nazi fervor at local National Socialist rallies. Even though Bern adopted a regulation in 1940 requiring that permits be obtained by organizers of political meetings, German citizens flouted such restrictions. The federal government finally cracked down on such foreign organizers when in October 1942 an antidemocratic rally presided over by Gauleiter Ernst Bohle, Nazi chief of all "overseas Germans," aroused widespread indignation among the Swiss. The analysis of Germany's parlous situation on its various war fronts was also likely partially responsible for Bern's new decisiveness.[31]

A contretemps known as the "Däniker affair" became a notorious symptom of the pockets of Nazi rot in the Swiss polity. The episode was emblematic of how some elements of the army were attracted by the disciplined strength of the new Reich. Colonel Gustav Däniker, a senior army officer and former commander of the military school at Walenstadt, possessed an unblemished reputation except that he was openly pro-German in his political views—though not to the extent of being a part of the country's political lunatic fringe. Shortly after Henri Guisan's passionate declaration on the Rütli the prior summer, Däniker's Berlin-leaning convictions led him to write Guisan to declare he had faith in neither the general's program nor his ability to lead the country. Rather than discipline his subordinate and risk publicly revealing what he judged to be serious divisions in the army command structure, Guisan responded with a private letter to the colonel in which he said he was satisfied of the "public's confidence," even if he didn't have that of all his officers.

After completing an assignment in Germany in May 1941, Däniker brought home a heightened conviction that Switzerland's salvation lay in accommodating itself to Germany—that by not resisting the "inevitable" the country would avoid a forced integration into the New Order when Germany won the war. Within five days of his return, he spelled out these beliefs in an intelligently reasoned memorandum boldly addressed to the nation's top army commanders and government leaders. Rather than advocating a coup, or a "march on Bern," as some of his like-minded confederates counseled, Däniker put his faith in the ability of Ernst Hofmann, leader of the largest Swiss Nazi party, to turn its *Nationalen Bewegung der Schweiz*—the Swiss National Movement—into an effective nationwide mass movement that would force the government to Nazify the country. But this time, Guisan saw to it that Däniker's challenge *was* released to the press.

Guisan soon found that two of his corps commanders were in basic sympathy with Däniker's views, which had spread into the air force as well. The general's immediate concern was not only for the successful completion of the massive redoubt program, an undertaking he knew would be jeopardized by defeatism in the highest echelons of the nation's military command, but also for the message it would give the world—especially Germany—if the nation's divisions were laid open.

The underlying message Guisan took from Däniker's efforts was that changes were necessary in the policies that were sapping the Swiss will to resist. Guisan began his mending by beefing up the national police and army security organizations, seeing to it that close watch was kept on all suspected pro-German organizations. Railway personnel, through their union membership, were encouraged to scrutinize all German and Italian trains transiting the country for any suspicious signs or activities. Work on the redoubt was speeded up, Guisan calculating that more German military victories—and these were still all too routine—would only deepen Switzerland's peril.

A sensitive spot remained the war's effect on public morale. Guisan understood that even though the great majority of the Swiss were eager to maintain their nation's independence and democracy, conflicting messages from a divided government and army were dangerous to national unity. That unity was, he knew, fundamental to resisting the German clarion. An organization called Army and Home, set up in late 1939 to oversee the welfare of soldiers and their families, was greatly expanded by

Guisan to fight the nation's apathy and fears of the unknown. Though the government objected to using Army and Home as a medium to reach civilians, the general convincingly argued that civilian-soldiers and their dependents *were* the nation.

Using his most trusted and persuasive officers, the organization arranged town and village forums in virtually every corner of Switzerland in which Guisan's message and vision of a free Switzerland were articulated and the citizenry was encouraged to ask questions or voice concerns. By the end of 1941, the organization had turned into a national media phenomenon that effectively spread Guisan's own deeply held belief that Switzerland would only by determination and preparedness come through Europe's trial a free nation. At the beginning of 1942, it was the general more than the federal government who was the real center of Switzerland. In the late summer of 1942 Guisan ordered Däniker finally removed from his position. [32]

By 1942, national morale was on the mend and the Swiss were beginning to believe that their efforts in resisting Germany's demand for Switzerland's *Gleichschaltung*—"incorporation" into the Reich—were going to pay off. And it became increasingly apparent that Germany was still guided by sound reasons not to invade—despite Swiss "provocations." "Why should Hitler attack?" some anonymous Swiss asked. "He would only gain four million more slaves. He has slaves enough now." [33]

· · ·

The Spaniards alone among the neutrals suffered anything like true war conditions at home. Still, in common with Eire, Sweden, and Portugal, the rationing-centered reality of Switzerland's home-front experience was often a painful one, especially when contrasted with the bountiful prewar life its citizenry had enjoyed.

From what had been a cornucopia in prewar Switzerland, the nation's larder had after 1940 shrunk to a carefully husbanded shadow of its former abundance. For a trade-dependent country whose good life was sustained by importing food and raw materials (in the 1930s it brought in an average of seven and a half million tons of foodstuffs and raw materials a year) and exporting manufactured goods, the array of import and export restrictions both warring blocs imposed on all the neutrals translated into difficult belt-tightening. If the situation had an upside, it was to stimulate Switzerland's capacity to provide for itself just about all of what it needed to keep its population healthy.

Though the basic rationing plan had been developed soon after the war started, by 1941 Bern was cranking out a river of new regulations meant to ensure fairness and caution in distributing the country's now finite food resources. (The three-month supply the government had urged all householders to stock in March 1939, renewing the request three months later, fortunately served as a cushion when the tougher rationing started.) Bread could, for example, only be sold forty-eight hours after it was baked, the theory being that few people would throw away stale crusts when new but still stale bread arrived. Wednesday and Friday were officially declared meatless days, emulating the *Eintopf Tag*, or "casserole day," which all German citizens were obliged to observe; unlike the Germans, the Swiss were able to stretch such meals with plenty of fish and eggs. By March 1941, rationing had come to include all sorts of basics: butter, limited to ten ounces per person per month; chocolate and dog food, cheese, tea and coffee. The bread for the butter—stale though it was—went on the ration from October 1942.

Swiss dietary planners originally set the national ration at a total of 3,000 calories a day, but by 1941 the amount was lowered by 600 calories, a big enough decrease so that the Swiss people soon came, in the aggregate, to display noticeably slimmer physiques.[34] Farmers were allowed extra calories, the government reasoning that they worked harder than most other people and that in any case it would be impossible to control how much they ate.[35] In the main, the Swiss wartime rationing system worked well, causing little resentment primarily because it was seen to be fair and levels of available food remained high enough so that no genuine hardship was suffered. The one public relations failing was that foreign visitors were fed without regard to any rationing, leading foreigners to report that the Swiss were waxing fat and happy while much of the rest of Europe teetered on the edge of malnutrition.

Despite the fact that the Swiss were one of Europe's biggest dairy producers, dairy products were rationed from October 1942 because Germany demanded huge quantities of milk (as well as fats) in exchange for the German coal Switzerland imported from the Reich for its energy needs.[36] When the Swiss balked at what they held to be extortionate exchange levels, the Germans simply threatened to withhold both coal and iron, as well as to withdraw the permits—*Geleitscheine*—that allowed the Swiss to pass a limited amount of trade through the German blockade. At one juncture, in the spring of 1941, such trade had been held up as a warning by the Germans, forcing the Swiss that summer into a new commercial agreement with the Reich in which Switzerland agreed to raise its credit limit to $350 million Swiss francs—about $16 million. These accommodations to Germany in turn prompted the British to tighten its own blockade of Switzerland, compelling Swiss envoys in London to constantly plead with the Ministry of Trade for greater understanding of their country's isolation.[37]

Clothing purchases were restricted from early in the war because of the difficulties in obtaining wool and cotton fabrics. But whereas their German neighbors had to get by on 100 clothing "points" per year, Bern allowed each Swiss a ration ten times as large. Still, each Swiss citizen was annually allowed but a single pair of shoes, a commodity that had virtually disappeared from Europe.[38] The shoes the Swiss did get were made of real leather, though, all but unavailable throughout most of wartime Europe.

For Switzerland to have survived the war years with its nutrition as good as it was, the government had to try to make up as much of the lost imports as possible. With only a quarter of its land surface arable— mountains, glaciers, pastures, and woods made up most of the remainder—Bern declared what it called an "agricultural battle," and set out to refashion every inch of fallow land into food gardens. In the four years following November 1940, the cultivated surface of Switzerland nearly doubled through the cutting down of 90 square kilometers of forest, the draining of 480 square kilometers of marshland, and the drastic reduction of livestock and reclaiming of pasturage for crop production.[39]

The characteristic look of Swiss cities metamorphosed as nearly every arable scrap of urban parks, civic plazas, football fields, roadside rests, and private lawns was converted to cultivating food. The government allowed the bounty from such private gardens to be used to supplement the official rations. Industrial companies were required to provide their employees with land on which to plant food, with each firm's staff from president to office boy pitching in after hours on these communal-type gardens.[40] The grounds of Geneva's League of Nations palace, that gray marble relic of a by now vanished era of democratic ideals, were turned into the nation's premier potato patch.

Tending some of these new plots were the thousands of foreign political refugees and interned soldiers chased into Switzerland by the advancing German armies. By late 1941 some 60,000 of the latter had entered the country, among them men from France, Belgium, the Netherlands, Denmark, Norway, and the United Kingdom—the most disgruntled probably the German aviators shot down when overflying Swiss airspace and interned by the Swiss for the duration. (The Swiss knew this infuriated the Germans, but not to have forced the German planes down would have made an empty argument of Switzerland's claim to the inviolability of its airspace.) Eager for a chance to earn a meager living, the refugees were organized into "work corps," given instruction in one of Switzerland's languages if necessary, and instilled with the basics of useful trades with which to underwrite their temporary Swiss lives.

Jews from Vichy France made up the heaviest influx of refugees. Two principal roads of escape existed for these frightened people, both starting from Savoy and centered on the French ski resorts of Megève and Chamonix. The first led westward from Megève, toward Geneva; the escapees on this route either rowed across Lake Geneva at night, mostly in the Nyon area, where the crossing was only two and a half miles wide, or else got across the land border with forged documents. The second escape path left Chamonix, clung to hazardous mountain trails around the base of Mount Blanc, and finally broached the border in the vicinity of the small Swiss town of Martigny. Neither the increased Swiss patrols in these areas nor the $1,000 price some of the local French citizens demanded of the escapees for their own border-crossing permits stopped the traffic.

Jews did not rate as "political" refugees, and were therefore neither granted asylum nor, barring special circumstances, exempted from the stringent Swiss immigration quotas. Despite the generally widespread disapproval of the Swiss citizens for this policy, the federal government refused to change it, one official callously declaring that "we cannot turn our country into a sponge for Europe." The "special circumstances" permitted the sheltering of about 23,000 Jews during the war, but another 10,000 applicants were turned away.[41]

One of the many shocks the Swiss suffered as a result of the war was inflation, an affliction little associated with the hard-as-diamonds Swiss economy. The wholesale price index of both imported and domestic goods, weighted at 100 in August 1939, had by April 1941 soared to 162.9. Virtually all necessities had increased in price during the period, generally by 25 to 50 percent; only rents, controlled by the government, remained stable. Wages increased only by about 10 percent during these twenty months, a clear and abrupt decline in the national standard of living. (By the standards of the rest of war-ravaged Europe, of course, the decline wasn't much more than merely troublesome.) To keep its businesses running in a trade-restricted environment, the government encouraged domestic spending; one group to take the advice with a vengeance was the hard-pressed hoteliers, who with an almost total loss of foreign tourism—one of the mainstays of the prewar Swiss economy— slashed their room rates and pushed hard to encourage domestic daytrippers.

Railways within Switzerland itself had, because of the inter-Axis trade—Germany to Italy and vice versa—become virtually German-owned. Railway yards were closed to the public, but through wire fences curious Swiss could see mile after mile of German and Italian freight carriages heading for the Lötschberg, Simplon, and St. Gotthard tunnels. Most prominent were the coal cars carrying the lifeblood of Mussolini's Italy from the mines of the Reich; on their return northbound journey, the just-emptied cars were refilled with fruit and green vegetables from Italy and ores—lead, chrome, manganese, bauxite—from the Axis-controlled Balkans, all destined for the increasingly straitened German war economy.

Coupled with the shortages caused by the Allied blockade and the Axis's counter-blockade, Switzerland was forced to work around the myriad transportation headaches to which a continent at war was unavoidably subjected. Not only were the war's consequences beginning to destroy much of Europe's transportation systems, but voracious military needs had made ships, freight cars, and trucks increasingly rare and valuable commodities. Further, the operating ports and docks and railway stations that constituted the continent's transportation infrastructure were painfully overcrowded, and as the war progressed increasingly victims of bombing raids. The whole lamentable mess heightened the hardships inherent in the blockade.

Though the Swiss chartered their own collection of variously flagged freighters to supply them at several European ports, Genoa acting as the confederation's primary port of entry, getting the goods from their docks to Switzerland often created logistical nightmares. At the peak of the war, the Swiss employed some 70,000 freight cars that were sent across the continent to whichever port or other depot received goods the Swiss had bought. After Greece's neutrality ended in the spring of 1940, that country's ships—carriers the Swiss had at the war's outset depended on for their supplies—could no longer enter the Mediterranean, and now began to off-load at Portuguese and Spanish Atlantic ports. But from Iberia to Switzerland still represented a journey of traumatic proportions: the Spanish rail system remained in primitive condition, and even when the goods could be gotten across Iberia to the French border, the Swiss often weren't able to find workers willing to transfer their purchases from the Spanish broad-gauge tracks to the French narrow-gauge. The principal solution to the problem was the hiring of Spanish and Portuguese tramp freighters to pick up transatlantic goods from Iberian ports and transfer them to Genoa, and from that Axis port by rail to Switzerland.

An enormous potential danger to all wartime shipping—even that of neutral countries—was posed by the virtually unrestricted submarine warfare prosecuted by Germany's U-boat fleet. To counter this threat, the Swiss set up an office in their Berlin legation expressly for the purpose of informing the German naval authorities of the precise locations and routes of freighters carrying goods bound for Switzerland, information the mission continuously received over its own powerful radio equipment. Together with their itineraries, the Swiss gave the Germans detailed descriptions of all such ships, along with silhouettes, designed to make it harder for U-boat captains to mistake these neutral carriers bound for Genoa or other ports open to Swiss shipping—Trieste and Marseille were two such subsidiary ports—from those headed for Allied ports. As a result of this cooperation between Bern and the German Admiralty, not a single ship chartered or owned by the Swiss was torpedoed on its way to off-loading goods destined for Switzerland.

To enter their "home ports," the Swiss-chartered ships were provided with precise maps that enabled them to negotiate the heavily mined waters skirting virtually every belligerent harbor in wartime Europe. To further their own ends, the Allies were reported to have photographed these ships as they entered Mediterranean harbors, the pictures giving them a safe—that is, unmined—route to follow into the ports against the day Allied landings would get underway.[42]

Switzerland had at the war's outset established an air link with the outside world between Locarno and Barcelona, but this connection was severed in June 1940 when Italy entered the war, the route now overflying a war zone and thus unusable.[43] In exchange for a liberalization of the navicert limits in late 1940, London proposed a direct air link between Britain and Switzerland, the British motivated by a means to get the relatively small treasures of Swiss precision manufacturing—watch and timer movements, scientific instruments, field glasses—through the German economic blockade. (Switzerland's trade with Britain—17 percent of its total before the war—had dropped to virtually nothing by 1941.) The Swiss turned down the proposal as unworkable, prompting London to counterpropose a Swiss Air flight to London via Spain and Portugal. Neither the Spanish nor the Portuguese thought this a good idea, presumably on the logic that the Germans would know exactly why the air link was being established. In the end, no such wartime connection was ever set up.

Switzerland's trade problems linked the country almost wholly to Germany. In April 1941, Britain further squeezed Swiss imports when it refused to issue navicerts for U.S.-Swiss trade in bulk foods and many other materials, Whitehall fearing the material would end up finding its way to the Nazis. And after the onset of the Soviet-German war, any hope Switzerland entertained of trading with the Russians—a $23 million trade agreement had been signed between the two mutually antagonistic countries in February 1941—evaporated when the trade route through Germany and Poland was broken.

What the Germans wanted from Swiss industry mirrored the Allies' wishes: the sort of high-tech weaponry and instruments at which the Swiss excelled, weaponry with which Switzerland would credibly be able to defend itself. The irony was, of course, that Switzerland was forced to arm its only real enemy while it was arming itself against that enemy. After Swiss free trade virtually halted with the fall of France, the Swiss switch from normal peacetime production to the manufacture of armaments and other war materials found its sole significant market in the Axis—with the Axis setting the prices. Not only did these weapons and armaments constitute the country's lone major valuable commodities, but to stop such goods would have meant the closing of factories, which would have led to widespread unemployment, thus putting the newly jobless squarely under the seductive lure of Germany's call to "accommodation." Furthermore, the factories themselves were only able to remain open because they received German raw materials—coal and iron and all the other necessities the Swiss didn't possess in their Alpine homeland—and the Germans only sold to the Swiss because they fully expected the fruit of the factories to come flowing back to the Reich in the form of arms, ammunition, and the other items of war the Wehrmacht needed.

·   ·   ·

In the face of so much menace, Guisan continued to affirm Switzerland's intent to destroy the Alpine tunnels if the Germans invaded, the possibility remaining uppermost in the general's strategic thinking that Hitler's appetite for conquest might outweigh what he stood to lose. By the end of 1941, the national redoubt—Fortress Switzerland—had been transformed from concept into a practical refuge where the critical core of a Swiss government and army would survive a Nazi invasion.

Essential to the redoubt's success was the fail-safe capacity to blow up the Alpine tunnels, conduits without which a German takeover would make little strategic sense as long as Italy remained dependent on German energy supplies. An elaborate demolition system was installed in the tunnels, as well as in the Alpine road passes and the mountain bridges. These achievements of thousands of workers and engineers over decades of modern Swiss history were so wired that once the signal to destroy was given by Guisan no German counterforce would be able to stop the blasts. The timing of the destruction in case of invasion was, of course, variable: the works could be destroyed either at the outset of a German onslaught, to keep the Wehrmacht from crossing the Alpine barrier, or at such invasion's end, when as a last act of resistance it would signal Guisan's pullback into the redoubt.

Functioning together with the redoubt, the forward defense line continued as a major element in Guisan's strategy. The armed line, closely following the national borders, was maintained both to give a feeling of assurance to the bulk of the population not within the redoubt's perimeter and to help slow down an invading force while demolition was put into effect. The second, closer-in perimeter was abandoned on the logic that it would represent a dangerous dispersion of the limited troops available. Guisan placed the heaviest concentrations of defense forces in the portals to the seven main valleys that entered the protected region, openings that came to be known as the "doors to the redoubt."[44] At each of these points stood heavily armed fortresses, together protecting the center of the mountainous redoubt from forced entry. Wherever within the redoubt it was judged that German paratroops might be able to land, additional specially armed units were placed to thwart such eventuality.

Aside from the fact that work remained to be done on the redoubt facilities, the general knew that the redoubt and the scorched-earth policy associated with the tunnels weren't an entirely foolproof deterrent to a German invasion. Hitler might reason that the Alpine passes were of less value than the part of Switzerland that *would* be left to Nazi exploitation. The Swiss flatlands with their fertile soil, skilled urban workers, and valuable engineering resources might represent an irresistible enticement to a German dictator who saw the continued existence of a neutral, democratic, mostly German-speaking country on his own border as a personal affront. To remove the lure of the part of Switzerland left out of the redoubt became Guisan's next objective.

Beginning in late 1941, 16,000 Swiss military engineers and special demolition experts undertook the systematic placing of demolitions in hundreds of factories and other strategically valuable installations all over the country, and by early 1942, over a thousand such facilities had been wired for destruction in the event of a German invasion. The general ordered the wiring of everything of any conceivable attraction to the Germans. Factories were sowed with dynamite that would destroy them and present invading Germans with the blown-up remnants of useless Swiss industrial plants. The industrial sites were wired for demolition often in the face of heated antagonism by the plant managers, who, not as aware as Guisan of the danger Germany still presented the country, vehemently challenged the commander-in-chief's apocalyptic deterrents. In fact, the general would have to swallow the hostility of such owners until June 1943, when the Federal Council finally confirmed Guisan's authority to carry out a scorched-earth policy in the event of invasion.

This then remained the fundamental Swiss defense posture through the latter part of 1942. At that time, when the Axis armies were becoming fatally exhausted by the failing Russian gamble, Guisan began once again to envision saving the greater part of the country in case of an invasion by a potent but weakened Wehrmacht. And with more than a touch of irony, at the turn of 1943 it was the vision of an Allied preemptive invasion that would concern Guisan as much as an Axis assault.

· · ·

That the neutral states were playing fields for spies was one of their principal attractions to both warring blocs. Both Lisboners and Istanbulis savored their cities' reputations as *the* beehives of World War II boulevard espionage, but it was Switzerland where many of the truly important moves in this game took place: the confederation's relatively free and democratic government, its location in the center of the continent, its outstanding postal and rail communications systems, and its borders that remained open throughout the war all contributed to the nation's usefulness to the belligerents' intelligence services. Fortunately for the Allies, Guisan well understood that a triumphant Germany would spell the end of his nation's independence and thus render its neutrality irrelevant; owing in large part to this realization, the Swiss commander-in-chief would allow an American named Allen Dulles to become one of his country's principal partners in its discreet tilt toward an Allied victory.[45]

Switzerland's own intelligence service had before the war been, at best, of limited value. In common with many of Europe's liberal-left politicians and public, the Social Democrats in power for much of the interwar period stubbornly clung to the notion that to prepare for conflict was to invite it, and consistently engineered national budgets leaving the country militarily shortchanged. When in 1936 this attitude finally began to be corrected by the growing threat of European politics, the civilian and military intelligence capabilities correspondingly rose with the nation's defense preparations. Nonetheless, at the outbreak of war a mere ten officers were assigned to Swiss military intelligence. This number rose sixteenfold by the time the conflict was in full swing. Headed by Colonel Roger Masson, the service was charged with keeping Guisan and his high command fully apprised of what the neighboring armies were up to, especially where the 300-kilometer-wide "critical zone" around the nation's borders was involved.

In June 1942, another element entered the Swiss intelligence picture as a result of the Office of Strategic Services having been established that month by the United States government. The new agency was designed as the executive branch's arm charged with furthering America's position in the espionage war. The American spy agency had been deliberately modeled on Britain's Special Operations Executive, the organization of saboteurs, spies, and couriers who acted on Churchill's famous directive to "set Europe ablaze."

The OSS's three principal divisions were intelligence, operations, and research, together contributing to America's ability to foment confusion in enemy territory through propaganda and disinformation, to gather intelligence wherever it could, and to carry out sabotage behind enemy lines.[46] William J. "Wild Bill" Donovan, the first OSS chief, chose as the agency's first Swiss field activities director an old friend, forty-nine-year-old international law attorney Allen Welsh Dulles. It would be Dulles who would, through extraordinarily skillful work, be responsible for some of the most fruitful intelligence successes to come out of the entire Allied espionage effort in World War II.

Dulles arrived overland in Bern in November 1942, just hours before the Germans took over Vichy France and closed off its borders with Spain and Switzerland. His official assignment was to be attached to the American diplomatic mission as the minister's "special assistant." Unofficially and in reality, he was the OSS head in Europe, Donovan's primary agent for finding out as much as possible about what was going on in Germany, who was doing it, how to get in contact with them, and for evaluating the chances of success for the various German resistance groups; Washington told Dulles to seek out "disillusioned" Germans "actively at work" trying to overthrow the Third Reich.[47] To carry out this formidable agenda, Dulles established two primary objectives for himself: to make contact with as many Germans in Switzerland—both exiles and businessmen—as he could and to attempt to coordinate his own activities with those of the highly skilled Swiss intelligence services. The spymaster also approached every American in Switzerland to enlist their aid, and most agreed to help.

Dulles's arrival in Switzerland and its significance had not been hidden. The Swiss press announced that he was Roosevelt's "secret and special envoy," an exaggeration which Dulles tried only halfheartedly to disclaim and which likely contributed to his initial successes in establishing important contacts. He set up his residence in a beautiful old mansion in the Herrengasse, overlooking the Aare, and immediately removed the light bulbs from the streetlamps outside his door so nighttime callers could arrive and depart with less likelihood of being observed.[48]

Over the course of his mission in Bern, Dulles would be the catalyst of peace feelers from Germany, Italy, Rumania, and Japan.[49] Disappointingly, the first months of his efforts in the Swiss capital produced less than acceptable intelligence, data often discounted in Washington and for which he would receive official rebukes.[50] But the canny lawyer was reprieved when his most extraordinary espionage coup came into fruition, one involving an unassuming minor bureaucrat in Berlin's Foreign Ministry who wanted very badly to share what he knew.

Fritz Kolbe—known by the OSS code name "George Wood"—provided the United States with some of its most valuable German intelligence during the war.[51] The forty-year-old Kolbe was an aide in Ribbentrop's liaison office with the German military high command. His anti-Nazi convictions led him in mid-1943 to seek an appointment as a diplomatic courier authorized to travel freely throughout Europe, a freedom that would allow him to visit Switzerland, nearby to his duty posting in Salzburg. Once in the Swiss capital, after first talking to a German émigré friend he eventually reached Gerald Mayer, one of Dulles's aides. To Mayer he proposed providing the Americans with documents from the bulging top-secret files of his Berlin ministry. As a sample of what he could offer, he showed Mayer nearly 200 pages of microfilmed cables he had sneaked out of the ministry strapped to his leg. Impressed with the trove, Mayer and Dulles realized Kolbe could be enormously damaging to Germany.

To explain his willingness to commit high treason against his fatherland, the German claimed to be a Foreign Ministry cell member of the *Schwarzkapelle*, the "Black Orchestra" anti-Hitler opposition group operating in the German government.[52] Dulles had Kolbe/Wood checked through Washington, and came to the conclusion that his intelligence was authentic, though serious doubt would continue to exist—even after the war—as to whether Kolbe might have in fact been a German plant.

Over the next year, Kolbe provided Dulles with 1,600 cables from the Foreign Ministry, many of which involved diplomatic trivia of little importance, but some of which the Americans were able to use against the Germans with notable success, more for their ability to further their understanding of German ciphers than for specific intelligence content. Some were, however, useful from the pure intelligence standpoint, as, for example, a communication revealing the departure date of a convoy from a U.S. port, information allowing the enemy to station U-boats to destroy Allied shipping; the information permitted Bern to notify Washington in time to change the convoy's departure date. Kolbe informed Bern when he found that his employers had broken one of the Allied codes, leading London and Washington to change their ciphers. Another spectacular bit of Kolbe intelligence supplied Dulles with the exact battle order of the Japanese imperial fleet. By the time of the July 1944 attempt on Hitler's life, Kolbe's espionage activities had become so dangerous that he was forced to desist, and in early 1945 the courier turned spy escaped permanently into Switzerland.[53]

A major part of Dulles's mission was to coordinate his own activities with those of his host nation. Thanks in large part to General Guisan's recognition that in spite of the country's official neutrality Switzerland's interests would best be served by Swiss intelligence discreetly cooperating with Allied intelligence, Dulles was able to establish high-level contacts with his Swiss counterparts. Foremost among them was Major Max Waibel, head of N1, the Swiss military intelligence service, headquartered in Lucerne and charged with gathering information on the Axis powers. Dulles also met with Colonel Roger Masson, the chief of Swiss espionage, the two establishing a friendship that led Dulles to the tricky realization that Swiss intelligence services were also in touch with their German and Italian counterparts, a relationship Dulles finally and wisely concluded would only serve to help him gather more information than otherwise would have been possible. The full extent of the American's relationship with his Swiss counterparts isn't known with certainty, but it is generally believed that Dulles wouldn't have been able to achieve what he did without Swiss cooperation and even assistance.

Dulles's most celebrated involvement at his Swiss post—one that very likely shortened the European war and saved untold lives in the process— would come in the violent spring of 1945 as Hitler's Wehrmacht, still lethal, disintegrated in a final frenzied snarl. More on this episode in the next chapter.

·   ·   ·

Though Switzerland remained indisputably a democracy throughout the war years, there was little sympathy for those few Swiss who turned traitor. Some of the handful of Swiss citizens who betrayed their country to the Germans—no one was ever convicted of betraying the country to the Allies—did so for reasons of conviction, others for lucre. But irrespective of their motives, Swiss military courts were capable of handing down ruthless punishment to the transgressors who came before them. For endangering national security, the charge brought for spying for a foreign country, imposition of the death penalty was within the court's power, and by the end of the conflict thirty-three such sentences were passed. Fifteen of them were in absentia, and seventeen men were executed—fifteen Swiss, one Frenchman, one Liechtensteiner; one man was pardoned. As soon as appeals were voted down by parliament, the condemned traitor was immediately taken to the stake and there shot by members of his own unit. The doomed men included three officers, of whom the highest-ranking was a major, eleven noncommissioned officers, and three civilians.[54]

Dublin

As the war's third year overtook a world now bowed down by fighting, a single issue came to overshadow Eire's place in the conflict: the newly belligerent America's move into Ulster and its repercussions on the incendiary issue of Irish unity. To its already combustible politics, the American presence in Northern Ireland threatened to further bedevil the sundered island's social composure.

Between the German invasion of the Soviet Union in June and the onset of virtually unbounded world war in December, the citizens of the Twenty-six Counties in their blinkered isolation could do little other than duck the dangers. Having so recently suffered a small but terrifying sample of the aerial devastation now making wildernesses of Europe's cities, the Irish more staunchly than ever resolved to guard their neutrality. Though the threat of a German invasion subsided with the Axis assault on Russia, the government by no means assumed the Germans wouldn't still hit Eire hard if it were to cooperate openly with Britain. The signs of Germany's problems continued to be subtle, and overwhelming Nazi victories in Russia—obvious even in the closely censored Irish press—still made it appear in late 1941 that Europe's future would be written in Berlin. Even the massive aid the Americans were giving the British in the latter half of 1941 hardly translated into an assurance of Britain holding back—let alone defeating—the Axis menace. Moreover, few Irishmen believed Britain mightn't still strike out against the Irish to improve their strategic position against a German Navy continuing to cripple Britain's vital sea supplies and with them its capacity to persevere.

In the midst of this intensely gloomy time, the effects of the war even in this neutral land continued to bite deeper, daily more strongly paral-

leling the measure of life the British were enduring. To darken the
melancholy, Britain's prime minister persisted in his anathematization of
Eire and more punishing trade cutoffs to the island. In a December 1941
directive to the Chancellor of the Exchequer, Churchill spoke remarkably bluntly:

> The straits to which we are being reduced by Irish action compel a
> reconsideration of the subsidies [to Ireland]. It can hardly be argued that
> we can go on paying them to our last gasp. . . . Pray let me know how
> these subsidies could be terminated and what retaliatory measures could
> be taken in the financial sphere by the Irish, observing that we are not
> afraid of their cutting off their food, as it would save us the enormous
> mass of fertilizers we have to carry into Ireland through the de Valera-
> aided German blockade.[55]

As Eire was bereft of a merchant marine of its own, many of the
normal essentials of a modern society now became all but unavailable,
and without the raw materials required for its industries, both production
and employment tumbled—automobile production, for example, fell to
less than half its prewar levels. Only the demands from British industry
and the ensuing emigration to Britain kept unemployment from developing into a dangerous crisis; in fact, the eastward traffic across the Irish
Sea became so great by 1942 that the government had to stanch the
exodus to keep enough workers available for bringing in the harvests. It
should be noted, though, that besides taking the pressure off domestic
supplies, the 100,000 or so Irishmen working in Britain were depended
upon for the money they could send home, with some communities,
especially those in the poor western counties, almost entirely dependent
on these funds for survival.[56]

In the spring of 1941, the Dublin government set up an organization
called Irish Shipping Limited, its mission to obtain—in any way it
could—chartered ships to help maintain the country's minimum essential supplies. Two of the freighters the new board hired were American,
and another sailed under Panamanian registry. A fourth vessel, a pint-
sized 2,000-ton Yugoslav steamer, was taken over, having been attacked
and abandoned off the Irish coast, whence repairers salvaged and refur-
bished it for Irish use. Three ships belonging to the Baltic states had been
seized in Irish ports when Russia repossessed those ill-fated countries;
though their exiled owners disputed their Soviet "ownership"—since the
Soviets were at war, Dublin felt justified in taking them—the Irish High
Court agreed they could be held and used by Eire for at least the duration.[57] This motley fleet, whose total weight didn't reach 30,000 tons,

was helpful but hardly capable of significantly relieving the country's supply crisis.

Ominously, the stocks that Supply Minister Seán Lemass had ordered be laid in before the war were by the end of 1941 starting to run out. Coal for household use—of which there was no domestic supply—became a rarity, often replaced by the country's peat turf; great piles of the peat marred the country's appearance, even lining every inch of driveway in Dublin's once beautiful Phoenix Park. Gas and electricity were rationed (the former, laboriously generated from coal, was only supposed to be turned on at mealtimes), leading eventually to a suspension of the Dublin tram system. Intercity rail service dwindled to a shadow of its prewar schedule, and the lack of repairs and replacements on the Irish rail system took a toll that wouldn't be remedied until many years after the war ended. Hoping to replace the dwindling supplies of imported raw materials—principally coal—with ersatz substitutes, the government set up an organization called the Emergency Scientific Research Bureau, at the same time establishing another body, the Mineral Exploration and Development Company, to look for domestic energy sources other than coal.

Gasoline and rubber for private motoring became unavailable in 1942, and even for ambulances and tractors were in critically restricted supply. The disastrous shortages of imported fertilizers, which had long contributed heavily to Eire's own food supply and to the raising of cattle, the country's only big export, led to coastal farmers utilizing seaweed and their inland brothers to the use of animal manure to replace unavailable man-made fertilizers.[58] With additional government-mandated burdens on crop plantings coupled with the fertilizer shortages, Ireland's soil would—like its rails—be damaged to an extent that would take years to be redressed.[59]

The attitude of Britain—that is substantially to say the attitude of Churchill—toward helping supply and feed neutral Eire forced the de Valera government to think hard about how the island's people were going to make it without the traditional imports on which they relied for much of their diet. In November, the government conducted a census on which to base a national register for issuing ration books, though seven months would pass before a full rationing system came into effect. But food and drink shortages—especially of the national sustenance, tea— were becoming serious enough to create public alarm. Tea had been doled out since January, when each person received four ounces, which was halved and halved again by the end of the year; the *Connacht Telegraph* advised its readers to make do with a mix of common ash and hawthorn leaves, but the more usual remedy was to re-brew tea leaves until the resulting liquid approached water in clarity. Bread, the staple of virtually every diet in Ireland, went the way of tea. The milling of white flour became illegal, resulting in a sodden brown loaf concocted of whole-wheat flour and stretched with potatoes and barley, which has left the Irish with a prejudice against brown bread that persists to this day.[60]

Clothing rationing soon followed in the wake of food rationing, when British cotton imports were cut by 75 percent. Women were perhaps hardest hit, new stockings becoming as rare as full tea caddies with the end of silk and rayon imports. If smokers of Aftons saved up 175 of the coupons found in each pack, they could redeem them for a pair of silk hose, though the recipient still had to hand over one official ration coupon. Simpler still was the technique that in World War II hit Ireland just as it did the rest of the world: "stockings" painted on with tan makeup and finished with a *faux* seam carefully drawn with an eyebrow pencil. Only shoes remained generally available, since the Federation of Irish Tanners had struck a deal with British tanners to barter Irish rawhide for finished leather, an arrangement that even allowed Dublin to develop a small export trade in shoes to Britain.

Serving soldiers got the same rationing outlay as civilians. A number of coupons equal to the uniform provided by the quartermaster was deducted from each serviceman's total, with the result that soldiers rarely had enough coupons left over to get any kind of civilian articles. A man's suit, for example, took 40 coupons, a nightshirt 17. Anyone wanting to buy a kilt had to be prepared to turn over 18 precious coupons for the privilege.[61]

With the drop in goods and manufacturing came a sharp fall in the national standard of living, cutting deeply into the old norms of Irish life: with a base of 100 points in 1914, the cost-of-living index had risen to 173 by 1938—and then soared to 284 as 1942 turned into 1943. Costs sky-rocketed, but not wages and salaries, the latter held in check by the government's Emergency powers.[62] Though that action controlled the inflation that would have been inevitable with a rising money supply, it came at the cost of real hardships in the lives of the Irish people.

Still, whatever hardships the Irish endured didn't alter the nearly unanimous agreement of Irish citizens with their government's neutrality policy. Though by 1942 only an estimated tenth of Eire's citizens were anti-British in their attitudes toward the war, and tens of thousands of Irish men and women were serving in the British forces and working in Britain's industry, the unwavering stand in the Twenty-six Counties remained one of support for the Taoiseach's determination to keep his country out of the fighting. Those few antagonistic to the Allied cause found themselves the butt of some sharply pointed humor about the country's reliance on its big neighbor. One story making the circuit had to do with the Irishman who told the Englishman he'd be glad to see the Germans occupy Britain. "But don't you see," the Englishman said, "the next step would surely be an occupation of Ireland." "No, no," says the Irishman, "the Royal Navy wouldn't allow it."

.   .   .

The Dublin government regarded censorship as one of its principal tools in maintaining its neutrality unblemished, with the censor becoming a force in Eire the likes of whose authority even Eamon de Valera seemed not to surpass. Not surprisingly, the lengths to which censorship had to be carried to keep the Twenty-six Counties hermetically clean of the passions and propaganda of war very often crossed into the realm of the ridiculous. An early 1942 newsreel included scenes taken at a London zoo in which children were feeding elephants. But slung over the young-sters' shoulders were the omnipresent signs of wartime Britain, gas-mask canisters. Rather than let the sight of tykes forced to carry these sad instruments lead to sympathy for the children and thus for Britain, the censors ordered the scene cut.

Any mention of the worldwide conflict in cinema newsreels—during the war years one of the most popular sources of news—led to mad snipping of censors' scissors. Lines such as "London was blitzed out . . ." and "releasing men for the fighting services" (an item about female employment in Britain) were sure to be slashed. No pictures ever appeared on the screen of Hitler, or of Mussolini, or even of Churchill—or, for that matter, of any of the warring nations' leaders. No mention was ever made of fifth columns, or sabotage, or refugees—all taboo subjects and thus automatically cut from any film. Neither were battle incidents ever shown. The fine imposed on any cinema operator for offending the censorship regulations was £50 per offense.

Not only films but newspapers—now in reduced sizes—were rigorously expurgated. No speaker in the Dáil who spoke critically of any action of the government could expect to see his remarks in print. "IRA" was a proscribed term. The press could not refer to de Gaulle's forces as the Free French, but was instead required to call them "de Gaullists," as though the nonmention of the name by which they were known around the world would make them less threatening to Ireland's safety. Perhaps the apotheosis of the ridiculousness of Eire's censorship policy regarded an Irish sailor in the Royal Navy, a man well known in Dublin for serving in the British forces. The sailor was saved when his ship, the *Prince of Wales*, was sunk off Malaya shortly after Pearl Harbor. His friends, anxious to let it be known that the young man survived the disaster, wanted the fact published in the newspapers. But the censor refused to associate an Irish citizen with the calamitous British loss. Finally a solution was jury-rigged: a paragraph appeared in which it was with due gravity announced that the sailor had been picked safely out of the water "after his recent boating accident."[63]

· · ·

The IRA and its embrace with German espionage remained a constant in the catalogue of dangers to Irish stability. In view of the organization's potential for troublemaking, a significant part of Germany's espionage offensive in wartime Ireland involved the Irish Republican Army, though Berlin inexplicably placed its faith in some of the most bumbling agents the Reich's espionage services ever employed. Two days after the war started, Churchill, as First Sea Lord, wrote a memorandum to the Naval Staff, in it castigating the IRA connection: "What does Intelligence say about possible succouring of U-boats by Irish malcontents? If they throw bombs in London, why should they not supply fuel to U-boats? Extreme vigilance should be practised."[64]

As it happened, most Irishmen wanted as little to do with the IRA as possible: if the Allies were frustrated with de Valera's neutrality policy, Germany must have felt that frustration in spades at an Ireland in which the vast majority rejected any replay of the civil disorder that had so vexed Britain in World War I.[65] Though Berlin made halfhearted efforts at obtaining IRA cooperation against the British, Germany plainly equivocated when it realized that after de Valera's 1939 crackdown the organization had become too weak and disunited to be of any real service to the Axis.

A large portion of the now fractured IRA persisted in its embittered conviction that the Dublin government and its de facto acceptance of a partitioned island represented a greater threat to its aims than did a totalitarian, militarily threatening Germany. Since 1938, when it became committed to its campaign of terror, the IRA rejected peace with both of the island's governments. So earnest was the organization's hatred of the British "interloper" that it sought help from virtually any sympathetic quarter, even from Nazi Germany, in achieving its goal of a totally independent Ireland.

Except in Ulster, where the organization continued in the early war years to grow and where it possessed a large and lethal armory of weaponry and munitions, the IRA by 1942 had become a seemingly spent force, its prestige mauled since the beginning of the European conflict and de Valera's virtual declaration of war against it. Most southern Irishmen saw the war and a possible German victory—the latter still very much viewed as a possibility in 1942—as a far more lethal danger for Ireland than partition. By 1942, bolstered by public support, de Valera's now feisty government decided that the use of the name "Irish Republican Army," or even its initials, was provocative and thus an illegal act. Other such edicts, usually more symbolic than substantive, soon followed: official government notices of executions of condemned IRA prisoners could not be reported with editorial comments or additions, nor could they be printed on principal news pages. Even the size of newspaper type used to print these grim announcements—no larger than eight points—was set by government fiat.

Though de Valera's post-1939 campaign against the IRA severely hurt the organization, it nonetheless remained a thorn in the government's side. Between 1939 and 1945, more than 600 members of the organization found themselves imprisoned in central Ireland's Curragh Camp, Ireland's Aldershot and once the storied home of Queen Victoria's Irish army.[66] After the already noted Phoenix Park raid, two decrees—the Emergency Powers Act and a newly beefed-up Offenses Against the State Act—gave the government leave to impose the death penalty on anyone convicted of any of a long list of offenses, crimes typical of the IRA's modus operandi and that included murder, high treason, sending or possessing messages "endangering national security," acting to damage the defense authorities, firing weapons to resist or prevent arrest, kidnapping, possessing arms or munitions to endanger life, possessing explosives or causing an explosion, or being an accessory to any of these transgressions.[67]

Eduard Hempel, the perspicacious German minister in Dublin, was himself chary of the IRA's extremism, and correctly deduced that the organization had lost public support. (He nonetheless believed the outlawed society could on occasion be used profitably, particularly in Ulster, where its intelligence gathering on the Northern Ireland government might be helpful to Germany.) In the Twenty-six Counties, the envoy took care to see that agents in Germany's employ didn't act against the state, shrewdly unwilling to hand the de Valera government a legitimate grievance against Germany. He also judged that if the IRA-German connection were too obvious, the Allies might step up their pressure on

Dublin to break its ties with Berlin, a move Hempel feared probably more than any other for personal reasons: it would mean his leaving the safety of Ireland for the exceedingly dangerous uncertainties of war-torn Germany.

By 1943, the government's control of German espionage in the Twenty-six Counties had become nearly total. The Dublin authorities were effectively able to pick up the few agents still sent from the Reich, usually within hours of their coastal landings or parachute jumps. De Valera ordered his secretary of external affairs, Joseph Walshe, to protest these violations of Eire's neutrality to Minister Hempel. To forestall a British or American ultimatum that the German legation be ordered to give up its radio transmitter, Walshe also demanded that that apparatus be either handed over or destroyed. Hempel asked if instead it could be placed in a bank vault to which two keys would be required, one held by himself, the other in the keeping of the Department of External Affairs. De Valera agreed, and on December 21, 1943, the German mission's only radio capable of transmitting messages was officially sealed away in a Dublin bank.[68]

．　．　．

With America's entry into the conflict, the passionately sensitive issue of the island's sovereignty again erupted in all its bellicosity.[69] Northern Ireland was suddenly being "invaded" by a foreign army—that of the now wholly belligerent United States—leading to what would be the bitterest exchange yet between Dublin and the Allies. That Britain claimed every legal right to treat Ulster as its own soil was passionately rejected by an angry Taoiseach, de Valera maintaining that the entire island constituted the "national territory" of independent Ireland.

The genesis of the idea to station U.S. troops in Ireland seems to have begun with the American war secretary, Henry Stimson. Though Stimson balked at Roosevelt's plans to dissipate American strength by spreading it too freely in the service of the British war efforts, the secretary told Britain's Lord Halifax in October 1941 that the still neutral United States "could put a force of two or three divisions into Southern Ireland," a comment Halifax immediately wired to Churchill. The British prime minister, highly interested in getting an American military presence closer to the European war, knew such troops could not be placed in Eire. But Churchill jumped at the possibility of putting them in Ulster, where de Valera's permission was irrelevant. Churchill wrote the American president that it would be a very great reassurance and military advantage of the highest order if you were able to place a United States Army Corps and Armored Division, with all the Air Force possible, in the North of Ireland (of course at the invitation of that Government as well as of His Majesty's Government). . . . [The] arrival of American troops in Northern Ireland would exercise a powerful effect upon the whole of Eire, with favorable consequences that cannot be measured. It would also be a deterrent upon German invasion schemes.[70]

Aside from the fact that American troops in Ulster would enable Churchill to remove British forces already there to more effective use elsewhere on Britain's distant fronts, he undoubtedly harbored the hope that Washington would by stationing its troops in Northern Ireland psychologically nudge the Twenty-six Counties into the war. Churchill continued to underestimate the will of de Valera.

The United States was willing, at Britain's invitation, to send technicians to build bases under Lend-Lease provisions in Northern Ireland, "to make a fortress of Ulster," as Roosevelt put it—though it should be noted that Professor Warner Moss of Virginia's William and Mary College warned Secretary of State Cordell Hull against acquiring "a vested interest in a keg of dynamite." Democratic senator Elbert Thomas of Utah agreed: "whether Northern or Southern, the presence of American armed forces on Irish soil will involve us in domestic Irish politics."[71] Thomas's warning was to prove prophetic in light of the fireworks shortly to ignite.

The south's concern about the American presence in constructing British bases immediately surfaced, with de Valera querying the American government on both October 15 and November 16 as to the "purpose of the activities and of the intentions of the American government." He was told by Washington that the American contract was, in effect, with the *British* government, which Washington considered sovereign in Ulster, and that if Dublin had further questions they should be addressed to Whitehall. Eire retorted that it considered its government sovereign over the *entire* island. Here the matter basically stood until Japan intervened.

At 1:30 on the morning of Monday, December 8, 1941, the Taoiseach was awakened by an aide at his private home, Teach Cuilinn in the Dublin suburb of Blackrock. A critical message from Winston Churchill had just been received by the British legation, and was within the hour being personally delivered by Sir John Maffey. Since learning the previous evening from the BBC of the attack on Pearl Harbor, de Valera had feared the British response to the Japanese shock still reverberating around the world. He assumed it would be a demand for the return of the ports, a demand the now belligerent United States would forcibly back up. Half an hour later, Sir John arrived at the residence in Cross Avenue. The British representative to Eire handed over the type-written note:

> Following from Mr. Churchill for Mr. de Valera. Personal. Private and Secret. Begins. Now is your chance. Now or never. "A Nation once again." Am very ready to meet you at any time. Ends.[72]

Churchill's somewhat overwrought message to his Irish antagonist was written from the emotional heights of realization that his nation had very likely been saved by the events in the Pacific—that with the United States in the anti-Axis alliance, the chances had been enormously increased that Britain would not now lose the war. His own euphoria he hoped might somehow be transferred to de Valera, a euphoria that would per-suade the Irish leader to enter, even belatedly, in the fight against the greatest menace the world had ever known, and thus even win back the "respect" Churchill believed the Irish had forfeited for their inexplicable neutrality. The cryptic "A Nation once again" was evidently Churchill's pledge that Irish unity might still be the payoff for Irish co-belligerency in the now fully Anglo-American fight.

Churchill erred. The Taoiseach wasn't about to trade away neutrality for unity. He told Sir John just that, that he "saw no opportunity at the moment of securing unity, that our people [are] determined on their attitude of neutrality . . ." Neutrality was a policy the Irish people fully supported, whereas a vague pledge of unity from the British leader was a promise de Valera couldn't trust. Besides, the Taoiseach suspected that Irish unity to Churchill would more likely mean some stale version of the old Home-Rule-within-the-Empire scheme than it would the true island-wide republic de Valera envisioned.

In any event, Churchill soon realized that his message would be interpreted as a sort of Balfour Declaration if Eire did in fact come into the war. He "clarified" himself with the explanation that "I certainly contemplated no deal over partition. That could only come by consent arising out of war comradeship between North and South."[73] Still, it was made clear to Dublin that only participation in the war would enable the Twenty-six Counties to establish a footing for postwar cooperation with Ulster. De Valera thanked the British prime minister for his message, but explained that the best way to make progress on the matters dividing the two islands would be for a high British official to visit Eire and there be informed personally of its problems by the Irish prime minister.[74]

But the immediate repercussion in Ireland of America's entry into the

Allied coalition—its presence in Ulster—brought de Valera to his most serious crisis since the dangers of the summer of 1940. Churchill flew to Washington at Christmas 1941 to meet with his new war partner, there to jointly plan an Allied military strategy. At Churchill's suggestion (according to the notes of meeting participant General George Marshall), the American president agreed to help relieve the hard-pressed British troops of their defense responsibilities by stationing replacement American troops in Ulster.[75] Such a move would clearly demonstrate American resolve to soon get involved in the European war, and it also might deter the Germans from sending western occupation troops to the Russian front, where they were critically needed. Likewise, it might serve as a deterrent to the Germans against any thought of an invasion of Britain, then held as an unlikely but by no means negligible risk.[76] Though Roosevelt sent de Valera a note reminding him that "Ireland's freedom is at stake" in the war, he neither asked the Irish leader about stationing GIs in Ulster nor informed him that within a month he intended to do exactly that.

The first American troops landed in Ulster in the third week in January. There they were greeted by the premier of Northern Ireland, who repudiated the Taoiseach's claim to speak for all Ireland. "Northern Ireland," he said, "is in the fight for freedom and intends to see it through."[77] De Valera's first comment was to deride the Americans for recognizing a "Quisling government" in Belfast.[78] Immediately Eire's minister in Washington, Robert Brennan, protested to the State Department that the maneuver was a tacit recognition and approval on the part of the American government of Ireland's partition, to which protest Sumner Welles, the under secretary of state, told him that Ulster was British and that fact formed the basis of the American move. When Brennan further protested that Dublin considered the troops a danger to the Twenty-six Counties, his fears were brushed off as "incredible."[79]

De Valera's statement to the *Irish Press* on the American troop crisis provides a valuable insight to his thinking:

> Everybody knew . . . that Ireland had twenty years ago been partitioned and the Six Counties cut off from the rest of the country by an Act of the British Parliament, despite the expressed will of the Irish people.
>
> When the United States was entering the last war . . . President Wilson declared that America meant to fight for democracy and for the right of peoples to self-determination. The Irish people took him at his word and, in the General Elections of December, 1918, by an overwhelming vote—more than three for to one against—declared for National Independence and for the establishment of a Republic.

This decision was reaffirmed, after two years of conflict with Britain, in the General Elections of 1921, when the partition candidates returned were again less than one-fourth of the total representation.

Nevertheless, the British Government cut the nation in two, and set up separate Parliament for six of the thirty-two counties.

These six counties formed no natural, historic or geographic entity. The area was chosen solely with a view to securing a majority within it for the anti-national minority.

In one-half of the area, including the city of Derry and the whole territory adjoining the boundary within the Twenty-six counties, a majority of the inhabitants are against Partition.

To partition the territory of an ancient nation is one of the cruellest wrongs that can be committed against a people.

. . . the maintenance of the partition of Ireland is as indefensible as aggressions against small nations elsewhere which it is the avowed purpose of Great Britain and the United States in this war to bring it to an end.[80]

Roosevelt officially responded to these charges by declaring that the U.S. government had no intention whatever of either invading Eire or threatening its security. Dublin considered the response immaterial to what it held to be the central issue, that *Ulster was Ireland and that Britain was an interloper* with no justifiable rights whatever in the northern six counties. But it took de Valera nearly two months to respond officially to the President, clearly being careful to do as little as possible to widen the rift between Dublin and Washington.

The American government's seemingly unreserved recognition of [British] sovereignty, by sending its soldiers to the disputed territories without any reference to the Irish government, appeared to be a taking of sides and a worsening of Ireland's position vis-à-vis Britain, which the Irish government could not but deplore.[81]

On Roosevelt's order, the State Department ignored the protest, Washington to give Dublin the "absent treatment." But Churchill's response would prove far harsher than Roosevelt's. The British prime minister discouraged visits to Dublin by senior politicians, and would not reassure de Valera that Britain would honor Eire's neutrality. This attitude reverberated in the United States, where a press campaign of vituperation at Irish "duplicity" in its neutrality policy would gather steam throughout 1942,[82] a campaign whose principal moderating influence was the diplomatic skill of the Irish minister in Washington, Robert Brennan. With some irony, of the two major Allies the flag bearer *against* Eire was shifting from Britain to America. Yet Eire's deliverance from harm lay in the fact that now the fulcrum of the European war would move from the West to the East, putting the Emerald Isle safely in shadow.

As it happened, the buildup of the American forces in Northern Ireland progressed unimpeded by the Taoiseach's anger with the injury it did to the principle of Irish unity. Between infantry divisions and army air force squadrons, by the end of 1943, 120,000 Americans would be quartered in the province. Together with the troops went their support infrastructure: barracks, airfields, supply depots—an American military presence that used up much of Ulster's supplies of brick, cement, stone, tar, and bitumen, and whose construction employed enough Ulstermen so that the province's unemployment rate reached its lowest point in years. With the troops came the trouble usual to masses of soldiers plopped down in an alien civilian environment: GIs bored and mischief-prone, especially when confronted with the strict Ulster Sabbath customs, hucksters robbing unsophisticated soldiers closer to adolescence than to manhood, a local press quick to magnify small slights into large misdeeds. Sadly, the black American troops ran into the same bigotry they faced at home.[83]

Perhaps the most stinging words on the whole uproar came from the archbishop of Armagh and primate of Ireland, Cardinal MacRory, who sharply observed that the premier of Northern Ireland did not speak for Catholics in the North. Raging against both partition and the Americans in Ulster, he characterized the two as

> a flagrant and intolerable injustice against Catholics doomed to live under the narrow and unjust domination of the Belfast Parliament and Executive. When I read, day after day, that this war is being fought for the rights and liberties of small nations and then think of my own corner of my country overrun by British and United States soldiers against the will of the nation, I confess I sometimes find it hard to be patient.[84]

Madrid

The country heard the news of the German attack on Russia as an "explosion reverberating from one end of Spain to the other."[85] The immediate effect of the June bombshell was to create a vast ground swell of sympathy for Germany, for finally repudiating its iniquitous pact with Russia and joining battle against Bolshevism. Many Spaniards had remained suspicious of Hitler's Germany—its pitiless destruction of Catholic Poland, its mockery of the Vatican, its accord with Communist

Russia. But now they were able to discern, pointed out by the excitable Falange as well as by the enthusiastically pro-German press, their country's affinity with the Axis, plus the "fact" that the inexplicable Molotov-Ribbentrop pact had only been "tactical" in nature. The logic of the Civil War had been restored—a clear-cut struggle between Christian Europe and the atheistic plague of Communism.

Within five days of the assault on the Soviets, the first cries were heard in Madrid for the formation of a "legion" of Falanage-dominated volunteers to go to Russia to help the Wehrmacht in its fight with the common enemy, the prospect of assailing Communism on its own turf irresistible to thousands of Spaniards. After receiving his brother-in-law's blessing for the project, Serrano Suñer quickly approached the German ambassador in Madrid, to whom the foreign minister offered a Spanish contingent to leave as soon as possible for service on the Russian front. So as to forestall any assumption on Ambassador Stohrer's part that this meant Spain would soon join Germany in full belligerency, Serrano Suñer made it clear that the "gesture" was being made *outside* of any possible future Spanish declaration of war against the Soviet Union. Nonetheless, after Stohrer informed Ribbentrop of the offer, the envoy immediately accepted Serrano Suñer's proposal with "pleasure and satisfaction."[86] The time had come for the more radical elements of Serrano Suñer's gung ho Falange to "once more shoulder arms against atheistic Bolshevism and give vent to their pent-up emotions by ramming a bayonet down a Russian throat."[87]

But between Serrano Suñer's idealized "legion" and the Spanish Volunteer Division that would come into being—the Blue Division, so called for the color of the Falange uniform—was a substantive political difference. Careful that such a representation from Spain not be seen as merely a Falangist party token, but instead be fully representative of the nation's armed forces (many of whose ranking generals futilely protested it would bring Spain to the brink of war), Franco ordered that at least half of its men be volunteers and recruited from the regular Spanish armed forces; in the end, the proportion of professional soldiers considerably exceeded the 50 percent figure. It seems likely that Franco did, however, regard the division as a convenient means to rid himself of the hottest of his brother-in-law's Falangist hotheads, the fanatical element endlessly agitating for Spanish entry into the war.

In the years since World War II, one of the controversies enveloping the story of the Blue Division involves its status as a "volunteer" organization. The Allies charged that its members had in reality been coerced into joining by either the Spanish government or the Falange. To the degree that an uneducated and relatively unsophisticated private soldier in the Spanish Army of 1941 (most of which was made up of conscripts) was able to manage a genuinely "voluntary" decision, the *divisionarios* cannot be said to have been recruited against their will. There is, nonetheless, evidence that former Republicans were promised a clean slate for service on the Russian front.[88] At least, however, the men were not required to be Falangists, as we've seen Franco having purposely kept the unit a relatively balanced mix of regular army and Falange.

Though Serrano Suñer continues as the ranking member of Franco's wartime government to be excoriated by historians of the period for his fascist fanaticism, the shrewd foreign secretary may very well have regarded the Russo-German war as a respite for Spain, a chance for its government to catch its breath after the hitherto virtually nonstop demands from Berlin to join the Axis in war. Though the none too bright Ribbentrop may have considered the offer of the Blue Division a hopeful prelude to Spain's coming to its senses and recognizing the unstoppable march of German destiny, neither Franco nor Serrano Suñer viewed matters in quite that light by the summer of 1941. Though still cautious in their fear of German might—the Wehrmacht then stood at the apogee of its power—Franco and his mercurial foreign minister now saw Germany burdened with a two-front war and a crumbling Italian ally. It certainly wouldn't do to take disrespectful liberties with the German war machine, a machine fully capable, had Hitler wished, of propelling itself through Iberia, even in the face of Spanish opposition, to gain Gibraltar. But by carefully throwing the bone of the Blue Division in Hitler's direction, a bone both the Caudillo and his people could ideologically support, a small price would be paid to keep Spain neutral (at least for a while longer), to keep the Allies from choking off Spanish food and fuel to cataclysmic levels (at least for the time being), and to keep the Germans out (at least for now).

Furthermore, Franco could not foresee in June 1941 the democratic-totalitarian, capitalist-Communist coalition that would materialize as a result of Japan's attack on Pearl Harbor five months later. The pre-Pearl Harbor cooperative relationship between Britain and the Soviet Union, and much less openly between the United States and the Soviets, was grounded solely in a mutual desire to destroy Nazi Germany. In a few months' time it would become a Grand Alliance, whose impact would let Spain off Germany's hook altogether.

By July 13, the men of the hastily organized Blue Division were ready to entrain from Madrid's North Station for their German assembly camp. The assemblage consisted of some 15,780 private soldiers (as well as 38 female nurses of the Sanidad Militar) supervised by 2,272 NCOs and commanded by 641 officers, the whole divided into one artillery and four infantry regiments. It incorporated all the divisional subunits and special departments typical of any of the world's armies: veterinary (in an era when armies still depended as much on the horse as on the internal-combustion engine), pharmacy, engineers, communications, intelligence, and, to see to its spiritual needs, 25 chaplains from the Spanish Army's Cuerpo Eclesiástico del Ejército.

The commanding officer was General Agustín Muñoz Grandes, a forty-five-year-old Castilian and battle-tempered veteran of the Moroccan wars. He was also the survivor of a Civil War Republican tribunal, a miracle in itself. He was reputed to be a strict though scrupulously fair disciplinarian; his front-line troops tended to praise him while rear-echelon support personnel feared a rigorousness that had no compunction about sending men to firing squads for battlefield desertion. Though essentially moderate in his politics—he had asked to be relieved of his position as secretary-general of the Falange in 1939 to serve in a line command—he would by his leadership of the Blue Division become deeply involved in Francoist politics and emerge from the era as one of Spain's best-known figures. And because of his militarily laudable leadership on the Russian front, he also became Hitler's favorite Spaniard.

To a brass band's strains of "Deutschland über Alles," the Wehrmacht musically greeted Muñoz Grandes's men as they crossed the border at Hendaye in German-occupied France. The division's destination, reached on July 17, was Grafenwöhr, an old army maneuvering ground near Hitler's beloved Wagnerian shrine-city of Bayreuth, in Bavaria. The well-kept cemetery containing the graves of British, French, and Russian prisoners who died there during the Great War may have given the Latin troopers pause, but all in all the *divisionarios* were favorably impressed with the high level of amenities Germany provided its pampered Wehrmacht. Unfortunately, the division's Spanish-style military organization clashed with the Wehrmacht's idea of a proper military structure. After the Spaniards were reorganized and equipped along German lines into new regiments and support battalions (with 6,000 German horses thrown in), a few surplus troopers found themselves sent back to Spain because there was no place for them. A small contingent of Spanish Air Force pilots also joined their land-bound brothers to form a Spanish Volunteer Air Squadron.[89]

Here in Grafenwöhr, on July 31, 1941, the division—now officially the 250th Infantry Division of the Wehrmacht—took its *juramento*, or oath. To the accompaniment of "A las Banderas," each Spaniard raised the first two fingers and thumb of his right hand, vowing "obedience to the supreme commander of the German Army, Adolf Hitler, in the battle against Communism" (the wording was modified to specify only obedience "against Communism"[90]) and swearing to fight as a brave soldier and ready to give his life at any instant. The oath ended with "¡Sí, juro!"—"Yes, I swear!" A month later, the fully pledged and now fully equipped division left for the Russian front.

The forty-day progress into Russia turned into a nightmarish ordeal for the Latins. Roads jammed with German military columns made movement difficult, and since detraining at Suwalki, in Poland, the journey had become a route march on primitive Russian roads rendered into little more than muddy ruts by the first rains of September. With thousands of troopers falling to gastritis and diarrhea, these and other disorders partly caused by the still strange and heavy German army rations and infected foot wounds, they at least were doing better than their horses, the latter shot by the score every day as they broke legs in the slippery quagmire.

The division's destination was Novgorod, a by now mostly destroyed city of 70,000 people a hundred miles south of Leningrad. An ancient and historic town founded in the earliest days of the Christian era by the Scandinavian Vikings, Novgorod had grown in power and prestige over the centuries until it finally attained the status of a kind of republican commonwealth, with its own great walled fortress—or kremlin—guarding the town's wealth from the endless waves of invaders that swept back and forth over the steppes like the Russian snowstorms. In October 1941, the city's importance lay in its position at the Lake Ilmen headwaters of the Volkhov River, whose east bank was occupied by the Russians, the west by the opposing German armies then advancing on Leningrad. It would be across this sluggish waterway that the Spaniards and the Russians would pound each other into blood and bones for the next year, the men of Iberia shouting their war cries across the two hundred meters separating them from their adversaries: ¡Adelante! ¡Muerte al Comunismo! ¡Arriba España! The sentiment would protect them neither from the cold that soon set in nor from the withering shellfire of the unremitting Russian attacks.

Though within a week the Spaniards established a bridgehead on the east bank of the Volkhov, the Russians soon drove them back, with the two forces exchanging almost continuous artillery barrages. The toll on the Russians was always higher, but by the end of December 1941, when the Spaniards withdrew to the west of the Volkhov, the Blue Division had 718 dead and more than 1,900 wounded and missing. The Slavs fought in weather and on land to which they were accustomed. For the Spanish, in their inadequate uniforms—particularly footgear—illness and crippling frostbite were the everyday companions of their Russian adventure. To heighten their trial, when the Latins tried to negotiate with the local peasants for food and cold-weather footwear, the racial policies of the German armies fighting alongside ended whatever hope there may have been of cooperation between Spaniards and Russians.

Though the presence of the Spanish Blue Division in the "Great Patriotic War" contributed a mere drop to the sea of blood, its political effect on Spain would be profound. What Franco learned from the experiences of his *divisionarios* of the depth and endlessness of Russian strength would be a factor in his decision to pull back from the abyss of full-fledged co-belligerency with Stalin's enemies—and from the terrible retribution that Russia promised to inflict on those enemies.

Franco's *divisionarios* never considered their enemy *Untermenschen*, the Slavic "subhumanity" so drawn in the cant of Nazi ideology. To the Spanish troopers, the Soviet enemy—though despised for the Bolshevism of their government—represented a worthy opponent. The Spanish forte in this slaughter on the steppes was its soldiers' reckless courage. The Russian was its army's stoic tenaciousness.

For two years, the warriors of the division—men from Castile and Extremadura, León and Aragón, Galicia and Catalonia—would fight alongside their German partners in what was, for the Spaniards at least, a *"cruzada anti-bolchevique,"* a crusade to save Christian Europe from the onslaught of atheistic Communism. The division's commanders told their men that the battles they joined in the East were to be fought as though they were defending Spain itself—with the double inference that not only was their homeland being safeguarded from the Bolsheviks but their presence in Russia was frankly meant as a means to help keep Spain free from German control.

. . . .

As the *divisionarios* endured on the Eastern front, tantalizingly close to the besieged Leningrad, the news of Pearl Harbor sent yet another shock through Madrid. In the Pardo Palace, Franco sensed now that Roosevelt had gained a focus for America's sleeping might. And when Hitler with monumental miscalculation declared war on the United States four days later, that American muscle would, sooner or later, be dispatched to its island ally, transforming Britain into a giant base from which to strike out against Hitler and the democracies' enemies. For the Caudillo, changed circumstances meant a quick trip back to the drawing board.

With the United States in the war, Franco understood that the danger to Spain had been enormously increased. When America came to try to force open Europe—an inevitable undertaking given America's potential—Iberia would clearly represent a primary route through which to carry it out. On his trip to Berlin the prior month to renew Spain's membership in the Anti-Comintern Pact, Serrano Suñer had promised the Germans once again Spain's eventual co-belligerency. But both the foreign minister and the Caudillo now knew such a prospect was rapidly diminishing.

To quell what it correctly assumed would be Spain's new fears with the Americans now in the war, Britain made clear to Franco it wished neither to impinge on Spanish neutrality nor to step up its economic sanctions against Spain, regardless of Britain's now improved prospects. Still, the Spanish autocrat couldn't be sure of America's official attitude toward Spain—and he knew Churchill's course would be guided not by promises but by the requirements of the moment. What was more, a belligerent America would reinforce the economic blockade against Spain.

Shortly after the beginning of the new year, Franco decided to meet with Salazar to make sure his Iberian neighbor's policy lined up with his own. They met on February 12, 1942, in Badajoz, a small Spanish city hard on the Portuguese border, where some of the harshest Nationalist reprisals against Republicans had taken place. At the meeting it was Salazar who again insisted that remaining cool and staying out of the war was the only possible path for both countries. The Portuguese leader assured the Caudillo that overreaction to the dangers of Bolshevism would be a fatal mistake, telling Franco that "England and the United States would in fact oppose its extension on purely selfish grounds."[91]

In seeking the Badajoz encounter, Franco's intention was most likely a shaded approach to the Allies through Salazar and Portugal's singular links with Britain. The Spaniard wanted to know whether Salazar thought the Allies might use Spain as a landing site for their eventual return to the continent—and if so, would the Allies try to overthrow the Nationalist regime at the same time? Franco seemed relieved in the extreme to hear Salazar insist that no such danger existed, that he had in fact been assured by Sir Samuel Hoare that British intentions toward Spain were directed solely at keeping it neutral. The meeting served to verbally reinforce the Iberian Pact of Friendship and Nonaggression of 1939, and did much to ease both dictators' worries.[92]

Once again Franco's defensive fence-straddling came to the fore. Undertaking a tour of Spain for the first time since the end of the Civil War, for which the entire route through Andalusia—a region in which the opposition remained strong—had been meticulously cleared by jailing anyone with even remotely suspect political sympathies, the generalissimo vowed to the Spanish people that he was remaining faithful to "the people who shared our suffering," a careful indicator offered to Berlin of Spain's sympathies. "If one day the road to Berlin lay open, it would not be a mere division of volunteers but a million men who would offer to defend it against the Red horde." Franco could have had no idea that that road would lie open in three years' time. But in early 1942, a still potent Axis fighting the "common enemy" had to be paid proper respect.

Germany still continued to labor mightily to keep Spain in its column. Its embassy in Madrid, the largest German diplomatic mission in the world, worked day and night at influencing not only Franco's government but the Spanish people and even the Spanish-speaking peoples of the New World; the press attaché at the Reich's Madrid establishment was said to have more than 400 Spaniards on his extensive payroll.[93] The Reich's persistent influence over Spain's newspapers and magazines led Hitler to exclaim that the "Spanish press is the best in the world"—an understandable sentiment in light of its still near-universal support of the Axis in the war and corresponding condemnation of the Western Allies, most especially the West's Soviet ally-of-necessity.

·   ·   ·

Along the Russian front, 1942 greeted the *divisionarios* with dispiriting and deadly new pressure from their Russian opponent. A Wehrmacht which in its planning for the Russian campaign had—nearly beyond belief—given small consideration to the problems of winter weather could do little more than watch as its Spanish co-warriors struggled with the appalling cold. As the new year got underway, the Spaniards were forced to adopt primitive means to stay in the battle. Primary among them was a dependence on horses and sleighs to keep themselves in some semblance of mobility. Winter injuries plagued the Latins, with the temperature often dipping to − 50° Fahrenheit: frostbite and accidents on endlessly icy ground afflicted the troops to the point that scores lost their extremities (including ears) to amputation, all of which seriously decreased the division's battle capacity. Piled on top of these woes was the gratuitous indignity of having to endure the disdain of the German officers fighting on their flanks in the Wehrmacht's Army Group North.

The Germans, with their Prussian orderliness and National Socialist sensitivities, were deeply offended by the catch-as-catch-can, comparatively democratic attitudes of the Spaniards.

By the end of January, the German-Spanish elements on the Volkhov front had stabilized their lines as the Russian foe got bogged down for lack of supplies along overextended lines, giving the Iberian troopers a little free time to do something other than look down their barrels. Some busied themselves with turning out their equivalent of *The Stars and Stripes*, a mordantly anti-Communist troop newspaper called *Hoja de Campaña*. Others buried the mounting tolls of the dead. The main Spanish cemetery for the Volkhov front was at Porkhov, near Novgorod. There, under Latin crosses on which wood-carvers inscribed their names, the dead were interred in rows as neat as their surviving companions could manage. The living clung to the dubious hope that this small part of Spain might be respected after the fighting was over.

· · ·

It is impossible to say exactly when Franco finally deemed that the danger to Spain from any German invasion had ceased to exist (which might not have been until the Wehrmacht was dragged back from the Pyrenean border in 1944—if any such identifiable moment in fact occurred), but substantive fear of such an invasion must have lifted by mid-1942. Like Britain before it, Russia—now Germany's biggest problem—had not collapsed according to Hitler's timetable, the Russians' fighting capacity and resources beginning to show signs that they might be a great deal more potent than anyone believed possible a year earlier. Furthermore, the belligerent Americans were now possessed of an enormous tethered aircraft carrier with Great Britain, a springboard from which to eventually attack Germany and its interests. Though the Japanese war represented a danger to the Allies and a drain on their capacity to defeat Germany, the Battle of Midway in June 1942 demonstrated to an astute military observer that Japan's hopes of beating the United States were finished; it was too soon to say Japan was anything like beaten, but clearly that empire, a would-be ocean colossus with its navy mortally wounded, could not *win* its war against America and Britain.

Political conditions within Spain were in turmoil. Fears of invasion by either Axis or Allies still obsessed many who had little understanding of Hitler's military problems or Washington and London's determination to keep Spain out of the war. Nearly everyone of consequence either feared or hated the Falange, most especially the Spanish military establishment that saw the organization as determined to bring the country into the conflict on the Axis side. The Carlists and the monarchists increasingly added their voices to the opposition to the Falange, their relations deteriorating to the extent that in the spring and summer of 1942, Carlists and Falangists actually engaged in street brawls. And even within the Falange itself there were those who wanted the Blue Division returned, either for fear it was being destroyed on the Russian front or in the belief that it would strengthen their political position within Spain. Reports back from the Russian front concerning the high quality of American weaponry quickened the appreciation of many in the Falange for America as a potential adversary.

The beginning of the end for Serrano Suñer—and for much of the influence of the Falange he headed—came in mid-1942. Though the Falange's position in the government appeared secure to outsiders, especially with the Cuñadissimo holding the foreign affairs portfolio, Franco now was coming to realize that his brother-in-law might be more of a liability than an asset. It isn't known if Franco wholly understood the depth of Hitler's full-grown animosity toward Serrano Suñer, although he knew Hitler's esteem for him had declined since Hendaye; Hitler called him the "gravedigger of modern Spain,"[94] and believed that in spite of Serrano Suñer's pro-Nazi public stance the Spanish foreign minister's primary aim was not to further Spanish-German relations but to eventually form a "Latin union" consisting of Spain, France, and Italy. Some historians have even speculated that Hitler wished to use the Blue Division and its well-regarded commander-in-chief, General Muñoz Grandes, as replacements for Franco and his regime against the day when events in Europe would allow him to take revenge on the Spanish vacillating that had kept the Wehrmacht from Gibraltar.

The event—an unplanned and, on the face of it, inconsequential bit of political strife—that finally broke Serrano Suñer took place on August 16, 1942, in Bilbao, the capital of Vizcaya. General José Enrique Varela, the popular anglophile minister of war who was trying to saddle the Falange with responsibility for the country's debilitating black market, was the principal guest at a Carlist mass in the city's sixth-century shrine of the Virgin of Begoña. Outside the church, an argument between high-spirited political opponents broke out. The Carlists accompanying Varela stood against a handful of Falangist hotheads. Fearing that his outnumbered Falangist friends were about to get trounced by their Carlist antagonists, a young man named Domínguez threw a grenade into the Carlist crowd, wounding six of Varela's party.

The general, uninjured in the melee, jumped at what he quickly calculated to be an opportunity to strike a blow against the Falange. Presenting the incident as a premeditated act directed at the army and the monarchists, the court sentenced Domínguez to death. Though Franco balked at the judicial execution of a Falangist under such relatively trivial circumstances, knowing the damage it would inevitably do to the fascist organization, the sentence was nonetheless carried out.

Varela saw his chance to finally close the book on the primacy of the Falange's power in Spain. But matters didn't go quite as smoothly as the general wished. Franco viewed his war minister's ambition as a threat to his corporate state's carefully wrought and still delicate balance of power, and had no wish to see the Falange destroyed. But some indication would have to be made that the party was now on a reduced plane. Serrano Suñer's reign as foreign minister and head of the Falange was terminated on September 3, 1942.

Serrano Suñer's place was taken by General Count Jordana (giving Sir Samuel Hoare, the British ambassador, much joy at the prospect of dealing with a far friendlier figure than Serrano Suñer had ever been). Varela, too, was supplanted, by the Falangist general José Asensio, whom Franco knew would be far more beholden to him than to the party. Franco himself took the position of head of the Falange. The party was thus subtly downgraded in importance as the state made by far the greatest claims on Franco's time and energies.

The Falange would survive, but more as a "bureaucratic instrument" than as a central element of the ideology and governance of the Franco state.[95] It continued to serve the Caudillo as a kind of barrier against the demands of the other forces in Spain, primarily against a monarchist restoration uppermost in the desires of many who had fought on the Nationalist side in the Civil War. As historian Stanley Payne pointed out, "Franco's strength was based on the weakness and mutual hatred of his opponents"[96] that the Caudillo did his best throughout World War II to keep from being extinguished.[97]

However Serrano Suñer is judged by historians and his chroniclers— and few miss an opportunity to heap scorn on him—the facts show that he, in concert with his boss, did the most to preserve Spain's nonbelligerent course through the war, while it is beyond argument that of all the ranking Spanish leaders Serrano Suñer's views converged most nearly with the values of German and Italian fascism.

For the ordinary Spaniard, the high-level machinations from the Pardo Palace primarily coincided with and translated into more food and less music. As to the first, days after Serrano Suñer's dismissal a new agreement was reached with Argentina for the purchase of a million tons of grain,[98] the Allies allowing it through a blockade in which it had already permitted many holes to keep the Spanish quiescent. Second, because the Caudillo felt a need to show the Allies his tactically revised political sensibilities, all foreign-language radio broadcasts mixing words and music were forthwith banned in Spain, effectively neutering the highly propagandized but at least palatable musical programs from the Italian radio service.

• • •

Two hours after midnight on the morning of November 8, the new American ambassador, Carleton Hayes, a distinguished Columbia University history professor, telephoned Count Jordana, Spain's new foreign minister, telling him he had to see him right away. When the American arrived at the Jordana residence, he was carrying a letter that President Roosevelt wanted delivered to Franco immediately and without any pre-digesting—even by Jordana himself. Jordana suspected what was in the American president's message: notification that the long-expected Allied landings in Europe were coming through Spain—or, just as bad, that the Allies either were declaring war on Spain or were about to "requisition" Spanish territory to improve their strategic position.[99]

Memories were long in Spain, and few of the country's leaders forgot either the ravages caused by the many foreign armies that had fought on Spanish soil or the possibility that the Allies might choose Spain as their "highroad into Hitler's European fortress."[100] Without question, London and Washington weighed carefully the desirability of the Iberian Peninsula for a general European landing. But Jordana had worried as much about a North African landing as he had about the Allies coming through Spain itself: he knew a German counter-response to such a move might bring the Wehrmacht onto Spanish soil.

When Jordana called the Pardo Palace to find out whether Franco would receive the American that night, he was told that the Caudillo was on a hunting trip and that he and Hayes would have to wait until the morning. But Jordana's stricken behavior caused a sympathetic Hayes to take him into his confidence against the State Department's orders. Furthermore, the envoy knew that what was described in the message was already underway. When the ambassador told the foreign minister that the Allies were reentering Europe by means of preliminary landings in French North Africa, Jordana's relief was immediate and obvious. Hayes described the encounter:

I have never seen a man's face change expression so quickly and so completely as Jordana's. From one of intense anxiety, it was now one of intense relief. "Ah! he said. "So Spain is not involved."[101]

It wasn't only Jordana who was relieved. At the obvious softening of the foreign minister's face at the news that Spain wouldn't be involved, Hayes accurately inferred that Spain had no intention whatever of making any moves against an Allied invasion as long as its own territory wasn't threatened—an understandable worry to the American and his government given the large number of vociferous Germanophiles still occupying high places in the Spanish regime.[102] Apparently the Spaniard would leave his worries over a German counter-strike to another day.

At 9 A.M., Franco greeted Hayes in his notorious office, decorated with autographed portraits of both the Führer and the Duce. The foreign minister was also present, shorter in stature than Franco, both men being physically overshadowed by the tall, broad-shouldered figure of the American ambassador. (The only other person present was the official Spanish interpreter, the Baron de las Torres.) Appealing to the Caudillo's "vast military experience,"[103] in his letter Roosevelt explained why the Allies were undertaking the landings—"I am sending a powerful army to French possessions and protectorates in North Africa . . ."—adding that he believed "the Spanish government and the Spanish people wish to maintain neutrality and to remain outside the war." Most significantly, the American head of state declared that Spain would have nothing to fear from the "United Nations," as the Allies had now begun to style themselves. The letter ended, disingenuously but diplomatically, "I am, my dear General, your sincere friend, Franklin D. Roosevelt."

At the moment the Caudillo was reading the letter, American GIs were wading ashore on North African beaches, the ships they just left firing powerful salvos against their enemy; clouds of American aircraft were simultaneously attacking French installations from Casablanca to Algiers.[104] Roosevelt knew, and Franco knew he knew, that the outcome of the first great Allied offensive of the war depended to no small degree on Spain and whether that totalitarian state would continue to keep the Axis armies off its soil.

The news, though not welcome by Spanish leftist dissidents who would have very much liked to see an Allied invasion through Spain eliminating the Franco government they hated, was welcome indeed to the Caudillo—even though the North African landings brought land war closer to Spain than it had been at any moment up to then. He was even so relieved that it didn't take long for him to publicly proclaim his sympathy with and praise for the Reich's battle against Bolshevism, something he did in a December 7 radio broadcast, irritating the Allies in general while doubly angering the Americans because of the symbolic importance of the day—even though Hayes wired Roosevelt his joy in the Spanish Foreign Office's assurances that the government was "determined . . . to resist *forcefully* any attempt by *any* foreign power to invade Spanish territory."[105] Still, Franco surmised that what was in the best interests of the Allies at the moment might not be in their best interests in the future—and that Spain was in danger until one side or the other had completely trounced its opponents. Germany might yet demand permission to drive through Iberia to hit the Allies in their rear in North Africa. Such a move, still well within the Reich's military capacities if not its political will, would automatically lead to an Allied action against Spain.

Jordana continued to express fears of a German invasion to German ambassador Stohrer. Stohrer, one of Ribbentrop's more honest ambassadors, even though that honesty tended to diminish his influence in Berlin, wired the Foreign Ministry that he believed any German attempt to take Gibraltar—a move that was at the time considered a strong probability by many, Spaniards and Americans—or to attack the Allies from the rear in North Africa would involve Spain in total war, turning the country into a logistical and political nightmare for the Axis. Stohrer's advice to Berlin was to continue to supply Franco with weapons for the country's self-defense against an attempted Allied invasion of Spanish soil—and not to contemplate any drive by the Wehrmacht through the Caudillo's state. Hitler had already decided that Spain should retain its neutrality—the country being an economic basket case Germany didn't need—but he had no intention of becoming Franco's arsenal of last resort. The German dictator most likely derived some satisfaction from his Italian partner's concurrence in his view of Spain, Mussolini advising that Spain's co-belligerence would cost far more than it would ever be worth. The two consequently wrote off Spain, satisfied that as long as the Allies left Franco neutral, so would they.

But Ribbentrop got his own little lick in against Spain. On November 17, the German foreign minister was scheduled to meet the new Spanish ambassador to Germany, Gines Vidal y Saura. When Señor Vidal arrived at the station in Berlin to take up his posting, a message was waiting to inform him Herr Ribbentrop was otherwise detained. The insult left very little question of the Nazis' disgust with Spain's inconstancy.

So the equation for Spain ended up simply that neither belligerent bloc could afford to violate Spanish neutrality. Hitler believed that if he tried, it would provoke an Allied counter-response whose fires the Reich no longer had the wherewithal to extinguish. The Allies—Washington and London—believed that any incursion into Spain on their part would cause a massive German response and a subsequent endangering of the North African campaign's rear. As historian Raymond Proctor concluded, "each side had far more to gain at this time if Spain remained out of the conflict."[106] Spanish policy—clearly deliberate on Franco's part though seeming at the time more a matter of confusion—was to be neither too friendly nor too cooperative with either bloc, so that neither would have *sufficient* reason to act against Spain; it was a balancing act the Spanish would adhere to through almost the whole of the rest of the war. Franco's "luck" continued to hold.

· · ·

Now engaged before the city of Leningrad itself (having been transferred there from the Novgorod front in August 1942), the Blue Division continued its daily artillery duels with the Red Army, hoping to finally link up with Finnish forces to the north of the city. Far to the south, the last remnants of Hitler's enormous Sixth Army were being mauled in their militarily insane efforts to overpower Stalingrad. On the Leningrad front, Stalin's forces bitterly fought the Germans for every inch of ground, the *divisionarios* holding steadfast at the side of their fellow German troops. But it was becoming increasingly clear to every Spaniard, from the new commander, General Emilio Esteban Infantes,[107] down to the lowest private, that the Reich's crusade against the Soviets and Communism was miscarrying in the blood-soaked soil of this alien world.

As the Spaniards "celebrated" a second Christmas in frozen bunkers— the temperature seldom rising above the freezing mark—plans were being made for yet another push against the Reds. But the Latins' fingers and toes and ears continued to fall victim to the weather, and pneumonia swept over *divisionarios* who had neither the winter clothing nor the shelters that might have warded off the lethal virus. Red Army snipers became so skillful that venturing from the frozen bunkers involved a duel with death in which the defending Russians had gained the unquestioned upper hand.

What would save the remainder of the division would be politics—the demand by the Allies that this odious symbol of Spanish participation in Hitler's war must end.

Lisbon

Though the war continued to make a nervous Portugal ever more nervous, its people took some satisfaction from the observation that their country, particularly their capital city, was enjoying an importance not experienced since the days when Portuguese mariners turned their little corner of the continent into Europe's hub.

Almost every day the silvery American Clippers would dig fat furrows setting down in the broad river Tagus, Lisbon being now the only freely accessible air gateway to Europe from the Americas. The British, German, Italian, and Spanish land-based craft crowded the cosmopolitan airport in the shadow of the ancient royal palace at Cintra, crews and passengers ignoring one another as they unscrambled baggage in the diminutive terminal. And the capital itself—the beautiful city against the backdrop of its precipitous hills—had become a polyglot, urbane depot of refugees, escapees, and perpetual wanderers.

In spite of the constant fear of the war crashing in on their peace, most of Portugal's people went about their lives in a normal way that was in those years absolutely extraordinary. The citizens could get on as their talents enabled them, well fed with meals of commonplace foods that had already become dim memories elsewhere on the continent. Professor Salazar's government allowed no conspicuous displays of democracy, but for those willing to lead relatively apolitical existences, there was little reason to fear a knock in the night. The natives found amusement in the foreigners' propaganda battle for their hearts and minds, the belligerents all trying to outdo each other in the earnestness of their books and films and magazines delineating the world struggle. Anyone with time on his hands could sit at a sidewalk café and read these endless tracts on the greatness of the warlords and their war—bookstore racks carried *The Battle of England* in Portuguese next to the English-language *Anglo-Portuguese News*, both in the intimidating shadow of *The Great Thoughts of Hitler*, Nazidom's smash best-seller of 1942. All the Portuguese wanted was for their peace to continue unabated.

•   •   •

Although many did, not all the Portuguese regarded the German invasion of the Soviet Union as an undertaking guaranteed to keep the Wehrmacht safely occupied on the other side of the continent. On the contrary, there were those ranking Portuguese who viewed the enterprise as a fresh danger to their own country from an increasingly beleaguered Reich now forced to protect its rear. It was just such concerns Admiral Raeder had in mind when he forecast a month after the Russian invasion that if the United States occupied the Portuguese or Spanish islands the Wehrmacht would have no choice but to enter the peninsula to protect its own military interests. The Americans were now in the war, and this scenario looked all too real.

Soon after Pearl Harbor, the strategic concerns of the British and Americans in regard to Portugal's Atlantic islands publicly changed from a resolve that they be denied the Germans to one of employing them as bases from which Allied forces might better prosecute the war. At the end of 1941, the logical worry in Portugal was that the Germans would not permit this to happen. Though Iberia itself had of necessity receded in importance after the United States entered the war, the Azores did not. Allied shipping still suffered devastating U-boat losses in the Atlantic—in the first six months of 1942 German submarines sank just over three million tons of Allied shipping[108]—and the Allies' aircraft didn't possess the range to effectively attack the German submarines from available continental bases. Not only would a more southerly, and thus presumably safer, shipping route be open to the Allies with the use of the Azores, but naval escorts would have a refueling station and the aircraft based on the islands would serve as a major weapon in the war on the U-boats.

Through 1942 Washington and London war planners gave increasingly serious consideration to simply appropriating the Azores,[109] "by negotiation (London's preference), or, if necessary, by force"[110]—the rough-and-ready option that Washington had for some time already characterized as a "protective occupation."[111]

At the two 1942 Washington summit meetings, Roosevelt, Churchill, and their top military commanders discussed a wide range of options for waging war against the Germans, with the capture of both the Portuguese and the Spanish Atlantic islands debated along with other options relating to North Africa, France, and Spain. In the end, the war leaders turned down notions of taking any of the islands by force, and agreed the Allies didn't yet have the strength to risk a confrontation with the Germans in these peripheral areas when more important goals loomed on the horizon.

While the Allies deliberated their moves against the Atlantic islands, inter-Iberian affairs on the mainland took a dramatic turn. Toward the end of December 1942, the Spanish foreign minister, General Count

Jordana, paid a five-day state visit to Lisbon. The Portuguese premier held a great state banquet for the Spaniard, and the splashy event was given widespread and ostentatious publicity. The dictator and his guest spoke at the dinner of the Iberian Peninsula as a "zone of peace"—the first public expression of the formation of the imposingly named "Iberian bloc." The importance of the "bloc" lay in the fact that it meant that Spain continued to seek strengthened ties between itself and its peninsula neighbor that clearly valued its ties to Great Britain.

For its part, Spain quickly acted to make the implications of the new relations with Portugal clear to Washington. Juan Francisco de Cárdenas, Franco's ambassador in Washington, met with Secretary of State Cordell Hull two weeks after the Salazar-Jordana semi-summit. The envoy informed Hull that the Spanish and Portuguese governments viewed the pact's primary intention as having both governments "exert themselves to the fullest extent to preserve their neutrality and keep out of war."[112] This was just what Hull wanted to hear. As for Salazar, the pact greatly relieved his fear that Franco would react negatively to the Allies' Azores demands he knew he would soon have to face—and very likely acquiesce to.

But Salazar never failed to take into account Franco's underlying fear—both dictators well knew what it would mean to their regimes if Communism or Communist-supported regimes were established in Iberia as a result of a German loss of the war. Though not a naive man, Salazar couldn't understand Britain's moral antipathy to Franco's Spain or the British failure to see that country as a barrier to such a political future for all of Europe.[113]

•　•　•

Whatever Salazar's hostility toward what he held to be the mobocracy of the West, his attitude toward the Japanese was one of undisguised loathing. The war in the Pacific presented a direct threat to Portugal in the endangerment of its colonial possession, Timor, an island in the Lesser Sundas in the Malay Archipelago it shared with the Netherlands.

When by November 1941 a threat to the island from the saber-rattling Japanese appeared imminent, Salazar asked London for assistance in defending its colony. But days after the Japanese entry into the war, Australia and Dutch troops took it on themselves to preemptively occupy Portuguese Timor, infuriating Salazar that such an action should be taken without consulting him, let alone without his permission. Not only did he fear the Japanese would regard the Australian-

Dutch action as a violation of neutrality on Portugal's part; he worried that it might also endanger Macao, Portugal's tiny colony on the South China coast.

London apologized for its allies' actions, and Salazar sent a force of a thousand troops to the island from Lourenço Marques, capital of Mozambique—Portuguese East Africa. But in February, the Japanese struck, while Allied forces retreated inland to wage guerrilla warfare against the invaders. Hirohito's troops remained in control of Portuguese Timor until the end of the war, the Allies not wishing to expend the effort to push them off before the surrender. Only in August 1945 did Timor revert to Lisbon's colonial rule.

Vichy

The last of the continent's "neutrals" that would fall—if the French collaborationist state could in justice be called a neutral—collapsed in November 1942 with little more than a whimper. The Allied landing in North Africa violently changed the Reich's strategic situation. What had long been a relative indifference on Hitler's part regarding the Mediterranean—to the despair of Rommel and his Afrika Corps—changed overnight into a brutally graphic understanding of the danger the Torch landing represented. If allowed to succeed, the soft "underbelly" of his Festung Europa would come under a very substantially increased jeopardy from an Allied move to regain the continent.

At first, Hitler considered the notion of forcing Vichy France to join the Axis coalition against the Allies. When Pétain severed diplomatic relations with the United States on the morning of the Allied landings, the German dictator was encouraged in the hope that France's "chief of state" might also shore up Vichy's determination to defend French North Africa against the Allied avalanche. But it didn't take Hitler long to conclude that France—even the enervated France that Vichy represented— couldn't be trusted in any such crucial endeavor. The Vichy state would have to be seized and bent to the Reich's will.

In recognition of the new threat on his empire's southern flank, on the morning of November 11, 1942, Hitler's order to occupy the entirety of France was carried out, with Mussolini being thrown the bone of a go-ahead to have Corsica. Hitler also sent divisions into Tunisia in a successful drive to get there before Eisenhower's forces took that country from the west. The remaining French fleet, tied up at Toulon since the armistice, was scuttled by its crews rather than being taken over for use by the

Germans; the loss was a significant one to the Germans, who badly needed additional Mediterranean naval power to fend off the Allies.[114]

Though the "French state" was still formally headed by Marshal Pétain and retained its "capital" at Vichy as well as its shell of sovereignty, in reality all France now constituted simply another captive state—if perhaps the crown jewel—on Hitler's nearly completely captive continent.

CHAPTER V

DOWNHILL

Winter 1943–Spring 1945

The Eastern Front

The first months of Barbarossa saw truly astonishing German successes, so many successes the world supposed the Soviet state's death was inevitable. Leningrad was surrounded, Kiev fell and the rich Ukrainian farmlands with it, Moscow was nearly reached—all before the first winter set in. Then Russia's age-old ally—its hyperborean winters—brought the Wehrmacht to a halt. When the following spring the Germans set out to capture the oil fields of the Caucasus, they would finally be stopped at Stalingrad in a symbolic battle between the opposing ideologies; by February 1943, the Germans sustained their greatest loss in the war, surrendering 600,000 men at Stalingrad.

From this point, the Soviets, seemingly endless in number and endlessly supplied, took the initiative, ever more putting the Nazis on the defensive. By 1944, Stalin again controlled most of the Soviet Union proper, as well as the Baltics, eastern Poland, and much of the Balkans. In early 1945, East Prussia fell to the Red Army, then eastern Germany, then, in May, Berlin. Germany had underrated Russian resistance, manpower, distances, and weather, and Hitler's drive to destroy the Soviet Union—a campaign he expected to take but a few weeks—ended as the greatest military defeat in history.

Budapest

They were—and remain today—Sweden's Rockefellers. Tightly threaded through the most distinguished levels of Swedish industry, business, and church, the Wallenberg family had for generations stood at the peak of their nation's social and economic life. But to the world outside of Sweden, the name Wallenberg invokes a single member of that family, a man from one of its least moneyed branches, an international hero who no one to this day can even say with certainty is dead or alive. Raoul Wallenberg's life has served as a tragic lesson to the world, demonstrating how only a small collective effort to obstruct the holocaust might have diminished the most grievous stain on mankind's soul. The story played out its sad facts in Budapest, in 1944, when the city was about to be scourged.

Since 1941, Hungary had been an active if reluctant German ally in its war on the Slavs. Still, this ancient nation (though now an out-and-out German satellite) remained a sovereign state, and thus was free to opt out of those Nazi persecutions of Europe's Jews not suiting its purposes. The regency of Admiral Miklós Horthy[1]—the country remained theoretically a kingdom, with Horthy regent in the place of the defunct Habsburg dynasty—had long since turned over foreign Jews who had found refuge in Hungary, acquiescing to its Nazi ally's persistent demands. But though it had shorn them of many of their civil rights and expropriated much of their property, Horthy's government continued to shield native Jews from the maw of Auschwitz and Birkenau.[2] Such protection didn't spring from compassion. Rather, it candidly reflected Horthy's fear that if he eliminated the nation's Jews, who, though only 5 percent of the population, disproportionately managed Hungary's industry, the war-shaken economy very well might collapse.

At the beginning of 1944, Hungary possessed the only substantial Jewish community remaining on the European continent. It numbered something over 600,000. Of that total, perhaps 175,000 lived in the capital, Budapest, forming about a fifth of the city's populace. This latter community persevered largely intact in a city that had, so far, retained a normality fast disappearing from the rest of the continent's great metropolises. Over the prior century, Budapest's Jews had successfully assimilated—or, in the terms then current, "acculturated" or "Magyarized"—themselves into Hungarian society. The innate anti-Semitism Horthy shared with millions of his countrymen, reinforced by the regent's need to acquiesce to Hitler's insistent yapping at the kingdom to solve its Jewish "problem," had already translated into a glut of relatively "mild"—by the standards of the rest of Nazi-controlled or Nazi-allied Europe—anti-Jewish ordinances. But until March 1944, most of the city's native Jews were managing to lead almost normal lives.

When Germany's military began to shift to the defensive, Horthy openly set about abandoning Hungary's ties to the losing Reich. Since early in 1943, both popular opinion and official policy had been to extricate the country from the war, and that May the last of the Hungarian units were finally withdrawn from Russia. Only German pressure and Russian hostility prevented Horthy from formally declaring the country neutral.

When by the spring of 1944 the Russian advance moved in from the east, Hungarians were desperate to evade the coming storm. Though aware that Horthy's government had approached the Allies about a separate armistice, Hitler still badly needed Hungary both as an escape route for his Balkan armies and as a last barrier protecting Vienna from the advancing Red Army. But perhaps above all other concerns, he was enraged that the Hungarians continued to "coddle" their Jews, a situation the single-minded Himmler wanted "resolved" so his Führer could be at peace. Summoning Horthy and his cabinet to his presence like errant schoolchildren, the German leader handed the Hungarian head of state an ultimatum: dismiss his present vacillating prime minister and accept rigorous German supervision of the government, or face occupation by the Wehrmacht. After being held incommunicado for a day, Horthy chose the former, and an unequivocally German-oriented government was installed in Budapest's Royal Palace.

The new prime minister, Döme Sztójay, under the control of the Reich plenipotentiary, Edmund Veesenmayer, wasted no time emulating German methods. In forty-six days in the summer of 1944, Adolf Eichmann was allowed to destroy between 250,000 and 300,000 Hungarian Jews,[3] largely the poorer, non-Magyarized Jews from the provinces whose loss would be far less economically crucial than those in the capital. Eichmann scheduled the Budapest Jewish community for "action" on July 6. It was here the SS colonel found himself frustrated, Horthy having stepped in to cancel the deportations, the regent's actions likely motivated by fear of a postwar reckoning for the crimes he had already acceded to.

Meanwhile, international action had mobilized to stop what clearly was Germany's intention to kill every Hungarian Jew Himmler and his jackals could lay hands on. At the urging of Treasury Secretary Henry Morgenthau, in January 1944 the American president established the War Refugee Board to rescue the few remnants left of European Jewry. At long last, using American entry visas as a means of helping Jews escape

Hitler's clutches, the board's representatives also begged neutral diplomats to assume a role in attempting to rescue surviving Jews.[4] Tragically, when it urged the pope to threaten the Jews' persecutors in Hungary with excommunication if they didn't desist, Pius XII dithered for a month before contacting Horthy—by which time Eichmann had already done away with the non-Budapest Jews.

It became clear to the board that saving Hungary's remaining Jews would require a Daniel within the lion's den itself. Since the United States was at war with Hungary, a neutral agency had to be found to carry out a rescue mission. The board decided that Sweden, the country most willing to enlarge its diplomatic mission in Budapest, was the best choice. It is at this point—June 1944—that Raoul Wallenberg entered the picture.

Thirty-one years old and with a name that opened almost all doors in Sweden, by the time World War II was at its height Raoul Gustaf Wallenberg still was looking for direction in his life. Having been set on a path by his grandfather for a career in the family banking business, the tall, curly-haired young man decided instead to go to America. After exploring the wonders of the Far West, Wallenberg landed in Ann Arbor and architecture classes at the University of Michigan. On his return to Sweden in the mid-1930s, he characteristically jettisoned architecture to accept a family sinecure as a junior banker and businessman, his first two assignments taking him to South Africa and Palestine. It was in the latter post where he first heard the stories of Nazi persecution from the Jews beginning to reach the British Mandate and where he began to formulate the vision that would lead to his life's apotheosis. The fact that his maternal grandmother was a quarter Jewish—enough to have in all probability put her in one of Hitler's death camps had she lived in a Nazi-occupied nation[5]—likely increased the young Swede's sensitivity to the trial Europe's Jews were beginning to undergo.

In June 1936, Wallenberg left Palestine to return to Sweden, and when the war began he took a job as a foreign-trade representative for a Jewish-Hungarian exporter named Kálmán Lauer. As a Gentile with a Swedish passport, Wallenberg could go anywhere in Europe (his German was fluent), and he quickly became expert at dealing with the Nazi officials whose government was arrogating the continent. One of his principal destinations was Budapest, where through his employer's relatives he befriended many in the city's still functioning Jewish community. It was this background that in June 1944 brought Wallenberg's name to the attention of the War Refugee Board.

Looking for a Swede with an understanding of Hungary's bizarre politics, and one who would agree to travel through a continent now terrorized by daily Allied bombing raids, and who had the minimal qualifications to pass as a diplomat, and who spoke fluent German and at least some Hungarian, and—finally—who possessed the courage to attempt to rescue Budapest's remaining Jews, presented an intimidating challenge.

Kálmán Lauer—his offices, the Middle European Trading Corporation, were conveniently down the hall from the suite used for the American legation—was approached by the committee to see if he might know of someone who fit this unique description. Unhesitatingly, the Jewish businessman suggested as the ideal—quite likely the only—candidate his own employee Raoul Wallenberg, who had already volunteered to bring Lauer's own relatives out of Budapest to Sweden.

Wallenberg jumped at the chance, and bureaucratic wheels were immediately set turning to get the rescue mission underway. The Swedish Foreign Office agreed to confer diplomatic status on the candidate, with Wallenberg formally vetted to the Swedish legation to the Royal Hungarian Government with the rank of second secretary. The new diplomat opened a bank account with one hundred thousand American dollars, the first contribution from the American Jewish Joint Distribution Committee to the rescue mission's bribe funds. Impatient to get started, guarded only by his youthful enthusiasm and the wish to give meaning to his life, Wallenberg left Stockholm forty-eight hours later, and arrived in Budapest on July 9, 1944.

Wallenberg would draw on more than youthful enthusiasm, however, to save the 400,000 Jews remaining in Hungary. Wallenberg was endowed as well with an ability to organize, to get things done, to push himself forward, to see the right people, to use his inborn aristocratic hauteur in just the right way and with just the right people. Among Wallenberg's frightening discoveries was that the Nazis weren't the Jews' only nemesis: the *local* Nazis—the loathsome bullies who styled themselves the Arrow Cross—had with Eichmann's blessing become every bit as proficient as their SS mentors in terrorizing the city's Jewish community.

Arriving at the white Swedish legation overlooking the city from Gellért Hill, Wallenberg was presented with a sight that he would see repeated daily for the remainder of his days in Budapest: standing in front of the building was a long line of Jews, each desperate to obtain a Swedish visa—a *Schutzpass*—to escape from the doom all expected at the hands of either Nazis or Arrow Cross.

In his effort to shield them under the Swedish crown, Wallenberg's immediate priority was to find quarters in which to house the city's hounded Jews. Using his American funds, he rented thirty-two buildings, where eventually 15,000 Jews would be housed and fed, children schooled, sick nursed, orphans cared for. Still, these 15,000 represented but a fraction of the city's Jewish population, and the Swede learned to be inventive in finding ways to widen his safety net with the precious Swedish documents. Overcoming the resistance of Nazis and Arrow Cross with all manner of subterfuge and bribes, he found that one of the most effective threats was that of "postwar retribution."

While Wallenberg devoted his whole existence to the saving of lives, the Red Army and deliverance advanced toward the city. By November, desperate to beat the Russians and to secure a *Judenrein* Hungary—a Hungary "cleansed of Jews"—the monomaniacal Eichmann forced every Jew the SS could round up with the help of their Arrow Cross minions to march out of the city, through bitter cold, toward Poland and annihilation. Bearing down on one such column, Wallenberg demanded of its captors that those with his legation's passes be released, a breathtaking act of bravery for which Eichmann threatened to have the diplomat shot on the spot. Yet the Swede—through what courage and strength of will God only knew—convinced the SS to release 2,000 Jews from that doomed procession.

On Christmas Eve, the Red Army set siege to the city. Tens of thousands of Jews remained sealed in a ghetto in which their tormentors had caged them. When Eichmann ordered the ghetto liquidated—for which task 500 SS machine gunners stood ready—Wallenberg gave notice to the commanding German officer that if the order was carried out, he would see to it that the general was hanged as a war criminal. The commander—SS General August Schmidthuber—canceled Eichmann's order. In total, Wallenberg personally saved between 15,000 and 20,000 Jewish lives with his Swedish visas[6]—a small tally in a sea of six million dead, but far more than were rescued by any other single person, agency, or nation.

As the Soviets rolled into the city in the wake of the retreating Wehrmacht, Wallenberg's concern became the care and feeding of the wretchedly abused Jewish survivors. On January 13, 1945, he left the city to meet with the commander of the Soviet forces, hopeful of gaining help for the people for whom he had come to feel personally responsible. Instead of being received as the unique hero he was, the exhausted diplomat was arrested by the Soviet secret police, his captors apparently believing Wallenberg was a spy. In the paranoia produced by more than a quarter century of Communism, the deeply anti-Semitic Russians simply couldn't comprehend Wallenberg's compassion, zeal, and willingness to put his own life at risk in the service of "foreign" Jews.

The rest of the story is unrelieved tragedy, as Wallenberg disappeared into the abyss, one of the first victims of the Cold War. He was taken by the NKVD to Moscow, where he was first incarcerated in the infamous Lubianka Prison, there to be charged with spying. He received no trial: inquiries from the Swedish government were met with the reply that he had "probably" been murdered by the Gestapo. His presence in Russia was denied, but many witnesses to his incarceration came forward. A few years after the war he was said by the Soviets to have died from "natural causes," what was in fact a tacit admission of his abduction in the first place. Following stays at various Soviet prisons, in 1961—according to witnesses—Wallenberg was put in a mental "hospital," the horrific Soviet euphemism for a psychiatric prison. International pressure for information on him always met with Russian denials of any knowledge of his existence.

Finally, in the more open Gorbachev era, faced with an overwhelming number of witnesses who asserted they had seen Wallenberg over the prior forty-five years, the Soviets agreed to cooperate with an international commission created to look into the case. Few were surprised when the commission came up empty-handed, thanks to KGB stonewalling, the Russian secret police remaining utterly uncommunicative. As of today, the fate of Wallenberg—who could conceivably still be alive as a very old man, though the chances are sadly slim of surviving nearly half a century as a prisoner of the Soviet penal system—remains a mystery.

There are but a few citizens of any of the European neutrals in World War II who could by any definition be called heroes. But this one man stands so high he has become a worldwide symbol embodying the best impulses in humankind. Though hope diminishes daily that Raoul Wallenberg will ever again be seen alive, his memory remains the proof that neutrality need not mean apathy.

Stockholm

With the momentous change in the circumstances of the belligerents— reflected on fronts from Stalingrad to the South Pacific—had come a shift in Sweden's strategic predicament. Where the country had since 1940 dealt with the incontestable dominance of Germany, the Swedes would in this pivotal year of 1943 begin to be hectored by the ever more stringent voice of the flourishing Allies, the United States taking the unalloyed lead in this pressure. With a government less sensitive to centuries-old diplomatic punctilio, the Americans soon adopted a far more rigid position than Britain's where the neutrals' behavior was concerned. But both allies voiced their demands unambiguously: that Sweden cut back, and very soon suspend altogether, its trade with the Axis in critical matériel, most importantly in ball bearings and iron ore, the latter that year reaching its highest level in the war.[7]

Many in the United States felt that Sweden's reasons for its policy of neutrality were increasingly strongly guided by a sense of avarice looking toward the postwar world, a world in which an undamaged Sweden would enjoy tremendous commercial advantages—its plants intact, a fleet of freighters ready to supply a ravaged continent, its airliners available to link America with Europe.[8] Though it was undeniably aware of these factors in its future international relations, Sweden took a somewhat different view of matters. Instead of greed, it held its neutrality as a moral response to a world at war, and furthermore that as a neutral state it remained free to trade with *any* of the belligerents. Sweden remained critically dependent on the goods it received from Germany, and the only way it could get those goods was to in turn ship Swedish commodities to the Reich and its allies. Regardless of the justice of this stance, to many observers in Sweden, as in all the remaining neutral states, it had become evident by the early months of 1943 that Germany's chances of a victory were being daily reduced, and that postwar reputation was as much at stake as their economic role in that world.

The nation's bitterest domestic controversy remained the odious transit agreements. German soldiers and supplies continued to be carried across Swedish soil both to maintain neighboring Norway's subjugation and to provision the Reich's soldiers fighting alongside Mannerheim's army in Finland. Now much of the most vocal opposition to the transit arrangement sprang from organized labor. The principal workers group, the Landsorganisationen, angrily passed a resolution demanding the traffic be stopped, the statement's significance coming from the fact that this umbrella organization represented a million members—in a country whose total population was only 6 million. Hansson's government took no steps to silence the dissension, understanding that it might well serve to strengthen its own hand when the inevitable time came to face down Berlin over the issue.

Strongly backing popular anti-Nazi opinion was Sweden's press. Mirroring the tide of public sentiment, the majority of the country's papers now openly lashed out at the Nazis. Though the government still felt discretion dictated stifling some of the most vociferous press outbursts, and still even confiscated a few editions, the attacks went on. Outraged, the Nazis protested and labeled the Swedes "swine in dinner jackets"[9] and "vultures of neutrality,"[10] yet the Swedish newspapers continued to be increasingly hostile to the Nazi cause. The Nazi voice was still heard, though, now most strongly in the *Dagsposten*, a paper subsidized with German money; though its circulation was trivial, Swedes loved to quote the ludicrous claims of German victories it reported even as it was clear the Wehrmacht was beginning to retreat on almost every front.

Manifestations of sympathy for the Allied cause were to be seen nearly everywhere in Sweden. The movie *Mrs. Miniver* rang up box-office records in its Stockholm showing. American William L. Shirer's strongly anti-Nazi *Berlin Diary* sold more than 100,000 copies. John Steinbeck's *The Moon Is Down*, a play criticizing the foundations of the Nazi state, played to sold-out theaters all over the country; when the Nazi minister, Hans Thomsen, protested the continued showing of a drama he took—correctly—as a condemnation of everything his government stood for, the Swedish Foreign Office responded that the play did not name the "cruel invaders" it spoke of by nationality, this attempt at diplomatic "correctness" an only slightly veiled slap at the Third Reich.

The widespread support for the Allies was reflected too in popular wartime backing for Hansson's policies. In an early 1943 opinion poll, people were asked whom they would wish to have as prime minister should anything happen to Hansson. A large percentage of the respondents could think of no one else. Just as Churchill and Roosevelt dominated their nations, so did the rotund and ruddy Hansson dominate his. Though part of the explanation for his popularity rested on the special circumstances of a people struggling to get through the world crisis, the premier and his policies—especially that of neutrality—commanded the genuine support of the Swedish people. One consequence of Hansson's stance of keeping the nation in constant readiness to meet and repel any military challenge—a stance now directed implicitly at Berlin—was that it exacted an enormous part of the nation's treasure. (The national defense budget in 1943 was three-quarters of a billion crowns; three years earlier, it had been a third that amount.) Nonetheless, Hansson's coalition easily survived two entirely free elections between 1939 and 1945.[11]

An indication of the government's essentially pro-Allied posture was the gracious and compassionate treatment given Allied fliers who landed —often crash-landed—their crippled or lost aircraft in Sweden. On the afternoon of July 24, 1943, a lone battered B-17 Flying Fortress struggled to enter Swedish airspace, and after crossing the neutral coastline signaled it had to make an emergency landing. The fatigued crew that crawled out of the flak-torn bomber became the first ten Americans to seek refuge in Sweden.

Before the war ended, more than a thousand more such airmen sought and were granted temporary refuge by the Swedish government. Though officially state internees, all were treated as respected guests of the Swedish people. The fliers were fed, housed, and given medical care as good as that received by the Swedes. Three of the country's largest air bases became, for all practical purposes, internee air bases, their fields marked by scores of neatly lined-up Flying Fortresses and Liberators. The men themselves were generally initially accommodated in hotels, theoretically under guard. Their names, ranks, and serial numbers were reported to their diplomatic missions in Stockholm, which in turn immediately notified families of the downed fliers. All were under the supervision of the almost magically peripatetic Major Count Folke Bernadotte, whose far-reaching impact on the immediate postwar world would confer on this Swedish nobleman something approaching sainthood.

•   •   •

Though Germany was weakening, Sweden still had plenty of incentive to stay as much as possible in Berlin's good graces. Shortly after the New Year, the newly year-long *Lionel* and *Dicto* standoff boiled up again into a dilemma posing considerable danger for Sweden. Germany now decided to force a showdown on the issue. The legal ruling permitting the Norwegian ships to depart their Gothenburg anchorage for England, trivial as far as the two ships themselves were concerned, was a significant political victory for the Allies' side, and was, of course, read by Germany as such. Berlin warned Stockholm that if it continued in its defiance of German interests, the Wehrmacht would immediately stop the entire Gothenburg safe-conduct traffic—traffic that was, except for the occasional courier plane, Sweden's single and fragile sea lifeline to the democratic world. Receiving no such assurances from Stockholm, Germany decided to make good on its threat, and on the night of January 15 the Kriegsmarine blockaded Gothenburg's harbor. As for as the *Lionel* and *Dicto*, ironically the ships, two days after the blockade went into effect, made only one aborted effort to run to the relative safety of the open sea. Neither ship would, in fact, ever get away, though Britain was satisfied with the outcome, having seen Sweden formally take the Allied side on the issue.[12]

Though Berlin hinted it would lift its now total blockade if Sweden in turn made some concession—such as allowing increased German transit traffic—the Kriegsmarine continued to enforce the stoppage against the recalcitrant country for five months. In May, Berlin relented, finally realizing the stalemate could cause irreparable damage to the Berlin-Stockholm relationship when Sweden's cooperation and its supplies were now needed more than ever by the Germans. But the Reich felt it had made its point: that the tiny Gothenburg trading door could be militarily shut by Germany at any time. Still the Swedes, caught as they were between two irresistible forces, would have to make sure their policies didn't overly offend the Allies, who could now just as effectively slam shut the trading door as could the Germans.

Native productivity and inventiveness went a long way in replacing what the nation had lost to war-generated scarcities caused by the sort of extortion the Gothenburg standoff represented. Far the most important source for what it would have to improvise during the war years was the emerald sea of nearly virgin forests that blanketed vast tracts of Sweden. Swedes had for centuries built and heated their homes with wood, but during World War II they did much more with this almost inexhaustible resource. They dressed in wood, the kingdom's scientists having contrived durable fabrics from the rayon and cellulose wool extracted from the nation's trees. The Royal Swedish Air Force to a large extent flew its airplanes on fuel made from wood. Cattle were fed on wood-cellulose pulp mixed with 15 percent of molasses. A hundred thousand of the nation's automobiles and a smaller number of its motorboats were kept going on "gasoline" made from wood alcohol and charcoal, or, in some cases, from just plain firewood; enduring memories for wartime Swedes were the enormous mountains of such wood piled on every quay in the country. Finally, wood was drunk in akvavit, and it was even eaten—a form of albumin yeast derived from cellulose was transformed into a serviceable, however unpalatable, substitute for stringently rationed meat. [13]

Regrettably, a whole universe of goods existed to which Sweden's forests were irrelevant. Flour became one of the scarcest commodities, with a coupon required to order a single slice of bread in a restaurant. Shoes, which in a climate as cold and damp as Sweden's are required to be especially sturdy, could only be purchased at the rate of one pair every eighteen months. The soap available for washing and laundry amounted to about one small hotel-size bar for each citizen each week. Food shortages covered the spectrum. Every person was allowed one egg every two weeks, nine almonds every month. The average family's weekly meat ration came to one sausage the size of an ordinary hot dog, three slices of bologna, and six strips of bacon. Milk remained in fairly good supply, but only because the government banned cream, greatly restricted cheese production, and drastically cut the butterfat content of the milk. Coffee became virtually unavailable soon after the onset of the war, but a kind of substitute was concocted by grinding together beets and acorns (others tried this alchemy with barley and beets) and adding a dollop of a few wood shavings. Bad as it was, most Swedes reportedly preferred this bilge to nothing.

To keep track of their rationed lives, each Swede had to learn to juggle some ninety different coupon cards. Still, there were few food queues in wartime Sweden. Marketing cooperatives kept any substantial black market from developing, and the distribution of food was remarkably equitably handled by the government.

Little recognized by the outside world were the enormous losses sustained during the war by the Swedish merchant marine fleet. Despite the safe-conduct passes and navicerts issued Swedish ships, by mid-1943, 167 vessels were torpedoed or otherwise lost to enemy action—almost invariably German action—and on those ships, 788 Swedes died.[14] Many Swedish ships stranded outside the blockaded straits after the invasion of Norway were used to ferry goods between countries, some of which were belligerents, thus giving German U-boats "legal" leave to torpedo them; Sweden suffered a particularly large loss in the freighters participating in Allied convoys. Unlike the merchant fleets of many countries, these Swedish ships were not, incidentally, reluctant to enter the danger zone around the British Isles, a contribution to the Allied war effort worth noting when weighing Sweden's wartime actions.

• • •

In the spring of 1943 Sweden faced another and especially serious threat of German invasion. The previous autumn, Hitler had become unusually sensitive to northwestern Europe's security, primarily motivated by the expectation that Norway might become the focus of an Allied strike into Europe. Wehrmacht strength in Norway was accordingly increased to 25 panzer divisions manned by 400,000 troops, this when every unit that could be scraped together was vital to the deteriorating Russian front.

To secure the Reich's northern flank, Hitler ordered plans be drawn to strike in force through Norway into central Sweden and the Stockholm region. Though German military planners were aware of the anti-German bias of the majority of the Swedes, Berlin believed that most of the kingdom's officer corps would support a German occupation, especially since the commanding general, Olof Thörnell, was held to be both defeatist and pro-German. Berlin's strategy envisioned the Swedish defense forces quickly disarmed by a leadership that would sooner countenance a German victory than a destroyed Sweden.

The Swedish government was aware of its general outline, and anxious, since although 185,000 men were under arms at the beginning of 1943, only about 50,000 of them were considered genuinely battle-ready. But such a fantasy scenario never came to pass. Pressures on the Wehrmacht on other fronts were likely the primary reason the North never became a front itself: the Allied invasion of Italy and the fall of Mussolini soon led Hitler to siphon off a large part of the Norwegian garrison, thereby rendering any thought of invading Sweden unrealistic. After this scare, Sweden never again faced any concrete danger of German invasion.

But Stockholm sensed yet another terror brewing, this time on the country's eastern flank. In the spring of 1943 rumors of a forthcoming separate peace between Germany and the Soviet Union raced across Sweden like a forest fire, awakening in the Swedes their deepest fear of a Kremlin freed from its war with the Nazis. If the Russians were able to pursue unfettered their unsettled grudge match with Finland, Soviet Russian domination in the North would soon become the region's new nightmare. The *Social Demokraten* of Stockholm commented: "While surrendering hope of an absolute victory, the Third Reich now aims at a separate Russo-German peace. . . . The 1939 Russo-German pact of friendship goes to prove that the Soviet may be found willing to lend an ear to any reasonable discussion."[15] When on May Day Stalin announced his policy of unconditional surrender regarding the German enemy and a pledge to carry the war to final victory, relief in Sweden was palpable—even if the distrust of the Soviets was not entirely dispelled. The country would now wait until the United Nations victory before finding out what Stalin's designs on the North might be, but Swedes fervently hoped a victorious Anglo-American alliance would deaden Stalin's Scandinavian appetite.

·   ·   ·

Between 1939 and 1945, in all Axis-occupied Europe only a single nation saved its Jewish population from the murderous fate that awaited them: the people of Denmark succeeded, against long odds and in the face of deadly reprisals, in spiriting very nearly every Jew in the country, native or foreigner, to safety across the narrow strait to Sweden. Only because

Sweden remained outside the war was this unalloyed—and, by Berlin's reckoning, unneutral—wartime miracle both conceivable and achievable.[16] Its success hinged in large part of the active participation of the Swedes and their government.

In the early years of the German occupation of its Danish "model protectorate"—so designated because of the Nazi theory that the Danes were nearly as "valuable," racially speaking, as "genuine" Germans—the 8,000 Jews resident in Denmark (6,500 Danes and about 1,500 recent émigrés from Germany, Austria, and Czechoslovakia) were neither molested nor deported, remaining for the time being safe under the theoretical protection of the Danish government. The situation, of course deliberate on the Reich's part, fostered the illusion among Danes that their country remained sovereign and that their German overseers, though unpleasant, weren't quite the monsters they were elsewhere. True to the nature of Nazism, the illusion was soon to be dispelled.

When early in 1943 Hitler decided for security reasons that Denmark's relative independence needed clamping down, internal opposition quickly developed into a serious threat to the occupiers. Responding to the increase in the number of Danish resistance acts, the SS concluded that a good part of the blame for the growing disorder might profitably be laid on the country's Jews and the fact of their relative "coddling." To get its model fiefdom back in order, supreme security chief Heinrich Himmler decided to seize in a single stroke the country's entire Jewish population. The German sweep was set for the night of October 1, 1943— the Jewish New Year, when the country's small community could be expected to be celebrating in their homes and thus easy to ensnare.

Providentially, the Nazi plans were disclosed. Historians differ on how this happened. In the view of W. Glyn Jones, SS-Obergruppenführer Werner Best, Reich plenipotentiary for Denmark (Denmark's de facto ruler after Germany had assumed full administrative power two months earlier), surmised that the deportation would only create greater resistance from non-Jewish Danes.[17] Other historians, such as Lucy Davidowicz and Otto Kernberg, conclude Best fully concurred in the roundup.[18] For whatever reasons, Best divulged the deportation plans to his shipping attaché, G. F. Duckwitz, an anti-Nazi, who in turn leaked it to officials in the Social Democratic Party. From there, plans for a rescue operation were rapidly set in motion.

Working with extraordinary dispatch and resolve, the Danes were able to organize a rescue and, for once in its reign of anti-Jewish terror, the SS was nearly completely thwarted. Of the country's 8,000 Jews, all but 1,000 had been safely spirited away by their rescuers when Nazi security police arrived at Jewish homes.[19] Smuggled aboard a patchwork fleet of small vessels, the Jews were carried across the narrow Öresund strait separating Denmark from Sweden. Once in freedom, they were given refuge and a compassionate welcome by the Swedish people and government, who kept them safe until they were able to return to their homes at the war's end.

This action on the part of the Danes introduced into their country a spasm of German terror of the kind that had long since become a reality elsewhere in occupied Europe. Scores of alleged saboteurs were rounded up and shot, often without even a pretense of judicial process. Ordinary Danish citizens discovered with terrifying speed the true nature of Nazism when many were randomly snatched off the streets as hostages to be shot in reprisal for actions by the underground. Thugs of the Schalburg Corps, a native Danish SS unit recruited largely from released convicts, were encouraged by their employers to invent ever more fiendish brutalities to perpetrate on their own countrymen. The symbolic climax of this reign of terror was the murder by the Germans of Kaj Munk, the great Danish pastor, poet, and playwright, whose killing came to betoken more than any other the occupation's horrors.

Added to their embracing of Denmark's Jews—an action Berlin snarlingly characterized as "unfriendly and unneutral"—Sweden gained additional honor for its humanitarianism in the actions led by Count Folke Bernadotte. A nephew of King Gustav, Bernadotte represented the Swedish Foreign Ministry in an effort to free as many people as possible from the Reich's vast chain of concentration camps. Gaining a meeting with Heinrich Himmler, the Swede successfully pleaded for the release or transfer from Germany or German-held territory of 19,000 Scandinavian and other prisoners of war—French, Polish, Dutch, Czech, British, American, and even Argentine prisoners.[20] Without the Swedish nobleman's extraordinary efforts, which were fully supported by his government, there is little reason to assume those internees would have survived incarceration when in the war's closing months camp conditions descended to unspeakable depths.

•   •   •

As preparations for the Normandy invasion got underway, Allied pressure on Stockholm to curtail its trade with Germany escalated enormously.[21] The British tried to engage in preemptive buying of Swedish ball bearings and roller bearings, but to fulfill its commitments to the Reich as well as meet Britain's new demands, the main Swedish manufacturer, SKF, simply built new production facilities. To make its requirements that Stockholm renege on its contracts with Berlin somewhat more acceptable, Washington and London offered the Swedes manufacturing orders to compensate for the loss, as well as the extra attraction of 200 Spitfires.[22] When the Germans got wind of the Allied offer, Berlin in its turn promised to give the Swedes 200 Messerschmitts in exchange for a guarantee to keep the 1944 ball-bearing shipments at the 1943 levels.

Sweden's dilemma mirrored that of the other neutrals in the face of Allied demands: it knew that though reeling from Allied assaults, Germany still possessed the capacity to strike out at any small country that provoked it. What was more, Sweden continued to require Germany's coal to maintain any semblance of its normal standards of living—just as it knew the Allies had the capacity to cut off all supplies from the West if their demands weren't heeded. In fact, the Germans again stopped the Gothenburg traffic, from late 1943 until January 1944, while the Swedes negotiated these trade matters with the Allies; the continued presence of the *Lionel* and the *Dicto* was the formal excuse for the cutoff, but the more likely motive was to warn what would happen if Sweden broke its commitments to the Reich. In the end and after much wrangling with London and the more intimidating Washington,[23] it was the Russians who—unwittingly—came to Stockholm's rescue in its dilemma. With the Soviet fleet gaining all but complete control of the Baltic sea lanes, trade with Germany would now be prohibitively dangerous anyway, and when the Swedish government withdrew war-risk insurance for its ships in Baltic waters, no shipowner would put his vessel in jeopardy of Soviet torpedoes. Henceforth, the 50 percent or so of the traffic carried on Swedish ships was removed, and Germany, already desperately short of sea transport, couldn't take up the slack. In October 1944, the Swedes justified their action to Berlin by explaining that they were responding to German atrocities in Denmark and Norway rather than to any change in the country's policy of neutrality.

The thornier transit traffic issue remained more emotional for the Swedes, and, given the continuing German conviction of its necessity, more dangerous as well. Clearly, much of the drive to bring the transfer trains to a halt came from London and Washington, but the great majority of the Swedish people were equally anxious to have the humiliation over and done with.

In July 1943, with no small amount of trepidation, Hansson's government finally approached the Germans on the issue.[24] Ignorant of the fact that Germany had already given up any thought of mounting any military action against Sweden, the premier took steps to increase the armed forces from 170,000 men to 300,000. On July 29 the Swedish government officially informed Berlin's minister in Stockholm that the transference of German men and matériel across Sweden, to supply either Norway or Finland, must stop. The explanation given was that the concession had simply become too great a burden on the Swedish people and on their relationship with the Norwegian people, and—evidently to soften the blow—on the "traditionally friendly" German-Swedish relationship as well. The Swedish government concluded by assuring the minister that it would maintain to the full extent of its capabilities an "unconditional and armed neutrality."[25]

Berlin's reaction surprised Stockholm. Rather than erupting into one of his usual hair-raising frenzies, Hitler took the news with something approaching equanimity. Preoccupied with, among other things, Mussolini's ignominious dismissal by Italy's heretofore useless king, the German dictator could not contest the Swedish ultimatum, rationalizing the decision on the basis that the transit traffic had in any case become unimportant to the maintenance of the Wehrmacht in Norway. Nonetheless, the effect was an unequivocal indication that Stockholm's diplomatic bias would henceforth be directed westward.[26] The Swedes would not, however, break off relations entirely with Germany, as Washington demanded, Stockholm taking the view that such a move would be incompatible with both its sovereignty and its status as a neutral.

The country's new bearings were further amplified in a strengthened solidarity with the still tormented Norwegians and Danes. "Police forces" were trained from among those of both nations who had escaped to Sweden, the forces designed to be a kind of militia providing Norway and Denmark with ready military resources at war's end to counter any attempted Communist takeovers should a vacuum follow the German occupations. The Danish forces allowed to train in Sweden eventually numbered 500, the Norwegian 1,500 active members and 8,000 reservists.[27]

However much the government now tilted in the Allies' favor,[28] the Swedes themselves signaled no desire to get involved directly in the war, which after the Allied landings in France in mid-1944 clearly needed no Swedish intervention to ensure eventual Allied victory. However vociferously pro-Allied in spirit and deed, the Swedes themselves now conveyed nothing so much as a growing lassitude where the war was concerned. More and more, the average Swede's day-to-day preoccupations centered on the postwar world, a time when his irritating privations would end.[29] Though Sweden's "privations" were almost inconceivably petty compared with those suffered by the vast majority of Europeans, people nonetheless tend to view matters in the light of their own experience and standards.

Among Sweden's concerns for the postwar world was an ominous scenario that the Swedes themselves would be able to do little to control. If Norway and Denmark were fortunate enough to fend off Communist-controlled governments—an outcome most Swedes expected—Finland was a different matter. With the Finns fighting on the Axis side and with the Red Army increasing in strength every day, the specter of a re-Russianized Finland looked very much a possibility. For Sweden, the geopolitical configuration of Scandinavia would be radically altered if Finland became a Soviet satellite or—worse yet—"republic." For that reason, the kingdom's government made it a critical priority in 1944 to convince the Finns to get out of the so-called Continuation War while they were still independent and before the Red Army could overrun the country. After July 1944, Hansson tried to convince Marshal Mannerheim to assume the presidency and then somehow stop the war. Sweden closed its ports to foreign ships—in effect meaning German ships—in September, reasoning that the Russians might chase those German ships supplying the Wehrmacht in Finland all the way into Swedish ports and thus involve Sweden directly in the fighting. Germany, no longer able to effectively press its will on a noncooperative Sweden, had to swallow Stockholm's fiat, but its 170,000-man Twentieth Mountain Army nonetheless remained firmly entrenched along the Russo-Finnish border.

Finland had already been the victim of mass bombings by the Red Air Force, including the first catastrophic raid on Helsinki the prior February. On the twelfth of that month, the Finns approached their enemy through the Soviet ambassador in Stockholm, Madame Alexandra Kollontay. Knowing they had the Germans on the run, the Russians were in no mood to extend benevolent armistice terms to the Finns, a people whose army had exacted an enormous toll from the Soviet forces since their first encounters more than four years earlier. Mannerheim was told he had to agree to return his nation's borders to those established in 1940, at the end of the Winter War. The lesser demands—demobilizing its army, returning all Soviet prisoners, paying $600 million in reparations, and ceding the nickel-rich Petsamo area to the Soviet Union—were all inconsequential compared to the one really tough ultimatum Moscow laid on the table: as the price of peace, the Finns were expected to intern the German army within its borders.

Mannerheim refused the package. Though admitting that his government "had not surrendered to any illusions that a turn in world politics favorable to Finland will soon occur,"[30] the marshal insisted that acceptance of the Soviet terms would mean the end of Finland's sovereignty. The Finnish parliament unanimously agreed. On top of the shock of Moscow's demands, the Finns now had the Germans utterly distrusting them for their "perfidious" discussion of terms with the Soviet Union. The times had become desperate indeed for Finland.

They became a good deal more desperate on June 9, 1944, when the Red Army struck the Finnish front with the force of a tidal wave, the thunder of their artillery sounding 179 miles away in Helsinki like a summer storm. Nearly 800 guns roared along each mile of the Karelian forest frontier separating Finland from Soviet Russia, a sign the Red Army wasn't going to take any chances with an enemy that had so humiliated it in the 1939–40 war. Though the nearly half million Soviet soldiers were initially repelled by a Finnish force less than half its size and with much inferior armaments, they finally wore through Mannerheim's front-line forces to position themselves against the German army further north.

Still, the Finns held out on the Karelian Isthmus long enough for the relatively pro-German president, Risto Ryti, to resign and Mannerheim to succeed as head of state in August.[31] Immediately resuming talks with the Soviets, Mannerheim scrapped Ryti's earlier summer pledge made to Ribbentrop that the Finns wouldn't sign a separate peace with the Russians. Moscow repeated its demand that the Finns immediately break relations with Germany, but this time ordered only that all Wehrmacht forces be evicted from the country; the alternative to acceptance of these terms would be the immediate Russian occupation of Finland. On September 4, the Finnish government agreed to lay down its country's arms and thereby end the Continuation War.

Now Mannerheim's predicament centered on those German forces still firmly entrenched in Finland's north. Though Berlin understood the inevitability of its withdrawal from Finland, it nonetheless wished to bring its troops out in an orderly retreat and to retain as long as possible the critically important nickel mines in far northern Finnish Lapland. The German commanding general in Finland, Lothar Rendulic, told Mannerheim his forces would withdraw, but warned the new president that if the Finns showed any sign of using force to expel their former allies, the Wehrmacht would strike back with all the savagery it could muster. German disgust with the Finns and their "betrayal" boiled a mere fraction of an inch below the tension-filled surface of Finno-German relations.

Rendulic's task was immense. To withdraw his 170,000 men meant watching out for any sudden thrusts from the much larger Soviet forces to the east, making sure the Finns weren't pressed into attacking the Germans by their new Russian masters, and dealing with the fact that a possible retreat across Swedish territory had been eliminated by the now much emboldened Swedes, who made it clear that any German incursion would result in an attack by the Swedish Army.

With the Germans still in the course of their orderly and—to the Russians—leisurely departure, Moscow began to pressure the Finns into giving the retreating Wehrmacht a shove. Though Mannerheim tried as long as possible to accommodate the Germans, and used his army to actually form a buffer between the Wehrmacht and the Red Army, eventually the Finns were left with no choice but to strike at the Germans. It was all the justification Rendulic needed to make good on his pledge. His new tactics would be to leave behind him burned-out towns and countryside, a rending of the Finnish earth that effectively destroyed most of developed northern Finland.

As the German situation in Finland became near-impossible, with Royal Navy vessels now able to threaten any German evacuation down the Gulf of Bothnia and across the Baltic, Hitler ordered Rendulic to move his men and their accumulated supplies northward, across 300 miles of enemy-harassed arctic terrain crossed by only primitive roads, to their final goal of reinforcing the garrison in Norway. (The Lappish nickel mines were forgotten.) The undertaking represented almost unimaginable difficulties.

The Red Army soon began to tear the retreating Germans apart. Terrified of the consequences of being captured by the Soviets and inevitable internment in Soviet prisoner-of-war camps, the German soldiers fought like cornered tigers. As the Wehrmacht fell back, it followed its commander's scorched-earth orders to the letter, destroying every house and farm, school and hospital, and finally turning northern Finland into a lunar-like scene. As they crossed northern Norway's Finnmark province, Rendulic's soldiers followed exactly the same course of destruction they had visited upon Finland. The Soviets did not pursue the Germans across the Norwegian border because of the harsh weather and presumably to avoid the political complications of occupying Norway. By January 1945, the Wehrmacht was out of Finland, signaling the end of Finnish involvement in the war. Since the autumn of 1939, 86,000 Finns had perished. For the living, the greatest consolation was that no Soviet army occupied their ravaged nation.

· · ·

In the last months of the war, Sweden's shift away from Germany was so complete that the nation could, with ample justification, be termed a "pro-Allied non-belligerent state."[32] Trade with the Reich by 1945 had nearly come to a total halt. Because Germany wished to continue as good a relationship with the Swedes as possible—Berlin calculated it might receive some help from Sweden even in the waning days of the conflict—protests from Germany were feeble and generally couched in mild diplomatic language. Little, though, hid Sweden's hostility toward the dying Reich and its sympathy for the United Nations.

Hansson's primary concern now became the fate of his Scandinavian neighbors. Both Denmark and Norway continued to be occupied by large, well-equipped, and relatively undamaged German armies. In the so-called *Festung Norge* (Fortress Norway), the German occupying force was made up of roughly 350,000 men in May 1945; in Denmark, some 200,000 Wehrmacht troops constituted the occupation force at war's end. Even though a collapse might come about soon in Germany itself, there was no guarantee either of these Scandinavian armies of occupation would lay down its arms without a bloody fight to the finish; in Norway, Reichskommisar Terboven remained a particularly fanatical Nazi. Furthermore, the massive Red Army might still be diverted into Norway to expel the Wehrmacht—and end up settling in as a "protector" in the power scramble that would follow.

The Swedish defense staff prepared two plans, *Rädda Danmark* (Save Denmark) and *Rädda Norge* (Save Norway), for the intervention of Swedish military forces in both countries if Germans refused to surrender or if civil chaos threatened the region. Neither operation ever became necessary, partly because of Stockholm's recognition that the Allies had no plans to help—neither London nor Washington wished to divert forces to Norway that were still needed to bring Germany itself to heel—and partly because of the injury either could do to Sweden's continuing assertion of neutrality and its unwillingness to be drawn into the war even in its last days. The Danish and Norwegian "police forces" that the government had allowed to be trained in Sweden became the principal Swedish contribution to its neighbors' immediate postwar security concerns, this assistance being officially viewed by the Swedes as stretching their neutrality to its absolute limits.

However much the Swedes regarded their assistance to their neighbors as an imposition on their official neutrality, those neighbors—especially the Norwegians—in turn viewed it as too little and too late. The Norwegian government-in-exile hoped that a Swedish mobilization would convince the Germans dug in in their country to capitulate, if not before the official German surrender, then certainly in conjunction with it. The Swedish counter to this hope was the weak claim that such an action on Stockholm's part would simply cause the Germans to fight all the harder. It is perhaps difficult to sympathize with this rationale, but the Swedish government closed the matter with the assertion that it, rather than the Norwegian government-in-exile in London, could judge what would be the best course to follow when the German capitulation came about.[33]

Sweden's position of avoiding military involvement in the war's last days met with the approval of the Allied governments. A few days before the capitulation on the continent, the Norwegian government-in-exile in London again asked the Swedes for help, in this instance to seize strategic positions in Norway so the Germans could more easily be stopped if Terboven refused to surrender; the Norwegian leaders were especially concerned about vital industrial installations they expected to be destroyed by the cornered Germans. Stockholm begged the matter by referring it to the Americans and the British. Both advised Stockholm to take no action, implying that help would not be available from American and British forces already fully engaged.[34]

· · ·

One of history's tantalizing might-have-beens involved Heinrich Himmler and the Swedes, and came about in the chaos that surrounded Germany's collapse. Himmler, head of the Reich's security state-within-a-state and a man who considered himself the future German Führer, met on April 23 with Count Folke Bernadotte (in Germany on one of his Red Cross missions) in the Swedish consulate in Lübeck, the long since bomb-devastated Baltic *Hansastadt*. Calmly informing Bernadotte that "the Führer's great life is drawing to a close," *der treue Heinrich* ("the loyal Heinrich"), as Hitler had fondly called him, urged the Swedish nobleman to inform Eisenhower of Germany's willingness to surrender to the West; Himmler had assumed the power of negotiation from Hitler, whom he expected to be dead before much longer. The SS leader told Bernadotte he felt himself "responsible" for his country's future. Bernadotte agreed to pass along Himmler's offer only if it contained a promise to include all German forces in Denmark and Norway as well, to which proviso the Reichsführer agreed.

When five days later Hitler found out about these proceedings, his fury at his underling was unbounded, although the blow seems at least to have helped convince him the end of the Third Reich was now inevitable. As for the Allies, the offer was received with not so much even as contempt. But the Swedes took the surrender offer with some seriousness, expanding on Himmler's overture for a peaceful surrender of German forces in Norway. Hansson's government even suggested that Wehrmacht elements in Norway cross into Sweden and be interned.

The whole matter was finally dropped due to a lack of Allied interest. On May 21, Himmler himself was picked up at Bremervörde in northern Germany, and ended his life two days later by biting down on a cyanide capsule stored in his bridgework.

Sweden maintained its correct diplomatic relations with the Third Reich down to that empire's last day as a sovereign power. On May 7, 1945, the German minister in Stockholm was officially informed by the Swedish foreign minister that diplomatic relations between the two countries had ceased to exist.

Bern

Few Swiss realized at the time that the first weeks of 1943 were among the most dangerous of the war for the confederation. On January 6, Henri Guisan wrote a confidential report to the federal cabinet. The statement was a warning of what was, in his view, a danger from the Reich Switzerland hadn't faced since the perilous days of France's fall two and a half years earlier. Germany grew daily more preoccupied, the general wrote, with the concept of a *Festung Europa*—a Fortress Europe—as the farther ranges of its conquered territories were beginning to shrink under the onslaught of Anglo-American and Soviet armies.

In Guisan's concept of the danger, both Switzerland and its control of the Alpine passes would grow in strategic and tactical importance to the Reich's military planning, north-to-south communications now more critical than ever to Hitler in keeping Germany linked to its massive armies in Italy. Guisan theorized Berlin would increasingly fear Bern's permitting Allied armies access to Swiss territory to assault the Reich itself.

Guisan pointed out that Germany would in the near future require Swiss territory for quite different reasons than had been the case in 1940. During the Wehrmacht's halcyon spring, it had been primarily a matter of German territorial aggrandizement and Nazi dogma demanding that all European "Germans" be incorporated into a Greater Reich; if the Swiss had in 1940 carried out their threat to destroy the tunnels and execute a scorched-earth policy, it might well have been affordable to the Germans to simply repair the damage.

By 1943, the situation had substantially changed. At this point in the war the Germans required intact Alpine tunnels, and the Swiss industrial infrastructure of which Hitler now had such great need would be worthless if destroyed—it would be impossible for the strained Reich to get a destroyed Switzerland swiftly operational again. Only one way remained, Guisan hypothesized, for Berlin to turn Switzerland to its ends. It needed a coup that would serve up the democratic island intact. To make certain the Germans were thwarted in this scenario, Guisan told the federal government that the nation's total defenses would have to be placed on the highest state of alert, against both a foreign aggressor *and* the menace from within.

In this spring of 1943, Guisan calculated that the Allies planned to enter Italy very soon, and it was plain—thanks to the reports of his many intelligence sources in Italy—that when that happened the beleaguered Italians would withdraw from the war. But equally plain was the fact that Hitler was dispatching huge numbers of reinforcement troops to northern Italy, obviously with the intention of holding on to his clearly wavering ally. Whatever happened, the Swiss Alps would assume critical importance to the Wehrmacht's movements, and Guisan could envision the German dictator enhancing the Reich's position by incorporating those Alps into the overall German defense system. All this added up to vastly greater jeopardy for Switzerland and more need than ever for the country to be militarily able to hold its ground.

Though clear to Guisan, these dangers seemed much less so to the average Swiss, *and* to the men they had elected to govern them. In spite of political pressure on Guisan to scale back his enormously expensive, man-hour-consuming defense arrangements, the commander-in-chief defiantly refused.

Ironically, real danger to the confederation from German invasion was in the spring of 1943 more acute than at any other time during World War II. In March, a Wehrmacht operational plan against its neutral neighbor, *Fall Schweiz*—Case Switzerland—complete with its own invasion headquarters already set up in Munich, had been sufficiently developed to be presented at Hitler's personal headquarters. Even with the daunting appraisal of the Swiss situation by SS General Walter Schellenberg, head of the Reich's foreign intelligence service, that Switzerland would be a formidable and tenacious opponent if the Germans invaded, that a fifth column-led coup was not a realistic possibility, and that to take the country would require a massive military effort that would meet with a destroyed Swiss infrastructure and blown-up Alpine tunnels,[35] German preparations for an invasion nevertheless proceeded.

The proponents for Case Switzerland were Himmler and the SS, the opponents the regular army generals and the economic advisers.[36] But the voice that would turn out to be the most important in the matter—albeit a secret, silent voice—was Guisan's own informer, code-named "Viking Line,"[37] operating directly under Hitler's nose. When Viking Line reported back to Guisan that the Germans were on the verge of authorizing an invasion of Switzerland, the general ordered a meeting of his top military and intelligence personnel for two days later—March 20, 1943.

It was now that an uncharacteristically inept act on the part of Swiss intelligence both informed the Germans of the presence of the Swiss mole in the Führer's headquarters and led—incredibly—to a quick German decision to drop Case Switzerland. Swiss intelligence chief Roger Masson ordered one of his lieutenants to get in touch with Schellenberg to confirm the German's plans. Apparently believing in the SS general's desire to avoid war with Switzerland, Masson mistakenly concluded that Schellenberg's sympathies had transferred to Switzerland's deliverance. Masson's conclusion was wrong, but the results redounded to Switzerland's advantage.

Schellenberg's reaction was to ruthlessly comb the Führer's headquarters to uncover the spy or spies in the service of the Swiss. Though the leak was never found, security was strengthened, with the result that it became a great deal more difficult and dangerous for the informant to operate. Swiss intelligence's most valuable window into the top German command structure was severely compromised because of the misplaced trust in Schellenberg.[38]

Considering the disaster that would ensue from the destruction of the tunnels in keeping their northern Italian armies supplied, and with the realization that the Swiss would engage in vigorous and probably effective guerrilla warfare, the Wehrmacht would find itself facing almost insuperable problems. With all this, together with the knowledge that the Swiss knew what Berlin was up to—thanks to the Masson blunder—and that Guisan would use that knowledge to strengthen his defense posture, the German command came to the conclusion that its best course was to trust the Swiss general's pledge that Switzerland would resist *any* invasion—*even by the Allies*—and that functioning Alpine tunnels and reliable imports of Swiss manufactures represented the better bet.[39]

It isn't certain whether the Swiss found out about the abandonment of the German plans for invasion from its informer (or informers) or from Walter Schellenberg—he claimed after the war to have informed Masson of the decision to gain the latter's trust and thus, it was hoped, to get information from the Swiss on Allied intentions regarding a second front.

But still Guisan judged that the Germans remained mortally dangerous as their empire withered, and the general would keep his nation on its highest guard until the war ended.

•   •   •

While the general continued to muster the nation's defenses to meet any challenge, a different kind of struggle simmered between the Swiss and the Allies. The issue was the trade that continued to be carried out between Switzerland and its Axis neighbors.

Before 1943, the Allies weren't strong enough, militarily speaking, to force the Swiss to stop or at least radically curtail their lucrative and, in Switzerland's opinion, vital commerce with the Reich—nor were the Swiss willing to make any significant voluntary decrease in that trade. Switzerland, for its part, regarded the Axis trade as fulfilling perfectly legitimate obligations to deliver previously contracted materials—some of which were, admittedly, military in nature—to a Germany from whom the confederation in turn received vital energy supplies, which, to complete the circle, kept Swiss factories stoked and Swiss citizens employed, and maintained the confederation's capability to defend itself against the Nazi menace. Furthermore, the trade with the Reich was extremely profitable, a consideration never disparaged by the business-minded Swiss. But in 1943 the war's bearings were rapidly turning to the Allies' favor. Watching as Swiss exports to Germany reached new heights that year, London and Washington decided to bring the commerce to an end.

From the Allies' naive but understandable viewpoint, the situation looked to be a matter of Swiss iniquity. As the Allies put it in a letter from Dingle M. Foot, under secretary of the British Ministry of Economic Warfare, to Walter Thornheer, Swiss minister in London:

> If a neutral firm takes advantages of the war situation to increase its sales to Germany or her satellites, it is in effect choosing to assist the German war effort, and thereby helping to postpone the eventual liberation of Europe, an event which is as much in the interest of the neutral European countries as it is in that of the United Nations.[40]

Finally understanding the changed relationship of the belligerents to each other and to itself, on December 19, 1943, the Swiss government came to an agreement with the Allies that markedly altered Switzerland's economic course through the remainder of the war. Under intense Allied pressure, Bern undertook to biannually "revise" its exports to Germany, the revision intended, of course, to be in a downward direction. Since the

Swiss promised not to lower the price of their goods, the rate of price inflation since 1942 meant that ceilings set by the agreement would effect a 50 percent reduction in exports to Germany for 1944. To keep the Germans from spending all their money on the products most important to them, the Swiss also promised to limit every one of their exports to predetermined ceilings set at existing levels.[41]

In return for this good behavior, the Allies loosened their economic blockade a few notches, lifting an embargo on all navicerts and export licenses, including food, which the Allies instituted in March 1943,[42] and promised to quit blacklisting suspected Swiss firms unless specific proof of violations surfaced.

It should be noted that the United States was happy to be receiving from Switzerland a number of Swiss products vital to its own wartime economy, most particularly watches and jewel bearings. In 1943 and 1944, a third of all Swiss watches were exported to the United States (nearly nine million altogether). Export of standard nonmilitary watches was freely allowed by Germany, although many were distributed by the American armed forces to officers. The crucial supply of Swiss watches freed up American watch factories to convert to more critical manufactures for the pursuit of the war. The jewel bearings, tiny diamonds expertly engineered to serve in precision flight instruments, found their way to Americans bombers, each of which needed about 250 for flight instruments alone. Even German-made glass eyes, in heavy demand in the United States for injured GIs, were sent to America through transshipment from Germany arranged by Swiss agents.[43]

Though Switzerland was clearly the losing party in the economic standoff, it was also clear that the Allies were going to win the war and that it was those potentially vengeful Allies the Swiss would have to face *after* the war. Nonetheless, the Swiss navigated their way through the conflict's economic minefields with considerable skill and relatively little damage to their economy. During the final months of the fighting, Bern came to accept ever more of the Allied demands on cessation of trade with Germany. On October 1, 1944, it agreed to stop the export of all arms and ammunition, as well as airplane parts and other military supplies; soon thereafter, the government closed the Simplon tunnel to transit traffic, though it continued to keep the St. Gotthard route open to the Germans. Finally, it agreed to prohibit use of its territory to conceal ill-gotten German spoils, including money—a measure that would have substantial ramifications, for if the traditional blind Swiss bank refuge had been available to Nazis, the postwar restoration of stolen money would have proved nearly impossible.

. . .

As the war ground down to its final months, yet another source of danger emanated from the dying Axis. With Allied armies moving closer to Germany's borders, the idea of a redoubt modeled on the Swiss example began to look to many in Germany—most importantly to Himmler—like a workable way to preserve the kernel of the Reich. The SS chief thought refuge could be sought in the precipitous Alpine massifs running across the bottom of Greater Germany—perhaps in the Bavarian Alps or the Dolomites or Brenner Pass region, or possibly in the Austrian Arlberg. The same notion had occurred to the Nazi Party's Tyrol *Gauleiter*, Franz Hofer, but he never carried it beyond the initial planning stage for fear of Hitler's deadly reaction to anything that smacked of defeatism.[44]

As Himmler and Hofer toyed with the redoubt idea, so had the German army commanders in northern Italy. By late 1944 twenty-three divisions (about a million troops) were battling the Americans driving northward, and many Nazi commanders began to envision a redoubt into which to escape, possibly in company with the still relatively idle twenty divisions sitting in Austria. They took their thinking a step beyond those in the Reich itself. Their speculation gravitated to the already complete model they knew existed—Guisan's Swiss redoubt—and into which such a massive force could move opposed by only a relatively insignificant force.

At the time of the D-Day landings in Normandy, Guisan asked the government to order a general mobilization, sensing this danger (as he had so many others) from the forces by which the country was still surrounded[45]—especially the armies in Italy that would eventually have to fall back to the Reich. Again, as in 1943, he was refused, the cabinet deciding this was "unnecessary" and would be "misunderstood" by a general population that might be panicked by the "psychological shock" of a full mobilization. Cost-conscious, the council was equally fearful such mobilization would take farmers from their fields and thus jeopardize the nation's food production.

A week after the Normandy landings and with Guisan stubbornly persisting in trying to convince the government of the danger, the Federal Council finally agreed to order a partial mobilization of the frontier defense forces; after the Allied landing in the south of France on August 15 it upped the ante by authorizing a further limited troop call-up. Whether or not German armies would have used the Swiss option in a general retreat into the Reich, the open threat of a nearly fully militarily prepared nation was there for them to think about. That there was no

German incursion of Swiss soil in World War II was owed, at least in part, to the resolve of Henri Guisan.

·   ·   ·

Escaping invasion, Switzerland nonetheless found itself at the center of a final crucial incident of World War II—though it was a private citizen, not the Swiss government, on whom the affair's resolution turned. What became known as Operation Sunrise was a complex series of negotiations, double-dealings, and heartfelt optimism that anticipated and probably was predicated on the surrender of the German army in northern Italy. In the closing weeks of the war, that army was the strongest military force Hitler still possessed.

As the Reich's army was forced out of northern Italy, the possibility that it would follow a scorched-earth policy typical of prior Wehrmacht withdrawals horrified many, including the Swiss. Filled with historic cities and towns, most of which were matchless living repositories of art, the area also contained the industrial base critical to Italy's postwar construction.

In February 1945, as the concluding ordeal of the German home front at the hands of the Red Army was about to begin, an Italian baron named Luigi Parilli arrived in Zurich. Parilli, an industrialist with a stake in the region's economic fate, represented a like-minded group of his countrymen desperate to prevent northern Italy's destruction. Hoping to enlist Swiss help in arranging a separate truce between the Western Allies and the Germans in Italy that would stop the war as well as keep the advancing Soviets out of Italy, Parilli got in touch with a longtime friend in Zurich, Dr. Max Husman. Husman was an influential owner of a private school and a man respected by the old first families of northern Italy. He realized that Parilli's idea of splitting the Allies was illusory, but nonetheless believed there might be some way Switzerland could intervene to at least get the Germans in Italy to surrender. Husman introduced Parilli to Major Max Waibel, head of the Swiss military intelligence office in Lucerne. What followed over the next several weeks with Waibel may have had the personal approbation of Guisan (the general followed the events closely), who respected the intelligence officer and knew the magnitude of the stakes. But the enterprise did not have the official backing of the general; nor was the Swiss government privy to it. Waibel's attempt to end the threat to Italy would officially remain his own.

Taken with Husman's enthusiasm to save Italy from certain destruction, Waibel immediately contacted Allen Dulles. The American agreed that the idea of a separate peace between Germans and the West—one that would exclude the Soviets—was beyond the pale. Still, he promised to participate in the negotiations if the Swiss could bring high-ranking Germans to talks specifically aimed at their surrender in Italy.

When Parilli returned to Italy, he sent word that a delegation of top-rank German officers would indeed meet with the Swiss in Lugano, Switzerland's largest town in the Italian border region. Dulles's representative told the Germans that if they agreed to unconditional surrender in Italy, it would accrue significantly to their advantage after the Reich collapsed. When the Germans returned to their headquarters with this message, the high command—including the leading commander, Field Marshal Albert Kesselring—agreed to send a representative to meet with the Allies. The man chosen was SS Oberstgruppenführer (Colonel General) Karl Wolff.

Wolff, the German military governor of northern Italy and plenipotentiary to Mussolini's shadow Salò Republic, appeared the ideal German to hear out the Allied proposal. Youngish (forty-five), suave, urbane, and well spoken, Wolff had been responsible for abandoning Rome without destroying the city and was also credited with having saved Florence's art treasures during the Wehrmacht's retreat. Unknown then to anyone in Switzerland was the fact that as Himmler's assistant he was also personally responsible for the deportation of 70,000 Jews to Treblinka (after the war a grisly memo turned up in which he proclaimed his "special joy now that 5,000 members of the Chosen People are going to Treblinka every day"[46]) as well as the criminally brutal behavior of his SS men in dealing with Italians.

On March 6, Wolff arrived at the Swiss border. Received by Husman, he was immediately taken to Zurich and there met with Dulles at the OSS safe house. To Dulles, he promised to urge Kesselring to surrender unconditionally to the Allies, understanding that the German situation in Italy left him little to negotiate. When he later met with Waibel, the Swiss put pressure on Wolff, asking that the Germans immediately cease any action that might destroy Genoa and Savona, the two "Swiss" seaports in Italy, and that the Italian rail lines connecting those ports with the confederation's border be spared. Wolff agreed to the Swiss requests. Plans were set to surrender the German armies in northern Italy to the Allies at Caserta, with the Soviets invited to send a representative to the ceremony. All the participants knew that the surrender of this still potent army in advance of the anticipated general German surrender would save enormous losses in both lives and property, and could even hasten the end of the war.

On March 12, Moscow was informed of the talks and the ensuing arrangements by Russian spies in Switzerland. Believing a separate peace would allow the Wehrmacht to turn its full force against the Red Army invading the Reich on its eastern flank, Stalin threw a wrench into the works.

Sure that the West was about to sell him out, Stalin wrote (or had Molotov write) a nasty letter to Roosevelt, who especially wanted the negotiations to succeed so Allied soldiers in Italy could be released.[47] Appalled at this evidence of Stalin's paranoia, the president had General George Marshall and Admiral William Leahy jointly write a stinging letter disabusing Stalin of his suspicions. "It is astonishing," the message said,

> that a belief seems to have reached the Soviet government that I have entered into an agreement with the enemy without first obtaining your full agreement. . . . Frankly, I cannot avoid a feeling of bitter resentment toward your informers, whoever they are, for such vile misrepresentations of my actions or those of my trusted subordinates.[48]

Stalin was finally brought to heel when Churchill added his personal "association" to Roosevelt's message.

Still, no German surrender would take place on the original timetable. While Washington was allaying Stalin's suspicions, Hitler recalled Kesselring to Germany to take charge of its final defense on the Western front. The field marshal's replacement in Italy, General Heinrich-Gottfried von Vietinghoff, wouldn't agree to the Dulles-Wolff arrangement, believing, in the fullness of his ingrained Prussian sense of honor, that it would represent some kind of betrayal of Kesselring, whom he apparently fully expected to return to Italy as commander. So faced with Vietinghoff's implacability and stung by Stalin's suspiciousness about the undertaking, the Western allies decided to call the whole thing off.

Heinrich Himmler, learning of all these arrangements at a late remove, called his subordinate Wolff to Berlin to explain himself. Though he wasn't necessarily against the surrender, he wanted to make sure it would accrue to his personal advantage. Wolff obeyed the summons when he found out his family had been arrested as hostages. He managed to convince Hitler that he was only trying to keep Germany's options open, that contacts with the Americans and British would divide them against the Soviets.[49] Hitler told Wolff that there must be no thought of surrender in Italy, though. Wolff returned to Italy with instructions to get the talks back on track but to stall for time, knowing that Hitler's injunction against capitulation could lead to nothing but disaster for the Wehrmacht.

Vietinghoff, now more aware of the impending defeat of the Reich, gave in to Wolff. The SS general contacted Waibel with the news, stating he would come to Switzerland to implement the unconditional surrender of all German forces in Italy. While Dulles awaited instructions from Washington as to what to do, Waibel generously put up Wolff[50] and two aides at his own home on Lake Lucerne. Three days later—April 27— Dulles was instructed that the German surrender representatives should fly to Caserta, the Allied headquarters in Italy, to arrange for the capitulation. They arrived on April 28, and the surrender was set to take place at noon on May 2. (The final surrender was almost sabotaged by a series of arrests and counter-arrests among the German command, but Hitler's suicide on May 1 clinched the Caserta accord when news of it reached the German headquarters.[51]) For the ceremony, a Soviet delegation was present.

There is no doubt that had the surrender of the German armies in Italy awaited the general German capitulation a week later, the loss of life and the destruction in northern Italy would have been much greater. Many historians note that the surrender at Caserta precipitated the dis-integration of the remainder of the Reich's forces,[52] thereby shortening the war by some unknown—but certainly precious—period of time. And these precious days came about in large measure from the compassionate undertaking of officially neutral Swiss citizens acting in the best interests of humanity.

·   ·   ·

Official American attitudes toward Switzerland were markedly softened from the truculence displayed by Washington toward the other neutrals. That palliation was as much as any factor colored by Washington's rec-ognition of the broad range of humanitarian services the Swiss provided the Allies—and the cooperation it afforded for Allied intelligence gath-ering. Swiss monitoring of Axis prisoner-of-war camps was instrumental in ameliorating the jailors' mistreatment of their captives, and was espe-cially important late in the war when the conditions in the camps wors-ened. Further, the Swiss International Red Cross headquarters in Geneva acted as a kind of clearing office for Allied POWs, the confederation's representatives reporting back the conditions of the prisoners' captivity and relaying messages to their families. Cordell Hull wrote of American forbearance with Switzerland and expressed his government's gratitude in his memoirs:

> Toward Switzerland . . . our policy differed somewhat from that which we practiced toward other neutrals. We felt it essential, in presenting our

demands and in exercising pressure to reduce Swiss exports of strategic manufactured goods to Germany, to avoid pushing Switzerland into a diplomatic rupture, or worse, with Germany. This was the reason that Switzerland, representing us diplomatically in enemy countries, was our sole link with them.[53] We had to depend upon her representatives to ensure the welfare of American prisoners of war. We were keenly gratified by the conscientious manner in which Switzerland had endeavored to fulfill this task, even though her efforts in the Japanese area had been largely ineffective because of the uncooperative attitude of the Japanese military authorities and the barbarism of many of them toward prisoners of war. The British agreed with us that our approach to Switzerland, while strong, should not be of such nature as to destroy our only channel for representation to the Axis.[54]

An additional point in Hull's estimation of Switzerland certainly must have been Swiss treatment of American fliers interned in that country, which was fully as humanitarian as that shown by the Swedes. Wartime violations of its airspace were not regarded as inconsequential by the Swiss, regardless of the uniform of the violator. If military aircraft of any nationality crossed Swiss borders, the 300 or so pilots of the Swiss Air Force were quick to try to force down bombers in formation, though they remained under orders to ignore obviously accidental incursions of single-engine craft. Though some of these incidents were deliberate, most were the result of navigation errors—in April 1944 alone the Swiss counted 650 such incursions, by that date mostly Allied; many were British and American crews on their way to bomb Italian targets. Pilots who knew they couldn't make home bases often desperately struggled to cross the Swiss frontier to set their craft down in what was until France's liberation the sole friendly nation for many hundreds of miles in any direction.

By war's end, some 150 American B-17s and B-24s were parked on Swiss landing fields, mostly at Dübendorf, near Zurich. The crews were the relatively pampered guests of the Swiss state, their board paid by draft from the American government and the men given leave to freely visit Swiss tourist locations—though not to leave Switzerland. The aircraft themselves were held by the Swiss until after Japan's surrender.[55]

· · ·

Palm Saturday and April Fools' Day coincided in 1944. The winter's gloom was rapidly dissolving, and on this sunny early spring day forsythia blooms sprouted in Schaffhausen on the Rhine. The ancient town, long the traveler's mecca for the nearby Falls of the Rhine, bore—as it bears today—a scale and comeliness that have long pleased its visitors. But at about midmorning that April 1, the rush of the river and the gentle hum of busy townspeople were submerged by the drone of heavy bombers. The people of the town took little notice of the roaring engines, being by now long accustomed to almost daily fleets of Allied aircraft lumbering on their missions to destroy one or another of Germany's or Austria's or Italy's cities.

The Rhine River has for centuries formed the boundary between Switzerland, on the south, with Germany, on the north. But the city of Schaffhausen and its hinterland, a sort of anomaly of Swiss territory, lies on the north, or German, side of the river. Confusing at least to American fliers with limited knowledge of the region's geography and who assumed everything north of the Rhine was fair game for their bombs. That gap in the airmen's knowledge was to have tragic consequences for the ancient town.

Thinking they were over the nearby German city of Tuttlingen, thirty bombardiers of the American squadron let loose from their bomb bays nearly 70 tons of high explosives and incendiaries, falling directly toward the Swiss city lying five miles beneath their wings. Forty seconds later, the effects on Schaffhausen would be appalling. Sixty-six buildings—including the stately old History Museum—were totally consumed in flames and more than 500 damaged to a lesser extent, 450 people were suddenly homeless, 271 injured, and, most tragically, 40 were killed, 18 trapped in the burning railroad station alone. The Old Town's riverfront lay in ruins, as did the Mühlengasse and the industrial quarters on the Rhine. The white Swiss cross painted on so many of the roofs served no purpose, even though since sunrise it had been a luminous day.

As soon as the American legation in Bern learned of the raid, Minister Leland Harrison sent his military aide to Schaffhausen to assess the damage. He then went to see Pilet-Golaz. The Federal Councillor told the diplomat he could find no explanation for the attack unless it had in fact been deliberate, Pilet-Golaz's implication being that the Americans were evidently trying to coerce the Swiss into adhering to their demand that Bern stop all trade with Germany.

The Swiss public displayed no such rancor, probably, to some extent at least, because the government ordered newspaper coverage be subdued and factual. The first communiqués from the American headquarters lamely tried to explain away the bombing as an error of "navigation difficulties and bad weather."

General Carl Spaatz, commander of the American air forces in Europe, went personally to the Swiss chargé in London to apologize, and in

Washington Secretary of State Hull issued an official American apology together with an appreciation to Pilet-Golaz for not allowing any inflammatory reporting of the incident in the Swiss press. This mollified official Switzerland. More concretely, the American government immediately placed one million dollars at the disposal of the Swiss government to disburse as it saw fit to the victims of the bombing.[56]

Although there would be other "accidents" perpetrated on Swiss cities and towns, none was so devastating as that which had wounded Schaffhausen.[57] On February 22, 1945, the Swiss border towns of Stein am Rhein and Rüti were accidentally bombed, with the loss of eighteen lives, and on March 4, American bombs fell on the country's largest city, Zurich, resulting in five deaths; in the latter raid, the planes had been on their way to attack Pforzheim, in Germany.[58]

General Spaatz went to Bern to apologize to the now justifiably offended Swiss. He promised that the offending pilots would be punished and his bomber crews would be instructed in the future to refrain from attacking any German targets not positively identified as being in Germany if the Swiss border lay within fifty miles.

Full financial reparation for all these incidents was made by the American government in 1949, though the negotiations were marred by Swiss demands that interest be paid on the reparation amounts from the date of each attack; one American congressman from Ohio called the Swiss "impertinent" to insist on interest. But a draft on the U.S. Treasury for the equivalent of 62,176,433.06 Swiss francs—about $3.1 million— was accepted by the confederation's government "in full and final settlement of balance due on all claims for losses and damage inflicted on persons and property in all Switzerland during World War II by units of the United States Armed Forces in violation of neutral rights,"[59] and the matter was quietly closed.

Franklin Roosevelt directly involved himself in the Schaffhausen incident only a few days before his death. In a letter to the mayor of the town, the president graciously extended the regrets of his country for what had been, after all, relatively minor navigational errors in a war whose magnitude was unprecedented.

· · ·

The final trial with which the Swiss had to deal in World War II was the swelling flood of refugees. Various waves had already swept the country— the remnants of the French and Italian armies in 1940 and 1943 and the political refugees that came throughout the war. But in the closing months of the struggle, thousands of ordinary civilians fleeing the chaos of armies threatened to exceed the country's capacities, prompting one harried official to utter the memorable but, in hindsight, tragic comment that "the Swiss boat is full."

In the fall of 1944, the Allies began to worry about one category of refugees that might soon be knocking on the Swiss door and for whom no pity was due: the Germans and others who were fleeing from the punishment of the vengeful victors. Switzerland declared that its right of asylum was a "limited" one, one that could morally and justifiably exclude those guilty of crimes or who had taken actions injurious to Switzerland or its interests. Its only proviso, one the Allies accepted, was that it alone possessed the right to make such decisions about individuals and that the confederation would not bow to arbitrary decisions of the victorious Allies.[60]

As the war wound down, much of the Swiss fear of Nazi Germany began to be redirected toward concerns for the postwar world. The Swiss were highly dubious of the Allied claim that the Russians would be tamed and civilized after the war, made to "take their place" in a peaceful new order. In these last days of the war, the Swiss, almost to the man, regarded with horror the Soviet armies pressing westward through Austria, each day getting closer to Switzerland. The almost bottomless animosity between Bern and Moscow gave good cause for worry should the Red Army smash right up against Switzerland's eastern border. The thought of Russians sitting on the country's frontier engendered fears of a permanent Soviet presence in the heart of Europe, a presence that would eventually strangle the democracy that the Swiss had, almost alone, preserved for the past five years. Such a specter had, in large measure, governed the behavior of the vast majority of the peoples of all the European neutrals through the war.

Dublin

On St. Patrick's Day in 1943, Eamon de Valera went on the radio to give voice to his vision of postwar Ireland:

> Let us turn aside for the moment to that ideal Ireland that we would have. That Ireland, which we dreamed of, would be the home of a people who valued material wealth only as a basis of right living, of a people who were satisfied with frugal comfort and devoted their leisure to the things of the spirit; a land whose countryside would be bright with cosy homesteads, whose fields and villages would be joyous with the

sounds of industry, with the romping of sturdy children, the contests of athletic youths, the laughter of happy maidens, whose firesides would be forums for the wisdom of serene old age. It would, in a word, be the home of a people living the life that God desires that men should live. . . .[61]

No words could have more successfully evoked the paternalistic, moralistic, God-fearing nation that the Taoiseach envisioned. Though there were, as we've seen, many reasons official Eire stood apart from the Anglo-dominated world's battle with fascism, one of the most elemental was the fear that co-belligerency in such a war would have suspended—perhaps forever—the achievement of these aspirations for Ireland. Joining the world, as it were, would have brought the world's problems and temptations to the island, international confoundments unamenable to homegrown remedies. Much as their Iberian co-neutrals, the people of Eire wanted the world held at bay.

By 1943, it seemed as though Eire was on its way to achieving something of de Valera's vision for its postwar future. First, and perhaps most critically for the years ahead, the IRA had just about been paralyzed in its ability to seriously rend the south's social fabric. The government's tough policy of tackling and hamstringing the organization's thugs met with nearly unanimous popular concurrence, leaving only Ulster as a future locus for the canon of terror with which the IRA is today universally associated. Though the IRA continued to issue manifestos couched in grandiose terms, most southern Irish had lost sympathy with, if not its aims, then certainly the methods it advocated to achieve those aims. Even in Belfast and the north, the organization became, in historian J. Bowyer Bell's words, "a little huddle of men seeking refuge not action, holding on out of pride and habit, unable to act, barely able to keep in contact."[62] For the remainder of the war, and beyond, the IRA ceased to be a vital force in Eire, the belief having taken hold that partition would be ended by politics, not gunfire.[63]

If de Valera no longer was confronted with an effective IRA, he was more than ever vexed by the increasingly potent and antagonistic Allies. David Gray, the galling and unprofessional American minister, not only urged his own government to take a harder line against Eire but continued to pump Churchill to engage in ever harsher economic sanctions against the south. Gray's motive was, in Whitehall's view, to "bring home to a people who have been persistently misled by their Government as to the true basis of their economy."[64] Though the British prime minister never went so far as Gray urged, he did tell Anthony Eden that the Irish would be made clearly aware of the "ignominy of their conduct" if it were unmistakably pointed out at the upcoming United Nations food conference. Churchill also wanted to be certain that at the postwar peace conference Eire was "made to feel her isolation and shameful position."[65]

In 1944, the sniping shifted into high gear. Official relations between Eire and the Allies—especially the United States—sank to their lowest point thus far in the war, with Gray once again the chief mischief-maker. The presence of the Axis missions in Dublin since the first days of the war had been a subject of bitter feelings between de Valera's government and those of Britain and, more lately, the United States. When early in the year Gray wrote home recommending de Valera be made to close the Axis legations on the basis that they posed a threat to planning for the upcoming invasion of the continent, both Roosevelt and Churchill agreed with him. London's only proviso was that Washington initiate the action.

Armed with a letter (in diplomatic terms a demarche) from Roosevelt requesting—as "an absolute minimum"—the closing of the German and Japanese missions in Dublin, Gray arrived at de Valera's office on February 21, 1944. "Axis agents," the minister read, "enjoy almost unrestricted opportunity of bringing military information of vital importance from Great Britain and Northern Ireland and . . . transmitting it by various routes and methods to Germany."[66] A day later Sir John Maffey handed de Valera much the same message from Churchill.

De Valera was enraged by the Allied leadership's apparent belief that the government of Eire would idly stand by while Axis diplomats engaged in espionage aimed at the Allies, as well as by the presumption that Dublin would risk the nation's four and a half years of fragile neutrality by precipitating a possible declaration of war between Eire and the Axis. Nobody seriously believed that the personnel of either the German or the Japanese mission would pass up any opportunity to do mischief to the Allied cause, but preventing the opportunities for such mischief had, de Valera devoutly believed, been amply seen to.[67]

What most maddened de Valera was the imputation that Irish neutrality had been skewed in the direction of the Axis. The Taoiseach defended with considerable ardor his belief that his government's policy, while attempting to preserve its essential neutrality, had demonstrated time and again its fundamental sympathy for the Anglo-American cause. From its treatment of Allied fliers (who were almost always repatriated, and whose repatriation was a potentially dangerous and continual source of irritation to the German minister in Dublin) as against German airmen (invariably interned for the duration),[68] to the substantive assistance given Ulster, to the use of its ports for the rescue of downed U.S. and British aviators, to demanding that the German minister surrender his shortwave radio in 1940, to its willingness to permit scores of thousands of its nationals to serve in the British forces, Eire had clearly demonstrated in which direction its moral compass pointed.

In his reply to the demarche, de Valera noted that the undiplomatically sharp terms used in Roosevelt's letter were "out of harmony with the traditional friendship between the two countries." He added that it was "perhaps not known to the American Government that the feelings of the Irish people toward Britain have, during the war, undergone a considerable change, precisely because Britain has not attempted to violate our neutrality."[69] The Anglo-American insult was decried by virtually the entire nation. All political parties and all sections of the press rallied to the government's support. Even the pro-British *Irish Times* said that de Valera "was bound to refuse to accept dictation from any outside power, however friendly."[70] The London *Observer* concurred, noting in an editorial that

> it is probably to be regretted from our point of view. We in Britain respected Eire's neutrality in 1940/41 when it was an acute menace to us. To become a party in its breach now when it no longer more than a serious nuisance might undo what history may well regard as one of our most unselfish and most far-reaching acts in this war.[71]

One Irish historian—T. Ryle Dwyer—attributes David Gray's meddling and motives in the legation flap to more Machiavellian considerations. It is Dwyer's view that Gray believed an Ireland still divided at war's end would re-create the same sort of problem that existed when the American Congress rejected the Versailles Treaty and membership in the League of Nations. Namely, he now feared that disaffected minority groups in the United States would lobby Congress to turn down such an organization after the present war if those groups' European homelands weren't treated equitably. To prevent this from happening with the enormous Irish-American community and thereby derailing the United Nations organization, Gray thought it was a necessity for world peace for de Valera to be discredited. Since he would reject the American president's demand that he expel the Axis diplomatic personnel, these "undemocratic" actions on de Valera's part could be contrasted with Belfast's "correct" steadfastness in the war. The upshot of this reasoning was that the American Irish voters would thereby feel it would be "ungrateful to support Dublin in a dispute with Belfast,"[72] and the chances decreased of the UN organization's being derailed.

If David Gray was operating on the understanding that the American Irish policy was directed more at the United States' Irish community than it was at Ireland itself, it makes the seemingly amateurish behavior of Roosevelt's kinsman that much easier to comprehend. In fact, in the postwar period de Valera was never able to drum up much anti-partition support in the United States, undoubtedly because it was a relatively minor concern with a Cold War-dominated public, but also in at least small part because of the Irish leader's tarnished reputation as a neutral who thwarted the interests of the Allies in their fight with totalitarianism.

In March 1944, the Allies instituted a measure against Eire that clearly demonstrated their disgust with Dublin's whole policy of neutrality. Three months before the planned Normandy landings, the movement of Irish ships to and from continental ports was halted, an act restricting the island's trade but ostensibly carried out in the interests of preventing security leaks—and which appeared to Dublin very much like out-and-out punitive sanctions.[73] On March 19, Churchill wrote Roosevelt that he wouldn't institute further economic sanctions against Eire other than those already in place, but he obviously savored the notion that "we should let fear work its healthy process."[74] Though Roosevelt and Cordell Hull were in favor of further tightening the screws on Dublin, it was left to London to see to "its" Irish problem, and London wisely decided that since Eire's participation in the war was no longer needed it might as well let matters rest where they were. As far as Eire's people were concerned, it was de Valera who came out of the contretemps as the island's champion.[75]

In the last years of the war, de Valera faced the perils of democratic elections. Some Dáil members agitated for lengthening by fiat the constitutionally mandated five-year life of the legislature, but de Valera prudently stood against any such tampering. In 1943, economic conditions largely a result of the war were handing the opposition Labor Party a useful club with which to beat de Valera over his policies—tea was at 25 percent of its normal supply, textiles were 80 percent off, and there was no domestic coal whatever;[76] even Dáil candidates were able to get only eight gallons of gasoline each on which to electioneer around their constituencies.[77] In fact, the prime minister's party, the Fianna Fáil, failed to win a majority in the 1943 general elections (the one IRA candidate won 1,961 votes out of 34,472 cast in his constituency, an example of how badly all those considered "extremist" fared), and de Valera retained the premiership only because the other parties weren't able to unite in a coalition against him. (It would have taken a coalition of only 71 votes—a simple majority—to unseat de Valera.) The Taoiseach's voting majority was so slim that government supporters in the Dáil began to take their afternoon whiskeys in the legislative building's bar rather than sip them at their usual leisure a few blocks away, holding themselves ready to rush in to vote for the government.[78] Still, the one issue on which all parties were united was that the country remain neutral.

De Valera held on until he could manage another election the following year. When a technical transport bill failed to receive a majority, he grabbed at the excuse he needed to either demand a vote of confidence—which since the issue was merely a technical one he probably would have won—or call an election. He opted for the latter, primarily in hopes of enhancing his razor-thin parliamentary margin. The 1944 election resoundingly restored the Fianna Fáil's majority in the Dáil to 76 seats—14 more than all the other parties combined. This was in spite of the still arduous economic conditions, which can be understood perhaps most readily from the fact that throughout that summer even Dublin tram services had to be suspended and the national rail service had degenerated into a ghost of its prewar state. It is likely that the Fianna Fáil's 1944 victory was largely a reaction against the recent pressure from Gray and a feeling on the voters' part that they had best unite behind the one man who could stand up against those who would still try to compromise Eire's neutrality.[79] The election would afterward be remembered as de Valera's "greatest political triumph."[80]

Ironically, de Valera's "greatest political triumph" was followed within a year by his greatest political blunder. On April 30, 1945, in the Red Army-besieged inferno of the German capital, Adolf Hitler slew his dog Blondi, helped his new wife, Eva, poison herself, and, in what was in effect the symbolic end to his Thousand-Year Reich, bit down on a cyanide capsule as he pulled the trigger on the pistol that blew his brains out. On that same afternoon the prime minister of the Dominion of Ireland, in his capacity as minister for external affairs, called on the German minister resident in Dublin to officially express his and his nation's condolences at Germany's loss. The swastika still flew—though at half-staff—above the legation.

The Taoiseach's diplomatically correct but morally idiotic act, while not shocking to an Irish public long used to the absurdities of its government's punctilious neutrality, scandalized a good part of the rest of the world.[81] Over the prior few days the realities of the Third Reich's policies—realities that included, among endless other depravities, final proof of a network of concentration camps planted across Europe—were just coming out. Though he had been strongly warned against the visit by the Ministry of External Affairs, the headstrong de Valera decided to do it anyway. Noting that he could have feigned a "diplomatic illness," he later wrote that not to have called on the German representative would have been an "act of unpardonable discourtesy to the German nation." Furthermore, he added, "it is important that it should never be inferred that these formal acts imply the passing of any judgements good or bad."[82]

That de Valera had paid a similar visit at the American legation a few weeks before on Roosevelt's death, and had eulogized the American president in the Dáil, and that in his official position it was correct for him to pay a similar (if muted) courtesy call on Minister Hempel, was ignored in the Anglo-American press. Speaking at a London trade association luncheon, Board of Trade president Hugh Dalton caught the general tone of disgust:

> If I were Mr. De Valera—thank God I am not—I would open my remarks by condoling with you on the passing of a painter. I think, however, you would regard it as more appropriate to drink to the future disencumbrance of this foul brute who began as a painter but who degenerated in later life and who is now in physical life degenerating further. We will do our utmost, subject always to the need of finishing off the Japanese as we have finished off those for whom Mr. De Valera feels so soft a sentiment.[83]

It has been noted—by historian Dermot Keogh—that the total space allotted to this incident in the editorial columns of American newspapers exceeded that of any other single incident related to Irish policy during World War II.[84] It has also been suggested that the episode, whether or not its specifics were understood, shaped the immediate postwar Anglo-American public opinion of Eire's position in the war more than any other. Certainly many believed that country's role in that conflict of black-and-white morality was dishonorable for its neutrality.

The legation visit was poisonously remarked upon by de Valera's arch-foe, Winston Churchill, in his May 13, 1945, victory broadcast heard around the world. In an address marking the end of the German enemy Britain and its empire had fought so valiantly for nearly six years, the descendant of Marlborough spoke passionately of that empire's valor. But on Eire, the oratory turned to gall:

> Owing to the action of Mr. de Valera, so much at variance with the temper and instinct of thousands of southern Irishmen who hastened to the battlefront to prove their ancient valor, the approaches which the southern Irish ports and airfields could so easily have guarded were closed by the hostile aircraft and U-boats. This was indeed a deadly moment in our life and, if it had not been for the loyalty and friendship of Northern Ireland, we should have been forced to come to close quarters with Mr. de Valera or perish forever from the earth. However,

with a restraint and poise to which, I say, history will find few parallels, His Majesty's Government never laid a violent hand, although at times it would have been quite easy and quite natural, and we left the de Valera government to frolic with the Germans and later with the Japanese representatives to their hearts' content.

When I think of these days, I think also of other episodes and certain personalities. I think of . . . Irish heroes. . . . And then I must confess that the bitterness by Britain against the Irish race dies in my heart. I can only pray that in years which I shall not see the shame will be forgotten and the glories will endure . . .[85]

Hearing these embittered words, every Irishman felt as though he had been personally struck, and all Eire waited for de Valera to respond. He held himself silent for three days, though he was said to have had the first draft of his response ready the night after Churchill's broadcast. On May 16, he took himself to Radio Éireann, on the main thoroughfare of his capital. Anxious that the country's honor be defended, every citizen was nearby to a radio.[86] (The complete speech is presented in the Appendix.)

De Valera began his rejoinder by acknowledging that his people expected him to answer Churchill's fire with fire of his own, and admitted that that would once have been the character of his reply. But rather than adding "fuel to the flames of hatred and passion," he took the broadcast as a chance to demonstrate to the world the logic and morality of Eire's neutrality.

Noting Churchill's implication that Britain would have possessed the right had it violated Eire's sovereignty, de Valera also noted that such logic—that "when this necessity was sufficiently great, other people's rights were not to count"—was that which the United Nations were fighting so hard to conquer. He observed that others would have succumbed to it, but that "acting justly [had] its own rewards."

As to the justice of Eire's wartime position, de Valera introduced the festering wound of partition in defense. He asked how Englishmen would have responded under similar circumstances if a victorious Germany had in the 1914–18 war occupied England, and after a long and bitter occupation finally departed—except that six southern counties remained under German control so as to weaken England and its ability to "maintain the security of her own communications through the Straits of Dover." And afterward, in another great war in which Germany was fighting as the "protector" of small nations' rights, would an embittered England join Germany in the fight? De Valera judged it would not. And that Churchill would agree it should not.

With especial eloquence, de Valera remarked on Britain's pride in its lonely stand against the Axis after France's fall. Could not Churchill, he asked, show understanding for an Ireland that "stood alone not for one year or two, but for several hundred" against the depredations it endured at Britain's hands, and to which it never admitted defeat and never "surrendered her soul."[87]

Regardless of one's view of de Valera's and Eire's roles in World War II, the gracefulness and justice of his defense retains a potency nearly a half century after the relevant events passed into history. Whatever the right Britain had on its side, whatever the wrong it had done this island, whatever the justice or injustice of Eire's part, in his speech Mr. de Valera summed up centuries of ill will between these two small islands anchored as uneasy neighbors off the continental shore. He spoke pointedly and with tolerance of Britain's anxieties about his nation's neutrality. But with equal eloquence and certitude, he stated his and his nation's case for the world to decide its justice for itself. The Irish people could have expected no more.

Madrid

In these last years of the war, life had become for most Spaniards more miserable in some important ways than during the Civil War itself. For the Allies, Franco's fascist "nonbelligerent" state was a strategic blessing. But for the Spanish people, day-to-day existence under dictatorship meant a repression that intruded into every corner of the country and virtually every facet of life.

The golden rule of mid-war Francoism was orthodoxy: orthodoxy in religion, in education, in politics. Assuming the citizen adhered to this received doctrine, and further assuming a past free from Republican heresy, then the likelihood was that the ordinary Spaniard's only worries were those associated with keeping himself and his family alive in the face of the unrelenting food problems that plagued the country from Galicia to Andalusia. The military and ranking party and government bureaucrats encountered few difficulties in maintaining their comforts—a phenomenon nearly universal among repressive regimes, indeed a fundamental guarantor of such regimes' survival. But most Spaniards, including those who had unflaggingly supported Franco, continued to suffer, even if by 1944 the food shortages had been eased. When the Allies had been weak, economic policies toward Spain were comparatively generous to ensure continued Spanish neutrality. But with the good fortunes of the Anglo-American cause, Washington and London adopted ever tougher policies of restricting imports into Spain.

Though on the surface—the "surface" being the middle-class residential and business districts of the large cities—conditions in Spain seemed placid and free from the destruction that was tearing up most of the rest of the continent, the Civil War's scars continued to be inflamed. By mid-war perhaps half of the urban buildings damaged or destroyed had been rebuilt, but in the countryside the proportion was far lower. Many small towns remained in ruins, Guernica a prime example—only in 1945 did that symbol of fascist terror begin to return to life. University City in Madrid, the scene of famous and ferocious fighting in the Civil War, saw its first building reopened only in the summer of 1944. All over the country trenches left from the conflict had become subterranean kitchens for the destitute, the smoke rising from these pits a symbol of the still broken Spain.

The living standard in Spain had by the last few years of World War II fallen to an abysmally low point, with wages frozen at the 1936 level and kept there by the government despite the fact that the price index had risen from a base of 100 in 1935 to 450 by 1944. The average wage that year was 10 pesetas (90 cents) a day, with a woman earning, on average, one peseta for every four earned by a man. These wages, combined with the chronic food shortages, allowed the average Spaniard about a quarter to a half of the minimum number of calories needed to maintain good health. A man on the street summed up the nation's discontent: "They shed so much blood to give us this!"[88]

It was not only the body that suffered. The stifling of Spanish intellectual life during this zenith of Francoism repressed a part of the national spirit that wouldn't return for decades. In classrooms, the only kind of learning was the rote memorization and regurgitation of official state orthodoxy. Absolute adherence to the glories of God and Franco became the daily bread of every schoolroom in Spain. A primer published in Madrid in 1943 by the Vice-Secretariat of Popular Education extolled Franco in a homily climaxing with the words: ". . . Spain, freed from the poison distilled from envy . . . married her rescuer the Caudillo. They lived happily for many years, to the greater glory of heaven and earth. The End. Praise be to God."[89]

By an ordinance of March 2, 1943, martial law became an integral part of civil justice, so that civilians could be tried before *consejos de guerra*." Any disturbance of public order—including labor agitation or strikes—was punishable by death: the victim was dispatched by a firing squad against the bullet-pocked courtyard wall of one of a countless number of anonymous jails. The official decree defined those subject to the death penalty as anyone who "instigated, supported or favored armed revolt against the Chief of State, the Government or Government institutions."[90] The punishment also applied to rumormongers, conspirators, possessors of unlicensed firearms, saboteurs—and strikers. The law made strikes synonymous with "serious trouble to public order," and those convicted were included under the mandatory death provision.

The remnants of Spain's Republican Civil War armies continued to be hunted down with ferocity. Those who had found refuge in remote caves and sierras or with family or friends knew they could expect little mercy from the state if discovered. Besides these former soldiers, there were in post-Civil War Spain three million anarchists, socialists, trade unionists, and former Republican supporters of one degree or another. The judicial murders and score settlings disguised as executions against such persons carried out during World War II were conservatively estimated at 100,000, far exceeding the executions during the Civil War itself.[91] As late as 1944, at least a thousand executions of Republicans, both the newly uncovered and those who had been caged in the country's prisons for as long as four years, indicated the lack of any move toward national reconciliation on the part of Franco's regime.

Politically, 1943 was the year Franco publicly unveiled his new perspective on the various "groups" of belligerents. The Caudillo's nuances varied depending on his audience, the German ambassador getting a slightly different version from that which the British or American minister received. But, in short, the "two wars" theory he had postulated the prior year escalated in 1943 into a "three wars" doctrine. In the war between Germany and the Allies, Spain was "neutral," even though until sometime in 1943 or 1944 he apparently thought his regime could not survive a German defeat. As to the struggle between Nazi Germany and the Soviet Union (Franco in his convoluted thinking seemed to forget that the Soviet Union was an Anglo-American ally), he came squarely down on the side of the Reich. He regarded a Russian victory in this war, in the clear consensus of his biographers, as Christian Europe's death knell.

The Pacific war was the third part of his tripartite theory. From what had been a position of neutrality regarding this struggle in 1942, he now shifted to a pro-Allied stand, a move attributable in large part to his anger over Japanese treatment of Spanish consular officials in the Philippines. By 1945, Franco was even said to be interested in joining the Allies against their Japanese enemy if Washington would give the slightest encouragement. Unfortunately, a diplomatic blunder forestalled this unlikely scenario; a congratulatory 1943 Spanish telegram to the new quisling Laurel regime in Manila (initiated by a minor official in the Spanish Foreign Ministry and evidently not a calculated act on the part of Franco[92]) so angered the United States that Washington could never have even considered unofficially proferred Spanish help in the Pacific. Further, Madrid's reaction to that anger was a contributing factor in Spain's refusal to stop the wolfram trade with Germany and thus end the U.S.-initiated oil embargo.

Still, Germany kept as tight a leash as it could on Spain. Though Berlin had all but given up on any offensive designs on the country by 1943, it meant to see to it that Spain would resist any attempt by Anglo-American forces to land in the peninsula. By way of reminding Spain of the dangers of irritating the Reich, it had recently torpedoed two Spanish ships, the *Monte Gorbea* and the *Monte Igueldo*, both signals that Foreign Minister Jordana probably correctly interpreted as Berlin's way of saying Spain shouldn't "stray too far from the Axis."[93] To mollify an edgy Berlin, Franco allowed the Germans to maintain an espionage presence in Spain far outweighing that of the Allies. General Walter Schellenberg, after Canaris's 1944 arrest chief of German secret services, claimed that between 70 and 100 staffers in the German embassy in Madrid were primarily engaged in espionage and illicit broadcasting.[94]

Yet Franco continued to have a vision of Germany and the Allies joining in battle against the "real" scourge of mankind, Soviet Russia. With motives that were far more anti-Soviet than pro-Axis, in February he sent a memorandum to Ireland, Sweden, and Switzerland proposing the creation of just such an alliance, with Portugal slated for a leading role. All had to be ready "to intervene at the opportune moment . . . with an appeal in the favor of the cessation of hostilities for a common defence against the Bolshevist danger."[95] That this vision was a chimera—especially in light of the unified Allied demand for Germany's unconditional surrender—didn't lessen Franco's ardor.

On October 1, 1943, in an opulent reception salon of Madrid's Palacio Real, a setting in which it was hoped the grandeur of Spain's past would lend authority to the proceedings, Generalissimo Franco formally proclaimed Spain's unvarnished neutrality for the first time in three years.[96] The generalissimo was dressed not in his customary costume of the Falange Española, but in a naval uniform, and no party members were in sight. (Ambassador Hayes favorably noted that the German ambassador "was almost completely isolated."[97]) The impetus for the turnabout was a demand from the U.S. ambassador, Carleton Hayes, who on

July 29 formally handed to Franco a list of American grievances: primarily the grossly pro-Axis attitude of Spain's radio and press and the continued presence of the Blue Division in Russia. Though the Spanish dictator calmly reiterated his notion of neutrality in the Allies/Axis struggle and his partiality only in the Axis/Bolshevik war, he nonetheless agreed to ask Germany to return his soldiers and promised to see to a more evenhanded neutrality on the part of the Spanish radio and newspapers.

At the same time Hayes was imprecating Franco from the American perspective, Sir Samuel Hoare was doing the same from Britain's. What has come down in the history of these times as Hoare's "grand remonstrance" was the British government's own list of grievances it insisted Franco do something about—immediately. These included refusing the use of Spanish ports for the continued provisioning and fueling of German ships, withdrawing facilities Spain provided Germany to commit deadly mischief with its espionage activities, and barring the use of the country's airports for German planes to refuel after sinking Allied shipping in offshore waters. What Franco wanted for an affirmative reply to Hoare's "remonstrance" was some kind of promise that his regime would be allowed to live after the Allied victory. With such a promise, Madrid would begin to disengage itself from its still close and patently unneutral ties with the Third Reich. But the July collapse of Mussolini's Italy (though it was replaced with a northern Italian rump entity called the "Italian Social Republic," ruled from Salò, a "state" recognized only by Germany, its satellites, and Japan) made it painfully evident to Franco that the Allies would be calling the shots from now on.

Three days after the palace ceremony, the switch from nonbelligerency to neutrality was officially announced in the press. Except for the still lingering trade ties, Spain's eight-year-long tryst with the Reich had ended. And twelve days later, the first elements of the Blue Division began to be relieved by German troops.[98]

To German recriminations over this turning away from the Reich, Franco quickly asserted that the steps were taken only under Anglo-American economic duress. The Caudillo swore that he wished Germany all the best and that he would do everything he could for a German victory. (One can only speculate on Berlin's reaction to such nonsense.) Figuring that an Allied-dominated Europe would be committed to the restoration of the French empire and his hopes for a New Spanish Empire would thus go a-begging on Germany's defeat, the reasons why he still hoped to see Berlin triumph aren't hard to fathom.[99]

•   •   •

As Spain began to contort itself into an authentic neutral cast, the Anglo-American alliance's attitude toward it changed little. This was in large part the result of the Western Allies' principle (a principle with which all the neutrals had to deal) that as more concessions were granted, more were demanded. (The attitude of the Soviet Union toward *all* the neutrals was antagonistic, but Moscow reserved a special hatred for the government that had destroyed the Republic and sent the *divisionarios* to fight in Russia.) Wolfram was again the touchstone for Washington and London's anger, with Spain still sending useful amounts to Germany—in June 1943 alone, Spain sold 125 tons to the Reich.[100] Though Germany was no longer able to effectively punish Spain if Madrid were to stop the shipments, Franco seems to have believed a "debt of honor" required that the strategic mineral continue to flow northward.[101] The enrichment to the Spanish treasury that came from the heavy duties it imposed on the exports was likely a further consideration. But clearly part of Franco's motive also was to placate Berlin for his demand that the Blue Division be withdrawn, and he extended a $40 million credit for purchase of the mineral. In any event, he gambled that the more easygoing British would overrule any precipitate American move to force Spain to cut off the wolfram shipments. But the United States acted against advice from London not to overly rile a Spain still potentially able to help the Reich, and in fact proceeded to initiate a full-out oil embargo.[102] On January 28, 1944, with the power of the navicert system, backed by the guns of their navies, the Allies almost totally stopped oil shipments into Spain.

The results were devastating. Industrial activity and transportation were hardest hit, and in consequence of plant closings all over the country destitution rose rapidly. Private automobiles disappeared, and the only public transportation vehicles allowed to operate were buses and taxis fitted with cumbersome charcoal burners. With the disappearance of trucks, new food shortages in every part of the country reversed the recent easing of the nation's provisioning problems. Though the regime's finely honed tools of repression kept the masses from any serious protest, the hardship engendered by Franco's bluff—his way of demonstrating to Washington and London who was in charge in Spain, the calculated rebuff founded on his belief the Allies would prefer a Franco-ruled Spain in the postwar world to what he thought would be an anarchic void—simply meant yet more suffering for a long-suffering people.

Having thus demonstrated his macho to America and Britain, and knowing that the latter's inclination was to back away from applying any more pressure on Spain, Franco gave in and stopped sending wolfram to the Reich (as well as other products Spain had been supplying Germany). In May 1944 the petroleum embargo was called off. Franco made other concessions as well, including promises to expel German agents from Spain and to close the German consulate in Tangier (which served as an important base for German espionage in North Africa), as well as the final withdrawal of all Blue Division elements, concessions that were as much a part of the Allied strategy in launching the oil embargo as was the cessation of the wolfram trade.[103] All added up to a clear indication of the Allies' capacity to force their will on Spain. A further gesture, perhaps trivial, made an agreeable impression on the Allies: Franco finally took down the portraits of the Führer and the Duce from his Pardo Palace office. He replaced them with a picture of the pope.

The concrete Allied act of making peace with the reality of a postwar Francoist Spain came very quickly and in a notably dramatic setting—the House of Commons of the British parliament. On May 24, 1944, Winston Churchill publicly and decisively legitimized Francisco Franco's government. The British premier took the chamber's floor to tell his colleagues—and the world—that Spain had rendered services at a time when its "power to injure Britain was at its very highest," and that, in effect, though the Spanish people and their suffering at the hands of the Franco regime might be deplorable, it was no business of Britain. What was important to the United Nations, he went on, was the fact that Spain had remained neutral in the face of almost irresistible blandishments from the Axis, and that only a strong Spain could be expected to serve as a "strong influence for the peace of the Mediterranean after the war." It would be difficult to find an instance of more clearly expressed *Realpolitik* on the part of the Allied leadership during World War II.[104]

As historian Max Gallo concluded, Churchill was putting Franco on notice that if "you keep control of your country, we shall not intervene or let anyone else intervene in the internal affairs of Spain."[105] It wouldn't be long before Franco would be called upon to make *sure* Spain kept control of its affairs.

With the Allied liberation of France, the Spanish opposition that had managed to survive in France was freed from its Vichy/Nazi restraints. Joining forces with the left-wing underground inside Spain and marching to the cry of "¡Reconquista!,"[106] these opposition groups decided in the latter half of 1944 to try for an insurrection against the Franco regime. Some 12,000 entered Spain in September through the Arán Valley, on the rugged and isolated Pyrenean border west of Andorra. From Toulouse, they broadcast an appeal to their fellow Spaniards to join them in their crusade. Again, as in 1936–39, Franco's strength and ruthlessness of purpose carried the day against his adversaries' disarray. Though these primarily Communist or anarchist forces were able to cut down a few Guardia Civil units and temporarily disrupt communication lines, Franco's overwhelming superiority quickly eliminated a threat that never overly worried Madrid.[107] With no chance of organizing themselves effectively inside Spain, the guerrilla forces were overwhelmed by both the army and the bitterly wintry weather. Spain established a *cordon sanitaire* eight miles deep on its side of the border, and anyone caught within this forbidden zone was arrested or shot while "resisting" arrest.[108] The fate of captured resistants was often a quick death by firing squad, the "fortunate" ones consigned to Spain's fetid jails for as long as thirty years, many routinely put to torture.

Another potential problem for Franco was Don Juan, the legitimate heir and pretender to the Bourbon throne. Though Spain's monarchists, backed by large elements of the Spanish Army, urged Don Juan's restoration,[109] Franco saw little reason to give in to these pleas for a "legitimate" reversion to a sitting monarch.[110] In June 1943, he sent a halfhearted invitation to Don Juan to return to Spain, presumably to its throne, if he accepted Franco's supremacy and a retained Falange. Don Juan refused, loftily writing to Franco petitioning the "urgent installation of a new national regime, which, like that of the traditional Catholic monarchy, would find itself free from compromising positions and injurious ties and capable of carrying out the concepts of strict neutrality."[111]

In a return letter six months later, Franco bluntly told the son of Alfonso XIII that as Alfonso had voluntarily given up the throne in 1931, and the army, which had then risen up against the Republic, wasn't monarchist in character but instead "Spanish" and "Catholic," and the monarchists who participated in the nationalist crusade hadn't made up more than a mere fraction of that movement, his government had no obligation to recognize the *ancien régime*. Don Juan wrote back, expressing, in effect, how little he thought of the "nationalist-syndicalist" state, obviously having more of an eye to the future than to any present hope of assuming even figurehead status in Spain.[112] After Churchill's speech to the Commons a few weeks later, the playboy prince also became cognizant that Britain would very likely disappoint those monarchists hoping for Whitehall's support, the British prime minister clearly putting them on notice that Spanish problems were a matter for the Spanish to resolve.[113]

• • •

After the Normandy landings and the repatriation of France and Allied control of the Mediterranean, the war turned into a downhill run for Spain. No longer important, no longer more than a minor consideration in Allied councils (except to make sure the country didn't become a haven for Nazi criminals or Nazi loot), Franco focused on ensuring his survival. He agreed to a number of Allied requests regarding such matters as the internment of Germans fleeing France and adhered to the Allied demand that Spain not become a refuge for bolting Nazis; in fact, the United Nations War Crimes Commission never had to apply to Spain for extradition of any major Nazi war criminal.[114] Diplomatic relations with Japan were broken in April 1945, and Spain formally reestablished full relations with all the Allied governments-in-exile.

Finally comprehending the preposterousness of an Allies/German union against the Soviet Union, Franco had to contend with the fact that Stalin would likely be one of the supreme victors in the United Nations alliance. When one of his closest friends had asked him in the summer of 1943 what he planned to do to survive in the event of an Allied victory, he replied, *"Pasar la cuenta"* ("Pass the bill"), meaning that by not joining the Axis and by keeping the Germans out of Spain and Gibraltar, he had won favor with the "West," which, though paying lip service to Stalin, would be in final control of the world order.

As to the specifics of that control, he appears to have believed the real postwar leadership, at least in Europe, would be a British-Spanish alliance, as Italy, Germany, and France were all beaten and internally rotten and only the United Kingdom and his own nation could hold things together. Only in this way would a Christian Europe be kept out of Soviet clutches.[115]

At war's end, Franco self-righteously asserted, "Spain and the other neutrals *must* participate in the negotiations for the peace treaty," and would, in fact, be welcomed in the councils of the victors sooner than anyone could have foreseen. But even with a bit of democratic window dressing on his corporative state—a parliament (*Cortes*) with all its candidates appointed by the state had been set up during 1942 and 1943 and a bill of rights (*Fuero de los Españoles*) in early 1945—few were fooled into thinking Franco's Spain was on a road leading to genuine democracy.

. . .

Franco's behavior, clearly in character, on learning of Hitler's death caused nowhere the storm generated by de Valera's obsequies. Not only were masses held for Hitler but one Spanish municipality asked its citizens to "perpetuate the memory of one who continued until his death to defend the civilization of the Christian West . . ."[116] The newspaper *Informaciones* described Hitler as "a son of the Catholic Church, [who] died defending Christianity," adding that his tombstone should note: " 'He who lies here did not die. His death was the beginning of life.' . . . The war against Bolshevism has entered on its victorious phase. . . . And in Heaven there is much rejoicing."[117]

On the other hand, the death of Roosevelt, a sternly anti-fascist president who counseled leniency toward Stalin, was believed by most Falangists to augur well for postwar Spain. Ironically, however, it was Roosevelt's successor in the White House who would lead the free world in treating Spain in the first postwar years as an international pariah, probably a great deal more sternly than Roosevelt would have done—until the reality of the Cold War motivated the American administration to forgive Spanish fascism its transgressions in the name of NATO.

With the advent of peace in Europe, the Francoists and Falangists noisily proclaimed the wisdom of Franco's "neutrality," a neutrality that belied what Sir Samuel Hoare had called "an occupied country of the second degree."[118] It was transparently clear that these people were frightened of a future in which they might quite possibly be held to account for the crimes that had been so deeply sowed in the name of Christian order and the fear of Communist chaos.

As with the other neutrals, Spain was not invited to participate in the San Francisco Conference of the new United Nations. A Mexican initiative, easily adopted by the body that represented the war's high-riding victors, dictated that no state that had been brought into being with the help of one of the United Nations' late enemies would qualify for membership until such state changed its regime. The provision was expressly tailored for Spain. (Stalin wanted *all* diplomatic recognition withdrawn from Spain, but Truman and Churchill held him in check on this point.[119])

It is illuminating to consider, however, what a German-occupied Spain, or even just a German Gibraltar, would have meant to World War II at any point prior to the Allied invasion of North Africa. Would any Western leader have traded Franco's repression for the uncertainties of a

Spain in which the Republic had triumphed?[120] What Allied general would have exchanged the anonymous victims of the Franco state to gain as an ally the Spanish Republic? Would the cumulative world community have held the potential victims of Republican vengeance any more or less dearly than those who died at the Nationalist stake? Would a Republican regime in Madrid in 1940 have been able to ward off a German invasion that would have had Gibraltar as its goal? Would the West have wished for a Republican Spain and its nearly certain postwar association with Stalinist Russia? As Winston Churchill admitted in the most dangerous year of the war, Franco's Spain "held the key to all British enterprises in the Mediterranean, and never in the darkest hours did she turn the lock against us."[121]

Lisbon

He was Professor Henry Higgins, Ashley Wilkes, the Scarlet Pimpernel, and Romeo to Norma Shearer's Juliet. In 1943, Leslie Howard was one of Britain's most powerful propaganda voices, a man who from screen and stage scorned Nazi posturing and inspired his fellow Britons in their fight for victory. His death, a minor tragedy of World War II all but forgotten today, flowed out of the river of espionage that was wartime Lisbon.[122]

At midyear 1943, Lisbon held in its buoyant embrace what was probably the world's premier collection of spies and agents provocateurs. All competed for the crumbs that fell off the diplomatic and military plates served up at the embassies and missions in what historian Tom Gallagher called this "European Shanghai."[123]

The British actor had journeyed to Iberia to undertake a lecture tour, to enlighten Portuguese and Spanish audiences as to the nuances of his stage and screen skills, particularly that most trying and majestic of roles, Hamlet. On April 27, 1943, with his manager, Alfred Chenhalls, whose passing but hardly overwhelming resemblance to Winston Churchill would one day add a mythic dimension to an already strange tale, Howard left Bristol, England, on a flight bound for Lisbon. Nervous about flying, especially across a Bay of Biscay within easy range of French-based German fighter squadrons, the actor was further disinclined to get on his KLM DC-3 airliner after he noticed a row of neatly punched and repainted indentations on the side of the fuselage. On inquiry, he was frankly told they were scars of bullet holes from a recent German attack.

For the next seven and a half hours, the passengers scanned the skies nervously from their porthole windows while the Dutch pilots tried to keep within diving distance of clouds, the best means of escape in case any Luftwaffe fighters should show up. Not that the Germans attacked very often. The planes nearly always completed their journeys in perfect safety between the United Kingdom and Portela Aerodrome, outside Lisbon.

This flight, too, ended uneventfully, and Howard spent the first part of his five-week trip regaling Lisbon audiences with anecdotes of his theatrical experiences, as well as analyzing with understated brilliance the skills that had made the fifty-three-year-old actor a world-famous symbol of British savoir faire.

After the brightness and gaiety of Lisbon, Howard and Chenhalls left the Portuguese capital to spend the middle weeks of the trip in Madrid. Franco's first city was only four hundred miles away but seemed light-years distant in feeling from the relative lightheartedness they were leaving behind. Popular sympathy for Germany in the higher social reaches of Franco's Spain meant that Britons—particularly those patriotically associated with King and Country as was the popular Howard—were often treated with barely disguised scorn. Despite the chill, Howard carried out his twelve days of cultural engagements in Madrid with characteristic graciousness and wit. When passing Germans in the lobby of the Ritz—easily picked out by their slick-sided haircuts and Prussian demeanor—the actor made gentlemanly efforts to conceal his own contempt. He wasn't, of course, aware that among those Germans were agents reporting his movements back to Berlin.

Propaganda Minister Joseph Goebbels had seen Howard's 1941 film *Pimpernel Smith*, a modern adaptation of *The Scarlet Pimpernel*, the 1934 picture in which Howard took the part of an English aristocrat who rescued French nobles from the juridical mobs and guillotines of the French Revolution. In *Pimpernel Smith*, the Third Reich is ridiculed by Howard, who played an archaeology professor who traveled to Europe to rescue refugees from the clutches of the Third Reich. Goebbels decided to get the man who not only starred in this attack on the Reich but who directed and produced it as well.

Back in Portugal on May 21, Howard spent the remainder of the trip at Estoril's lush, palm-surrounded Hotel Atlântico. Lisbon's mini-Monte Carlo, overlooking the Tagus a few miles downriver from the city, was quite likely the most luxurious place on the entire European continent in 1943. But Howard quickly grew restless. He told Chenhalls he wanted to get back to London to take care of last-minute details on his new propaganda film, *The First of the Few*, in which he starred as the developer of the Spitfire airplane. Scheduled to leave on KLM on June 2, he had Chenhalls pull the necessary strings to get out a day earlier, on Flight 2L272 set for Tuesday, June 1, 1943.

The plane—called *Ibis*—had reached Lisbon on its journey from England the day before. The same aircraft and carrying the same Dutch crew as on Howard's April 27 inbound flight, it still bore the patched-up indentations from the earlier brush with the German fighters. Listed on the roster for the homeward flight were fourteen passengers, a number of whom might have been desirable targets to the Germans. An Ivan Sharp had been in Lisbon negotiating wolfram exports to the United Kingdom, and another, Mr. T. M. Shervington, Shell manager in Lisbon, was mistakenly thought by the Germans to be chief of the British Secret Service. There were, of course, "desirable targets" on most of these flights between Lisbon and free-world destinations, since many passengers were important to the war effort in one way or another. What kept them from harm's way was the fact that Axis sympathizers considered these flights useful too, a convenient conduit to important persons or important information. Flight 2L272 would prove the exception to the rule.

When Howard boarded the unpressurized DC-3, he could easily have been spotted by any number of observers from the Lufthansa offices and repair bays, facilities that stood within a few feet of the KLM buildings at the airport. The Germans could have with little effort been aware of his itinerary, and even the unannounced change from June 2 to June 1 wouldn't have protected the actor from any Axis agent keeping watch over the KLM activities in the terminal or on the runway.

Ibis took off from Portela Aerodrome at 9:35 A.M., slowly climbed to 9,000 feet, and set a course to make the last Iberian landfall at Spain's Cape Villano before heading out over the Bay of Biscay for the seven-hour run on to Bristol. On Cape Villano stood a powerful German omnidirectional radio navigation beam.[124] As *Ibis* passed this last land-fall, the beam caught the airliner firmly in its electronic embrace.

At noon, the KLM airliner was well over the Bay of Biscay. But it was also rapidly converging with a *Staffel* of Luftwaffe Junkers-88s, eight heavy fighters assigned to the Kerlin-Bastard airfield a few miles west of Bordeaux, whose usual targets were the military flying boats and C-47s that plied between Britain and North Africa. On this day, their leader had been ordered to sortie only a few minutes after Howard's plane left Portela. At some time just before 1 P.M., the eight Junkers fired cannon and machine guns at Flight 2L272, the Dutch pilot unable to reach the safety of the clouds below. In flames, *Ibis* dived for the sea. No one aboard survived. No records exist of the squadron's assigned target, but its shooting down of an unarmed civilian airliner was an act so rare that British authorities had refused to consider moving the routes farther out over the Atlantic or even to change flight schedules to nighttime hours.

The German reaction immediately afterward was undisguised glee. *Der Angriff*, Goebbels's paper, headlined: "Pimpernel Smith has made his last trip!"[125] The consensus in Britain came to be that the attack was entirely the doings of a trigger-happy German squadron leader and had no connection with the famous actor on board.

In later years, the most widely reported explanation for the shooting down of Howard's flight was that Winston Churchill had been the target. The British war leader had been in North Africa for a conference with his fellow war planners when these events took place. Many have surmised that a German agent in Lisbon/Portela mistook Howard's manager, Alfred Chenhalls, for Churchill, the latter presumably on his way home from the Algiers conference. Supposedly, this report led the Germans to order out the fighter planes to shoot down the airliner. Even Churchill seems to have subscribed to this theory, as he suggested in the *Hinge of Fate* volume of his history of World War II:

> The brutality of the Germans was only matched by the stupidity of their agents. It is difficult to understand how anyone could imagine that with all the resources of Great Britain at my disposal I should have booked a passage in an unarmed and unescorted plane from London and flown home in broad daylight. We of course made a broad loop out by night from Gibraltar into the ocean and arrived home without incident. It was a painful shock to me to learn what had happened to others in the inscrutable workings of fate.[126]

Not only would the Germans have been stupid to have acted as Churchill above suggests; the dates, too, are wrong. Surely the Germans were aware when the conference ended and when Churchill departed North Africa, his presence in North Africa having been fully reported. Howard's flight was shot down on June 1, but Churchill's flight returned from Africa to England nearly a week later.

There is to date no positive proof of what happened to Leslie Howard's flight. The events laid out here follow Ronald Howard's surmisal. Perhaps as Howard suggests, the real explanation might be that the *combination* of Leslie Howard, British patriot par excellence, and T. M. Shervington, would-be British Secret Service chief, was too much for the Germans not to shoot down.

The whole affair quickly blew over, the combatants getting on to more important killing. But Leslie Howard and *Ibis* sent Lisbon one of its sharpest frissons of excitement during the war, even though in payment the world lost, to quote Churchill, one "whose grace and gifts are still preserved for us by the records of the many delightful films in which he took part."[127]

· · ·

If Leslie Howard captured the world's fancy for Portugal in the closing years of World War II, the Azores problem continued to occupy the attention of the war's planners. Early in the war, Germany had viewed the Azores primarily as a mid-ocean platform from which to attack the United States as well as to renourish its prowling packs of U-boats. As the conflict's balance no longer favored the Reich, their use as a stepping-stone for transatlantic flights and a place from which to attack the U-boat menace became uppermost in Allied thinking, with Salazar trying to hold out as long as possible against Allied demands to station their forces in the islands.

Until 1943, Britain and America had to weigh their own plans to invade the Azores against the likely adverse effects on Portuguese and Spanish opinion. In mid-1941 Winston Churchill himself believed a preemptive occupation very well might invite an attack by the Wehrmacht on the Portuguese mainland, a situation which Britain, already bled white, would be nearly powerless to do much to check.[128] In consequence, and in spite of Senator Pepper's intemperate, if understandable, remarks in the American Congress (recounted earlier), it became Allied policy that the islands would be taken only if Germany tried to move on them or if either Portugal or Spain joined the Axis as a military co-belligerent.

Though Hitler contemplated an invasion of the Azores on a number of occasions in the early years of the war, his advisers always persuaded him of the folly of an occupation, for the substantive reason that the immensely strong Royal Navy could likely block any such attempt. There was the secondary but less measurable consideration that it would be foolish to turn Salazar into an enemy unless Germany planned to crush Portugal, something that became unlikely after the Reich changed its course eastward to the Balkans and Russia. Furthermore, German intelligence would have reported on the forces Churchill kept ready to take the islands if Spain were invaded by the Germans: with the imminent loss of Gibraltar, Britain would have little choice but to take the Atlantic islands—the Azores or the Canaries or both—with or without Madrid's and Lisbon's support.[129]

By 1943, however, Allied war planners had come to regard the Azores as a platform from which they could at little cost more effectively combat the enemy. Washington, the more insistent partner of the two where problems with the neutrals were concerned, determined to secure use of the islands at almost any cost.

Considering the stakes, this attitude was entirely understandable. Since 1942, Allied losses to U-boats had risen inexorably, and the number of new boats built by Doenitz began to exceed those the Allies were able to sink. It didn't take the U.S. military long to conclude that the most effective weapon against the submarine threat was air coverage. Even a single airplane over a convoy was enough to scare off the German submarines, and with long-range protection from the sky available for the greater part of the North Atlantic convoy run, the German advantage might very well be turned around.

In the vast central Atlantic, such air coverage was impossible. Even the fighters available on escort carriers were insufficient to protect all the convoys using the southerly route. But with Azores bases from which to roam, this could be reversed. What's more, escort vessels would be re-fueled from the islands at less effort and expense, and a new, direct, all-weather air supply route from the United States to Europe, Africa, and the Far East would be established.[130] A base in the Azores would also allow more effective strikes at the concentration of U-boats in the Bay of Biscay, as well as the area near the islands themselves where the German subs were known to be resupplied in the Kriegsmarine's innovative milch-cow technique. With such advantages, the military chiefs began to pressure the politicians and diplomats to do whatever was necessary to obtain the bases it needed.

How to obtain them now become a major problem to be worked out between the two leading Allies. At the May 1943 Trident Conference in Washington, the military chiefs recommended force, on the logic that simply asking Salazar's permission would be a waste of time. The Americans' biggest British supporter for this option was Winston Churchill, who noted that the Portuguese were so afraid of a German reprisal if they abrogated their neutrality in this manner that Salazar would never give in, and thus the islands would never come into Allied use. Churchill held that even the best diplomatic approach to the Portuguese would result in a negative response, and that in making such an approach the Portuguese would be forewarned of the Allies' urgent interests in the islands, so that the element of surprise in a military seizure operation would be lost.[131] For his part, Roosevelt thought Brazil should be approached to try to persuade Portugal to give in to the Allies—the colingual Latin American nation enjoyed a close relationship with Portugal—but the president wouldn't entirely rule out the use of force to take the islands.

But more moderate counsel prevailed. Churchill's most powerful political subordinates, Foreign Minister Anthony Eden and the deputy prime minister, Clement Attlee, backed by the weight of the Foreign Office as well as the Defence Committee, argued that the consequences of a forceful occupation of sovereign Portuguese territory were so serious that a diplomatic approach to the matter should certainly be *tried* before imposing a military solution, if only to avoid an irreparable breach between Portugal and the Allies. Eden and Attlee concluded that the six-century-old alliance between England and Portugal would be the best grounds on which to approach Salazar, Eden holding that once Britain was in on the basis of the ancient treaty, the Americans could be somehow slid into the islands too. With the concurrence of the rest of the British cabinet, the military heads of the Trident Conference gave the diplomatic faction leave to try their way first.

Diplomacy was embarked upon on a two-pronged approach. In London, Eden met with the Portuguese ambassador to ask for the necessary permission for Allied bases in the Azores, and in Lisbon the British ambassador sought an audience with Salazar, pointedly noting in his talk with the premier that "small nations [were] dependent on an Allied victory" and thus that such an arrangement would certainly benefit Portugal's interests.

It was, of course, Salazar with whom the final decision rested. First the dictator consulted with his under secretary for war, Fernando Santos Costa, who argued against such an accommodation on the grounds that it would destroy the nation's neutrality in the eyes of the Germans regardless of Portugal's legal declaration that it was granting facilities to a nation that could rightfully claim them under treaty rights. Warily but conclusively, Salazar nonetheless decided in Britain's favor, formally invoking the Anglo-Portuguese alliance of 1373—though the less formal rationale was more likely Salazar's assessment of the relative positions of the two belligerents at this point in the war.

Something even more important was on Salazar's mind in acquiescing to the British and the Americans. That was Portugal's colonial empire. The empire fabricated from the crusading bravado of the nation's long-ago explorers was Portugal's proud and valuable possession. It stretched across southern Africa through Angola and Mozambique, continued along the small jewels scattered on the Indian coast, and finally reached far out into the southwestern Pacific. Salazar knew that in the postwar world access to the empire would be largely controlled by sea lanes dominated by the war's victors. Perhaps in the back of his mind was the fear many European leaders were starting to experience in these years, of aspirations for independence among the captive colonial peoples of the non-European world. What Antonio Salazar wanted was an Allied guarantee that Portugal would be helped after the war to maintain his country's empire.

In acquiescing to Britain, Salazar imposed one significant limitation on his deal. There was to be no American presence in the islands. If he had to face an irate Reich over his deviation from hitherto strict "neutrality," at least he would have a six-hundred-year-old pact with England to vindicate his actions. If Americans were involved, no such excuse would be available, and Berlin would unarguably be justified in treating Portugal as an Allied partner.

To get as much as he could from his concession, the premier demanded new antiaircraft guns from Britain, to help Portugal protect itself from an aerial bombardment, an attack Salazar expected daily for the first few weeks after the Azores bargain was struck. The weapons were quickly delivered by London. It might have been Salazar's own wolfram weapon that proved the most useful in the whole affair: with Portugal promising not to reduce its shipments of the vital ore to Germany, Hitler may have "overlooked" that country's transgression. Even Churchill suggested as much, keeping quiet about wolfram shipments to the Reich.[132]

On August 18, 1943, the deal between London and Lisbon was formally concluded. For its part, the British received naval rights to facilities at Horta and air rights to Lajes airfield, on Terceira, with the date of possession set for October 8. For their part, the Portuguese got a promise that the British would withdraw all their personnel and facilities at the war's end and that the United Kingdom and the British dominions would fully back Portugal's postwar rights to sovereignty over its empire.[133]

This arrangement was, though, considerably less than what the Allies would have wished for. Not only did the United States envision the Azores as a key base in its postwar plans to establish a security network making the world safe for American power, but even in the short term Salazar's concessions fell far short of what was needed to best prosecute the war against the Axis. The British hadn't the resources to establish the naval and air facilities in the islands needed to wage worldwide war. London promised to try to talk Lisbon into allowing air facilities for the American Air Force, and unilaterally decided to include U.S. craft in mixed Anglo-American convoys, apparently with the hope the Portuguese would let such a technical violation of the agreement go without protest.

Though Roosevelt authorized a pledge be given to the Portuguese providing that the United States would join the British in guaranteeing the Portuguese colonial empire after the war, the American president wanted the concession held for a quid pro quo return on his investment. George Kennan, the U.S. chargé d'affaires in Lisbon, was certain Salazar wouldn't agree to an American presence in the Azores without such a guarantee, realizing the Portuguese dictator was still deathly afraid of Hitler's reaction, as well as Franco's, if the Americans were formally allowed into the islands.

In the end, Kennan was allowed to commit the United States to respect Portuguese postwar sovereignty in its colonies, and persuaded Roosevelt to write a letter to Salazar promising to evacuate and return to the Portuguese facilities which would be granted for its military and naval use for the remainder of the war. Salazar thus gave in to the Americans, encouraged by Berlin's and Madrid's relatively unbelligerent reaction to the agreement with Britain. And to add a legal fillip to his rationalization, the Treaty of 1773 with Britain contained a "Friends of Friends" provision (by which any friend of Britain was, ipso facto, a friend of Portugal), with which, Salazar reasoned, the Americans could be "legally" shoehorned into the agreement's provisions.

The Portuguese formally relented to an American presence in the Azores on December 2, 1943. The German response was summed up in Goebbels's diary entry on November 13: "Unfortunately [Salazar] has lost faith in us to some extent . . ."[134] It was an altogether accurate summary of the Portuguese leader's present attitude toward Germany. A week later, American air forces were using Lajes field as a mid-Atlantic refueling base for their heavy bombers, and by the following February, supplies were reaching the Far East in aid to China after being relayed through the Azores base. At the end of 1943, the new American ambassador in Lisbon (the post had recently been upgraded to ambassadorial level) prevailed on the Portuguese government to allow an addition to the Lajes airfield, as well as to start survey work for an entirely new base to be built on the island of Santa Maria, the latter to be slightly disguised as a Pan American Airways undertaking so as to preserve the last shreds of Portugal's formal neutrality.

To get permission to actually start building the new field and set up an American naval squadron's presence in the islands, Washington tried to lure Salazar with a promise to allow Portuguese troops to help liberate Portuguese Timor from the Japanese control under which it had suffered since 1942. But Salazar wasn't anxious to start a shooting war with the Japanese, afraid that if he did so their treatment of the Portuguese in Macao could go from bad to very much worse. But apparently on the basis of "in for a penny, in for a pound"—as well as the assumption that Portuguese honor was on the line in its determination to help free Timor—Salazar finally acquiesced to the Americans, insisting on as much camouflaging as possible of the American presence in the Azores. This final agreement between Portugal and the United States, allowing the latter to build and have exclusive use of an air base on Santa Maria, was signed on November 28, 1944.

By approaching the Azores problem on the diplomatic front rather than the military, both Britain and the United States turned out as winners. Though it is not possible to calculate how many Allied lives were lost and how much Allied shipping was sunk because Britain and the United States weren't able to use the Azores earlier, in moral terms the two countries ended up in a far stronger position, and Washington was able to convince Lisbon to continue to allow the United States to use its Azores bases for many years after the war.

．　．　．

May 2, 1945

Three days after Eamon de Valera wound his way through Dublin's streets on his visit to the Third Reich's diplomatic representative to Eire, Antonio Salazar undertook a similar journey through the streets of his own capital. The Portuguese radio had earlier in the day relayed the news from Bremen and Hamburg that Adolf Hitler had "died in action."

As the premier clung to his notions of "juridical neutrality" in the face of Germany's collapse, the Portuguese people went a different way. On V-E Day, the 300-foot-wide Avenida da Liberdade, Lisbon's greatest boulevard, was engulfed by a crowd, deliriously happy that a war that had only grazed their nation was over.

ACCOUNTING

*"There will be no hiding places in
future world conflicts."*
—JOHN MAJOR,
British prime minister

What the experiences of the European neutrals in World War II have revealed about the affairs of nations is, at a minimum, that declarations of neutrality are by themselves an insubstantial thing. That assumption weighs with undeniable gravity on the present. Even with a seemingly irreversible nuclear future, one guaranteeing that no nation will ever again be immune to the consequences of its neighbors' quarrels or ambitions or blunders, war has remained resolutely "conventional."

Until World War II, warfare had, in the main, been a contained phenomenon. Nation-states could generally stay out of harm's way by avoiding international quarrels and declaring neutrality. Even in World War I, the first case of modern general warfare where tactical considerations manifestly superseded "neutrality," a nation could still steer clear of the battle unless it had the misfortune of being vital to one of the belligerents, as in the most lamentable case of Belgium.

With World War II, such assumed immunity vanished. In the two regional struggles that coalesced to make up World War II—the European war and the Asian war—the belligerents, with tactical, strategic, or economic rationales, overrode rights of self-declared neutral states. So mauled was the concept of neutrality that at war's end the victors judiciously built into their new United Nations Organization forces designed to guarantee protection from aggression. But this international "law" would to the new world body prove nearly as illusory as it had to the weaker and less self-assured League of Nations. After 1945, the chimera of international law would attempt to secure its members' safety from hostile neighbors by the UN's employment, or authorization of employment by states acting in its name, of superior military strength. Such was the avenue by which Iraq's invasion of neighboring Kuwait was overturned in 1991. Though a state that is the victim of unwarranted aggression certainly is not always able to characterize itself as "neutral" in a conflict, the protection of any such state—"neutral" or not—is sought on the grounds of collective safety.

It is the kind of military strength employed by the United Nations that accounts, as much as any other factor, for the successful European neutrals' deliverance in World War II. At the beginning of the struggle, every country in Europe tried desperately to stay out of the German-Polish-British-French conflict. All the rest of Europe's states swiftly and solemnly declared their official nonpartisanship. But the nature of the Nazi state, its alliance with Soviet Russia, its ally Japan's aggression in Asia, and the formation of the worldwide Axis quickly and radically distinguished *this* war from those before it. And the leaders of those neutral states grew aware that the likelihood of the success of their neutrality was diminishing daily. Some formed alliances with the Reich, some sheltered their defenses under Moscow's precarious canopy, some laid great emphasis on the scrupulous impartiality of their dealings with both sides.

Each of the successful neutrals was shaped by a unique set of political and social conditions on its journey through World War II. None of them got through simply by opting out of the conflict, by declaring neutrality and expecting its declaration to be respected. It was, of course, an aggressive, expansionist, always potentially lawless Germany with whom the neutrals had to reckon. Of the five, only Eire ever stood a substantive risk of physical violation of its mainland territory from *both* sides in the conflict. Admittedly, this would not become clear to Spain until after 1942, to Portugal until after the Azores deal was consummated, or to Sweden until after Churchill abandoned his envisioned Norwegian enterprise. At bottom, though, for all the neutrals, the real danger emanated from Nazi Germany.

In the early days of the war, a misstep on the part of any of the five neutrals could have resulted in invasion and occupation by the Wehrmacht, the fate of the other European states that attempted the path of neutrality. As the war progressed, the power of the Allies to make the neutral capitals acquiesce to their demands increased in direct proportion to the decrease in Germany's capability to get its way by threats. But the danger from the Allies remained primarily economic thumbscrew-tightening and warnings of ostracism: the Allies never hung the threat of imminent destruction over the neutrals.

As we've seen throughout this book, a factor that played a critical role in the successful neutrality of these five states was their geography. Four lay on the periphery of the continent, outside the main concourses of the war, and thus comparatively removed from its worst dangers. The acquisition of any of the five would have been immensely desirable to the Reich. But as long as each remained amenable to the varying degrees of pressure Berlin applied, Germany chose not to occupy them—at least not while it still possessed the power to do so—to preserve its resources for other uses.

Postwar historiography has awarded first place as transgressors of the Allied cause to the Iberian states—particularly to Spain. This is irrefutable in terms of their antagonism to liberal, parliamentary democracy. Both Spain and Portugal viewed Western liberalism as the provenance of many of their problems, a view abetted by their deeply ingrained Roman Catholic doctrine. Spain had seen its empire fall to Anglo-American supremacy and to independence movements in Latin America. The painfully recent episode of a failed Spanish republican government caused the country's middle and propertied classes to cling to the simplicities and assurances of fascism. Fascist Spain had been helped into existence on the wings of the Condor Legion and the Duce's guns, and both Franco and Salazar had easily and quickly adopted the effective authoritarian methods of the major-league dictators consistent with their own values. Though Salazar's rule was gentler—was indeed described by many Westerners as the "best" and most benevolent of the dictators—neither Iberian autocrat had any desire to emulate the uncertainties and heresies of democracy.

In truth, Spain might well have entered the Axis camp as a cobelligerent had several factors interplayed differently: first, had Germany been overwhelmingly militarily successful in the fall of 1940, especially in relation to the fight against Britain; had Hitler not engaged in his pact with the Soviet Union, a state despised and feared by Catholic Iberians; had Hitler been able or willing to satisfy Franco's material and colonial demands; and had the Spanish themselves been less prickly, less proud, more yielding people. From Hitler's perspective, unquestionably the factor that kept Germany from simply taking what it wanted in Spain was that nation's ability to defend itself. As with Sweden and Switzerland, Spain represented a nut not worth cracking, at least not as long as its policies brought more good to the Axis than harm.

Though it was by no means clearly discernible in the fall of 1940 that the Reich had run into potentially fatal military obstacles in its war with Britain (and, importantly, with Britain's empire), to Franco it was nonetheless obvious that the United Kingdom was, for whatever reasons, maintaining itself. Behind Britain stood not only its vast and richly abundant colonial domain but also an America whose leadership was transparently and utterly inimical to a German victory. Franco refused to gamble everything on the Axis until Germany had unmistakably established itself as the European political force that would prevail.

As were all the successful neutrals, the Iberian states were horrified at Hitler's pact with Stalin and at the subsequent invasion and dismemberment of Catholic Poland. For Hitler, the Molotov-Ribbentrop pact was a political expediency, the German dictator not caring a particle about Russia's rejection of religion. But irrespective of Hitler's reasons, the deal Germany made with the Soviets in 1939 weighed significantly in the decision of the Iberian dictators to step back from closer ties to Germany.

At the end of its three-year-long Civil War, Spain lay ravaged. Yet it was still unable to end the war with itself, and hundreds of thousands of former Republicans and Republican sympathizers remained outside the uneasy and fragile Spanish political consensus. With his nation divided, exhausted, and parrying with famine, Franco well understood that any relationship with Germany couldn't remotely add up to one between equals. For his part, Hitler could not without dangerously overstretching his own capacities keep Spain's civil and military needs met, particularly in light of his plans to invade the Soviet Union. Nor could he satisfy Franco's colonial ambitions without forfeiting his admittedly tenuous plans to turn France into an active partner against Britain.

Less measurable but recognized by many historians as a factor in Spain's odyssey through World War II was the Spanish temperament. The Blue Division's experiences serving with the Wehrmacht made clear that Spaniards were psychologically incapable of assuming the junior status and Teutonic regimentation that German partnership would have involved. Torn by enemies from the days of Islamic expansion, most recently by Napoleonic imperialism, the country had just waged a battle to the death against the "foreign" ideology of socialism. Spain was loath to share sovereignty with yet another alien power. Franco judged that Hitler's objective was control of the peninsula, a control neither the

Caudillo nor any part of Spanish society, with the possible exception of pro-Nazi elements in the Falange, was willing to cede. Hitler's respect for the Spaniards' potential for resisting unwanted outsiders was what, in the end, decided him against moving uninvited into Spain in the sunlit days before Barbarossa.

Whether a victorious Germany in a postwar Europe might have taken on Spain, or whether in such a scenario Franco would have sent the invitation himself, or even if a more malleable puppet—perhaps Muñoz Grandes—would have drawn Spain into the role of a Vichy-like rump, is impossible to know. But in the way that history *did* play itself out, the choices Spain made worked overwhelmingly to assure an Allied victory.

The authoritarian Spain of World War II was a decidedly unpleasant place for opponents of the state, opponents both real and imagined, and its surface manifestations of sympathy for the Axis were bitterly resented by the Allies as well as by the legions of the Axis's victims. Franco's assistance to the Reich, while perhaps fathomable as payment for Berlin's help in raising his state to power, represented in the aggregate a terrible burden on the Allied cause—the granting of Spanish ports for the Wehrmacht, the sale of Spanish matériel to the Reich, the use of Spanish territory for German espionage and radar. The Blue Division, meant to placate the Germans, nonetheless killed thousands of Russians. And, quietly invidious, Franco's regime relentlessly spread pro-Axis and anti-Allied propaganda throughout Latin America, a sphere which it considered, by linguistic affinity, its own.

Sir Samuel Hoare (later Lord Templewood), London's wartime ambassador in Madrid, acidly portrayed Franco in his published account of his Spanish experiences. While admitting Spanish service to the Axis represented a kind of "Danegeld"—a tribute to secure peace—Hoare said that such Danegeld was significant in scope and freely given. Franco, according to the envoy, stayed out of the war in 1940 and 1941 not because of any love for Britain, but because "he believed he could obtain everything he wanted without fighting"—as well as the fact that almost all Spaniards opposed taking Spain into the conflict. It was an assessment shared by many other observers of Spain and World War II.

But the Germans *were* kept from acquiring a Spanish ally, from controlling an Iberian coastline, and—most consequential of all—from putting a fatal plug in the western entrance to the Mediterranean. Whether this was from a small accretion of happenstances, or—far, far more likely—from Francisco Franco's stunningly effective mastery of the art of diplomatic procrastination, is, in the end, for students of history to finally decide for themselves.

As for the state with which Spain shared its peninsula, getting safely through World War II was a case of both influencing and following Madrid. Portugal's fate was inextricably linked to Spain's in the world-wide struggle—an invasion of a hostile Spain by the Germans would have inevitably included Portugal. (Conversely, Germany knew there was no realistic way to occupy Portugal alone without gaining Spanish acquiescence or incurring Spanish hostility.) If the Germans entered the peninsula, either invited or by forcing their way, Premier Salazar took as a certainty that Portugal would come under German military dominion and be obliged either to enter the war as an Axis co-belligerent or else to endure the same dismal fate as all the other German-occupied former neutrals.

To spare Portugal this future, Salazar's key objective in the early, more dangerous years of the war was to persuade Franco, whom he knew to be under immense pressure to enter the conflict, to prevaricate with Hitler. The Portuguese dictator had little reason to think the Nazis would judge his regime of much account, and thought that Berlin likely would concur with the Falangists who asserted that Portugal had no justification to exist independently from Spain.

Throughout the war, Salazar's darkest nightmare vision was of mainland Portugal or its Atlantic provinces becoming battlefields. Once German forces established themselves in Iberia, there was a high probability that their presence would be contested by the Allies, perhaps immediately, more likely when the Anglo-American drive to regain Europe got underway. From 1940 on, a constant fear in Lisbon was of an American-led occupation of the Azores, which would—in Salazar's mind—surely prompt a German military response, if not against the islands themselves, then against mainland Portugal.

By mid-war came the realization in Lisbon that Germany's capacity to enforce its will in the peninsula was decreasing. Salazar could breathe easier, yield to Allied demands for an Azores base in the name of its antique alliance with Britain, and at the same time even line itself up a respectable place in the postwar world.

Though it would be misleading to make too much of Salazar's influence on Spanish neutrality, substantial credit must nonetheless be given the Portuguese leader. The assurances he proffered to Franco of Iberian military solidarity and the link Portugal represented between Iberia and the Allies helped allay Franco's fears of Spain's being used by the Allies as a site for future European landings.

Like its fellow neutrals—excepting only ideologically fascist Spain—Portugal opted for safety over collective security in World War II. Its people judged that a Nazi victory would have sooner or later meant the end of Portugal's autonomy, and that Nazism amounted to an unholy and barbarous order in which their Catholic faith would demand scant respect, an extension of the same fear engendered by Soviet Communism. The belief that the neutrals should have placed the continent's collective security above their own safety in their response to the Axis was the basis for the Allies' disgust with the European neutrals. Admittedly, the United States remained neutral for the first two and a half years of the war, despite its president's unambiguous understanding of the dangers of German fascism, until it was forced into that war by the stimulus of Japan's Pacific aggression. But with the zeal of the converted, once *in* the war America held the European neutrals to its own new standard.

The imperatives of collective security certainly made moral sense. The battle the Allies were waging against the Axis was a battle for all nations, for with a Nazi victory *no* people would be safe from the grotesque racial ideology and debased judicial system that characterized the Third Reich. The Nazis' adversaries and victim nations expected the neutral states to understand that reality.

Not surprisingly, the neutrals didn't view their dilemma with quite so exacting a moral compass. The governors of Eire, Sweden, Switzerland, and Portugal were often publicly hostile to Nazi ideals and German bellicosity. Within the limits of their circumstances (limits that were often extraordinarily confining), and without economically crippling themselves or angering the Nazi beast to the point of inviting attack, each (with the exception of Spain) adopted policies that tried to neutralize their contributions to the Reich and maximize their support to the anti-Nazi coalition, even in the early dangerous years of German supremacy. As the Reich's potency began to wane and the dangers correspondingly lessened, each bent its policies in varyingly unneutral shapes to the Allied cause. Afraid of the fate of the failed neutrals, none believed that active co-belligerency with the Allies would have any real effect on the war's outcome. Those worthwhile services each could perform as neutrals would have been forfeit—Sweden as a safe haven for its neighbors, Switzerland as the locus of international Red Cross activities, Portugal as an escape hatch from a tortured continent, timid Eire's help to bombed Ulster. None of these would have been possible had they been victims of the war against Hitler.

Sweden was the only one of the five European neutrals not to have its destiny controlled by a single dynamic individual in World War II. Franco, Salazar, Guisan, de Valera—these men were overwhelmingly the icons representing their nations' journeys through the war. But today few remember Per Albin Hansson, let alone regard his premiership as the key factor in the safeguarding of Sweden from a German invasion. Instead, King Gustav is more often held as the significant figure to emerge from Swedish history of the period, for although Hansson was responsible for Swedish policy, many historians believe the king's prestige was such that Hitler trusted him to abide by the form of neutrality that made Germany the principal beneficiary of Swedish economic policy.

In justice to Sweden, to retain its freedom, it had little choice. Cut off after the spring of 1940 from any potential Allied military assistance, the Swedes were forced to come to terms with the menacing presence across the two-and-three-quarter-mile-wide strait separating them from occupied Denmark. They judged that their policy benefitted conquered Norway by maintaining Sweden as a refuge. Many Norwegians, though, felt their neighbors were simply acceding to *Realpolitik* in permitting the Wehrmacht to replenish its Norwegian garrisons via Swedish territory. This consideration became a prime factor in Norway's postwar decision to join NATO—the Anglo-American-dominated alliance—rather than remain sheltered solely by the Pan Nordic bloc, with Sweden their primary helpmeet.

Stockholm's threat to destroy the ore fields critical to the German war effort would very likely not have stopped Hitler from invading Sweden had Swedish policy toward the Reich been less acquiescent. But even though the comparatively strong Swedish armed forces would not have been able to withstand a concerted German effort to occupy the country, the strength of the Swedish defenses and of the Swedish political consensus to keep them strong were unquestionably a deterrent. Had Sweden been adjudged by the German high command to be a military pushover, the occupation of that country might have been pursued along with that of Denmark and Norway in Operation Weserübung.

Sweden's sister "traditional" neutral shared this debilitating isolation through most of the war. After June 1940 Switzerland was surrounded by the Axis or by Axis-controlled territory, a reality that radically altered its behavior, policies, and options. Early on, Switzerland had stood the greatest chance of any of the neutrals of sliding into a kind of voluntary *Anschluss,* or union, with Germany. Gripped as were almost all Europeans with a fear of the Nazis, many of its politicians and leaders urged greater accommodation to the Reich. Businessmen and industrialists weren't anxious to risk their enterprises and their profits in a potentially disastrous confrontation with Germany, which most "reasonable" people felt was on its way to winning the war. In 1940, Switzerland stood at the edge of voluntary destruction.

One man represented the innate revulsion of the majority of the Swiss for Nazi Germany. Henri Guisan was for Switzerland precisely the right man at precisely the right moment. It was Guisan who took the initiative to defend his nation against the aggressor, and resolved to destroy the most valuable parts of the national infrastructure rather than turn them over to an invading Wehrmacht. With the unique authority of a wartime general that had been providentially built into the Swiss system of governance, Guisan stood up against vacillating politicians whose principal concern was too often the nation's balance sheet, and appealed to his countrymen's courage, dedication, and hard work to keep Switzerland free. Above all, Guisan recognized that neutrality without the means *and the will* to defend itself would mean little. As *Time* magazine put it, it was "dynamite, not diplomacy" that kept Switzerland an island of freedom in the middle of Hitler's Europe.

Though, as in the cases of the other successful neutrals, Switzerland was fortunate in that Germany simply never *had* to take it, the reverse is also true: Germany *would* have taken Switzerland if it had been easy enough. But the Swiss went to expensive lengths to convince Berlin otherwise, and that the advantages Berlin derived from peaceful coexistence would be violently denied if the Wehrmacht were to cross the border.

There was, however, a moral price paid by the Swiss. They provided one of the most evil governments in history with a vital part of the means by which it pursued its misdeeds. Swiss industry supplied the German economy, Swiss agriculture fed German soldiers and civilians, Swiss rails transported the muscles and sinews of the Reich to its Italian accomplice.

That said, a significant point needs to be made regarding the degree to which each of the neutrals accommodated Germany. A very major part of our revulsion with Nazism comes from an ex post facto understanding. Much of the beastliness of Hitlerism was, admittedly, evident as soon as the Third Reich began its life—its anti-Semitism, its disregard for justice, its totalitarian interference with all aspects of private life. But the overwhelming horror represented by the concentration camps, and the *Einsatz-kommandos*, and the plans for captive nations after a final Nazi victory weren't known or entirely appreciated until relatively late in the war, and were not, in fact, fully reported until after the Reich's collapse in May 1945.

Many evil regimes had with utter impunity tormented their own citizens. Yet for years after World War II it was fashionable in leading Western intellectual circles to deprecate criticism of the Soviet Union, a state governed since Stalin's accession with an iron brutality that in many respects equaled the worst depravities of Nazi Germany. The principal prey of the Nazi regime—Jews—were badly treated almost everywhere, and those who escaped from Hitler's murderous grasp found scant welcome wherever in the world they went. Nazi disrespect for the niceties of law and justice was between 1939 and 1945 at least partly mirrored in many nations around the world, and similar disrespect exists in plenitude even today.

These observations are not by way of excusing any nation's willingness to accommodate an evil that had already clearly shown its nature, but rather to suggest how in the war years things seemed far less clear to the neutrals than they would when revealed to the whole world in that war's aftermath.

Eire was a special case. The overwhelming majority of the dominion's citizenry hoped Hitlerism would be stopped—destroyed if possible—but that citizenry refused to take any central part in the struggle to achieve that end. Fueled by centuries-old hatred for England, depleted of 400,000 of its citizens by an almost literally thankless role in World War I, exhausted by a struggle for independence that was followed by a civil war, and, finally, embittered by the island's partition, Eire was determined to stay out of World War II.

Britain could, of course, neither appreciate nor even understand Eire's wartime behavior. That their languages and principal religions were different was ignored. Ireland was, to the British, simply a backward, but nonetheless inherent, part of their world. These attitudes, ingrained in generation after generation of Englishmen, would go very far in explaining Eire's unwillingness to share Britain's burden in its battle with Nazism.

As dearly as the Irish may have held their neutrality and sovereignty, their military capacity to defend such was never highly developed. That Britain retained Ulster after letting the rest of Ireland go its own way accounts in large part for the fact that Eire's neutrality was not violated by the Allies: Ulster was available to serve as a forward base from which to protect a part of Britain's sea lanes, and retaking the Treaty Ports thus never became an overwhelming necessity. Had it been and had any part of Eire been occupied by Britain, the ports would have become a legitimate German target, with all Ireland very well sliding into the war.

For the part of Ireland that remained British, the consequences of de Valera's wartime policies would leave a tragic legacy. To Ulster's Protestants, the decision to stay out of Britain's war was unforgivable, representing a moral failing on the part of the Catholic south that has helped ensure the barrier of distrust remains high between these two peoples.

•   •   •

Of the score of the continent's "neutrals" at war's outbreak, only this handful successfully maintained their outsider status. There were, to paraphrase one Swedish historian, more Norways—and Hollands and Belgiums and Hungarys and Greeces—than there were Swedens.

Even if mere declarations of neutrality may not have much meaning in a nuclear context, it would seem that, since the war, military capacity has been perceived as the most effective guarantor of neutrality, an observation borne out by the astronomical levels of military spending in virtually every country in the world. The deadly procession of quite ordinary wars has in the nearly half century since the last worldwide struggle gone on unabated. And while most of the several score of new states created in that half century have solemnly proclaimed their total neutrality in conflicts between each other and between the powers, they have nonetheless continued their small-time slaughters with an abandon that defies understanding.

The lessons learned about European neutrality in World War II seem most clearly to underline its failure, and remain all-too-depressingly valid today.

APPENDIX

Eamon de Valera's Reply to
Winston Churchill

May 1945

Certain newspapers have been very persistent in looking for my answer to Mr. Churchill's recent broadcast. I know the kind of answer I am expected to make. I know the answer that first springs to the lips of every man of Irish blood who heard or read that speech no matter in what circumstances or in what part of the world he found himself. I know the reply I would have given a quarter of a century ago.

But I have deliberately decided that that is not the reply I shall make tonight. I shall strive not to be guilty of adding any fuel to the flames of hatred and passion which, if continued to be fed, promise to burn up whatever is left by the war of decent human feeling in Europe. Allowances can be made for Mr. Churchill's statement, however unworthy, in the first blush of his victory. No such excuse can be found for me in this quieter atmosphere.

There are, however, some things which it is my duty to say, some things which it is essential to say. I shall try to say them as dispassionately as I can.

Mr. Churchill makes it clear that in certain circumstances he would have violated our neutrality and that he would justify his action by Britain's necessity. It seems strange to me that Mr. Churchill does not see that this, if accepted, would mean that Britain's necessity would become the moral code and that, when this necessity was sufficiently great, other people's rights were not to count.

It is quite true that other Great Powers believe in this same code in their own regard and have behaved in accordance with it. That is precisely why we have the disastrous successions of wars, World War Number One and World War Number Two; and shall it be World War Number Three? Surely Mr. Churchill must see that, if his contention be admitted in our regard, a like justification can be framed for similar acts of aggression elsewhere and no small nation adjoining a Great Power could ever hope to be permitted to go its own way in peace.

It is indeed fortunate that Britain's necessity did not reach the point where Mr. Churchill would have acted. All credit to him that he successfully resisted the temptation which, I have no doubt, many times assailed him in his difficulties and to which I freely admit many leaders might have easily succumbed. It is indeed hard for the strong to be just to the weak, but acting justly always has its rewards. By resisting his temptation in this instance Mr. Churchill, instead of adding another sordid chapter to the already blood-stained record of the relations between England and this country, has advanced the cause of international morality an important step, one of the most important indeed that can be taken on the road to the establishment of any sure basis for peace. As far as the peoples of these two islands are concerned, it may perhaps mark a fresh beginning toward the realization of that mutual comprehension to which Mr. Churchill has referred and for which he has prayed and for which I hope he will not merely pray but work also, as did his predecessor who will yet, I believe, find the honored place in British history which is due to him; certainly he will find it in any fair record of the relations between Britain and ourselves.

That Mr. Churchill should be irritated when our neutrality stood in the way of what he thought he vitally needed I understand, but that he or any thinking person in Britain or elsewhere should fail to see the reason for our neutrality I find it hard to conceive. I would like to put a hypothetical question. It is a question I have put to many Englishmen since the last war. Suppose Germany had won the war, had invaded and occupied England and that, after a long lapse of time and many bitter struggles she was finally brought to acquiesce in admitting England's right to freedom and let England go. But not the whole of England, all but, let us say, the six southern counties. Those six southern counties, those commanding the entrance to the narrow seas, Germany however singled out and insisted on holding herself with a view to weakening England as a whole and maintaining the security of her own communications through the Straits of Dover. Let us suppose further that, after all this had happened, Germany was engaged in a great war in which she could show that she was on the side of the freedom of a number of small nations. Would Mr. Churchill as an Englishman who believed that his own nation had as good a right to freedom as any other, not freedom for a part merely but freedom for the whole, would he, while Germany still maintained the partition of his country and occupied six counties of it, would he lead this partitioned England to join with Germany in a crusade? I do not think Mr. Churchill would. Would he think the people of partitioned England an object of shame if they stood neutral in such circumstances? I do not think Mr. Churchill would.

Mr. Churchill is proud of Britain's stand alone after France had fallen and before America entered the war. Could he not find in his heart the generosity to acknowledge that there is a small nation that stood alone not for one year or two but for several hundred years against aggression, that endured spoliation, famines, massacres, in endless succession, that was clubbed many times into insensibility but that each time on returning consciousness took up the fight anew, a small nation that could never be got to accept defeat and has never surrendered her soul?

Mr. Churchill is justly proud of his nation's perseverance against heavy odds. But we in this island are still prouder of our people's perseverance for freedom through all the centuries. We of our time have played our part in that perseverance and we have pledged ourselves to the dead generations who have preserved intact for us this glorious heritage that we too will strive to be faithful to the end and pass on this tradition unblemished.

Many a time in the past there appeared little hope except that hope to which Mr. Churchill referred that, by standing fast, the time would come when, to quote his words, "The tyrant would make some ghastly mistake which would alter the whole balance of the struggle." I sincerely trust however that it is not thus our ultimate unity and freedom will be achieved though, as a younger man, I confess I prayed even for that and indeed at times saw no other.

In later years I have had a vision of a much nobler and better ending; better for both our peoples and for the future of mankind. For that I have now been long working. I regret that it is not to this nobler purpose that Mr. Churchill is lending his hand rather than by the abuse of a people who have done him no wrong, trying to find in a crisis like the present an excuse for continuing the injustice of the mutilation of our country. I sincerely hope that Mr. Churchill has not deliberately chosen the latter course but if he has, however regretfully we may say it, we can only say "Be it so."

Meanwhile, even as a partitioned small nation we shall go on and strive to play our parts in the world, continuing unswervingly to work for the cause of true freedom and for peace and understanding between all nations. As a community which has been mercifully spared from all the major sufferings as well as from the blinding hates and rancors engendered by the present war, we shall endeavor to render thanks to God by playing a Christian part in helping, so far as a small nation can, to bind up some of the gaping wounds of suffering humanity.[1]

NOTES

INTRODUCTION

1. Though often counted as one of the successful European neutrals of World War II, Turkey is not, of course, primarily European; nor did it end that conflict as a neutral: Ankara declared war on the Axis in February 1945, chiefly to gain the qualification for charter status in the new United Nations Organization. (Sweden would become a UN member in 1946, while Portugal, Spain, and Eire were admitted in 1955; Switzerland is not a member.)

2. Plus the tiny independent territories of Andorra, Liechtenstein, and Vatican City.

3. Iberia, or the Iberian Peninsula, is the great southwestern European peninsula occupied by Spain and Portugal; it is so called for the ancient name of the Ebro River, the Iberus.

4. Kay, 124 ff.

5. Gordon, 4.

6. Loenroth, *Scandinavian Journal of History*, February 1977, 89–105.

7. There is some difficulty in what to call the non-British part of the island at this time. "Eire" was the co-official Irish (Gaelic) language name, but officially it theoretically included Northern Ireland as well. Legally a British dominion, the south wasn't yet the "Republic," a status it wouldn't achieve until 1949. Just calling it "Ireland" doesn't distinguish between the south and Northern Ireland (commonly called Ulster). Perhaps "the Twenty-six Counties"—a term often used during the war in Ireland and Britain—is the clearest name. Although Northern Ireland was (and still is) called "Ulster," this term isn't perfect either; the ancient province of Ulster contained nine counties, only six of which constituted "Northern Ireland." (Monaghan, Cavan, and Donegal joined the south; Londonderry, Tyrone, Fermanagh, Armagh, Down, and Antrim remained British-governed.)

8. Quoted in Schwarz, 155.

CHAPTER I: Provenance

1. Quoted in Shirer, 598–599.

2. This did not stop the Swiss general staff from holding joint defense talks with the French, about which more later.

3. Early in 1939 the British and the French issued the same sort of pledge regarding the Netherlands, Belgium, and Switzerland: the Swiss rejected it, telling London and Paris they would ask for help if and when help was needed.

4. Schwarz, 6.

5. Bonjour quoted in Schwarz, 7.

6. Today Gustloff is remembered—if at all—for little other than that one of the fun ships of the Nazi Kraft durch Freude (Strength Through Joy) vacation organization was named for him. That ship's February 1945 sinking by a Soviet submarine as it evacuated Germans from an East Prussia being overrun by the Red Army ranks as the greatest civilian maritime disaster in history—more than 7,000 of its 8,000 passengers drowned in the catastrophe.

7. The 1938 Austrian *Anschluss* was the amalgamation of that independent republic into the German Reich.

8. Lyon, 152.

9. After which the entire country is called today (somewhat as the Netherlands is commonly called Holland after its nucleus territory).

10. Werner Richter, "The War Pattern of Swiss Life," *Foreign Affairs*, July 1944.

11. Even if, as historian William Martin suggests, this defeat wasn't the actual cause of Switzerland's decision to stay out of other nations' affairs, it did represent the peak and the end of Swiss military glory, and certainly within a few years the nation's leaders came to see the benefits of neutrality. Discussed in Soloveytchik, 160.

12. Quoted in Black, 21.

13. Bonjour, 112. The League nonetheless acknowledged Switzerland's "peculiar position" of longtime neutrality and guaranteed its territorial integrity.

14. Hughes, 150.

15. A smaller tunnel, the Tauern, connected Salzburg and the Tyrol with the gateway to the Italian far northeast—Venice and Trieste.

16. Schwarz, 4.

17. Such was the case in 1939; today the Ministry of Agriculture and Industry has been renamed Public Economy, and Posts and Railways is now Transport, Communications, and Energy.

18. Munro, 780–782.

19. German, French, Italian, and Romansch are the four official languages of the Swiss Confederation, the last recognized as coequal with the first three in 1937.

20. A general can also be elected in times of "national emergency." In peacetime, corps commander constitutes the highest rank.

21. The Gothic historian Jordanes wrote of Scandinavia as the "matrix and mold of the [East Germanic] peoples."

22. "Rus" is nearly the same as the modern Finnish and Estonian word for Swedes. The word "Rus" comes from the district on the east coast of Sweden called Roden, or Rots.

23. Quoted in *Sweden: A Wartime Survey*, 24.

24. The essentially ceremonial office of president (and thus head of state) was held by Douglas Hyde.

25. DGFP, Vol. VII, 422–423.

26. DGFP, Vol. VII, 471–472. Italics mine.

27. Longford, 349.

28. "Celt," or "Kelt," is a cognate of the word "Gaul."

29. Pronounced "shin fane."

30. Gunther, 371.

31. *Eamon de Valera Centenary*, 13 ff.

32. *Time*, March 25, 1940.

33. The parliament itself was called the Oireachtas; its equivalent of a House of Lords was the Senate, with minimum powers; the Dáil was the lower but far more powerful chamber.

34. Northern Protestant leaders were responsible for leaving the three less Protestant counties of Ulster—Donegal, Monaghan, and Louth—out of the new entity; northern politicians feared that otherwise the overwhelming Protestant majority in the seceding six counties would be watered down.

35. The 1937 constitution did not recognize the *permanent* partition of the island, but held that the constitution applied only to the "former" Free State's territory pending the reintegration of the northern six counties into the whole. The constitution was considered by Dublin to apply to the "whole island of Ireland, its islands, and its territorial seas."

36. Although "Ireland" was still official, "Eire" was considered the *first* official name. Both names were meant to apply to the whole island, awaiting reintegration of Ulster.

37. Pronounced "Cove."

38. Toynbee, 234.

39. Fisk, 9.

40. *Time*, November 18, 1940.

41. Nowland & Williams, 15.

42. Hughes, 302.

43. Thomas, 16.

44. Thomas, 31.

45. Gunther, 218.

46. Within a year, Franco would merge the two parties—the Falange and the

Carlists—into the Falange Española Tradicionalista, thereafter the Nationalists' official party, or *partido único*.

47. Payne, A *History of Spain and Portugal*, 654.

48. John C. Cudahy, *Life*, March 31, 1941.

49. Some historians question whether the crash was an accident.

50. He was the youngest general in any European army when promoted in 1926 at the age of thirty-four to flag rank.

51. Today solemnly called El Ferrol del Caudillo.

52. Whealey, 135.

53. Hitler also dispatched a number of tank units as well as sundry specialist personnel to the Spanish fronts.

54. Whealey, 11.

55. He would be executed in November 1936.

56. Whealey, 103. Thomas says 50,000 Italian soldiers fought in Spain.

57. The anti-clericalism was more likely uncontrolled mob action than official policy of the Azaña government.

58. Communists wouldn't enter the Popular Front government itself until September, when the socialist Francisco Largo Caballero replaced the liberal José Giral as premier.

59. Hughes, 308.

60. Jackson, 50.

61. Taylor, 120.

62. France did ship twenty Potez aircraft to the Republic just before the Non-Intervention Agreement went into effect on August 8.

63. Calvocoressi & Wint, 61.

64. Gunther, 232.

65. Earlier, on taking Badajoz, near the Portuguese border, 4,000 captured Loyalist civilians and militiamen were machine-gunned in a gruesome fusillade in the city's bullring. Gunther, 222.

66. Franco would often and loudly decry Basque (and Catalan) demands for autonomy as undisguised efforts to Balkanize Spain and thus weaken its central government.

67. Thomas, 607.

68. Eubank, 69.

69. Whealey, 135.

70. This illegitimate son of Pedro the Cruel was, incidentally, the first foreign monarch to receive the Order of the Garter, England's premier mark of chivalry.

71. Figueiredo, 94.

72. Gallagher, 10.

73. Kay, 17.

74. *Life*, July 29, 1940.

75. The Portuguese equivalent of Harvard, Oxford, Cambridge, and the École Polytechnique put together.

76. Portuguese names are a combination of patronymic (first) and matronymic (second); the shortened version of one's name is generally the matronymic.

77. Gunther, 234.

78. This was his salary in 1941. With the resources of the state at his disposal, it is likely he made the salary go a long way.

79. *Life*, July 29, 1940.

80. Portugal had its own version of the German Hitler Jugend and the Italian Ballilla, called the Mucidade. All were distinguished by their straight-arm salute.

81. Gallagher, 52.

82. Payne, *A History of Spain and Portugal*, 663.

83. Marques, 214–215.

84. Salazar's opponents did make common cause with the Republic, though; a Portuguese warship mutinied in the Tagus, planning to go to the Loyalists' aid—Salazar ordered it blown out of the water.

85. Franco's Burgos-based regime was formally recognized by the Portuguese government in May 1938.

86. The leader of the Spanish insurgency, General Sanjurjo, was on his way home from a Lisbon airfield at the beginning of the insurgency when, as many historians have it, he was assassinated.

CHAPTER II: The War Begins

1. Moos, *Yale Review*, September 1943.

2. Meier, 266.

3. Guisan, of course, spoke perfect Schwyzertüsch, the "Swiss-German" dialect that Germans revel in ridiculing.

4. During World War I, he had been attached to the Allied armies as an observer.

5. Schwarz, 2.

6. The general also placed heavy troop concentrations at the portals of the two critically important Alpine tunnels, the St. Gotthard and the Simplon; the area around the Swiss entrance to the St. Gotthard tunnel soon came to be the most heavily fortified place in the world, its defenses exceeding even those at the ends of the Panama Canal.

7. The war was anything but dormant at sea, however.

8. Hughes, 151–152.

9. Schwarz, 15–20.

10. Gordon and Dangerfield, 37.

11. Before the war, Switzerland had imported annually 1.8 million tons of coal from Germany and 300,000 tons from Britain; the coal imports from Germany rose during the war until 1942, when they started to slide, reaching virtual zero by 1945, while imports from Britain were almost completely halted with the onset of war.

12. Schwarz, 91.

13. Schwarz, 132.

14. In World War I, many POWs and deserters fled to Switzerland and there received refuge. Marrus, 154.

15. Toynbee, 205–206.

16. As Switzerland only had about 9,000 native Jews, there were few co-religionists to effectively lobby Bern for less harsh immigration policies. Marrus, 155.

17. Marrus, 252.

18. The latter part of his title honored Gustav's ancient forebears; there is also still a city of Gothenburg and an island of Gotland in Sweden to commemorate these ancient Nordic warriors.

19. At the time of his accession in 1907, only 9.5 percent of Swedes were eligible to vote in a country in which property ownership was still a requirement for suffrage.

20. Queen Victoria had died in 1930.

21. Lady Louise was born Princess Louise of Battenberg; her long Anglicized family dropped its royal status and took on British nobility (the family name was anglicized to Mountbatten) in the anti-German hysteria in Britain during World War I.

22. Later in the war he would become Chief of Combined Operations, and after the war the last viceroy of India and its first governor-general.

23. Gunther, 500.

24. Gunther, 500.

25. Iron ore wasn't the only fruit of Sweden's soil that was catnip to the Germans. There was also arsenic, a mineral from which a poisonous gas can be made; such gases based on arsenic had been one of the grislier discoveries to emerge from World War I. Sweden's arsenic mines, discovered after the end of the Great War, were located at Boliden, west of the port of Skelleftea on the Gulf of Bothnia. The mines were first exploited by Ivar Krueger, the "Swedish match king," whose suicide in Paris in 1932, a result of his financial empire's crumbling in the chaos of international bank failures, dominated headlines around the world. Though the mines were first thought to contain only gold, the discovery of the richest arsenic source in the world sent a collective scare through Sweden: the country knew that, like its iron ore, arsenic was another mineral that would enhance Sweden's appeal to a belligerent dictator.

26. Sweden Speaks, 1939.

27. Toynbee, 177.

28. Toynbee, 179.

29. Fox, 120.

30. Fewer than 5 percent of enlistment-age men would be exempted—primarily on grounds of physical shortcomings—by 1941. Sweden: A Wartime Survey, 28.

31. As in the United States after December 1941, Swedish automobile man-

ufacturers turned their production to military aircraft after the German attack on Poland. Similarly, Swedish match manufacturers switched the bulk of their production to ammunition, and hunting-rifle makers transformed their production into machine guns.

32. Elting, 106.

33. In formal terms, the main Nazi representative in Sweden in 1939 was Prince Viktor zu Wied, head of one of the largest German embassies Ribbentrop's Foreign Ministry maintained.

34. Root, Vol. I, 76.

35. Shirer, *The Challenge of Scandinavia*, 327.

36. Most of the world sympathized with the Finns; though Germany half-heartedly defended its Soviet co-conspirators, Italy and Japan publicly deplored the Soviet demands.

37. Engel and Paananen, vii.

38. Shirer, *Challenge*, 330–331.

39. Fodor, 126.

40. Engle, 143.

41. Fodor, 156.

42. Quoted in Mansergh, 64.

43. Fisk, 114.

44. Quoted in Carroll, 19.

45. Quoted in Mansergh, 75.

46. Referring to the IRA's terror campaign in Britain, unrelated directly to the war. See below.

47. Churchill, *The Gathering Storm*, 382.

48. Fodor, 178.

49. DGFP, Vol. VIII, 241.

50. Duggan, 127.

51. Eden was still convinced of the need for at least a minister-surrogate in Dublin, but he thought anyone called an ambassador would be too "portentous." Incidentally, as far as London was concerned, Maffey remained *officially* "United Kingdom Representative *in* Eire." Fisk, 106.

52. He didn't leave the post until November 1949.

53. Quoted in Longford, 353.

54. Longford, 354.

55. Keogh, 116.

56. Nowland, 20.

57. Longford & O'Neill, 348.

58. Longford & O'Neill, 348.

59. Young, *An Cosantóir*, September 1989, 33–38.

60. Young, 36.

61. Share, 45.

62. Stewart, *The Nation*, January 31, 1942, 140.

63. Longford, 356.

64. Fisk, 85.
65. Fodor, 179. Bell 102.
66. Quoted in Mansergh, 61.
67. Longford, 358.
68. *Time*, January 15, 1940.
69. Gervasi, 263.
70. Gervasi, 264.
71. Roucek, 369.
72. Root, Vol. II, 84.
73. Gallo, 87.
74. Irrespective of his sympathy for a fellow Catholic state, the Caudillo held Poland at least partly responsible for the war with Germany because of its refusal to compromise on the issue of the Corridor. Payne, *The Franco Regime,*256.
75. Toynbee, 266.
76. Franco envisioned turning Vigo into Spain's chief seaport (in place of Barcelona), with the hope that it would replace Lisbon as the European terminus for transatlantic flying. *Newsweek*, December 11, 1939.
77. Fodor, 79.
78. When the pact was announced, the leading Falangist newspaper headlined it "Surprise, a Tremendous Surprise." Payne, *Franco Regime*, 255–256.
79. Gallo, 86.
80. Payne, *Franco Regime*, 256–257.
81. Hughes, 231.
82. Fodor, 78.
83. Payne, *Falange*, 212.
84. Payne, *Falange*, 224.
85. The authorities made amends by roping off a section of the beach solely for diplomats, but when it got around that the city's sewer emptied into the bay just beyond the privileged part of the strand, diplomatic bathing at San Sebastián lost its cachet.
86. Hamilton, 207.
87. Hamilton, 209.
88. Gervasi, 264.
89. Hills, 334.
90. Whipple, 48.
91. Much of the same realization struck Mussolini. Despite his longings to return Italy to a new Roman imperial era, he quickly declared his neutrality in September 1939, largely because 80 percent of Italy's imports came by sea, and since Britain controlled that sea, it could cut off those goods if the Duce made war against Britain and its allies.
92. Kay, 128.
93. David Scott, *News Chronicle*, September 10, 1940.
94. Salazar was from 1936 to 1947 his own foreign and war ministers.
95. Figueiredo, 90.

96. Figueiredo, 97.

97. DGFP, Vol. VII, 290.

98. DGFP, Vol. VII, 441.

99. During World War II, Portugal would in fact lose one of its overseas colonial possessions, not to the British but to the Japanese. Portuguese Timor, an island in the Lesser Sundas in the Malay Archipelago, which it shared with the Netherlands, was occupied by the Imperial Japanese Army in February 1942.

100. Figueiredo, 97.

CHAPTER III: War in the West

1. Quoted in Shirer, *Rise & Fall*, 681. Admiral Raeder himself also pointed out the implications to Sweden of the operation: "If Germany occupies Norway, it can also exert heavy pressure on Sweden, which would then be obliged to meet all our demands." Fox, 131.

2. Quoted in Elting, 45.

3. Quoted in Wright, 65.

4. So called because of its size relative to standard battleships—about 12,000 tons displacement compared to 35,000 tons. "Pocket battleship" was their Western name; the Germans called them *Panzerschiffe*, or "armored ships."

5. Thinking Britain would agree to peace, Hitler held the *Graf Spee* in check for three weeks after war broke out.

6. Swedish intelligence was able to inform both the Norwegians and the Danes of the impending attack several days before it was launched, but neither country believed the reports were accurate. Scott, 504.

7. The loss of Denmark quickly highlighted the importance of Greenland and Iceland, the former a Danish colony, the latter an independent state tied to the mother country by a common king. The United States immediately took over Greenland, an island that clearly could not be allowed to come under Nazi control; the Danish minister in Washington reported that a large German force was gathering in northern Norway preparing to leave for Greenland. The Icelandic government renounced its last tie with Denmark—allegiance to its king— after Denmark fell. Though it would have preferred to sit out the war without any foreign troops on its soil, Iceland knew it was vulnerable to a German invasion, and invited U.S. and British forces to station themselves there to protect the country. Root, Vol. I, 54.

8. The German surface fleet suffered losses in the Norwegian campaign from which it never recovered, though these losses were not decisive in the campaign itself.

9. In their planning for Weserübung, the Germans knew that supplying Narvik by sea would be extremely difficult, and fully expected to "request" permission from the Swedes to use Swedish railroads to supply their garrison there. West, 77.

10. Hitler considered ordering the commander to take his troops into Sweden and internment before allowing them to be captured by the Allies and the Norwegians.

11. Lewin, 106.

12. DGFP, Vol. IX, 142.

13. The Swedes would not be able to turn to the Hague treaties to seek the protection of international convention on the German demands; the framers of those treaties never considered the possibility of this sort of use of a neutral's territory by a belligerent. Kansas City *Star*, May 5, 1943.

14. Toynbee, 178–182.

15. West, 76 ff.

16. Shortly after the invasion of Norway, Swedish Army chief of staff Axel Ruppe assessed the situation: "To the extent the Germans can maintain their sea communications with Norway intact we may not be subjected to such heavy pressure, but if this is not possible there will certainly be immediate demands on us to make territory and railroads available to them. . . . The most immediate demand would probably be to ship supplies to their troops in Narvik." West, 76.

17. Nissen, 105.

18. Fox, 129.

19. Scott, 505.

20. DGFP, Vol. IX, 245–246.

21. Fox, 128.

22. DGFP, Vol. IX, 226.

23. DGFP, Vol. IX, 245.

24. West, 79.

25. DGFP, Vol. IX, 258.

26. New York *Post*, May 1, 1940.

27. West, 78–79.

28. The Germans had granted Sweden safe-conduct passes—their own version of navicerts—for a small number of ships to pass through their net, but goods bound for Allied countries were strictly banned. Both blocs closely checked this Swedish shipping: Germans to make sure nothing was intended for reshipment to Britain, the Allies to make sure no goods for Germany were sent on the return leg. Small amounts of matériel bound for Britain could get out through Petsamo, in northern Finland, but this represented a tiny fraction of the 70 percent of its prewar exports to countries other than Germany. Gordon, 62 & 75.

29. Through intelligence sources of their own, both King Leopold of the Belgians and Queen Wilhelmina of the Netherlands had warned the British the prior November 7 of imminent German attack, an attack that had been planned but postponed. Bradford, 309.

30. Churchill wished governments of countries overrun by the Germans to form "free Allied governments" in London, not only to serve as a rallying point for whatever fighting forces could be gotten out of those countries but also to

allow the legal Allied appropriation of any funds outside the captured countries. Bradford, 317.

31. Hitler was also concerned about the succession of water lines around Dunkirk, obstacles he feared would ensnare his tanks.

32. These figures vary by source; quoted figures are from Wright.

33. De Gaulle led the only real French counterattack in the entire Battle of France; he advanced to within a mile of Guderian's forward headquarters before massed Stukas drove him off.

34. Keegan, 85.

35. The entire ceremony was repeated the next day, in Italy, where the French delegation was flown, so Mussolini could savor the same experience.

36. Schwarz, 37–38.

37. Schwarz, 29–31.

38. Switzerland would for another two years maintain a semi-open window on the outer world, through its short frontier with Vichy France, in the Geneva area.

39. This was Pilet-Golaz's second term in the presidency; he first held the office in 1934.

40. Historian George Soloveytchik has noted that Pilet-Golaz was handicapped by having followed a genuine statesman and internationally respected Swiss, Giuseppe Motta, who died in January 1940. Probably Switzerland's greatest diplomat, Motta had dominated his nation's public life for a quarter of a century at his death. The tragedy of Motta's later years was his attachment to Mussolini, an ardor that remained strong long after the Italian dictator's excesses had become evident. Nonetheless, his carefully nurtured image as a "simple Swiss democrat" had for many years endeared him to the Swiss people. Soloveytchik, 227 ff.

41. Schwarz, 38.

42. His Council colleagues, Philipp Etter and Enrico Celio, simultaneously repeated the speech in German and Italian.

43. Soloveytchik, 253.

44. Quoted in Schwarz, 53–54.

45. DGFP, Vol. IX, 364–365.

46. DGFP, Vol. VIII, 772.

47. Kimche, 64.

48. Throughout the Battle of France, German planes that strayed over Swiss airspace were fired at and sometimes shot down by the Swiss Air Force. After June 1, any German plane planning to cross Swiss territory was required to request an escort of Swiss Me-109s, doubly incensing the Germans because the Me-109s had been bought from Germany. Schwarz, 32.

49. Schwarz, 49.

50. Guisan had public opinion sampled to ascertain popular acceptance of

the plan, with the results showing that the majority of the people, evidently fed up with German threats, supported the commander-in-chief. Fodor, 50.

51. *Fortune*, September 1941, 74.

52. The Reich even demanded that the Swiss extend credit to German buyers, a practice which the normally cash-and-carry Swiss sometimes were forced to accept. *Fortune*, September 1941, 74.

53. *Fortune*, September 1941, 114.

54. Thueren, 157.

55. Schwarz, 18–24.

56. *Time*, November 18, 1940.

57. West, 80.

58. West, 86.

59. West, 86.

60. West, 87. On the other side of the equation, the cost of an occupation was a factor in Berlin's thinking, as was the conjectured reaction of Germany's nominal ally, the Soviet Union.

61. West, 89.

62. West, 90.

63. The pertinent section of the telegram: "Great Britain's official attitude will for the present be that war must go on, but Butler assured me that no opportunity to reach compromise peace would be missed if reasonable terms were obtainable, no diehards would be permitted to stand in their way. He considered that Great Britain had stronger negotiating power now than might be the case later on and that Russia would play a more important part than the United States if conversations were to start. During our talks Butler was called in to Halifax and returned with a greeting to me saying 'common sense, not bravado' would dictate British Government policy. Halifax added that such a message would be welcomed by the Swedish Minister, but that it must not be interpreted to mean 'peace at any price.' From talks with other MPs it would appear that if and when the prospect of negotiations should arise possibly after June 28 Halifax might succeed Churchill."

64. West, 91. Historian John M. West speculates on whether the threatened "coercive measures" would really have been implemented in the form of a German attack on Sweden; he cites the lack of evidence for a substantive German buildup targeted at Sweden, but also notes that in the case of Yugoslavia an attack was carried out with very little advance preparation time involved. Further, West notes that German troops were not at this precise time tied down with attacks on any other fronts. Notes, West.

65. The press was also informed of the decision, but was not immediately allowed to publish it. Toynbee, 184.

66. Toynbee, 184.

67. West, 93.

68. Toynbee, 184.

69. Britain informed Sweden that even if the Americans had been willing to

sell the aircraft, the United Kingdom intended in any event to block their actual delivery. Toynbee, 185.

70. Joesten, *Background: The Key to Current Events*, 13.

71. *Sweden: A Wartime Survey*, 193–194.

72. Root, Vol. I, 77.

73. Root, Vol. I, 78.

74. Root, Vol. I, 78.

75. *Background: The Key to Current Events*, July 1942, 13.

76. Joesten, *Hitler's Secret Ally*, 14.

77. Mansergh, 69.

78. Mansergh, 69.

79. Mansergh, 66.

80. Longford, 372–373.

81. David Gray, the American minister, said in August that de Valera was pursuing so anti-IRA a policy that the best the Taoiseach could expect if the Germans ever got control of Ireland was "to be liquidated painlessly." Dwyer, 210. Bowman, 212.

82. Hempel didn't share the Taoiseach's concern about the strength of the IRA. In a telegram to the Foreign Ministry in Berlin, he said: "The danger of internal disturbances on the part of the IRA, which might obtain a large increase in members, would not be sufficient against the strong resistance of de Valera. . . . I assume at the same time, however, especially in the case of a German intervention in advance of one by England, that . . . it would be, on the whole, a reliable tool in the hands of the Government and would obey its orders." DGFP, May 23, 1940, Vol. IX, p. 423.

83. Donald W. Mitchell, *The Nation*, January 31, 1942, 136.

84. Mansergh, 72.

85. From September 1939 through June 1940, the Allies had lost 702 merchant ships totaling 234 million tons; after France's fall, the losses rose precipitously—rising to 1,235,000 tons from January to March 1941 alone. *Times Atlas of the Second World War*, 48.

86. *Irish Press*, November 6, 1940. In a March 1938 House of Commons debate, Churchill himself had taunted Chamberlain with blame for relinquishing the ports and said Britain would have no right to retake them, saying to do so and thus violate Irish neutrality would bring the United Kingdom international scorn. It was probably because of Churchill's comments on that occasion, historian Nicholas Mansergh surmises, that Hempel repeatedly counseled his government that there was little likelihood Britain would move on the ports. Mansergh, 65.

87. Quoted in Mitchell & Snodaigh, 224.

88. Quoted in Fisk, 172.

89. Because Chamberlain had as prime minister been the moving spirit behind the return of the Treaty Ports, Churchill entrusted him with the responsibility for these negotiations. Bowman, 220.

90. Fisk, 486. Longford, 366.

91. Toynbee, 239.

92. Bowman, 224.

93. Bowman, 228.

94. Quoted in Bowman, 231.

95. *The Times*, July 5, 1940.

96. Manchester *Guardian*, November 21, 1940.

97. And as a result of which the historic and lifesaving Lend-Lease program was instituted by the United States.

98. Churchill, *Their Finest Hour*, 479–480. Italics the author's.

99. Fisk, 159 ff.

100. Loewenheim, Langley & Jonas, 127.

101. Fodor, 181.

102. *Time*, November 18, 1940.

103. Fisk, 368.

104. Quoted in Longford, 377.

105. Fodor, 181.

106. *Newsweek*, May 20, 1940.

107. *Daily Herald*, January 7, 1941.

108. Longford, 380–381.

109. Duggan, 138.

110. This compares, for example, to the Coventry raid in which 554 were killed; the Belfast raid was one of the most devastating on the British provincial cities during the war.

111. Historian Robert Fisk concludes that the German fliers may have inadvertently dropped their bombs on civilian areas, having mistaken them for the harbor. Fisk, 486.

112. Fisk, 505.

113. It might be noted that no Irish were conscripted during World War I, when all Ireland was under British rule.

114. Quoted in Longford, 384.

115. Quoted in Fisk, 513.

116. Longford, 385.

117. Quoted in Longford, 386.

118. *Newsweek*, June 9, 1941.

119. The connection wasn't quite as neat as it might have been. The railroad cars of France and Germany, running on a 4-foot-8½-inch gauge, would find themselves unable to proceed on the Spanish lines, built on a 5-foot-6-inch gauge. Admittedly, the Spanish railways in the early 1940s were in such poor repair they wouldn't have done the Wehrmacht much immediate good anyway.

120. Franco was parroting Mussolini's use of the "nonbelligerent" label in Italy's prewar relationship with Nazi Germany. Historian James Cortada writes that "neutrality" connotes "a state of impartiality in a conflict between two or more powers," while "nonbelligerency" is a "legal state . . . signifying 'various

shades of partiality toward the contending parties, but stops short of war in the full legal sense,' allowing a nation to make commitments to a belligerent short of war but without violation of neutrality or state of war clauses in international law." Cortada, *Wolfram and World War II*, 30–31.

121. Gallo, 108.

122. For example, the amount of oil allowed into Spain through the navicert/embargo system was dropped, reducing the country's stocks to a level that would last it only for two and a half months, an amount London felt would not entice the Spanish into selling or trading what it could get by without to Germany for foreign exchange.

123. Hitler reportedly intended to turn the bastion over to Spanish sovereignty if German troops seized and secured it. Ansel, 41.

124. Beaulac, 2. In an effort to demonstrate its own sympathies for Spain's imperial aspirations, the British government announced it approved of Spain's taking "her rightful place . . . as a great Mediterranean power . . ." in seeking an expanded zone in Morocco. Payne, *The Franco Regime*, 274.

125. Churchill, *Their Finest Hour*, 443.

126. Toynbee, 286.

127. Churchill wrote to Roosevelt on this point on November 23, 1940: ". . . The Rock of Gibraltar will stand a long siege, but what is the good of that if we cannot use the harbour or pass the Straits? . . . We must gain as much time as possible." Churchill, *Their Finest Hour*, 452. Some high-ranking members of the Wehrmacht believed that Britain would not fight to the death over Gibraltar. In his war diary, General Franz Halder wrote that "Gibraltar is merely a symbol of prestige. I think it is by no means impossible that the British might evacuate Gibraltar of their own accord in the face of preparations for an assault, since a voluntary evacuation would not be as much of a blow to their prestige as would be the loss of the fortress after a struggle. Should the British decide to hold, however, we would find it necessary to secure the entire peninsula right down to its southern tip, or else it might become another Alcázar." Burdick & Jacobsen, 1200. In his own war memoirs, Churchill writes that so great a danger to Britain was posed by the loss of Gibraltar that "for nearly two years we kept constantly at a few days' notice an expedition of over five thousand men and their ships, ready to seize the Canary Islands, by which we could maintain air and sea control over the U-boats, and contact with Australasia round the Cape, if ever the harbour of Gibraltar were denied to us by the Spaniards." Churchill, *Their Finest Hour*, 443–444. In April 1941, Churchill wrote again to Roosevelt on this subject, telling him that "the moment Spain gives way or is attacked we shall dispatch two expeditions which we have long been holding in readiness, one from Britain to one of the islands in the Azores, and subsequently to a second island, and the second expedition to do the same in the Cape Verdes." Churchill, *The Grand Alliance*, 121.

128. In June, the British foreign secretary asked Churchill if offering to negotiate Gibraltar's status at war's end mightn't be a useful way to gain Spanish

sympathy. In a perspicacious reply, the prime minister wrote: "I am sure we shall gain nothing by offering to 'discuss' Gibraltar at the end of the war. Spaniards will know that, if we win, discussions would not be fruitful; and if we lose, they will not be necessary. I do not believe mere verbiage of this kind will affect the Spanish decision." Churchill, *Their Finest Hour*, 546. Allegations from Francoist Spain arose after the war that from 1940 onward Churchill had made promises to Spain to negotiate the postwar status of the Rock, even as far as ceding it outright. In *The War & the Neutrals* (272), Toynbee asserts such Spanish allegations were unfounded.

129. Gallo, 107.

130. Feis, 67.

131. Feis, 52.

132. Cordell Hull's cancellation of a U.S. loan to Spain in December was largely dictated by fear of the American public's anger had such a loan been approved by the administration. Manchester *Guardian*, April 4, 1941.

133. Feis, 54.

134. *The Times*, October 19, 1940.

135. Historian Stanley Payne describes Beigbeder in 1939: "like many of Franco's senior officers . . . Beigbeder was relatively pro-German but not fanatically so." Payne, *The Franco Regime*, 255. Beigbeder, aside from being of the wrong political complexion at the moment, also made his own situation worse with inappropriate love affairs in a sexually prim regime.

136. Feis, 64.

137. Toynbee, 287.

138. Spanish Morocco consisted of 7,700 square miles with three-quarters of a million people; Río de Oro and Adrar contained only 840 white persons on 109,200 square miles; Ifni, Spanish Guinea, and Fernando Po and its surrounding territories formed the rest of the Spanish African empire. The Canary Islands were considered a part of metropolitan Spain.

139. Feis, 69.

140. Unsigned memorandum, Francisco Franco to Adolf Hitler, DGFP, Vol. IX, 509–510.

141. The trip had the corollary consequences of causing the United States to reconsider a pending Spanish loan request; Serrano Suñer assured Ambassador Weddell that the trip wasn't "official" and thus presumably wouldn't alter the status quo.

142. The Tripartite Pact between Germany, Italy, and Japan would be signed in Berlin on September 27.

143. Feis, 81.

144. DGFP, Vol. IX, 201.

145. Churchill, *Their Finest Hour*, 447. Between July and November 1940, the British evacuated about 16,700 persons—mostly dependents—from the Rock. Carrington, 32.

146. Feis, 93.

147. Unsigned memorandum, DGFP, Vol. IX, 375.

148. Churchill, *Their Finest Hour*, 447.

149. Such chunks might have been the Channel Islands.

150. Quoted in Toynbee, 280.

151. Beaulac, 11.

152. Beaulac, 11. Hitler was reputed to have told Mussolini at Florence a few days later that he would rather have "three or four teeth pulled" than go through another experience like the one he had just had with Franco. Churchill quoting Ciano's papers in *Their Finest Hour*, 447. To Mussolini, Hitler would rail at Spain's demands being "absolutely out of proportion to their strength." Churchill, *Their Finest Hour*, 447.

153. Feis, 95.

154. Avni, 57–58.

155. *The World at Arms*, 82.

156. The distance from Gibraltar to the nearest point on the African shore; a little farther west, only nine miles separates Europe from Africa.

157. Conn & Fairchild, 79.

158. Toynbee, 280.

159. Churchill, *Their Finest Hour*, 451.

160. Feis, 115.

161. Beaulac, 15. While these discussions were going on, both German and Spanish army units were practicing their assaults on Gibraltar—the Germans using a mountain in the French Jura that resembled the Rock, the Spaniards practicing on their own territory. Bridges were also being strengthened on the French-Spanish border for the passage of German units. Though Franco may not have really envisioned Operation Felix actually launched, he certainly wanted Canaris—and Hitler—to think he was negotiating in good faith. Feis, 123.

162. Cortada, *Wolfram and World War II*, 16.

163. Quoted in Churchill, *The Grand Alliance*, 10–11.

164. Beaulac, 16.

165. Feis, 126.

166. Feis, 102.

167. Manchester *Guardian*, April 4, 1941.

168. The duke would be killed two years later while on active duty in the RAF.

169. Quoted in Fodor, 88.

170. The British censored all transatlantic mail and required that it be deplaned in Bermuda, where scores of censors plowed through the mail bags, removing any security-sensitive matter before allowing the rest to be sent to its destination.

171. *Daily Telegraph*, October 24, 1941.

172. Robinson, 88.

173. Toynbee, 325.

174. Serrano Suñer said that it was the Germans who had suggested to him that Spain should absorb Portugal and that the Spanish government instantly rejected this suggestion. There is, however, no evidence of any such suggestion in the German war records. Toynbee, 327.

175. The Azores were an integral part of metropolitan Portugal, as was Madeira; the Cape Verdes were a colony, as were Angola and Mozambique.

176. Weiss, 4.

177. Toynbee, 331.

178. Churchill, *The Grand Alliance*, 119.

179. Quoted in Toynbee, 333.

180. Pepper later entered the House of Representatives.

181. Weiss, 12.

182. Quoted in Langer, 369. Britain had at the same time a plan, called Shrapnel, to secure the ten islands and five islets of the Cape Verdes if Portugal would give its treaty partner permission to "maintain naval control of the crucial stretch of the route around the Cape." Churchill, *Their Finest Hour*, 531.

183. Langer, 368.

184. The papers of Franklin D. Roosevelt quoted in Weiss, 13.

185. Stanley Payne wrote that just as Germany had no concrete plans for a first-strike invasion of Iberia, neither did Britain; neither side knew this until after the war, of course. Payne, *The Franco Regime*, 269 ff.

186. DGFP, Vol. XII, 731–733.

187. Quoted in Langer, 517.

188. Quoted in Fodor, 90.

189. The terms "wolfram" and "tungsten" are interchangeable for the ore; whereas "tungsten" is more commonly used today, during World War II "wolfram" was more frequently heard in describing the unprocessed ore. Finished tungsten's chief nonmilitary use is in incandescent-lamp filaments.

190. America's Westinghouse Electric estimated it had found some 1,500 uses for tungsten in goods manufactured for World War II; historian James Cortada suggests the Germans undoubtedly used the ore for an equally broad range of purposes. Cortada, *Wolfram and World War II*, 19.

191. So too had the United States since 1941 purchased the ore from leading South American suppliers, both for its own use and to damage Germany's war effort. Cortada, *Wolfram and World War II*, 20.

192. Ambassador Hayes says that Franco's action was based on the fact that Germany had been sending arms to Spain, and for a "militarist" like Franco there could be no question of jeopardizing the flow of those weapons. Cortada, *Wolfram and World War II*, 46.

193. Gordon, 115.

194. Gordon, 115.

195. Kay, 180.

196. West, 94.

197. West, 93.

198. DGFP, Vol. XIII, 12.

199. Though in November 1938 Hungary had been happy to share in the spoils of Czechoslovakia when Budapest annexed parts of Slovakia and sub-Carpathian Ruthenia; five months later, it occupied all of Ruthenia.

200. Hungary remained formally a kingdom throughout the war.

201. Hughes, 336.

CHAPTER IV: World War

1. Conn & Fairchild, 127.

2. Langer & Gleason, 827.

3. Washington never declared war on Finland, and neither of the Anglo-American partners would ever engage in hostilities with the Finns.

4. Carlgren, 114.

5. The German minister in Stockholm cabled Berlin that "the decision of the Swedish Government encountered extraordinary political difficulties. The negative views within the Cabinet itself and in the parties of the Riksdag almost led yesterday to a Cabinet crisis." DGFP, Vol. XIII, 21.

6. DGFP, Vol. XIII, 13.

7. Historian Henrik Olsson takes the view that the king never seriously intended to abdicate, but rather that it was Prime Minister Hansson who used the threat of a royal veto to bring the Social Democratic government around to his way of thinking. Henrik A. Olsson, *Statsvelenkapalig Tidskrift*, 1963, 28–49.

8. DGFP, Vol. XIII, 20.

9. Also sometimes called the Oslo Division.

10. Fodor, 135.

11. DGFP, Vol. XIII, 68–69.

12. Carlgren, 118–119.

13. Carlgren, 119–120.

14. Carlgren, 122.

15. During the war some 1,200 British flights between Scotland and Sweden made the hazardous run carrying 500 tons of ball bearings and roller bearings. Fodor, 127.

16. *Sweden Speaks*, 1939.

17. Fodor, 137.

18. Carlgren, 125.

19. Terae, 226–248.

20. Carlgren, 126.

21. Root, Vol. I, 81.

22. Carlgren, 129.

23. Carlgren, 135.

24. Carlgren, 138.

25. Toynbee, 190.

26. It is interesting to speculate whether under the same circumstances the Swedes might have been invaded had they been a Slavic people rather than Nordic.

27. Toynbee, 229.

28. Toynbee, 212. *Hakenkreuz* means swastika.

29. *Daily Telegraph*, July 30, 1941, cited in Toynbee, 213.

30. Toynbee, 214–215.

31. Toynbee, 215–216.

32. Kimche, 67–72.

33. *Fortune*, September 1941, 74.

34. In 1944, the Swiss daily calorie intake sank below 2,000. Marron, 252.

35. Schwarz, 70.

36. Root, Vol. II, 125.

37. Ogley, 148.

38. Root, Vol. II, 125.

39. Schwarz, 71.

40. Schwarz, 72.

41. Lerman, 150.

42. Schwarz, 79–80.

43. Schwarz, 77.

44. Schwarz, 58.

45. Kimche, 76–77.

46. Russell, 100–101.

47. Smith, 210.

48. Brown, 274.

49. Meier, 297.

50. Brown, 277.

51. Donovan biographer Anthony Cave Brown says that "Wood's" identity as Kolbe was "probable" but not "certain." Brown, 278.

52. Brown, 279.

53. Russell, 104–105.

54. Schwarz, 116–117.

55. Quoted in Nowland & Williams, 33–34. In point of fact, by 1941 British phosphate fertilizer exports to Ireland had already fallen to 7,000 tons, from 89,000 tons in 1939 and 74,000 tons in 1940; no fertilizers at all would arrive from Britain in 1942. The decline in feedstuffs would be just as precipitous: from 8 million tons in 1930 to nothing in 1942.

56. *Newsweek*, March 27, 1944.

57. *Fortune*, March 1942.

58. The bad luck of an outbreak of foot-and-mouth disease in 1941 further reduced at a critical juncture the country's cattle industry.

59. Nowland & Williams, 37.

60. Share, 38.

61. Share, 41.

62. Nowland & Williams, 35.

63. *Daily Telegraph*, February 10, 1942.

64. Churchill, *The Gathering Storm*, 381–382.

65. Toynbee, 245.

66. Ireland's largest military training establishment served also as the country's sole internment camp, one in which Allied and Axis aviators found themselves quartered next to each other.

67. Carter, 27.

68. Longford, 397.

69. A Gallup poll taken in January 1943 revealed the ironic fact that 47 percent of the American people didn't realize Eire hadn't entered the war against Germany. *Newsweek*, January 18, 1943.

70. Quoted in Longford, 425.

71. Cronin, 93.

72. This version of the message is from Longford's biography of de Valera, Longford acknowledging but not explaining the difference from the version in Churchill's wartime memoirs. (Churchill, *The Grand Alliance*, 511: "Now is your chance. Now or never! I will meet you wherever you wish.")

73. Bowman, 247.

74. Such a meeting took place when Lord Cranborne was sent to Dublin by Churchill. Little came of it except for a chance for de Valera to reiterate his well-known views on a united Ireland. Longford, 394–395.

75. Cronin, 95.

76. Mansergh, 161.

77. Quoted in Elliott & Hall, 481.

78. *The Nation*, February 7, 1942.

79. Cronin, 95.

80. *Irish Press*, January 28, 1942, quoted in Mitchell and Snodaigh, 230–231.

81. Quoted in Cronin, 95–96.

82. Bowman, 249.

83. Concerned about violence toward American military personnel in Ulster, in 1943 the State Department had the FBI prepare a study of the IRA on the grounds that as proponents of a united Ireland the organization was a danger to GIs in the British province. Ironically, the Irish-Americans among the U.S. troops were held responsible for the increased tensions between the GIs (as a whole) and the British in Ulster because the former were thought "susceptible" to Irish Nationalist sentiments and thus considered "sympathetic" to the IRA. Cronin, 92.

84. Quoted in Elliott & Hall, 481.

85. Quoting Sir Samuel Hoare in Proctor, 115.

86. Proctor, 117.

87. Payne, *Falange*, 233.

88. Moats, 90.

89. In a later greeting of these air elements at Berlin's Tempelhof airport the Luftwaffe band played not the anthem of Nationalist Spain but that of the defeated Republic, a protocol error that caused greater embarrassment for the Germans than it did for the amused Spaniards. Proctor, 132–133.

90. Scurr, 6.

91. Quoted in Gallo, 115.

92. Portugal might have had its own version of Spain's Blue Division fighting alongside the Wehrmacht in Russia if a proposal the German ambassador in Lisbon made to Salazar had come to fruition. In a telegram dated July 2, 1941, the ambassador reported to the Foreign Ministry in Berlin that "in the course of today's conversation with Salazar the talk turned to the establishment of a corps of Spanish volunteers to fight Bolshevism and to the question of carrying out a similar demonstration in Portugal. I informed Salazar that we were receiving daily applications from Portuguese to be taken into the German army. . . . Salazar explained that . . . in Spain it was somewhat different . . . that Spain had a debt of gratitude to pay for the help in the Civil War." (The telegram doesn't say which man broached the topic, but from the drift of the conversation it appears the German was the instigator.) Salazar managed to disengage himself, and said he would "perhaps" organize a "Portuguese Legion" demonstration on behalf of the German fight on the Russian front. The diplomat's reply was that even this gesture would find a "strong response not only in Germany but all over the world." The subject was apparently dropped, though, except that the German raised it one more time in October, at which time Salazar responded only that he hoped the ambassador didn't want an immediate reply. Nothing further came of the idea. DGFP, Vol. XIII, 69–70.

93. Payne, *The Franco Regime*, 299.

94. Proctor, 203.

95. Payne, *Falange*, 237.

96. Payne, *Falange*, 238.

97. In a public address shortly after the war's end, Franco referred to the role of the diminished Falange as "not really a state political party, but a sort of administrative 'instrument of national unification.'" Payne, *Falange*, 240.

98. Gallo, 118.

99. Two weeks earlier, Churchill had written to Roosevelt about notifying Franco and Salazar of the landings. "I am satisfied that it is important to inform both the Spanish and Portuguese Governments of British participation, if only to remove any suspicion about the object of our own concentrations at Gibraltar. . . . There will be no question of our publishing the full text of our declarations to Spain and Portugal on zero day. We should of course say to both Spaniards and Portuguese that what we tell them about our share in the operation is for their strictly confidential information." Loewenheim, 261. Salazar was given the same information that evening by the British ambassador in Lisbon, Sir Ronald Campbell; like Jordana, Salazar was mightily relieved that neither Spain nor Portugal was the object of Allied military landings. Fodor, 91.

100. Hughes, 264.

101. Quoted in Proctor, 213.

102. Sir Samuel Hoare had warned the planners of Operation Torch: "The Germans will be on General Franco's back, dinning into his ears, 'Now is your time.' Let no one underrate the power of this temptation of thinking that because nine Spaniards out of ten do not want war, General Franco might not risk it for the big stakes that it might offer him." Clark, 54.

103. Gallo, 118.

104. Hughes, 262.

105. Hughes, 264.

106. Proctor, 217.

107. Esteban Infantes replaced Muñoz Grandes on December 13, after the latter had been ordered back to Spain.

108. *Times Atlas of the Second World War*, 88.

109. As late as May 1941 Hitler had still been hazily looking forward to eventually gaining a long-range-bomber base in the islands, saying as much to Raeder, who responded with the same advice as that tendered at all earlier mentions of the subject—that at no foreseeable date could the German Navy militarily hold the Azores or keep them adequately supplied. Toynbee, 330.

110. Weiss, 18.

111. Langer & Gleason, 669.

112. Quoted in Watson, 176–177.

113. Kay, 155 ff.

114. Shirer, *Rise & Fall*, 924–925.

CHAPTER V: Downhill

1. Horthy had been an admiral in the Austro-Hungarian Navy during World War I, when the Dual Monarchy still possessed an Adriatic coastline from which to launch a navy.

2. Jews brought under Hungarian control when parts of Czechoslovakia, Rumania, and Yugoslavia were ceded to Hungary were not regarded as "native," and Budapest did not extend protections to them.

3. Shirer, *Rise & Fall*, 972.

4. Werbell & Clarke, 16–17.

5. Germany's 1935 Nuremberg Laws defined a Jew as anyone with at least one Jewish grandparent.

6. About 120,000 Jews survived in Budapest—the largest Nazi-controlled Jewish community in Europe to survive—many because of Wallenberg's influence over their tormentors.

7. Iron ore shipments to Germany in 1943 were 10.1 million tons, or 27.5 percent of Germany's total supplies of iron ore that year. Nissen, 371.

8. *Christian Science Monitor*, July 10, 1943.

9. Scott, 508.

10. Dahlman, *The American Swedish Monthly*, New York, March 1943, 5.

11. In the 1943 election, the Communists elected 3 members out of 230 to the lower house, 1 out of 150 to the upper chamber. Chicago *Sun*, May 8, 1943.

12. Carlgren, 142–143.

13. Dahlman, 5.

14. San Francisco *Chronicle*, May 16, 1943.

15. Quoted in the New York *Herald Tribune*, May 7, 1943.

16. Davidowicz, 373. This humanitarian action had a politically successful precedent on a smaller scale in Norway, which was again possible because of the proximity of a neutral safe haven. Partly because of the presence of a collaborationist government under Quisling, the story of the Norweigan Jews didn't end as happily as in Denmark: about half of the 1,800 Norwegian Jews died in Nazi concentration camps.

17. Jones, 177–178.

18. Davidowicz, 373. Kernberg in Goldberger, 189.

19. The Germans captured about 400 Danish Jews, all of whom were sent to the "model" concentration camp at Theresienstadt. None, thanks to the insistent efforts of the king and the Danish Red Cross, were sent from Theresienstadt to Auschwitz. Fifty-one died in Theresienstadt. Davidowicz, 374. W. Glyn Jones gives the figures at 472 arrested and deported and 52 deaths. Jones, 178.

20. Toynbee, 193.

21. In the fall of 1943, Churchill wrote his foreign secretary suggesting that Sweden, as well as Turkey, be brought into the war "of their own volition"; how this was to be accomplished he didn't specify. Churchill, *Closing the Ring*, 247.

22. Fox, 138.

23. One explanation for the less intimidating tone in Anglo-Swedish relations was London's anxiety for its postwar relations with the Swedes and its concern that the Soviets not establish themselves in Stockholm; though the tenor of the two principal Allies toward Sweden often differed, there was no question that the final goal of each was for the Swedes to break off all relations with the Germans, both diplomatic and economic. Carlgren, 203.

24. There has never been more than the most transparent pretense that this traffic represented anything but a breach of Swedish neutrality—"one of the burdens," Hansson said that April, "which our country had had to bear as a consequence of the war." McInnis, Vol. IV, 270.

25. Carlgren, 154.

26. Nissen, 273. It was an equally clear indicator that the Swedes sensed the approaching defeat of the Nazis, and would move toward a clear separation between their country and Germany.

27. Nissen, 273.

28. In May 1944 the Swedes informed the Germans that even the mail and courier services the Wehrmacht conducted on Swedish railways must end im-

mediately; the grounds presented Germany involved numbers of maps of Sweden found in the goods in transit.

29. Nissen, 275.

30. Elting, 178.

31. The Finnish parliament passed enabling legislation to allow Mannerheim to assume the presidency without an election.

32. Nissen, 291.

33. Nissen, 312.

34. Denham, 166.

35. Kimche, 100–101.

36. Ogley, 151.

37. Only a handful of Swiss intelligence officers knew the identity of the Viking Line informer. The intelligence from this source continued until the end of the war. Kimche, 91.

38. Kimche, 102.

39. Kimche, 102.

40. Quoted in Meier, 289.

41. Meier, 290–291.

42. Toynbee, 78.

43. Meier, 294–295. Historian Heinz K. Meier believes "Germans never gave the same emphasis to economic warfare as the Allies and that they underestimated the value of Swiss products to Allied war efforts."

44. Kimche, 120.

45. Only on August 28, 1944, when the Americans reached the Franco-Swiss border, did Switzerland cease to be surrounded by Axis forces.

46. Simons, 26.

47. A belief in the existence of a German Alpine redoubt was a major reason the Allies wanted the Germans out of Italy, a redoubt into which Washington and London figured the Germans could retreat. Padfield, 573.

48. Quoted in Simons, 28.

49. Kimche, 143.

50. Dulles would save Wolff after the war, but in 1962 he was convicted on charges of abetting the murder of Jews and sentenced to fifteen years in prison; he was released on health grounds after serving nine years. Padfield, 584.

51. Calvocoressi, 506.

52. Schwarz, 148.

53. This was a factor of great importance in Washington and London's reluctance to pressure Switzerland into difficult choices. At their peak, Swiss diplomatic missions in 35 countries assumed a total of 219 mandates to act as protecting power, sometimes simultaneously for countries at war with each other—Switzerland was the protecting power for the United States in Germany and for Germany in the United States. Schweiz, 132.

54. Quoted in Meier, 309.

55. It might be pointed out that Polish pilots were not treated to quite so much luxury. Since there were no support payments for the Poles, these fliers were put to work by the Swiss to compensate for their room and board.

56. Meier, 314. On September 12, 1944, the Swiss turned the country's lights back on, lights that been extinguished at German demand early in the war. Knowing the Germans could no longer take any effective retaliation, Swiss border towns again shone brightly at night in an effort to alert Allied aircraft crews of the difference between lit-up Switzerland and pitch-black Germany.

57. Neither had the Schaffhausen incident been the first such accidental bombing of a Swiss city: in December 1940, the RAF accidentally bombed the railroad station in Basel.

58. Gilbert, 644–645.

59. Quoted from the *Federal Register* in Meier, 316.

60. Toynbee, 225–226.

61. Mitchell & Snodaigh, 231.

62. Bell, 233.

63. Bell, 235.

64. Quoted in Hachey & McCaffrey, 133.

65. Hachey & McCaffrey, 133.

66. Bromage, 283.

67. Mansergh, 163.

68. De Valera differentiated his repatriation policies according to a certain logic: those airmen on operational flights—which German fliers invariably were—were detained; those on training flights—which Allied aviators were almost always *seen* to be—were released. Longford, 401.

69. Quoted in Mansergh, 163.

70. *The Irish Times*, February 23, 1944.

71. *The Observer*, March 13, 1944.

72. Dwyer, 218–219.

73. Longford, 408.

74. Quoted in Coogan, 120.

75. Longford, 408.

76. Nowland, 36.

77. *Time*, July 5, 1943.

78. *Newsweek*, March 20, 1944.

79. One of the party's slogans in the election was "Vote for Fianna Fáil or the bombs will fall." Coogan, 119.

80. Mansergh, 163.

81. Not Ramón Serrano Suñer, however. The former Spanish foreign minister wrote Leopold Kerney, Irish diplomatic representative to the Franco government, his appreciation: "The brave, Christian, and human attitude of President [sic] de Valera moves me write you these lines to express to you my

admiration for your country and to assure you again of my friendship." Quoted in Keogh, 194.

82. Letter to Bob Brennan in Washington, quoted in Keogh, 192.

83. Manchester *Guardian*, May 4, 1945.

84. Keogh, 196.

85. *Vital Speeches of the Day*, New York, June 1, 1945, Vol. XI, No. 16, 482–483.

86. Some people had to make quite an effort to do so—there were only 169,000 sets for Eire's 3 million people. *Newsweek*, March 27, 1944.

87. *Vital Speeches of the Day*, New York, June 1, 1945, Vol. XI, No. 16, 485–486.

88. *Fortune*, March 1945.

89. Quoted in Gallo, 135.

90. *Daily Telegraph* (date unclear—March 1, 1944?).

91. Avni, 54.

92. According to Ambassador Hayes's memoirs.

93. Toynbee, 298.

94. Avni, 64.

95. Quoted in Gallo, 125.

96. Toynbee, 301.

97. Fodor, 86.

98. Gallo, 131. The last duty on the Russian front of the Blue Division's commanding general, Emilio Esteban Infantes, was to visit the cemetery at Mestelevo, where 2,000 of his soldiers were buried. The first returning *division-arios* crossed the border back into Spain on October 29, 1943. A Volunteer Legion—unofficially called the Blue Legion—remained in Russia; it numbered between 1,000 and 1,500 men. In just over two years of fighting, the Blue Division had suffered 12,726 casualties: 3,934 dead, 8,466 wounded, 326 missing. At the beginning of 1944, the Blue Legion volunteers were ordered home, finally reaching Spain in April. Thereafter, about 150 Spaniards ignored the closed frontier with France and volunteered their services to the Axis cause; they were incorporated into Waffen SS units. The last Spaniards serving Hitler were fighting around the Chancellery rubble in Berlin as Nazi Germany expired. Of the Blue Division's prisoners taken by the Red Army, the last to reach Spain alive did so in April 1954. Scurr, 27–31.

99. Cortada, 72.

100. Feis, 210.

101. Some observers acidly note that Franco might have viewed the British- and French-led embargo of arms to the Republic during the Civil War as incurring as much of a blood debt as had Hitler's and Mussolini's gifts.

102. A 400-million-peseta credit to Germany—"repayment for Civil War debts," Franco called it—helped push the Allies into their drastic response. McInnis, Vol. V, 185.

103. Historian Juan Pablo Fusi theorizes that the true Allied intent for the embargo may have been to "keep tension alive in order to justify, if necessary, the invasion of Spain in support of the planned landings in Normandy." Fusi, 59.

104. Churchill's view of Spain's contribution to the Allies was by no means shared by everyone in his cabinet, and a large body of public opinion on both sides of the Anglo-American alliance remained utterly opposed to any accommodation to the Franco government. Toynbee, 309.

105. Gallo, 141.

106. An echo of medieval Spain, the term is used in Spain to refer to the seven centuries of dislodging the Moors from the Iberian Peninsula.

107. Small numbers of survivors managed to harass Franco forces until 1951 from their hideouts in the north and from Andalusia and Extremadura.

108. *Newsweek*, November 6, 1944.

109. Watson, 178.

110. American ambassador Hayes wrote the State Department in January 1943 that he believed it possible Franco would soon "seize the initiative" in restoring the monarchy, making himself regent. Watson, 178.

111. *Newsweek*, October 18, 1943.

112. Fusi, 60.

113. Speaking on the monarchy in November 1944, Franco said that "the question of a monarchy today does not constitute any problem for the Spanish people. There are graver problems. However, when this difficult phase of world history has passed, and if such a step is in the interests of Spain, then would be the time, exclusively in accord with the will of the Spanish people and without damaging Spain's unity or weakening its governmental authority, when we could arrive at the establishment of a monarchy." Manchester *Guardian*, November 6, 1944. This is basically what would happen thirty years after the end of the war.

114. Toynbee, 304.

115. Trythall, 189.

116. Quoted in Gallo, 151–152.

117. Quoted in Gallo, 152.

118. Hoare 286. Hoare's role in Spain received perhaps its highest praise from the man Hoare so often vilified, Ramón Serrano Suñer, who wrote of the British diplomat: ". . . no other Allied mission in Spain was as useful, as productive, as his was. By his presence and influence in Spanish politics he succeeded, to an appreciable degree, in counterbalancing German influence, and even in causing numerous sectors of opinion to abandon their faith in Axis victory and in the advantages such a victory might bring. He conspired successfully; he defended his cause with tenacity; he raised spirits; he was in a real sense a power within Spain." Quoted in Beaulac, 159.

119. Toynbee, 310.

120. The Spanish Communist Party would in 1940 endorse the Molotov-

Ribbentrop pact, and most likely would have that same year cooperated fully with the Reich had it been in a position to do so. Hills, 427.

121. Churchill, *Their Finest Hour*, 443.

122. This account is based on the research of Ronald Howard, the actor's son, for his 1981 book, *In Search of My Father: A Portrait of Leslie Howard*. Its conclusions differ from those which had been written earlier (even by such a renowned figure as Winston Churchill), a difference that will be explained at the end of this section.

123. Gallagher, 105.

124. When the British had first found out about the beam, they decided that trying to get the Spanish to close it down would involve endless wrangling. So instead they turned its use to benefit the Allies as well as the Germans. Howard, 221.

125. Quoted in Howard, 225.

126. Churchill, *The Hinge of Fate*, 721.

127. Churchill, *The Hinge of Fate*, 721.

128. Churchill, *The Grand Alliance*, 120.

129. Churchill, *Their Finest Hour*, 531.

130. Weiss, 21.

131. Gallagher, 102.

132. Kay, 179. When in the following year Salazar finally embargoed all wolfram shipments to Germany, the result was a loss of £2 million to the national treasury as well as tens of thousands of jobs lost in the wolfram-mining industry. Robinson, 91.

133. Livermore, 337. Weiss, 25.

134. Quoted in Figueiredo, 100.

APPENDIX

1. *Vital Speeches of the Day*, New York, June 1, 1945, Vol. XI, No. 16, 485–486.

BIBLIOGRAPHY

Books, Articles, and Works Cited and Consulted

An Cosantóir: The Defence Forces Magazine. Dublin: Army Authorities, September 1989.

Andrews, Allen. *Proud Fortress: The Fighting Story of Gibraltar*. London: Evan Bros., Ltd., 1958.

Anger, Per. *With Raoul Wallenberg in Budapest: Memories of the War Years in Hungary*. New York: Holocaust Library, 1981.

Ansel, Walter. *Hitler and the Middle Sea*. Durham: Duke University Press, 1972.

Avni, Haim. *Spain, the Jews, and Franco*. Philadelphia: The Jewish Publication Society of America, 1982.

Beaulac, Willard L. *Franco: Silent Ally in World War II*. Carbondale: Southern Illinois University Press, 1986.

Bell, J. Bowyer. *The Secret Army: The IRA 1916–1979*. Cambridge, Mass.: The MIT Press, 1970 & 1979.

Beus, Alexei A., ed. *Geology of Tungsten*. Paris: UNESCO, 1986.

Black, Cyril, et al. *Neutralization and World Politics*. Princeton: Princeton University Press, 1968.

Bonjour, Edgar. *Swiss Neutrality: Its History and Meaning*. London: George Allen & Unwin, 1946.

Bowman, John. *De Valera and the Ulster Question 1917–1973*. Oxford: Clarendon Press, 1982.

Bradford, Sarah. *The Reluctant King: The Life and Reign of George VI 1895–1952*. New York: St. Martin's Press, 1989.

Bromage, Mary C. *De Valera and the March of a Nation*. New York: The Noonday Press, 1956.

Brown, Anthony Cave. *The Last Hero: Wild Bill Donovan*. New York: Vintage Books, 1984.

Brown, Terence. *Ireland: A Social & Cultural History 1922 to the Present.* Ithaca: Cornell University Press, 1975.

Burdick, Charles B. *Germany's Military Strategy and Spain in World War II.* Syracuse: Syracuse University Press, 1968.

────── & Hans-Adolf Jacobsen, eds. *The Halder War Diary 1939–1942.* Novato, Calif.: Presidio Press, 1988.

Calvocoressi, Peter, & Guy Wint. *Total War: The Story of World War II.* New York: Pantheon Books, 1972.

Campbell, John, ed. *The Experience of World War II.* New York: Oxford University Press, 1989.

Carlgren, W. M. *Swedish Foreign Policy During the Second World War.* New York: St. Martin's Press, 1973.

Carrington, Charles Edmund. *Gibraltar.* London: Oxford University Press, 1956.

Carroll, Joseph T. *Ireland in the War Years.* Newton Abbott: David & Charles, 1975.

Carson, William A. *Ulster and the Irish Republic.* Belfast: William C. Cleland, Ltd., 1956.

Carter, Carolle J. *The Shamrock and the Swastika: German Espionage in Ireland in World War II.* Palo Alto: Pacific Books, 1977.

Childs, Marquis W. *Sweden: The Middle Way.* New York: Penguin Books, 1948.

Churchill, Winston. S. *The Second World War* (six volumes). Boston: Houghton Mifflin Co., 1949.

Conn, Stetson, & Byron Fairchild. *U.S. Army in World War II. The Western Hemisphere: The Framework of Hemisphere Defense.* Washington, D.C.: Office of Chief of Military History, Department of the Army, 1960.

Connery, Donald S. *The Scandinavians.* New York: Simon & Schuster, 1966.

Conquest of the Balkans. Alexandria: Time-Life Books, 1990.

Coogan, Timothy Patrick. *Ireland Since the Rising.* New York: Praeger Publishers, 1966.

Cortada, James W. *United States–Spanish Relations, Wolfram and World War II.* Barcelona: Manuel Pareja, 1971.

────── , ed. *Spain in the 20th Century World: Essays on Spanish Diplomacy 1898–1978.* Westport, Conn.: Greenwood Press, 1980.

────── . *Historical Dictionary of the Spanish Civil War 1936–1939.* Westport, Conn.: Greenwood Press, 1982.

Cronin, Seán. *Washington's Irish Policy 1916–1986: Independence Partition Neutrality.* Dublin: Anvil Books, 1987.

Crowl, Philip A. *Traveller's Guide to Historic Ireland.* Chicago: Contemporary Books, 1990.

Crozier, Brian. *Franco.* Boston: Little, Brown & Co., 1967.

Dankelmann, Otfried. "Zur Spanischen 'Nichtkriegführung' in Zweiten Weltkrieg," *Zeitschrift für Militärgeschichte.* Halle: September 6, 1970.

Davidowicz, Lucy S. *The War Against the Jews, 1933–1945*. New York: Holt, Rinehart and Winston, 1975.

Davies, R. E. G. *A History of the World's Airlines*. London: Oxford University Press, 1964.

Denham, Henry. *Inside the Nazi Ring: A Naval Attaché in Sweden 1940–1945*. New York: Holmes & Meier, 1984.

Derry, T. K. *A History of Scandinavia*. Minneapolis; University of Minnesota Press, 1983.

Detwiler, Donald S. *Die Frage des Spanischen Eintritts in den Zweiten Weltkrieg*. Wiesbaden: Franz Steiner Verlag Gmbh., 1962.

Documents on German Foreign Policy, 1918–1943, from the Archives of the German Foreign Ministry, published jointly by the British Foreign Office and the U.S. Department of State, Series D, 1949–56.

Drozdov, Georgii, et al. *Russia at War 1941–1945*. New York: Vendome Press, 1987.

Duggan, John P. *Neutral Ireland and the Third Reich*. Dublin: Gill and Macmillan, 1985.

Durá, Juan. *U.S. Policy Toward Dictatorship and Democracy in Spain 1931–1953*. Seville: Arrayan Ediciones, 1985.

Dwyer, T. Ryle. *Irish Neutrality and the U.S.A. 1937–1947*. Dublin: Rowman & Littlefield, 1977.

Eamon de Valera Centenary. Dublin: Institiúid Ard-Léinn, 1982.

Elliott, W. Y. & H. Duncan Hall, eds. *The British Commonwealth at War*. New York: Alfred A. Knopf, 1943.

Elting, John R. *Battles for Scandinavia*. Alexandria: Time-Life Books, 1981.

Engle, Eloise, & Lauri Paananen. *The Winter War: The Russo-Finnish Conflict, 1939–40*. New York: Charles Scribner's Sons, 1973.

Epstein, M. *The Statesman's Year-Book 1941*. London: Macmillan and Co., 1941.

Eubank, Keith. *The Origins of World War II*. Arlington Heights, Ill.: Harlan Davidson, Inc., 1969–90.

Feis, Herbert. *The Spanish Story: Franco and the Nations at War*. New York: Alfred A. Knopf, 1948.

Figueiredo, Antonio de. *Portugal: Fifty Years of Dictatorship*. New York: Holmes & Meier, 1976.

Fisk, Robert. *In Time of War: Ireland, Ulster, and the Price of Neutrality 1939–1945*. Philadelphia: University of Pennsylvania Press, 1983.

Fodor, Dennis J. *The Neutrals*. Alexandria: Time-Life Books, 1982.

Foreign Affairs, various issues.

Foreign Relations of the United States: Diplomatic Papers. Department of State publication. Washington, D.C.: U.S. Government Printing Office, 1964 & 1965.

Forster, R. F. *Modern Ireland 1600–1972*. London: The Penguin Press, 1988.

Fortune, September 1941 ("Switzerland Sits Tight"), March 1942 ("Cable from Eire"), March 1945 ("Spain: Unfinished Business").

Fox, Annette Baker. *The Power of Small States: Diplomacy in World War II*. Chicago: University of Chicago Press, 1959.

Friis, Henning. *Scandinavia Between East and West*. Ithaca: Cornell University Press, 1950.

Fryer, Peter, & Patricia McGowan Pinheiro. *Oldest Ally: A Portrait of Salazar's Portugal*. London: Dennis Dobson, 1961.

Furtenbach, Boerje. "Planlaeggingen RN-RD," *Aktuellt och Historiskt*, May 1956.

——— and Herman Muellern. "Vi Var Beredda," *Aktuellt och Historiskt*, May 1962.

Fusi, Juan Pablo. *Franco: A Biography*. New York: Harper & Row, 1987.

Gallagher, Tom G. *Portugal: A Twentieth Century Interpretation*. Manchester: Manchester University Press, 1983.

Gallo, Max. *Spain Under Franco: A History*. New York: E. P. Dutton & Co., 1974.

Garlinski, Jozef. *The Swiss Corridor*. London: J. M. Dent & Sons, 1981.

Garratt, G. T. *Gibraltar and the Mediterranean*. New York: Coward-McCann, 1939.

A General Report on Swedish Internment: Internees of the American Air Force in Sweden. Washington, D.C.: Collection of the Library of Congress, 1945 or 1946.

Gervasi, Frank. *The Violent Decade: A Foreign Correspondent in Europe and the Middle East 1939–1945*. New York: W. W. Norton & Co., 1989.

Goldberger, Leo, ed. *The Rescue of the Danish Jews: Moral Courage Under Stress*. New York: New York University Press, 1987.

Gordon, David L., & Royden Dangerfield. *The Hidden Weapon: The Story of Economic Warfare*. New York: Harper & Bros., 1947.

Grimm, Bruno. *Gau Schweiz?* Zürich: Jean Christophe Verlag, 1939.

Gunther, John. *Inside Europe*. New York: Harper & Bros., 1940.

Hachey, Thomas E., & Lawrence J. McCaffrey, eds. *Perspectives on Irish Nationalism*. Lexington: University Press of Kentucky, 1989.

Hägglöf, M. Gunnar. "A Test of Neutrality: Sweden in the Second World War," *International Affairs*, 1960.

Hamilton, Thomas J. *Appeasement's Child: The Franco Regime in Spain*. New York: Alfred A. Knopf, 1943.

Harper's Magazine, September 1943.

Hayes, Carleton J. H. *Wartime Mission in Spain 1942–1945*. New York: The Macmillan Co., 1945.

Hills, George. *Franco: The Man and His Nation*. New York: The Macmillan Co., 1967.

———. *Rock of Contention: A History of Gibraltar*. London: Robert Hale & Co., 1974.

Hoare, Sir Samuel (later the 1st Viscount Templewood). *Ambassador on a Special Mission.* London: Collins, 1946.

Hollis, Christopher, ed. *Neutral War Aims.* London: Burns & Oates, 1940.

Holmquist, Bengt M., & Birgir Gripstad. *Swedish Weaponry Since 1630.* Defence Matériel Administration of Sweden, Royal Army Museum, 1982.

Howard, Ronald. *In Search of My Father: A Portrait of Leslie Howard.* New York: St. Martin's Press, 1981.

Hughes, Christopher. *Switzerland.* London: Ernest Benn, 1975.

Hughes, C. J. *The Parliament of Switzerland.* London: Cassell for the Hansard Society, 1962.

Hughes, Emmet John. *Report from Spain.* Port Washington, N.Y.: Kennikat Press, 1947.

Jackson, Sir William G. F. *The Rock of the Gibraltarians: A History of Gibraltar.* London & Toronto: Associated University Presses, 1987.

Jacobsen, Hans Adolf. *World War II Select Documents with Commentary, Strategy & Policy.* Santa Barbara: Clio Books, 1979.

Joesten, Joachim. *Background: The Key to Current Events* (Report No. 1: "Sweden: Hitler's Secret Ally"). New York, 1941.

———. *Stalwart Sweden.* Garden City, N.Y.: Doubleday, Doran & Co., 1943.

Jones, W. Glyn. *Denmark.* New York: Praeger Publishers, 1970.

Kay, Hugh. *Salazar and Modern Portugal: A Biography.* New York: Hawthorn Books, 1970.

Keefe, Eugene K., et al. *Spain: A Country Study.* Washington, D.C.: U.S. Government Printing Office, 1985.

Keegan, Jon, ed. *The Times Atlas of the Second World War.* New York: Harper & Row, 1989.

———. *The Second World War.* New York: Viking Press, 1989.

Keogh, Dermot. *Ireland & Europe 1919–1989: A Diplomatic and Political History.* Cork & Dublin: Hibernian University Press, 1990.

Kimche, Jon. *Spying for Peace.* New York: Roy Publishers, 1961.

Kleinfeld, Gerald R., & Lewis A. Tambs. *Hitler's Spanish Legion: The Blue Division in Russia.* Carbondale: Southern Illinois University Press, 1979.

Kreis, Georg. "La Suisse Pendant la Guerre: Etat Démocratique en Etat de Siège?" *Revue d'Histoire de la Deuxième Guerre Mondiale,* 1981.

Lalaguna, Juan. *A Traveller's History of Spain.* New York: Interlake Books, 1990.

Langer, William L., & S. Everett Gleason. *The Undeclared War 1940–1941.* New York: Harper & Bros. (published for the Council on Foreign Relations), 1953.

Lash, Joseph P. *Roosevelt and Churchill 1939–1941.* New York: W. W. Norton & Co., 1976.

Lerman, Anthony, et al., eds., *The Jewish Communities of the World: A Contemporary Guide.* New York: Facts on File, 1989.

Lewin, Ronald. *Hitler's Mistakes*. New York: William Morrow, 1984.

Life, various issues.

Livermore, H. V. *A New History of Portugal*. Cambridge: Cambridge University Press, 1976.

Lloyd, Alan. *Franco: The Biography of an Enigma*. Garden City, N.Y.: Doubleday & Company, 1969.

Loenroth, Erik. "Sweden's Ambiguous Neutrality," *Scandinavian Journal of History*, February 1977.

Loewenheim, Francis L., Harold D. Langley & Manfred Jonas. *Roosevelt and Churchill: Their Secret Wartime Correspondence*. New York: Da Capo Press, 1975, 1990.

Longford, The Earl of, & Thomas P. O'Neill. *Eamon de Valera: A Biography*. Boston: Houghton Mifflin Co., 1971.

Louda, Jirï, & Michael Maclagan. *Heraldry of the Royal Families of Europe*. New York: Clarkson N. Potter, 1981.

Luck, J. Murray. *History of Switzerland*. Palo Alto: Society for Promotion of Science and Scholarship, 1985.

Lukacs, John. *The Last European War: September 1939/December 1941*. Garden City, N.Y.: Anchor Press, 1976.

Lyon, Peter. *Neutralism*. Leicester: Leicester University Press, 1963.

Mahoney, Lawrence. *The Early Birds: A History of Pan Am's Clipper Ships*. Miami: The Pickering Press, 1981.

Manning, Maurice. *The Blueshirts*. Dublin: Gill & Macmillan, 1970.

Mansergh, Nicholas. *Survey of British Commonwealth Affairs: Problems of Wartime Cooperation and Post-War Change 1939–1952*. London: Oxford University Press, 1958.

Marques, A. H. de Oliveira. *History of Portugal*. Vol. II: *From Empire to Corporate State*. New York: Columbia University Press, 1976.

Marrus, Michael R. *The Unwanted: European Refugees in the Twentieth Century*. New York: Oxford University Press, 1985.

Marton, Kati. *Wallenberg*. New York: Random House, 1982.

McInnis, Edgar. *The War* (six volumes). London: Oxford University Press, 1945–46.

McPhee, John. *La Place de la Concorde Suisse*. New York: Farrar, Straus & Giroux, 1983.

Medlicott, W. N. *The Economic Blockade*. London: His Majesty's Stationery Office, 1952.

Meier, Heinz K. *Friendship Under Stress: U.S./Swiss Relations 1900–1950*. Bern: Herbert Lang & Co., 1970.

Millward, Alan S. "Could Sweden Have Stopped the Second World War?" *Scandinavian Economic Historical Review*, 1967.

Mitchell, Arthur, & Pádraig ó Snodaigh, eds. *Irish Political Documents 1916–1949*. Dublin: Irish Academic Press, 1985.

Moats, Alice Leone. *No Passport for Paris*. New York: G. P. Putnam's Sons, 1945.

Moe, M. Lorimer. *Sweden and the War*. New York: The American-Swedish News Exchange, Inc., 1942.

Morales, Victor Lezcano. "Las Causas de la No Beligerencia Española, Reconsideradas," *Revista de Estudios Internacionales*, May 3, 1984.

Mosley, Leonard. *The Reich Marshal*. Garden City, N.Y.: Doubleday & Company, 1974.

Muellern, Herman. "Tyskt Anfall mot Jaemtland och Haerjedalen," *Aktuellt och Historiskt*, 1963.

Munro, William Bennett. *Governments of Europe*. New York: The Macmillan Co., 1938.

The Nation, various issues.

Neutrals in Europe: Switzerland (Conference Papers 10). Stockholm: The Swedish Institute of International Affairs, 1988.

Newsweek, various issues.

Nissen, Henrik S., ed. *Scandinavia During the Second World War*. Minneapolis: University of Minnesota Press, 1983.

Nowlan, Kevin T., & T. Desmond Williams. *Ireland in the War Years and After: 1939–1951*. Dublin: Gill & Macmillan, 1969.

Ochsner, Charly R. *Neutrality in World War II: Its Origin, Its Application and Its Value*. Washington, D.C.: Unpublished master's thesis, 1945.

Ogley, Roderick. *The Theory and Practice of Neutrality in the Twentieth Century* ("The World Studies Series"). New York: Barnes & Noble, 1970.

Olsson, Henrik A. "Abdikationskrisen, 1941," *Statsvelenkapalig Tidskrift*. 1963.

Omang, Reidar. "Norges Frigjoering 1945," *Internasjonal Politik*, January 1958.

Padfield, Peter. *Himmler: Reichsführer SS*. New York: Henry Holt & Co., 1990.

Papen, Franz von. *Memoirs*. London: Andre Deutsch, 1952.

Payne, Stanley G. *Falange: A History of Spanish Fascism*. Stanford: Stanford University Press, 1961.

———. *Franco's Spain*. New York: Thomas Y. Crowell Co., 1967.

———. *A History of Spain & Portugal* (Vol. II). Madison: University of Wisconsin Press, 1973.

———. *The Franco Regime 1936–1975*. Madison: University of Wisconsin Press, 1987.

Pollock, James K., & Homer Thomas. *Germany in Power and Eclipse: The Background of German Development*. New York: D. Van Nostrand Co., 1952.

Proctor, Raymond L. *Agony of a Neutral: La Division Azul*. Moscow, Idaho: Idaho Research Foundation, Inc., 1974.

Ready, J. Lee. *Forgotten Allies*. Vol. I: *The European Theater: The Military Contribution of the Colonies, Exiled Governments, and Lesser Powers to the Allied Victory in World War II*. Jefferson, N.C.: McFarland & Co., 1985.

Rich, Norman. *Hitler's War Aims: The Establishment of the New Order*. New York: W. W. Norton & Co., 1974.

Rings, Werner. *Schweiz im Krieg 1933–1945: Ein Bericht*. Zurich: Verlag Ex Libris, 1974.

Robinson, Richard A. H. *Contemporary Portugal: A History*. London: George Allen & Unwin, 1979.

Root, Waverley. *The Secret History of the War* (two volumes). New York: Charles Scribner's Sons, 1945.

Rosenberg, J. L. "The Consecration of Expediency: The Wartime Neutrality of Ireland," *Australian Journal of Politics and History*, 1979.

Roucek, Joseph S., ed. *Contemporary Europe: A Study of National, International, Economic, and Cultural Trends*. New York: D. Van Nostrand Co., 1947.

Ruffieux, Roland. "La Suisse Pendant la Guerre: De l'Ordre Nouveau à la Nouvelles Préoccupations. La Débat Idéologique en Suisse Romande," *Revue d'Histoire de la Deuxième Guerre Mondiale*, 1981.

Russell, Francis. *The Secret War*. Alexandria: Time-Life Books, 1981.

Sanchez, José M. *The Spanish Civil War as a Religious Tragedy*. Notre Dame: University of Notre Dame Press, 1987.

Schwarz, Urs. *The Eye of the Hurricane: Switzerland in World War Two*. Boulder, Colo.: Westview Press, 1980.

Scott, Franklin D. *Sweden: The Nation's History*. Minneapolis: University of Minnesota Press, 1977.

Scurr, John. *Germany's Spanish Volunteers 1941–45: The Blue Division in Russia*. London: Osprey Publishing, 1980.

Seger, Otto. *A Survey of Liechtenstein History*. Schaan: R. Lingg, 1970.

Share, Bernard. *The Emergency: Neutral Ireland, 1939–45*. Dublin: Gill & Macmillan, 1978.

Shirer, William L. *The Challenge of Scandinavia: Norway, Sweden, Denmark and Finland in Our Time*. Boston: Little, Brown & Co., 1955.

———. *The Rise and Fall of the Third Reich*. New York: Simon & Schuster, 1960.

———. *The Nightmare Years 1930–1940*. Boston: Little, Brown & Co., 1984.

Simons, Gerald. *Victory in Europe*. Alexandria: Time-Life Books, 1982.

Smith, R. Harris. *OSS: The Secret History of America's First Central Intelligence Agency*. Berkeley: University of California Press, 1972.

Smyth, Dennis. *Diplomacy and Strategy of Survival: British Policy and Franco's Spain, 1940–1941*. Cambridge: Cambridge University Press, 1986.

Snyder, Louis. *Encyclopedia of the Third Reich*. New York: Paragon House, 1989.

Soloveytchik, George. *Switzerland in Perspective*. London: Oxford University Press, 1954.

Solsten, Eric, & Sandra W. Meditz, eds. *Finland: A Country Study.* Washington, D.C.: Federal Research Division, Library of Congress, 1990.

Sorrell, Walter. *The Swiss: A Cultural Panorama of Switzerland.* Indianapolis: Bobbs-Merrill Co., 1972.

The Spanish Government and the Axis: Documents. Washington, D.C.: Department of State, 1946.

Sweden: Ancient and Modern. Stockholm: Swedish Traffic Assn., 1939.

Sweden: A Wartime Survey (Public Authorities). New York: Albert Bonnier, 1949.

Taylor, A. J. P. *The Origins of the Second World War.* Greenwich, Conn.: Fawcett, 1961.

Terae, Martti (Lt. Col., Finnish Army). "Ruotsi Saksan Sucinnetelmissa Vuosina 1940–1941," *Historiallinen Aikakauskirja,* 1967.

Thomas, Hugh. *The Spanish Civil War.* New York: Harper & Row, 1961.

Thueren, Georg. *Free and Swiss: The Story of Switzerland* (tr. R. P. Heller & E. Long). London: Oswald Wolff, 1970.

Time, various issues.

Toynbee, Arnold & Veronica M. Toynbee, eds. *The War & the Neutrals.* Oxford: Oxford University Press, 1956.

Trythall, J. W. D. *El Caudillo: A Political Biography of Franco.* New York: McGraw-Hill Book Company, 1970.

Turner, Paul St. John. *Pictorial History of Pan American World Airways.* London: Ian Allan, 1973.

Unsigned. "Los Planes Militares de Hitler Sobre España en 1942–43," *Ejercito,* 1964.

Valentin, Hugo. "Jews in the Kingdom of Sweden," *Contemporary Jewish Record,* March–April 1940.

Vital Speeches of the Day. New York: City News Publishing Co., 1945.

Watson, Bert Allan. *United States–Spanish Relations, 1939–1946.* Washington, D.C.: Unpublished doctoral dissertation, 1971.

Weiss, Kenneth G. *The Azores in Diplomacy and Strategy, 1940–1945* (Professional Paper). Alexandria: Center for Naval Analyses, 1980.

Werbell, Frederick E., & Thurston Clarke. *Lost Hero: The Mystery of Raoul Wallenberg.* New York: McGraw-Hill Book Company, 1982.

West, John M. *The German-Swedish Transit Agreement of 1940* (Scandinavian Studies). Denver: Colorado Women's College, 1978.

Whealey, Robert H. *Hitler and Spain: The Nazi Role in the Spanish Civil War 1936–1939.* Lexington: University Press of Kentucky, 1989.

Wheeler, Douglas L. "The Price of Neutrality: Portugal, the Wolfram Question, and World War II," *Luso-Brazilian Review,* February 23, 1986.

Whipple, A. B. C. *The Mediterranean.* Alexandria: Time-Life Books, 1981.

Willomott, H. P. *The Great Crusade: A New Complete History of the Second World War.* New York: The Free Press, 1989.

Wourinen, John H., ed. *Finland and World War II*. New York: Ronald Press, 1948.

Wright, Michael, ed. *The World at Arms: The Reader's Digest Illustrated History of World War II*. London: Reader's Digest Association, Ltd., 1989.

Wyden, Peter. *The Passionate War: The Narrative History of the Spanish Civil War*. New York: Simon & Schuster, 1983.

Yahil, Leni. *The Rescue of Danish Jewry: Test of a Democracy*. Philadelphia: The Jewish Publication Society of America, 1969.

Yale Review, September 1943.

Young, Peter, ed. *The World Almanac Book of World War II*. New York: World Almanac, 1981.

INDEX

Boldface entries indicate maps

Achilles (cruiser), 133
Act of Paris, 1815, 12–13
Admiral Graf Spee (pocket battleship),
133
Admiral Scheer (pocket battleship), 133
Aiken, Frank, 184–85
Ajax (cruiser), 133
Åland Islands, Soviet demands regarding,
232
Alarcón de la Lasta, Luis, 197
Albania, 204
Alfonso XIII, 211
deposed, 46
dies, 212
Algeria, 198
Allied naval blockade
German counter-blockade, 79–80,
253
impact on Sweden, 243–44
impact on Switzerland, 14, 78–80,
158, 319
navicert system, 78–79, 158, 197, 254,
304
Allies
aid to Spain, 210–11
benefits of Swedish isolation, 169
control of Swiss trade, 158, 251, 253,
254–55, 319
demands regarding Spanish neutrality,
340–42

embargo petroleum to Spain, 226,
339, 341–42
halt Irish shipping, 332
invade Italy, 305
liberate France, 342
North African invasion, 284–85, 291
postwar sentiments regarding Sweden,
169
pressure Eire on Axis diplomats, 330
pressure Sweden, 88, 164, 168, 243–
44, 299–300, 307–8
on Spanish "nonbelligerent" status,
189–90
trade blacklist, 319
treatment of Spain, 118
withdraw from Norway, 165–66
Alsace incorporated into Germany,
146
Altmark incident, 133
American Air Force
Azores base, 354–55
bombs Swiss cities, 325–27
American Army in Northern Ireland,
268–69, 271, 273
American Export line, 215
American intelligence operations
in Switzerland, 258–60, 324
American Jewish Joint Distribution Committee, 297
American Lincoln Battalion, 53

For the sixty-eight months from Blitz-krieg to V-E Day, Europe suffered a war of unprecedented barbarity. Just five nations on that tormented continent managed to keep their peace. This is the story of how, against overwhelming odds, they did it.

—FROM THE INTRODUCTION

At the outbreak of the war, in 1939, over thirty independent states spanned the European continent. As the Nazi war machine advanced across Europe, consuming almost everything in its wake, only five—Switzerland, Sweden, Spain, Portugal, and the Republic of Ireland—preserved their sovereignty and protected their populations from devastation. These were the "neutral" nations of the Second World War, which survived through a combination of strategy and sheer luck, and continual, strained negotiations with the Axis and Allies.

Neutrality, in practice, often meant accommodating warring neighbors and appeasing the ascendant power. Until Germany lost its edge in 1942, it threatened invasion to exact costly compromises: Switzerland complied with press censorship and granted the Germans access to Italy via their Alpine tunnels; Sweden permitted transport of Nazi troops and war matériel to the Norwegian front. Spain's and Portugal's right-wing dictators paid homage to Hitler, and Franco went so far as to send Spanish soldiers to the Russian front. The Republic of Ireland, fearing British occupation as much as Nazi attack, maintained relations with the Germans, isolating themselves